15.000+ Positive Affirmations

Life-Changing Affirmations for Health, Wealth, Happiness, Confidence, Self-Love, Self-Esteem, Sleep, Healing - Includes Motivational Quotes That Will Drastically Boost Your Mindset

Victoria Griffith

©Copyright 2021 - Victoria Griffith, Mary Adaly, Willie Brown - All rights reserved

The content within this book may not be reproduced, duplicated, or transmitted without direct written permission from the author or the publisher.

Under no circumstances will any blame or legal responsibility be held against the publisher, or author, for any damages, reparation, or monetary loss due to the information contained within this book, either directly or indirectly.

Legal Notice

This book is copyright protected. This book is only for personal use. You cannot amend, distribute, sell, use, quote, or paraphrase any part, or the content within this book, without the consent of the author-publisher.

Disclaimer Notice

Please note that the information contained within this document is for educational and entertainment purposes only. All effort has been executed to present accurate, up-to-date, and reliable, complete information. No warranties of any kind are declared or implied. Readers acknowledge that the author is not engaging in the rendering of legal, financial, medical, or professional advice.

Table Of Contents

Affirmations for Women 7
Introduction 8
Chapter 1 What are Positive Affirmations? 11
Chapter 2 Why Use Affirmations? 18
Chapter 3 The Power of Positive Affirmations 23
Chapter4 Does Positive Affirmations Work? 25
Chapter 5 Power Up Your Affirmations 29
Chapter6 How to Eliminate the Feeling of "Not Good Enough" 36
Chapter 7 The Beginning of Greatness 40
Chapter 8 Be Proud of Who You Are 43
Chapter 9 We are All Humans and no Human is Inferior 46
Chapter 10 Use it to Your Advantage 50
Chapter 11 How do I Make Financial Affirmations work for Me? 54
Chapter12 Affirmations for Positive Energy 64
Chapter 13 Affirmations for Feeling Healthy 81
Chapter 13 Affirmations for Weight Loss 99
Chapter 14 Affirmations for Spirituality 108
Chapter 15 Affirmations for Achieving Goals 116
Chapter16 Affirmations for Overcoming Obstacles 122
Chapter17 Affirmations for Happiness and Gratitude 144
Chapter 18 Affirmations for Friends and Family 172
Chapter19 Affirmations for Health and Fitness 182

Chapter 20 Affirmations for Better Sleep... 214

Chapter 21 Affirmations for Career, Success, and Wealth...................... 219

Chapter 22 Affirmations for Gaining Confidence.................................... 258

Chapter 23 Affirmations for Leadership 276

Chapter 24 Affirmations for Love and Relationships............................. 288

Chapter 25 Affirmations for Work and School.. 305

Chapter 26 Affirmations for Black Parents to Become a Confident Parent 309

Chapter 27 Affirmations for Self-Worth and Self-Love.......................... 316

Chapter 28 Affirmations to Motivate Yourself Daily.............................. 353

Chapter 29 Affirmations for Black Women that will Change Their Lives 371

Chapter 30 Don't Reflect it... 378

Chapter 31 Understand What You Present... 382

Chapter 32 The Only Obstacle That Can Stop You in Life..................... 386

Chapter 33 Nobody is Useless – be a Blessing and Not a Curse............ 389

Chapter 34 Know Who You Are... 393

Chapter 35 Take Responsibility for Your Life 396

Chapter 36 Self-Image, Mindset, and Results... 399

Conclusion 405

Affirmations for Men.. 407

Introduction 408

Chapter 1 Positive Affirmations... 410

Chapter 2 The Power of Affirmations... 418

Chapter 3 Daily Affirmations for Positive Thoughts 422

Chapter 4 We Are All Humans and no Human is Inferior 429

Chapter 5 Why You Should Love Yourself 432

Chapter 6 How to Eliminate the Feeling of "Not Good Enough" 436

Chapter 7 Take Responsibility for Your Life 439

Chapter 8 The Instigator of Confidence 442

Chapter 9 We all Need Good Counselors 445

Chapter 10 The True Test of the Value of Your Desire 448

Chapter 11 Use It to Your Advantage... 450

Chapter 12 You Deserve It 453

Chapter 13 The Choice is Yours to Make 455

Chapter 14 Affirmations for Self-Esteem 457

Chapter 15 Affirmations for Self-Love.. 472

Chapter 16 Affirmations for Accepting Yourself 497

Chapter 17 Affirmations for Controlling Yourself and Your Surroundings 509

Chapter 18 Affirmations for Relationships and Supporting Others 525

Chapter 19 Affirmations for Taking Accountability and Responsibility 537

Chapter 20 Affirmations for Self-Confidence 550

Chapter 21 Affirmations for Increasing Productivity and Improving Decision Making... 573

Chapter 22 Affirmations for Success 589

Chapter 23 Affirmations for Building, Keeping, and Growing Wealth 606

Chapter 24 Affirmations for Attitude and Relationship with Money..... 634

Chapter 25 Affirmations for Handling Professional, Work, and Business Stress 651

Chapter 26 Affirmations for Protecting and Improving Your Mental State and Confidence.. 661

Chapter 27 Affirmations for Gratitude 673

Chapter 28 Financial Affirmations for Every Day 686
Chapter 29 Breaking Bad Habits 717
Chapter 30 Building Constructive Habits 723
Chapter 31 On Sadness 730
Chapter 32 On Happiness 736
Chapter 33 Setting Short-Term Goals 743
Chapter 34 Setting Long-Term Goals 750
Conclusion 757

Affirmations for Women

Life-Changing Affirmations for Confidence, Wealth, Health & Self-Love That Will Drastically Boost Your Mindset and Increase Your Happiness

Mary Adaly

Introduction

Self-perception influences how you feel about yourself and the way you react to daily events, including social situations. Life experiences, and your interpretation and relationship to those events, have an impact on self-perception, whether positive or negative. On the other hand, do you have a clear knowledge of how memories are formed? Overestimating the importance of our words and would be an understatement of extreme difficulty.

For young individuals, low self-esteem is mostly caused by the interactions they've had with the people they've encountered throughout their lives, including their parents, siblings, classmates at school or at work, instructors, and other adults.

The majority of children grow up in environments where they are not constantly exposed to experiences that cause them to question their own identities and feel less confident in themselves. By contrast, a minority of them grow up in environments where they are constantly exposed to experiences that cause them to question their own identities, among other things. Many youngsters grow up in surroundings where they are continually exposed to situations that drive them to doubt their own abilities and make them feel less secure in their own skin. This is especially true for girls, in particular young women.

You have formed a perspective of yourself and your life as a result of everything that has happened to you. Everyone and everything has played a role in why you feel the way you do about yourself and your life. The first step in changing such a perspective is to understand the conditions that led to them and then to begin the process of mental reconfiguration from there.

As a result of the negative and derogatory words their mothers or someone very close to them used on them on a regular basis when they were much younger, I have had some beautiful young girls and adult women come to me feeling self-conscious about their appearance and body image. They are less confident in their appearance and physique. Some young women have confided in me that they believe they would never amount to anything meaningful in life as a result of the things they have heard about themselves from others. Because of such harsh words or events, some women have allowed their mental health to be badly affected to the point where they are no longer motivated to pursue anything useful in life as a consequence.

Some individuals continue to hold themselves responsible for the trauma they suffered as children and use this to define themselves, while others are less confident in themselves as a result of their skin color and our collective past, among other things.

Pay attention, young lady: you have no control over your past experiences, particularly those that occurred when you were young and vulnerable, with little or no ability to manage your emotions. It's important to pay attention to this. As a result, continuing to define yourself and your life in terms of awful events that have occurred is both erroneous and destructive, particularly when you have had no control over the circumstances.

Whatever you may think, you are not the result of the horrific events that have happened in your life. You are the cause of those occurrences! Nobody can make you feel insecure because you are not the derogatory names that others have called you or make you feel insecure about yourself because of the irresponsibility, meanness, and thoughtlessness of anyone who has ever done something bad to you that has caused you to feel self-conscious. That incident should not be recreated in your mind, and you should not allow it to determine how you behave and live your life. It is also past time for you to stop blaming people for your negative self-image.

Regardless of something like the events that have occurred in your life, you have the ability to alter your view of yourself as well as your perception of others. Because you have been mistakenly reading your previous negative experiences as an accurate representation of who you actually are today, you continue to feel bad about yourself and have less confidence. The moment to reinvent yourself and claim your proper position in the world has never been greater than right now, and this book is intended to assist you accomplish that goal.

This book aims to assist black women in recognizing themselves for who they truly are, reprogramming their brains to see themselves in a better and more positive light, and encouraging them to strive for the best that life has to offer because they truly deserve to be successful.

As you move through this book, you will notice a positive shift in your self-thoughts and self-talk, as well as an increase in your self-esteem and self-confidence. With the assistance of this wonderful self-help book, you will have a terrific time enhancing your mind and your life.

Chapter 1

What are Positive Affirmations?

If you've ever found yourself consumed with positive or negative thoughts, you'll admit that the words you feed yourself, as well as what you hear from others, can affect your wellbeing. Words are powerful tools with the potential to transform our behaviors and thought processes. Past occurrences or events that are yet to happen influence our thoughts. Although you are not defined by your past mistakes, they can infiltrate into your conscious and subconscious minds. They generate negative perceptions about your ability to manage current or future situations. For this reason, you must affirm yourself. Incorporating daily positive self-talk into your life will help.

Affirmations are simply positive self-statements of what you want to happen now or in the future, as though they have already occurred. Affirmations assist with taking a hopeful and confident perspective about life and work. People who are hopeful and confident hold good assumptions about what is to come. Hopefulness is a superior feeling of prosperity despite life's challenges. It facilitates elevated levels of adapting, wellbeing advancement practices, and accomplishment in forming relationships.

Affirmations differ in their content and conditions. By content, I mean that they are unique words to help you stay committed to a specific goal. Leadership affirmations, for instance, consist of words like "I can make positive change", or "I'm confident and ready to deal with any obstacle tossed before me". This indicates a person's desire to get to the top or remain there. They differ from affirmations composed of words like "I have all I need", or " I'm deserving of what I want".

Affirmations also vary by their conditions. They tell you what actions one will take and when. The person's weight loss journey will begin immediately, starting with a change in diet after a statement like "From today, I will eat more healthy foods and avoid junk foods".

Throughout this book, affirmations are classified according to content and condition to guide you as to when to use them.

We gain and retain our confidence as black women via affirmations, which are regularly used to navigate the intersection of race and gender issues. Despite the fact that we are often referred to be strong, we make the mistake of clinging to things and people that are not beneficial to us. This may be exhausting, and we need to hear words of encouragement to help us lift ourselves and one another up.

When it comes to being a black woman, it's difficult to accept myself for who I am, and I've made the mistake of comparing myself to others way too many times. Finally, I'm learning to enjoy every facet of myself, from my skin to my hair to my physique to my freckles, and I'm having a lot of fun doing it.

What is an affirmation?

With an affirmation, you are expressing your belief in your ability to overcome negative thoughts and feelings. They contribute to the reinforcement of positive feelings and attitudes. Reciting an affirmation first thing in the morning may help you think more effectively, have a more optimistic attitude, and, as a result, impact you approach you're the day's challenges.

Many of us are prone to negative thinking and engage in it on a daily basis. When we think negatively, our self-esteem, attitudes, and perspectives may all suffer as a result.

Negative thoughts have the ability to turn into a self-fulfilling prophecy. As a result of this delusion, we believe we are unworthy of success. This has a detrimental influence on our personal lives, relationships, and professional endeavors as a consequence.

Your capacity to maintain a happy attitude and speak in a positive manner determines the tone of your emotional life. Positive affirmations are phrases used to show optimism about one's life, emotions, career, and other areas of one's existence. They are also known as "affirmations of faith."

To put it another way, you are expressing what you want to see, regardless of the facts. Affirmations are more than simply words you say; they are a step further, allowing you to identify with them. In short, these words become yours. They become your values and serve as the foundation for your belief system.

These positive affirmations assist in overcoming the negative ideas that might keep you trapped in a never-ending cycle of agony, pity, and inefficiency. When you say them enough times and believe them, you will begin making the required adjustments in your lifestyle. The trick to affirmations is that you have to keep repeating them over and over.

Positive affirmations are seen negatively by some as a waste of time. Others dismiss it as nothing more than wishful thinking. However, if you look at them in the same way that you look at physical exercise, you'll understand that they have much more significance. In this instance, you're exercising your mind to maintain a good attitude on life. Consider positive affirmations as mental exercises that help you remodel your subconscious mind.

Although it is not always possible, if we deliberately think favorably about ourselves, the results may be equally as strong and far more helpful.

How affirmations work

When you speak or write down positive statements, it affects your brain. It broadens your general viewpoint to lessen the impact of negative emotions. This can be either by activating the reward and positive valuation centers of the brain. You reflect only on rewarding and positive experiences that have happened in your life and can expect future positive events.

Affirmations also have the power to regulate emotions. They ensure you're enriched with positive thoughts and feelings. When you regularly say positive words or statements to yourself, it will cause you to change your behavior and veer from practices that reduce your self-worth.

Affirmations take practice, commitment, and effort before you can start seeing results. All you need to do is start with small sections of your positive statements daily for a specific duration of time. Then, maintain consistency throughout the week. If you do this often, you will create the habit of uttering positive affirmations to yourself.

To begin creating and using affirmations, you'll need the following:

- **A book and a pen:** You'll write your positive statements in present tense in this book. This will deceive your mind into believing that something has already occurred.

- **Focus your mind** only on positivity and avoid negativity.

- **Choose affirmations from this book:** Each chapter contains affirmations tailored to a specific goal. You can mix affirmations or only choose from the chapter that you want to excel in.

- **Write your affirmations down** in your book as how they appear in this book.

- **Schedule time to recite your affirmations:** It doesn't matter how much time you allocate to memorizing your affirmations. You must set aside a specific time of day to read them. This is the most crucial step of the process. You can also connect your affirmation to an activity you do every day. This will help you set a routine.

- **Read each positive statement out loud:** By reading aloud, your affirmations will be stored in your brain and you're more likely to remember them.

- **Change your mindset to believe that what you're saying is happening:** As you read your affirmations, picture only good things happening and becoming part of you.

- **Be repetitive with your affirmations:** This will help store them in your conscious and subconscious mind.

Importance of positive affirmations

When you feed yourself with positive self-statements, it activates the pathways in your brain that control arousal and motivation. Motivation increases your drive and desire to do your best work. It gives you a sense of purpose and autonomy and encourages mastery. Motivation also elevates your drive to accomplish your goals by enhancing mental toughness and increasing the ability to focus. When you're focused, you'll start working on your goal, and your desire to continue working toward it will increase. Motivation boosts confidence and creates mental preparation. This is needed to dominate difficult situations. Motivation will help to increase or maintain the amount of effort you put toward achieving your goals.

Repeating your affirmations will focus your attention on your goals. Goal achievement is helped by keeping your mind on the desired result. Affirmations shift your concentration away from disappointments or deficiencies. They direct concentration toward your current qualities and those you need to create. Without focus, one might forget the correct way to maximize their potential. Positive affirmations will make it easier to devote your work to your objectives. You'll have the choice of deciding where your attention will be directed, making it simpler for you to devote your time and energy to that area. For example, if you want to become an entrepreneur, it become a focus in your life.

Affirmations help you become confident about you and your ability to accomplish goals. You'll feel more positive about yourself as you rehearse them. When you feel confident, you will be more successful in the things you do. In turn, your confidence level will increase. This positive cycle brings achievement and bliss. You will need to act on these statements daily to optimize their benefit. Through practice, you can convince yourself that you're now confident. These affirmations will guide your thought process on how to achieve such goals.

Daily positive affirmations are necessary to enhance self-efficacy. Self-efficacy is the faith in one's ability to organize and execute the necessary game plans to deliver a given result. So, when you make saying positive statements a habit, it will act to reinforce the beliefs you have formed after accomplishing a goal. When you have a high feeling of self-efficacy, you will be able to do the following:

- View difficult issues as undertakings to dominate.
- Structure a more grounded feeling of commitment to your interests and activities.
- Foster further interest in the activities you enjoy.
- Recuperate from difficulties and disappointments.

Benefits of Positive Affirmation

Successful black women like Oprah Winfrey and Viola Davis are prominent preachers of positive affirmations. It's evident that positive self-talk has produced incredible results in their lives.

You are next in line!

With positive affirmations, you can achieve the following:

- Erase negative thought patterns
- Boost your mood, confidence, and self-worth
- Gain motivation for an enriching life
- Unlock amazing potentials and possibilities
- Fill your life with boundless success
- Live a life of happiness and fulfillment

Prepare yourself by making sure that you're comfy and calm before beginning your affirmations session. Affirmations are most effective when received just after waking up or just before going to sleep. You may, however, listen to affirmations throughout the day; for example, when taking a stroll or while driving.

Chapter 2

Why Use Affirmations?

Affirmations are a great tool for making positive changes in your life. That is all there is to it. The well-established law of "like attracts like" is as powerful as gravity. Although it may be more difficult to describe, this does not make it any less effective. In the mornings, do you get out of bed with a grin on your face and a desire to take on the difficulties of the day? It's not always as simple as it seems if you're anything like me. Positive affirmations are like snow tires in the storm of life, keeping you grounded and focused.

Your brain is the first computer, and it's also the first smartphone, although considerably more powerful than the average one. However, you must understand that what you put in or program is what your brain will spit out as a result. It is only a mechanism, although one complicated by sentiments and emotions. Let's seize the reins and train our brains to assist us achieve the goals we set out for ourselves in life. It is possible to have good health, riches, and tranquility, as well as financial success and fulfilling relationships.

It is important to speak in the present tense as though the affirmation is occurring right now or coming to you in clear sight. For example, "Today, I shall..." or "I am..." should be spoken. This makes your brain think that these things are already here. So now your reality has no choice but to catch up quickly.

I encourage you to write down any affirmations that speak to you and put them in your house where you can see them multiple times throughout the day. Use colors and even stickers to awaken your mind. Your mind will respond much stronger if colors or sparkles are added.

Neurologists believe that visually stimulating yourself has a greater effect on putting your goals into action than a non-visual stimulus. You will need to make your desires as strong as possible so they are forced to become your reality.

This book is intended to be read daily, although it is not required to do so. If you feel inspired, skip ahead and read different affirmations; no problem if you miss a day. This book can be used year over year, and you can never get enough of these affirmations. The more you repeat them, the closer you will get to your goals. Each year, commit to setting some new goals; you can then use this book to transform your new yearly goals into reality. If you feel that you can't get enough affirmations, read as many as you like. The days are just a starting point to keep you on track in reading affirmations daily.

Goal Setting

Before beginning the daily affirmations, I suggest setting some clear goals for yourself. Then as you read each affirmation, you can apply it directly to one of the goals. I would recommend either writing down 4 or 5 master "BIG" goals and putting the list on your wall as well as creating a vision board, big or small. You can also put your list in your smartphone's notes if you are always on the go. If you are making a vision board with poster paper, get some magazines that interest you and go through them, cutting out anything you are attracted to without judging yourself. Glue the pictures to poster paper; even one or two magazine pictures of important things taped to your bathroom mirror are better than nothing.

Some goals might be:

- I find a new, enjoyable and lucrative career
- I meet my soulmate
- I help my body become healthy and fit
- I buy a new car
- I buy my own house

- I earn an extra $1,000 before the end of the year

Written goals should have some or all of these qualities:

- Specific
- Measurable
- Achievable
- Realistic
- Time-bound

This is known as the S.M.A.R.T. acronym for goal setting.

Now that you have decided precisely what you want, you must outline the steps you will take to achieve your goal. If your goal is to be healthy, write out a plan statement such as:

Goal: To become healthy and fit

Plan: I will accomplish this by eating less sugar and exercising every day

Goal: To earn $10,000 extra this year

Plan: I will accomplish this by selling the 100 wooden tables I have made

As much as we would like to think our goals will magically manifest themselves, with zero effort on our part, that is just not the case. This is both the good news and the bad news. The good news is that change will only come to people who desire it, and the not-so-good news is that you have to make an effort to start the process. If you desire wealth, the only way to real fortune is to provide a service or sell something of value to others.

This does not imply that you must work harder to make additional money. Look at the most financially successful people; most of them have set up their businesses very well so they can sit back and enjoy themselves. You can have this too; think about new ways to serve people. There are ways to leverage yourself so that the amount of work you do is minimal compared to the reward. You just need to be open to some new ideas.

Don't worry if you don't yet have a plan for all your big goals. Maybe you want to buy your own house and need $100,000 for a down payment. It might take a while to come up with a viable plan. Keep this in mind as you do your daily affirmations and manifest a good solid plan. Plans for big goals can take time to uncover, so be patient.

In addition to consciously manifesting the goals on your list or poster board, there is a huge unconscious, unexplainable power at work. I have a personal story: in my 20's, my cat had passed away. I wasn't even looking for a new kitten, but a friend brought me one as a gift. It was the cutest, fluffiest, little orange male kitten. I kept him, and he was my cat for many years. When he was about a year old, I took another look at an old poster board I had made years before receiving the kitten. As I was looking through the pictures of houses and tropical destinations, I found glued in the corner a tiny picture I had cut out of a fluffy orange kitten.

Be warned that powerful energy is involved when you start listing your goals and taking the steps to manifest them. Like a magnet turned on, these goals are slowly moving closer to you. Visual stimulation adds another level of incredible power to your brain.

In addition to your big goals, I would also suggest a list of some daily attainable goals as well:

- eat less sugar
- get more exercise
- practice patience
- go to bed on time

These will help you feel good daily to focus and use your energy to achieve your big goals.

Chapter 3

The Power of Positive Affirmations

Positive affirmations have long been recognized as having a significant amount of self-motivating power. If you tell yourself anything negative about yourself, you will either feel better or feel worse about yourself as a result of your actions. Depending upon what you tell yourself, even if true, you will either embrace or reject yourself, become confident or insecure, happy or unhappy, or a combination of these emotions.

The repetition of these lines as soon as you find yourself in a scenario that causes you to feel afraid or worried can assist you in overcoming it and bringing about the changes you want. It is critical to treat oneself with love and care during the process in order for these transformations to be good and long-lasting in nature. To put it mildly, you should approach yourself in the same manner that you would approach a friend under comparable circumstances.

It is not always easy to lose weight for health or cosmetic reasons, and it is far more difficult to maintain a healthy lifestyle over the long term after you have lost the weight. We will be able to achieve motivation and self-esteem more simply and faster if we utilize positive affirmations to help us along the way.

What are positive affirmations?

In order to make positive affirmations that are credible, a person must speak out loud to themselves (preferably in private!) and believe what they are saying. Your actions are beneficial when you provide words of encouragement that boost the emotions of others in the immediate vicinity. When you consider the great outcomes, the fact that it seems weird at first look does not imply that it is risky to give it a go.

If you want to retrain your brain to think more positively, you should make positive statements about your health, your career, your own self-confidence, your relationships, or any other aspect of your life that you are proud of on a regular basis.

One's ultimate goal is to provide joy to others just by stating anything. When hearing something for the first time, it might be difficult to believe what someone is saying in its totality. The simple act of repeating phrases that are diametrically opposite to our beliefs forces the brain to accept them, and we ourselves come to accept them. It is necessary to first earn our confidence before these affirmations can have a true impact on our lives and our decisions.

How to Create a Powerful Positive Affirmation?

The start of a new year gives a chance to take stock and set goals that are both hard and motivational in nature, as well as to reflect on the preceding year. You may have thought about it, but have you given any consideration to what you want to accomplish, achieve, and become in the year 2022? Now is the moment to get started if you haven't already. This is an excellent moment to start thinking about your alternatives if you haven't previously. Do you have a plan in place to achieve your goals? Our recommendation is that you write down strong positive affirmations for each of your objectives to help you achieve them more quickly.

Chapter 4

Does Positive Affirmations Work?

Yes, positive affirmations work. And no, the problem is not you. There is a strong link or impact between the words you speak and your mind. When your mind is able to enter into a cycle where the words you speak feed it, and it meditates on these words and then feeds your speech in return, you generate an energy that opens you up spiritually and mentally to the things you have spoken about. This leads to a manifestation of those things in your life. The process by which this happens is simultaneously complex and very straightforward.

How exactly do affirmations work?

There is a biblical quote that says, "as a man thinks in his heart, so is he." This expression may have Christian religious roots, but every culture, faith, and philosophical practice has a version of this very same statement. Almost everyone supports how the mind fuels our experiences. Cognitive-behavioral therapy experts will tell you that in order to develop new habits and change or get rid of the old ones, the first place you have to start working is with your mindset. Affirmations also work this way. It all starts with your mind. The moment we are born into this earthly world, the mind is a blank slate. As we grow up, it is shaped and colored by our experiences, our upbringing, and the words that are spoken to us as well as the input from people in our closest circle. Unfortunately, a lot of these things are not always positive.

Some societies oppress their citizens and, in some situations, specific genders are being oppressed in every way. Even if that oppression is not a physical experience, people in such conditions grow up with limitations placed on their capabilities and, until they push past those boundaries mentally, they will remain within the confines of that structure.

Positive affirmations are about reprogramming the mind and aligning it with your expectations. It doesn't mean that you are going to overhaul everything you have learned throughout your lifetime. Instead, it focuses on specific things, as I have said earlier when defining positive affirmations, and then it highlights your intention, which is where the mind comes into play.

Let me put it in practical terms: wanting something is not going to be enough for you to get it. Putting in the work to get that thing might only be enough to get you so far. It is like having the seed, the soil, and the water. Two elements out of these might be able to get you some growth, but you need the third element to manage that growth into a fruit. Your goals and your hard work are like the seed and the soil. Working hard for your dreams might get you some growth, but your mindset is what determines the fruit. You need to program your mind to see that dream, aspiration, or expectation in a positive light at first, and then you need to speak that vision into existence. When you speak the words, your mind absorbs them. With consistency, you internalize what you affirm until you become "it."

The first time you speak the words, you will face many disagreements within yourself. This is definitely going to happen if the thing you are aspiring for is way outside your comfort zone, or if it is something beyond the limitations placed on you. But when you make it a very consistent habit to speak these words, which is where repetition comes in, you will find that your mind becomes more receptive to the new message. With each passing day, your mindset will transcend the level of doubt and enter into expectation. You'll stop seeing life from a place of "this is not possible" to a place where you start thinking, "maybe I can get this." With more repetition, you will finally be in a place where the dream is the only possible outcome. When you get to this point, the experiences you have on the outside will begin to sink in and fit together like a puzzle that will eventually manifest your vision.

Is there a right way to use positive affirmations?

There is no fixed manuscript on how to activate the power of positive affirmations in your life. If you were hoping for a particular ritual and technique for achieving success in this area, I'm sad to say that there isn't one. However, some requirements must be met. The first thing on that list is conviction. You must have faith in what you are saying. It's great to search the internet for affirmations, but you need take it a step further.

Speaking affirmations that you have no faith in and expecting results is like attempting to use a feather to break a solid iron. It is going to be a pointless and useless exercise. One way to build confidence in the words you speak as affirmations is to ensure that they are in alignment with the vision you have set for yourself and your future. In other words, the affirmations you speak daily have to be very close and personal to you.

When you personalize your affirmations, you create a deeper connection and when that connection is present, you become emboldened. And when you make your affirmations from this point on, the universe responds to your conviction in the words you are speaking.

The second requirement is "sight." You have to see yourself living in the reality of the words being affirming. Let the image of the future you want to manifest become so real and vivid that you can live the details like taste, smell, and other sensual experiences. Let us say that you are affirming good health. Try to visualize yourself as the picture of good health. What would you do if you are healthy in every sense of the word? Are you enjoying a run outdoors in the morning sun? How are you spending your healthy days? How do you feel about it? These questions will provide answers which in turn will help you "see" the life you want to manifest.

I remember one particular experience I had during my early days of practicing positive affirmations. I was trying to manifest a life of abundance as it was very important for me to step up financially. Because of this, I was into financial affirmations. At first, I chose those specific affirmations because they sounded good, but over a period of time I became frustrated because they began to feel like empty words.

This prompted me to make some adjustments based on what I wanted. One major tool that helped me at that point in time was to identify why I wanted those things. When I was able to clearly define my reasons, I gained enlightenment regarding the future I wanted. The more I saw, the bolder I felt. This greatly impacted my affirmations; it was at this point that I connected with what I was saying because right after that, the manifestations began.

Next, I am going to expand on this process so you can replicate it in your life and get the kind of response and results you are seeking. Our next stop on this exciting new journey is to explore some of the myths surrounding affirmations.

Chapter 5

Power Up Your Affirmations

By now, you have written down the words that you feel best reflect your vision of the future. The next step in the journey is empowering those words so they can take effect. According to what I said at the start, there is no clear pattern to follow to come up with affirmations that work. If you put this in the equation, you increase the likelihood of those affirmations becoming your reality.

Consistency in the things you say

When you are consistent, you do the same thing over and over again with the same enthusiasm and excitement. This is known as repetition. If you remain consistent with your affirmations, it is impossible to stray from your routine. No matter what is going on around you or how you are feeling at the moment, your ability to remain consistent in your affirmations is not governed by your circumstances or your feelings.

The very first valuable thing you will notice when you wake up in the morning is that you are mindful of the fact that you are opening your lips and pronouncing the words you intend to use to bring about the reality you want. Maintaining consistency is not always a straightforward task. Distractions will always be competing for our affection and attention: we will always have things to deal with. To see the effects from your affirmations, you must be constant in your use of them.

To become more consistent with your affirmations, create a routine. Have a set time during the day dedicated to declaring affirmations. It could be in the morning when you wake up or sometime during the day when you enjoy some free time. You could even choose to do it at night. Choose a time when you are mentally heightened so the words you speak are not driven by emotions or sentiments.

You need to focus on the words while holding the vision in the forefront of your mind. Another thing that helps, besides having a set time, is creating a space where you can make the affirmations. They do not have to be done within the four walls of your home. You could do it on the road, on a plane, or even at your work desk in the office. You simply need to pick a spot free of distractions, but you have to make sure that the time you choose is suitable for the space.

Within the first few days of your affirmation cycle, you might find that it is easy to be consistent. But as time goes on, the routine becomes boring and mundane, mostly because you haven't yet seen the physical manifestation of those things you are speaking about. This is not the time to pull back, switch your routines, or change the wording of your affirmation. Instead, this is when you put more thrust on yourself to stick to what you are doing. It is not going to be easy. I have said this several times, but if you make up your mind, it will be worth it. A huge part of being consistent is being committed. The next section is going to focus on this.

Commitment to the process

Commitment is not a symbolic gesture to follow through on certain things. Some people feel that a commitment in marriage is in the ring you use to wed your spouse. Don't get me wrong, the ring shows the world who you have chosen to identify with and it is symbolic, but commitment is about the choices you have made. Commitment is getting up every morning and choosing to do a specific thing regardless of how you feel or where you find yourself. Commitment is directing your focus to the thing you have chosen and keeping your focus on it no matter what is going on externally. Given the fact that life is constantly throwing challenges at us, the question to ask yourself is, "How do I remain committed in the face of disruptions?"

The first thing to do is to strongly connect with the reason behind your actions. Why are you saying these affirmations? What does it mean to you to get these affirmations to become manifestations? When you connect with the "why," you strengthen your will and are able to remain consistent in what you do. You know that no matter what happens, the outcome of your action is far greater than the temporary relief you might get from letting go of your commitment to bear the burden of your present challenge.

Speaking of challenges, if you are going to remain committed to your affirmations, the second thing you need to do is focus more on the smaller victories, rather than the challenges you are going through. Your victories allow you to create a positive internal atmosphere that will continue to motivate you. On the other hand, focusing on the challenges excessively can drag you down mentally and emotionally, causing you to become less resistant to stepping back from your responsibilities. You have to learn to take your wins wherever you may find them.

In closing, I recommend you participate in a system that requires you to be responsible to someone other than yourself. This will assist you in remaining committed to your affirmations. It is more likely that you will have greater confidence in your commitment if you are accountable to someone other than yourself since you will be more conscious of the fact that you have obligations or responsibilities. While it is very understandable that you may be inclined to prioritize your own needs above those of others, the knowledge that someone else is counting on you to fulfill your obligations under a contract may give you the incentive needed to keep moving ahead. It is important to remember that affirmations are not about your ability to employ a range of words or your elocution abilities while utilizing them. They are primarily concerned with your ability to be constant and forceful in your assertions about the things you want to happen in your life, rather than the things themselves.

The cause must be championed with unwavering dedication at all times. Make an investigation into what inspires you to act in the way you do. Learn to share a common ground with the hunger that drives you on your journey. Depending on the circumstances, it may be important to go outside of your comfort zone. Stay consistent and steadfast in your commitment until you get the desired result as a consequence of your affirmations, which you will notice when certain things begin to blossom as a result.

Conforming to the new mindset

When powering up your affirmations, mindset is everything. I have talked about mindset before, but this is the point where you put everything you have learned into action. You cannot afford to have a mediocre way of life as the template with which you launch your affirmations. You have to change the way you think and act from the inside.

I talked about changing the internal environment to foster a more suitable place for your affirmations. You need to start learning to take actions that correspond with this internal environment you have created. It is one thing to think about it and altogether another when you meditate on it. It is an entirely different matter to activate it. Your new internal system means that you cannot continue to do things the way you are used to doing.

In order to boost the impact of your affirmations, you must begin to put into practice what you are preaching. In its most basic form, this implies that as soon as you glimpse the future you want to confirm, you must start taking steps to become the person who will live in that future as soon as possible.

Consider yourself in a situation or circumstance where you are attempting to demonstrate your better health and fitness. If you want to begin working with a positive frame of mind right away, you cannot afford to be slouching when you should be exercising. It is not possible to eat junk food while simultaneously indulging in dangerous activities such as smoking, which does absolutely nothing to promote good health.

Conform to your new attitude by recognizing any actions that compromise your goals to live in the future you have pictured and removing them from your life as quickly as possible. You may be able to begin to reproduce the reality you are now feeling on the inside by doing this simple deed. Eventually, if this is allowed to continue for an extended length of time, it will manifest itself physically in every other element of life. It is also possible to employ this method to manifest other aspects of your life, such as a good relationship, a meaningful job, or even financial success.

Sometimes the thing you are trying to manifest might be an object; you might ask yourself, "How do I make it works in alignment with the internal mindset I have created for this?" I am going to use a car as an example. You have envisioned the specific type of you want and have created images in your mind. So, what can you do or what will you do to help make this vision a reality even as you are making your affirmations?

First of all, you need to ask yourself if you can drive. This is a step that a lot of people skip, and I am not talking specifically about cars and driving. When you want something, you don't think about what you will to do when you get that thing. Look at those specifics and then start working on the things you can do right now so when that most awaited time comes, you are already prepared for it.

While you prepare for the unexpected, you have to ensure that you are making preparations for the things you are hoping to come to your life. If you are trying to manifest a dream job, start looking at how prepared you are to work in that position. Do you have the necessary qualifications needed? Are you making the right connections? And so on. Start thinking in these directions, and you will find that your affirmations are more empowered every time you speak them.

Containing contradictions through conscious reminders

Your experiences may contradict the things you are declaring into existence. For example, you might be speaking to acquiring wealth and find that in your present circumstance, you can barely afford your next meal. Allowing this to discourage you from continuing with your affirmations is a mistake. Disassociate your present from the future you want to see. Think of your current circumstance as the stepping stone to where you want to go, rather than focusing on the challenges you are facing. When challenges become your focus, you will find yourself constantly complaining. This will mess up the internal dynamics you have worked so hard to build.

Never take your eyes off the goal or objective. Life is a journey that takes you up and down, but that vision you have for your future should remain a focal point. It will help draw out the doldrums and motivate you to keep moving.

How can you use conscious reminders to help you contain the contradictions you see daily? The very first step is create a vision board. A vision board brings together elements that make up the dream you have for the future. It could be a dream house, a dream car, or whatever you want. You can use certain images to symbolize or represent what you are aspiring for. Put them together in an aesthetically appealing way on a single board and then position the board in a place so you can see it every day when you wake up.

This will give you a visual reminder of the goals you are working towards. Another thing I like to do is to write down little notes containing smaller affirmations that help me stay focused. I call them my little fairy lights because they help to shine the way when you are feeling down. I usually leave them by the door where I can see them whenever I am going out or coming in, or paste then by the mirror I use every morning and evening. I type them in beautiful fonts and print them out. They are excellent tiny reminders.

Another thing I have found very helpful is journaling, but not the everyday type. At the beginning of my journey of affirmations, I took the time to write down the vision I had for the future and included as many details into this picture as possible. Then, whenever I am feeling down or discouraged, I revisit this writing and get the opportunity to relive the positive experience I have had when I first started writing it.

Sometimes, I even add some extra information to stay on track with my affirmations and remind me of the reasons behind my decisions. You have to understand that life is not essentially a race for the swift. Affirmations are not going to manifest immediately. It is going to be a process, and part of that process is ensuring that you keep your head up in the game.

Keep in mind always that you are the most important component of this jigsaw. Because you have the ultimate authority, the choices and actions you choose now will have a significant impact on the results you may experience tomorrow.

Chapter 6

How to Eliminate the Feeling of "Not Good Enough"

Today's wisdom: The most common cause of insecurity in most people is self-comparison.

Affirmation: I am enough.

Encouragement:

The realization that you are unique and unlike anybody else and that you cannot, as a result, be like anyone else allows you to begin living life and enjoying it. Self-comparison is one of the major hurdles when it comes to self-expression. It has led so many people to cocoon themselves in self-dissatisfaction, causing them to believe that they are just not good enough and are insufficient.

Individuals sometimes compare themselves to others, saying things like, "Oh, why don't I have that?" and similar statements. My life is so different from his, I wonder why that is. Oh, why don't I have the confidence to stand so tall? What is it about my nose that makes it different from everyone else's? What is it about my skin that makes it different? My only regret is that I'm not black since I believe I could have gotten away with it... What about my physical appearance leads me to be so small? What I would give to be a part of their family, even for a moment... etc.

As a result, they will turn their focus away from themselves and onto people they feel are superior to them. What self-comparison may do is keep you from recognizing yourself for who you are and inculcating the belief that you are not deserving of acceptance.

Being enough means coming to grips with one's own identity and accepting the reality one has formed as perfect and complete from the beginning. It is the capacity to see oneself as a unique person and embrace all that distinguishes oneself from others.

Everything about you is perfect, and you do not want a certain look or a precise quantity of belongings in order to feel whole or adequate in your own right. Everything you've done so far has been sufficient.

It seems that some of us are going through an identity crisis, unable to recognize or grasp who we are. As soon as the media throws anything at us, we accept it without question and begin to shape ourselves to conform to the picture that the mainstream media is portraying. As a result of allowing others to brainwash us into believing that there is something wrong with the way we are, we have begun to feel ashamed about our physical appearance and are seeking to conform to the media image of what we should look like.

No one will ever be able to make you feel whole or competent. You will experience a similar sense from the inside as a consequence of the growing understanding of your own uniqueness and identity. In order to figure out what is causing this unpleasant feeling of not being enough, you must go deep inside yourself and address the basis of the issue.

I have never experienced trying to fit another man's notion of who he feels you should be for him to accept you . It's unlike anything else on the face of the earth. To put it simply, conforming is all about complying with other people's notions of oneself, and the only person who conforms to other people's perceptions is someone who does not know and understand themselves.

Not some stranger who knows nothing about you, but only you have the ability to choose what is acceptable and undesirable about yourself. Never allow anybody or anything to have an impact on your identity or what you do. Change your look only if you believe that doing so enables you to live a greater quality of life as the proper option for your situation. It should not be done to make oneself acceptable or seem good enough in the eyes of others who aren't even concerned about whether or not you are still living.

Whatever you do for yourself should not be motivated by a desire to rectify what you perceive to be a flaw; but rather, it should come from the conviction that you deserve the best and to be the finest version of yourself that you are capable of being. Maintain your self-assurance and comfort in your own skin. Understanding, accepting, and respecting oneself for who you are is critical to one's well-being. No one can make you feel good enough or capable; only you have the capacity to instill that sense of self-worth and competence in yourself.

There isn't anything that needs to be improved about you at all. There is nothing more essential than being yourself, and you should never consider or listen to anybody who tells you otherwise or leads you to feel differently than you already do. That is correct; you are more than adequate! Yes, you are up to the effort! Congratulations! This is something you should be conscious of at all times since you are the only one who has the ability to define who you are and make yourself feel good about yourself in the first place!

Declare these words aloud to yourself:

- I am made complete in all aspects
- I am enough in all aspects
- Everything about me is good
- Nothing is lacking or missing in me
- I will never wish to be like anyone else

- I will never allow my feelings or anyone to make me feel ashamed or less of myself
- I will always see and appreciate the awesome qualities in me
- I will never undermine myself in anyway
- I know I have been made complete
- I am good enough for the good things of life

Chapter 7

The Beginning of Greatness

Today's wisdom: If you want it and why you want it is strong enough, then nothing can be able to stop you from having it.

Affirmation: I will aspire to be great.

Encouragement:

To aspire is to hope or dream to become someone great in a chosen profession or occupation. Without aspiration for something, there can be no determination to achieve it. Aspiration is the first step to achieving greatness, and most of us don't seem to be want more or better than we already have.

One of the problems I've observed in most black people living in the hood lately is that some of us are settling for mediocrity. We've conditioned our minds to accept the status quo view that we're no longer motivated to strive to get ourselves out of our pitiable situations. We seemed to be satisfied with being in the hood and not wanting to go beyond it. We are failing to dream big and offer ourselves a more quality life than we are already having.

Look, you have great potential in you, but you cannot reach it if you don't stretch yourself to achieve heights far beyond your comfort zone. You can reach any height that you can imagine in life, but you first have to aspire for it.

When you look far beyond your existing position, you may see yourself living a life of much higher quality than your current one. This is the definition of ambition. The realization that you are worthy of a better life will push you to do whatever it takes to provide yourself with the life you desire and deserve, regardless of your current circumstances.

Before anything can be accomplished, a great desire to achieve must be shown. Being confined to one area and bemoaning the economic marginalization that some of our communities have experienced in our nation will not, in the long run, resolve any difficulties. For many of us, the moment has come to get up on our feet and start working toward the changes we want to see in our lives and communities. In order for us to repair ourselves, we must be in a positive position at the time of the repair.

You've been the don or local champion of your neighborhood for too long, it's now time to aspire to become one of the champions of your province, city, state, country, and world. You have the ability to become whatever you desire, but it's your aspiration that will activate such an ability and spur you to utilize them accordingly.

We all have to start aspiring for a better life. If you don't aspire, you will never push yourself to do whatever it takes to make it happen. Let's stop settling for life in the ghetto. Let's stop settling for a minimum wage job. Let's stop having minimum wage qualifications and skills, etc.

It's time to go higher. It's time to climb higher. Because no one will ever provide you with whatever it is you feel you deserve, you should never hold out hope that someone will. Instead, make the most of any chance that comes your way. If you want anything, you can have it. If you want to attain any height, you can reach it. All you need to do is to aspire to become it, and you will find yourself doing whatever it will take to have it.

You will not be hindered if you choose to be at the summit of the mountain, but no one will hinder you if you wish to be at the base of the mountain. Create lofty goals for yourself to ignite the passion that will ultimately lead to the determination that will propel you to the pinnacle of success - where you belong. Expect to see us at the summit of the mountain!

Declare

- I can be more than this
- I can be better than this
- I can attain any height in life
- All I have to do is to aspire to it
- desire for it
- be determined to have it
- and work toward having it
- And I will have it.
- I refuse to settle for a life of mediocrity

Chapter 8

Be Proud of Who You Are

Today's wisdom: If you must seek validation from anyone, let that person be yourself.

Affirmation: I am proud of who I am.

Encouragement:

You are the only one who can approve of yourself. You are the only one who can validate yourself. No man or woman on earth can make you feel good or better about yourself than you already make yourself feel.

What exactly am I attempting to communicate to you here? All I am saying to you is that your validation is within or should I say, with you.

Your validation is in how you feel about yourself and how proud you are of yourself. No man can make you feel this way, only you can. If you mistakenly try to get your validation from people, you will never get it. They will take advantage of you, and you will feel much worse about yourself than you already do. That much is guaranteed.

Your validation is in your hands; you can only get such validation be seeing and appreciating yourself for who you are, that is, seeing yourself as the awesome creation of the creator.

Put on your best face and tell me if you notice anything that makes you feel good about yourself. It's that simple. What about the awesome qualities buried inside of you crying out for expression?

Brother, you're like a precious gem whose worth cannot be quantified. You're a man of inestimable value worth being proud of. Always be proud of who you are, your personality, and your individuality. Be proud of who God has made you to be, as well as the great skills that have been placed upon you. Respect yourself, respect your swag, respect your blackness, and respect everything about yourself that you are proud of.

You will never be able to actualize yourself until you accept yourself for who you are and feel secure in your own skin - no matter where you are. There is no one better than you. There is no one more important than you. There is no one more deserving of the wonderful things in life than you. The fact that you exist in a universe and a class of your own speaks volumes about your character. You can't be compared to anybody else since you're so distinct from everyone else!

You have a slew of impressive characteristics that most males of other races would kill to have. You should be proud of your incredible physical fitness as well as of your self-assurance, strength, and perseverance. You should also be proud of your tenacity and fighting spirit in the face of the storm of obstacles and oppression we face.

Men of other races would not be standing on their feet and holding their heads up if they had gone through half of what you have and are now going through. You're indestructible and simply too much of a valuable gemstone to be broken. Consequently, you should be proud of everything about yourself.

You are the product of the craftsmanship of the creator, a well-thought-out creation that has been fearfully and beautifully formed. You should feel pleased with yourself. So take pride in your accomplishments.

Declare these words aloud to yourself:

- I can never be ashamed of myself
- I am proud of who I am

- I am proud of what I am
- I am proud of the little progresses I have made
- I am proud of who God made me to be
- I am proud of everything about myself;
- I am proud of my "Africaness"
- I am proud of my blackness
- I am proud of my life

Chapter 9

We are All Humans and no Human is Inferior

Today's wisdom: Nobody can make you feel inferior if you don't think you're inferior.

Affirmation: I am not inferior to anyone.

Encouragement:

Please keep in mind that you are not inferior to anybody else, and that your race is not inferior to any other race, despite the fact that you may seem as such to others. We are all sprung from that one man and one woman, according to the Bible, who were both created by God when mankind was first formed. Consequently, we were all treated on an equal basis, and we continue to be treated on an equal basis in all respects.

Furthermore, race is a differentiation that has been created by man only for the purpose of gaining political advantage. The exploitation, slavery, and persecution of those who have physical characteristics that are significantly different from their own are the primary sins of these individuals. Their authoritarian impulses were legitimized by a slew of erroneous ideas that served as justification for their actions and beliefs.

Do you know why blacks were singled out for oppression? It was because blacks were discovered to be very tough, strong, skillful, productive, not easily infected by disease or broken down; we are people who can easily adapt to any weather condition. Hence, white get intimidated by our wonderful traits; and since they have governmental power, they have used it to subjugate us, oppress us, and try to limit us so that we wouldn't manifest our true potential and greatness.

Others are intimidated by our toughness, strengths and abilities. Did you know that we are responsible for the development of the United States, the United Kingdom, and some of the world's most industrialized countries? Yes, that is a fact! Go and read your history book and discover the truth of your greatness. Our skills and resources were exploited all in the guise of colonialism and slavery.

We were used to build nations because we were skillful, strong and tough, not because we were inferior. Can a skillful person be inferior? Can a tough and strong person be regarded as inferior? Read between the lines. They intended to break us down with their oppression and negative tags; yet we are still standing strong and pushing harder to show them that we cannot be broken.

They are even using the law and armed forces to systematically weigh us down just as they have always done, but we are pushing harder, trying to let them know that they can never stop us from taking our rightful place.

They are intimidated by us, they are scared of our toughness, they are scared of our strength, and they are scared of what we can achieve should we be given the chance to express ourselves freely without interference like every other race out there. That is their fear and why they are trying to break us down and stop us from manifesting our true potential with their unjustifiable hate and oppression.

We have to keep keeping our heads up. Don't allow them to break you, don't allow them to stop you from dreaming, don't allow them to stop you from aspiring for greater heights, don't allow them to stop you from believing in yourself and working hard to attain the future you desire.

Despite their best attempts, however, we have managed to retain our calm throughout the storm. Taking a glance at the map allows you to see how far we've come thus far on our journey. Consider how far we've come in the face of slavery and injustice over the course of many centuries. Now consider a few of the upgrades currently in the process of being implemented. Our voices are beginning to be heard as a consequence of our efforts, and we are on the verge of being enthroned as a result of our dedication and determination. Let us maintain our composure and continue to collaborate in order to attain our mutual aims. Their fear of us grows as our height rises, and their influence over us and our actions diminishes as our altitude increases.

Neither you nor anyone else is inferior, nor are you capable of being inferior. You should never act or behave in a subservient way toward anybody, even your own emotions, and you should avoid doing so at all costs. God did not create a race in the traditional sense; rather, humanity, which is what we refer to as the human race, is a product of the Creator of the universe. None of your gender should be victimized by someone who criticizes, discriminates against or mistreats you on the basis of your skin tone or other characteristics. Your race is beyond your control, and neither you nor anybody else has the power to alter the reality of your personal identity.

It was planned that every facet of your being would serve a specific purpose; you were created with the goal of being great, and you were supposed to be a black person. In recognition of the fact that you were created whole and beautiful, and that no one is more superior to you, you should embrace your blackness and be proud of your roots. You are great!

Declare these words to yourself:

- I am created by God;
- I am created for a purpose
- I am created to be awesome
- I am created to be great

- I am created black.
- I am not inferior to anyone

Chapter 10

Use it to Your Advantage

Today's wisdom: The easiest way to get unnoticed is to be like everyone else.

Affirmation: I appreciate my differences and uniqueness.

Encouragement:

Being different is a good thing. It makes you easily seen and stand out from the crowd. Imagine someone different from everyone else being exceptional at whatever he does; such a person will easily get noticed and talked about.

I think it's high time we start using our differences to our advantage. Being one of the few black students or employees in a class or organization provides a tremendous chance for me to work even harder and become one of the top students or workers; and as a result, I am able to achieve even more success.

Some people may feel threatened or intimidated by you and your exceptional performance, but that is a good thing. It's good for you to make them feel threatened and insecure around you with your exceptional performance or personality than for them to make you feel threatened because they think you can't measure up.

I must tell you that there's a special way you feel when you're very good at what you do when in the minority. You command attention and respect easily, and everyone get scared to mess with you because they know you're the real deal.

Have you noticed that most people of other races - mostly the racist ones who feel very uncomfortable in the presence of a successful black person or a well exposed and educated black person. They try to comport themselves around the black person. Your being different is a plus. It puts you in the spotlight and is a very great opportunity for you to let those around you know what you're made of by flaunting your uniqueness.

Now is the time in our lives to stop holding back and instead go all in for what we want. In every situation, we should try to be among the finest in the world, no matter what or who we are dealing with. Because of our genius, we have been able to free ourselves from the chains of servitude. It is only when people recognize that they will never be able to compete with us that they will stop themselves from being prejudiced against us or speaking badly about our achievements. We are in charge of businesses and have influence over some of the most powerful people in society. Doesn't it make sense that anybody would want to be associated with such individuals?

Our distinctiveness has already supplied us with a competitive advantage, but we must recognize and capitalize on this advantage if we are to be successful in our endeavors. Many are putting up a tremendous effort to prevent us from rising and demonstrating our grandeur, but no one can hold a great man down for a lengthy amount of time, especially who does not choose to be kept down. The tools we need to overcome our challenges and become heard and seen throughout the world are already in our possession.

Most of our people have risen from obscurity into the limelight even with the rampant oppression, subjugation, deprivation and economic alienation that people of our kind are subjected to. You too can do it. You can make a difference. You can get yourself seen and heard – not for something bad but for something very good.

The tide is beginning to turn and more and more opportunities are beginning to be made available for us. We have to take such opportunities: not just take them but excel in them and make others understand that we truly deserve being given a shot.

You and I are placed in a special position; we can use that position to make ourselves seen and heard by choosing to be exceptional. We have it in us, and we shouldn't be scared to manifest our greatness wherever we find ourselves.

Individuality and distinction define you; you were not supposed to be the same as everyone else; rather, you were formed to be distinct and different from everyone else on the planet. Every one of your talents and skills was predetermined to be unique to you from the moment of your conception. You were created to set yourself apart from the rest of the wolf pack, and you have done it successfully.

Your uniqueness and ability to command respect everywhere you go is God's intention for you throughout your time in this world. Your uniqueness extends to every aspect of your personality! In almost everything you do, you emit a unique and engaging personality that pulls people to you and keeps them interested. It is your personal individuality that differentiates you from others in this world. Examine your uniqueness as a source of pride, and discover how to use it to your advantage.

Remember to be proud of your individuality, as it is a distinguishing feature of your personality. Unless you desire to be like someone else, you should never strive to be like them. Even though you may want to be like everyone else, you should never wish it. You will lose your capacity to express yourself in a creative manner. It is your particular personality and set of talents that have contributed to you being the person you are now. Employing your imagination to your advantage will ensure that your endeavors are effective.

Declare these words to yourself:
- I was created to be different
- I was created to be special
- I was created to stand out

- I was created to be unique
- I will use my uniqueness to my advantage

Chapter 11

How do I Make Financial Affirmations work for Me?

Financial affirmations can help you boost your positive thinking to new heights. As a result, your attitude toward money will change. You will finally succeed in transforming your financial situation as a result of this new way of thinking, which is backed up by necessary action.

If you want financial affirmations to work for you, follow these steps.

Have an open mind

As a result of this being your first experience with a financial affirmation, you may be skeptical about its effectiveness in your particular scenario. This shouldn't bother you, though, because one of the things you'll need is an open mind; that is, the ability to remain extremely receptive to its efficacy. Affirmations only work if you believe in the process.

Trust the process

Financial affirmation can assist you in achieving your financial objectives. Your belief determines the effectiveness of the affirmation. As you take action, trust the process and believe in yourself.

Put in the work

Knowing how to build the optimal mental environment for wealth isn't enough. By working hard, you should be able to make it work out for you. You will work smarter than others who do not use financial affirmations. According to scientific evidence, thinking positively encourages the brain to strive toward the goal you seek.

Are you trying to make ends meet right now? If so, you are not alone. While you're at work, repeat the following financial affirmations to help you succeed faster. You'll make more money than you've ever made before you know it.

Consider these money mindset affirmations:

Repeat after me:

1. I'm not poor; I'm on my way to living a happy life.
2. More money in my bank account doesn't make me a bad person.
3. Riches is a tool that can help me enhance my situation.
4. I can create the fiscal picture I desire with simple work and creativity.
5. I am deserving of a good fiscal foundation.
6. More riches will flow back to me as a result of my great generosity.
7. I am a highly skilled individual who can overcome any wealth barrier.
8. I have the potential to become financially independent.
9. My fiscal goals aren't served by negative thoughts about wealth.

10. I'm not concerned about my finances because I have a plan in place.

11. When it comes to managing the money that comes into my life in order to achieve my financial objectives, I am confident in my abilities.

12. I am deserving of a prosperous existence.

13. The benefits of life find me open and sensitive to all that they have to offer.

14. Money comes to me quickly and easily.

15. My financial situation improves beyond my wildest expectations.

16. I have the ability to attract money and fortune into my life.

17. Unexpected funds are accepted and received by me.

18. I effortlessly and effortlessly attract money to me.

19. I let go of any reluctance to attract money.

20. When it comes to money, I am a winner.

21. I'm one step closer to reaching my financial objectives.

22. I own financial success, and I accept it now.

23. Every action I take will help to sow the seeds of prosperity.

24. I make sound financial judgments and have faith in my system.

25. I'm ready to achieve my financial objectives and desires.

26. I'm excited to get started and set some financial goals.

27. I am a savvy money manager.

28. It's simple for me to change my financial story.

29. I restore my financial authority.

30. I'm looking forward to getting more money.

31. I'm overjoyed at the prospect of earning extra money.

32. Because I'm willing to put in the effort, manifesting money is simple.

33. Every dollar that comes in now goes to work for me, allowing me to make more money.

34. Making money is enjoyable for me.

35. I'm effortlessly generating more cash and wealth.

36. Making money is simple.

37. I always have enough money.

If you are a salary worker consider these financial affirmations for salary earners:

Repeat after me:

1. Riches are a valuable resource that I can obtain.

2. I can use my wealth to better my family and sisters.

3. My earnings are sufficient to cover my expenses.

4. I'm confident in my ability to win more money.

5. I am deserving of the opportunity to set my own pay schedule.

6. With enough time, I will amass all the fortune that I desire.

7. I have sufficient wealth to make the most of my daily life without reservation.

8. In my life, there are countless opportunities to increase my wealth.

9. My laborious work will pay off handsomely.

10. I have the right to adequate remuneration for my skills and efforts.

11. I recognize the accumulation of wealth from various sources.

12. I'm on my way to being wealthy.

13. My pay offers a lot of room for growth.

14. Every instant, money is being drawn to me.

15. Money miraculously appears in my lap.

16. Money is a tool, and I intend to master its use.

17. I make the decision to be organized and fiscally prudent.

18. My savings will continue to increase, ensuring my financial security.

19. To protect myself, I'll set aside money in an emergency fund.

20. I overcame every stumbling block in my path to financial achievement.

21. The challenge of saving more money appeals to me.

22. Being wealthy is a part of my identity.

23. My financial situation is under my control.

24. Money becomes effortless no matter how I feel or what I do.

25. I'm going to be debt-free. I have the authority to bring it about.

26. I feel there is sufficient funds to meet everyone's needs.

27. I am financially independent.

28. I have plenty of cash on hand.

29. I have a lot of money.

30. Everyone has enough money in the cosmos.

31. I have the ability to achieve financial independence.

32. Financial independence will not be a pipe dream for me; it will become a reality.

33. I have far more money than I will ever be able to spend.

34. I am able to contribute and serve abundantly as I gain money.

35. Well-spent money is a source of excellent and beneficial outcomes.

36. I can give and serve generously because I have money.

37. I'll be conscious of my money so that it can benefit me and others.

38. My earnings enable me to live a life I enjoy.

39. Every money I spend is multiplied and returned to me.

40. Money is beneficial because I put it to good use.

41. Being wealthy allows me to help innumerable individuals around the world.

42. I become wealthier the more I contribute.

43. My prosperity and abundance assist others.

Practice saying these affirmations for effective money planning:

Repeat after me:

1. It's fun to figure out how to have a good time while being frugal.
2. I can spend my wealth on the things that are most important to me.
3. I can keep track of my expenses and stick to a budget.
4. I appreciate the challenge of putting more money aside.
5. My commitment has no power over me.
6. I have the authority to make difficult financial decisions now in order to enjoy a simpler life afterwards.
7. My expenses are under my control.
8. When I consistently shine through my riches, I am happy.
9. Each dollar saved brings me closer to a larger financial opportunity.
10. I have the ability to achieve huge wealth.
11. To be safe, I'll set up a back-up stash.
12. With careful planning, I can make my fantasies a reality.

13. I make the decision to go over my assets carefully.
14. Today, I will make judgments that will generate income for me.
15. I can set up a budgetary education foundation for you.
16. I want to keep all of my money.
17. I am focused on cutting all obligations that don't contribute to a good life.
18. Attracting money is one of my favorite things to do.
19. Right now, I have everything I need to start building riches.
20. In each venture I undertake, I am a magnet that attracts money.
21. I am in awe of my power to manifest money whenever I need it.
22. With my thinking today, I am constructing a rich future.
23. Right now, more money is pouring in for me.
24. I've chosen to concentrate on money flowing freely to me.
25. I'm surrounded by examples of abundance.
26. Money always picks me.
27. I imagine myself having money, and I imagine myself receiving more money.
28. Money is always drawn to me.
29. Money just appears in my lap.
30. My earnings are steadily increasing.

31. I am deserving of more money.

32. I make money doing what I enjoy.

33. I'm always attracting possibilities to make more money.

34. It is simple for me to make money.

35. In my life, I would welcome an endless supply of money and fortune.

36. I am able to generate enough revenue to support the lifestyle I choose.

37. I am entitled to more money.

38. I am open to new sources of money.

39. For anything I require, I always have more than enough.

40. Regardless of what happens, I choose to focus on abundance.

41. I have the appearance of a wealthy person.

42. I am wealthy, and I can buy anything I want.

43. I adore money because it adores me.

44. I am deserving of the fortune I seek.

45. Over money, I release all negative energies.

46. Money is the source of happiness and satisfaction.

47. Money and spirituality may live in peace together.

48. Money and love can be friends.

49. I can use money to make a positive difference in the world.

50. I make the decision to spend my money wisely.

51. I have the financial means to spend money on the things that are most important to me.

52. Money is utilized to make my life and the lives of those I care about better.

53. Having money gives me access to new experiences and chances.

54. More money will flow back to me as a result of careful generosity.

55. I am content with the money I spend and earn.

56. Money can broaden my life's possibilities.

57. When I spend my money wisely, I feel content.

58. I can use money to make a better life for myself.

Chapter 12

Affirmations for Positive Energy

You may have heard that nothing worthwhile can be done in this world with a negative mindset. That phrase, as cliche as it may seem, does have some truth to it. Our attitude has a significant impact on the amount of energy we focus not just toward ourselves but also toward one another. Think about it: are you being productive and doing your best while you're sulking on the sofa and allowing your mind to ruminate on everything that makes you feel bad? Without a doubt, this is not the case! All of your emotions are entirely legitimate in their own right at any given moment, but at some point you must brush aside the negativity and embrace a more optimistic energy in order to finish the tasks at hand.

Using affirmations to produce good energy in your life is the subject of this section of the book. As a compilation of words, affirmations are intended to elicit an emotional response or shift one's mental frame of mind. Earlier, we mentioned how the objective of affirmations is to counteract negative thinking with positive thinking.

What exactly is positive energy and why is it so crucial to generate good energy, especially for black women? If you are surrounded by positive energy, it does not imply that you are consciously disregarding all of life's unpleasantness. No, not at all. Positive energy, on the other hand, indicates that you are aware of the bad yet choose to rise above it. It won't make the pain go away, confronting your difficulties with a positive attitude can offer you a greater feeling of control and will increase your resilience.

It is a sad reality that, despite the fact that significant progress has been achieved in the direction of change, there are still many unpleasant components of society that create a great lot of difficulty and suffering for people of color. However, while spreading good energy will not solve all of the issues that black women are faced with, it will be enough to kickstart a movement.

The contagion of optimism is crucial for black girls—in fact, it is urgent—because they are subjected to so much unwarranted criticism and negativity from so many different sources (Harris, 2015). Being faced with so many systemic issues, all of which want to kill you at your core, means that positive energy is your most effective weapon for keeping happiness and good health in this environment.

Every part of life, even optimism, has a negative side that must be avoided. Positive energy is not the same as a false sensation of deluded optimism, which is quite different. Toxic positivity is described as an overt emphasis on the positive even when the reality of an optimistic view is not always feasible, such as in the case of tragic circumstances when toxic positivity may be harmful. A positive attitude is obviously beneficial, but it is not the only or even the most important remedy.

Consider the possibility that you have a broken leg for a minute. Positive energy will undoubtedly aid you on your journey through the healing process. Having a lousy attitude with a broken leg, after all, will only result in feeling worse for the whole period it takes to repair the injury. You will, however, have to undertake a significant amount of effort and healing on your own to adequately repair that limb.

It takes a significant lot of time and work to repair and restore anything of significance. It may even need the assistance of others in certain cases. Everyone will experience negative things at some point in their lives, no matter how positive their outlook. Your positive energy, on the other hand, is significant because of its ability to supply you with the stamina you need to get through challenging situations.

The question is, how can we recognize when we are leaning on a poisonous positivity? To determine if your optimism is beneficial to your present situation, the only thing you must do is ask yourself this question. You will almost certainly need to either re-evaluate the circumstance or change your approach to dealing with it to be successful in your endeavor. You should also consider whether you are using the garb of optimism to conceal the underlying source of the issue in question. Affirmations centered on positive thoughts and energy are only effective to a certain extent. When things get challenging, it is up to you to figure out what to do next. If you are going through a tough period, you should put your positivism on hold and prioritize receiving the support you need.

Knowing when to seek assistance is an important skill. The fact that you are seeking assistance from others does not imply that your good energy has failed. No, not at all. It is an indication that you have the inner fortitude to be vulnerable and put your own needs above those of others. It also displays a high degree of trust in other people, which is particularly important if you rely to friends and family for help while going through difficult circumstances. After all, we are a complex web of connections and interactions that are linked throughout our lives.

Affirmations are a powerful source of positive energy in and of themselves. By design, they are intended to bring about only positive outcomes in our lives. The question is, how can you customize them to produce more good energy? The first thing you'll want to keep in mind is what kind of people and situations you want to bring into your life. If you concentrate on anything negative, such as "today I will not do this," you are unintentionally introducing negative energy into your affirmation. Consider this: the negative implications of the term will not indicate that the behavior or action you're contemplating is bad if used correctly. After making a mistake and engaging in harmful activity, you will experience feelings of guilt as a result of your actions.

As an alternative, you could concentrate on utilizing affirmations to direct your attention toward good habits. Spending time thinking about and rewarding yourself for positive behavior rather than obsessing on a habit you are trying to avoid is more helpful for your mental health. This inflow of positivity will serve to reinforce the positive action in your thoughts, thereby increasing the effectiveness of the affirmation significantly. You may feel lingering sorrow if you make a mistake and are unable to complete your affirmation; nevertheless, it is more likely that you will concentrate on failing to do a good action than erroneously indulging in a bad activity if you do make a mistake.

Positive energy is important, particularly for a black woman. The ability to retain a positive attitude when presented with instances of institutional racism may be difficult to achieve. If you want to maintain your integrity, you can't afford to disregard these basic problems. The ability to maintain high levels of energy, on the other hand, is a crucial survival strategy. Consider it this way: there will undoubtedly be many circumstances that are difficult for you, but you must learn to accept them to go on.

However, you must be aware of which ones are worthy of a negative reaction in order to respond appropriately. With a negative attitude toward all of the challenges in your life, it is doubtful that you will make considerable success in your endeavors. Additionally, having a good attitude as a black woman helps to ensure that you do not allow bad circumstances to bring you down long term.

- I attract only good things in my life.

- There is nothing that I cannot accomplish.

- I will achieve all my aspirations.

- I will push myself to, and beyond, my limits.

- I am capable of much more than I know and give myself credit for.

- I am a beacon of joy and light.
- I have faced a setback, but it only exists to make me stronger.
- I have done well in all my endeavors.
- I have done even better than I expected.
- My life is full of comfort and happiness.
- I receive plenty of love and support in my life.
- I always have what I need.
- I live my life to the fullest.
- Nobody gets to tell me how big my dreams can be.
- With every passing day, I am becoming increasingly conscious of my power and my abilities.
- I am becoming wiser and happier every day.
- My life is a treasure to me, and I will always cherish it.
- I am a worthy and deserving person.
- I deserve to have a wonderful life.
- I can confidently address any challenges that come my way.
- I am willing to take risks that will benefit me in the long run.
- Every day is a brand-new opportunity to be happy and healthy.

- Today is going to be a fabulous and fruitful day.
- Life is too short to be ordinary – so I'll be extraordinary!
- All things are hard before they finally become less challenging.
- The unknown does not scare me.
- My life begins at the moment I step out of my comfort zone.
- My life does not have to be perfect to be outstanding.
- Everything happens for a reason.
- I am putting in all the effort to do the very best I can.
- I am trusting the process of life.
- I am allowing myself to grow.
- I am creating this life for myself.
- I am the sole author of my story.
- I'm not going to become somebody I don't want to be.
- I accept each situation as it is and do not try to change it.
- I am not afraid of anything.
- As I inhale confidence, I exhale fear.
- I ignore the judgment of others.
- I welcome all new opportunities and experiences.

- I am pursuing my dreams and achieving my goals.
- I am one step closer to my goals than I was yesterday.
- I can be anything I want.
- Imagination creates reality.
- My potential has no limits.
- Someone else's success only empowers me to keep going.
- I try to learn from my coworkers and share my ideas with them, as well.
- I always stay positive and happy.
- I work hard and never give up.
- I am open to criticism and never stop learning.
- I surround myself with warm, happy, and genuine people.
- I am passionate about my career.
- I am wealthy, and I am happy.
- A new car is a sign that I am blessed.
- It is not what I have that makes me rich, but what I am.
- I am the only person who can give my children a happy mother.
- I am a blessing to my children.
- I am caring and compassionate.

- I am becoming a better mom each day.
- I am calm and relaxed.
- My body is strong.
- I always teach my children new things.
- There is no influence as powerful as that of a mother.
- I am exactly what my child needs.
- Motherhood has made me a better person.
- No language can communicate the strength, beauty, and courage of a mother's love.
- My family appreciates my passion and hard work.
- Being a parent is my superpower.
- I trust all my intuitions as a mother.
- Motherhood is just a part of me, but not all of me.
- I know that I'm not a perfect mom all the time, but that is okay.
- I only know I want to be beautiful and inspiring.
- My weight does not define my worth.
- I don't compare myself to others.
- I am beautiful by being the way I am.

- No one can keep me from becoming the best version of myself.

- Nothing in this world is impossible. The word itself says, "I'm possible."

- I am fortunate beyond measure.

- My mental health and well-being are my priority.

- I love myself unconditionally.

- No one is me, and that is my superpower.

- I am flawed and fabulous.

- I am learning to accept my body.

- Beauty is not "one size fits all."

- Nobody is ugly – it's just that we live in a judgmental society.

- I accept my imperfect self.

- Society does not define my beauty – I define it.

- I believe in myself.

- I prioritize my well-being.

- I feel beautiful because I have decided to be myself.

- I don't have to fit in to belong.

- I am kind, intelligent, elegant, and charming.

- Challenges only help me grow.

- I have realized that beauty is not just physical. True beauty lies in my heart and shines from within me – it brightens up my surroundings.

- Loving myself is the most crucial part.

- I am worthy of love and time.

- I am worthy of the incredible things life has to offer.

- I am enough.

- I feel blessed to know people who love me every day, in every way.

- I love me first!

- I radiate love, and it shines from within.

- I am keeping my heart open to love.

- I am focusing on myself because I know that my soulmate will find me.

- I deserve unconditional love.

- I believe that something extraordinary is in store for me.

- I am in search of a partner who will respect me and love me wholeheartedly.

- All things are possible for me.

- I can achieve anything that I can conceive in my mind.

- I have the talents, skills and knowledge I need to succeed.

- I am naturally and effortlessly disciplined, hardworking, and motivated.

- I have full faith, trust, and pride in myself and my abilities.

- Everything is working together for my good.

- I am constantly attracting great opportunities.

- I am a magnet for wealth, good health, and loving relationships.

- I succeed in everything I put my mind to.

- Any resources I need to attain my goals are attracted to me.

- I am a true optimist at heart.

- I see the good in every person and the good in every situation.

- I love my life.

- I am in complete command of my emotions.

- I have the power to do anything.

- I am grateful to live a life that I love.

- I always feel full of energy and vitality.

- Each of my positive thoughts rewires my brain for effortless optimism.

- I am proud of the things that I have accomplished and the things that I will accomplish in the future.

- Being positive is a natural part of who I am.
- I am overflowing with joy and happiness.
- I am constantly growing and becoming better each and every day.
- I have the power and the strength to conquer any obstacle.
- I have good habits that are easy for me to maintain, and get me closer to my goals.
- I have a clear mind, a strong will, and an able body.
- I look forward to my future.
- I choose to feel happy every day.
- I deserve and attract the very best that life has to offer.
- I am always doing my best and my best is enough.
- Every day brings new opportunities and new excitement.
- I am successful in all areas of my life.
- I am energized by my life and the possibilities for my future.
- I have enthusiasm that is contagious to those around me.
- I have a zest for life that draws people to me.
- I am strong, confident, and unstoppable.
- I approach all situations with confidence.
- I am full of love, and a light to all those around me.

- I wake up every morning feeling great and looking forward to what the day will bring.

- Things are looking up for me, and getting better and better all the time.

- I am grateful for my present, and excited about my future.

- Anything I want, I can make happen.

- I know that the possibilities are endless for what I can achieve.

- I make the best out of every situation.

- My future is bright and brimming with possibilities.

- I am a co-creator of my life.

- I am grateful for every part of my past, present, and future.

- I am always looking ahead with optimism and confidence.

- Each day gets better and better.

- I go after the things that I want with optimism and confidence, and in turn I receive them.

- I am able to make the visions in my head come true in my life.

- It is only a matter of time before I achieve everything I want.

- I know I can have, be, or do whatever I want regardless of what other people may think.

- I am always learning, always growing, and always evolving.

- I am grateful for the person I am becoming as a result of the pursuit of my goals.

- I create my own luck.

- I am full of energy and vitality.

- I have a naturally carefree spirit.

- I am surrounded by beauty.

- It is expected that good things will happen to me.

- I am grateful to be in an environment that inspires me.

- Each day I wake up filled with energy and excitement about my life.

- Luck and good fortune follow me everywhere I go.

- People look at my life and wonder how did I get so lucky.

- I wholeheartedly believe in my goals whether other people do or not.

- I possess an unshakeable positive energy that keeps me happy and optimistic regardless of what's going on around me.

- I am the originator of my own good fortune.

- My positive energy is so strong that I am unmoved by other people's negative energy.

- My physical body is healthy and strong.

- My physical body gets stronger and stronger every day.

- I radiate a youthful and excited energy.
- I am grateful to feel a true sense of happiness that comes from within.
- I am currently living a life that I used to only dream about.
- My life serves as a beacon of hope for other people.
- I live a life that is balanced and successful in all areas.
- I have great ideas.
- I'm going to take a chance.
- When I move beyond of my comfort zone, my self-confidence increases.
- I have faith in myself.
- I stand up for my beliefs.
- I have many unique gifts and talents.
- I am brave.
- With every breath, I feel stronger.
- I can do hard things.
- I am capable.
- I stand up for things I believe in.
- I am courageous even when things are unknown to me.
- I embrace change.

- I am confident.
- I listen to my inner wisdom.
- I can handle this.
- I have the courage to be myself.
- My choices are my own.
- I have everything I need.
- I've arrived precisely where I'm supposed to be.
- My confidence increases every day.
- No matter how hard it is, I can do it.
- I trust myself.
- I am awesome.
- I understand that obstacles provide a chance to learn and improve.
- I can make good choices.
- I believe in myself.
- I can totally do this.
- I am a hard worker.
- I can be a leader.
- I have the words I need to express myself.

- I stand up for myself.
- I am not afraid to tackle big things.
- I can say no.
- I will get through this.
- I can do anything.
- I am strong and determined.
- I have courage in everything that I do.
- I can do whatever I focus my mind on.
- I can achieve my dreams.
- I can and I will.
- Being true to myself is what matters.

Chapter 13

Affirmations for Feeling Healthy

You will find in every self-help book on the world that your health is the most essential thing to consider and that you will not be able to solve your issues until you first take care of yourself. The reason that it may appear tedious at times is that it is an essential part of making long-term changes in your life. This will enable you to spend more of your time and energy on other parts of self-improvement in the future. Consider the following scenario: if you put a runner in a marathon who does not have the appropriate physical and mental health, he or she will collapse sometime along the course. This applies to the rest of us who don't take the required efforts to ensure we are in the greatest possible mental and physical form is the same.

This does not imply that your health will be restored to its previous state by magic. Some of you consider your healthiest to be someone else's bare minimum, and vice versa. Everyone's mental and bodily states are vastly different from one another. It is possible that some of you who are reading this are already in fantastic physical and mental health, whilst others may be facing internal concerns with physical and mental health of their own. Especially when other problems such as chronic health concerns and impairments are thrown into the mix, the situation becomes much worse. Your primary emphasis should be on doing the best you can within the confines of your talents and limitations. If you attempt to push yourself harder than you are capable of, there are several ways in which you might cause catastrophic injury to your body.

The most important thing to remember while using affirmations to improve your physical health is to concentrate on becoming the healthiest version possible. Focusing on smaller, more realistic objectives is essential for success. The likelihood of seeing significant success in weight loss is low if you are staring in the mirror every day and telling yourself, "I'm going to lose weight."

For starters, the scope of your affirmation is way too wide in terms of its concentration. Instead, pay attention to the details. Alternatively, center the affirmation on a daily job that you are capable of doing. Simply confirming that you are going to go for a walk or doing a specific number of sit-ups in the morning will help you achieve your health goals. Another option is to concentrate on the things your body is capable of doing. Certain individuals will never be runners or weight lifters, for whatever reason. Consider what your body is capable of in order to maintain your health.

When it comes to eating healthily, we aren't necessarily going to concentrate on what meals are good for us versus what foods are bad. Instead, think about what meals provide you with nutrition and delight. If you want to be healthy, it doesn't mean you have to live on boring salads for the rest of your life. Affirm the advantages provided by your food and urge yourself to explore a range of different, nutritious foods to stimulate your taste buds. Having a strong belief in your ability to eat for health rather than weight reduction is also important. When we put an excessive amount of attention on eating just for the sake of weight reduction, it may have the unintended consequence of leading us to categorize foods as either good or bad, causing us to feel horrible if we ingest a "bad" item.

Mental health is an important element of our overall health and well-being that is sometimes overlooked. When it comes to health, many people prefer to think only about the physical aspects. It's true that having a healthy body also means having a healthy mind. As it turns out, the opposite is also true. We lose the motivation to take care of ourselves and our bodies when our mental health is in a bad condition, which has an effect on our physical health as well.

For black women, in particular, mental health may be a difficult issue to broach. It is not unusual for women in general not to be taken seriously when it comes to their mental health; but for black women, this is compounded by the fact that they are both female and of African descent. Consider the fact that mental health isn't as often discussed in black communities and certain physicians may not take your mental health seriously.

There is also a stereotype of the "strong black lady," who is self-sufficient and does not need the assistance of others. But, after all, we are human! There may be occasions when you will not be able to maintain your strength, and this is entirely normal. You can't be strong in every situation all of the time. It is critical to recognize when you need to reach out and speak with someone about the problems you are experiencing. Asking for assistance with one's mental health is not a sign of weakness, particularly when one's mental health may be such an unacknowledged burden, as it can be for black women in particular.

In part, the fact that black women have so much to cope with contributes to the importance of mental health in this population. Several scars on the skin of black people have been left by centuries of tyranny and discrimination. There have been generations of pain and suffering as a result of systemic problems. Then there's the fact that any kind of racism you may encounter in your day-to-day existence is both detrimental and distressing. As a result, it is vital to be honest with yourself about your emotions and take your mental health seriously.

When it comes to improving mental health, positive affirmations are one of the most utilized methods available. Do you recall that we stated that affirmations have the ability to reprogram your thinking and mental processes? A large part of mental disease, such as depression or anxiety, is characterized by persistently negative thoughts. These are the kinds of ideas that bring you extreme anguish and have a negative influence on your mental health. Affirmations, on the other hand, are an excellent tool for combating some of these negative beliefs. For the sole purpose of the simplicity and clarity in our discussion, we will limit ourselves to the more prevalent disorders of anxiety and depression, despite the fact that there are several other types of mental illnesses and health concerns.

Physical health is one of the most important building blocks of a happy and successful life. When we are in our best physical condition, it seems that everything else falls into place. This results in greater overall health, more confidence in our bodies, and more energy to dedicate to other aspects of our lives. You can't possibly have an impact on physical health by using positive affirmations, can you? Actually, you most certainly can! "Mind above matter" is a saying often heard. Consider why you want to be healthy in the first place. If the response is for the sake of someone other than yourself, you need to reevaluate your values and priorities.

Self-affirming statements may also be an excellent tool for inspiring yourself to maintain good physical health. It might be as easy as telling yourself, "I will drink enough water today," or "I will set aside some time to engage in a physical activity that I find enjoyable." The most effective method of reinforcing these specific affirmations is to simply practice them. In terms of our health, just saying the words isn't enough. We must also act on them. Improved physical health requires a significant amount of effort on your part, which you should be prepared to put up. Instead, make certain that your affirmations include contain specific activities you can participate in to enhance your health, such as exercising and eating healthily as well as getting enough sleep and being hydrated.

- Today, I'm going to fuel my body with nutritious food and physical activity.

- Today I will do something nice for my body.

- Today I will participate in an exercise that I enjoy.

- My body is the vessel that carries me through this life. I am grateful for all that it does for me.

- Exercise sustains and fuels me.

- I will eat foods that nourish and enrich my body and mind.

- When I take care of my body, I feel more in control of my life. I am strong in my physicality.

- My body is a strong and powerful vessel.

- There is nothing that my body cannot accomplish.

- I thank my body for all the ways it has cared for me over the years.

- I am a good and worthy person and I don't need to feel bad about myself for not doing my best today.

- I enjoy using my body's strength to nourish my life through this exercise.

- I enjoy being physically active.

- This exercise brings me great joy to do.

- I am grateful that this food provides me the energy I need to go about my day.

- I put my health and healing above everything else and strive to live a good life.

- I am enough. I have my back.

- I deserve the best and am ready to start over.

- I am at ease with my pain since I know it will heal soon.
- I know the power of love will cure all my sufferings.
- I have no doubts and fears regarding my abilities.
- My immune system is healing my body.
- I accept my flaws and work towards becoming a better person.
- My body is strong and healing.
- I know how to care for myself.
- I am courageous and can face the challenges lying ahead of me.
- I deserve peace to ensure my mental well-being.
- I try to visualize my highest self to take good care of my mental health.
- I always treat myself with the utmost compassion, kindness, and love.
- I give ample time and space to my soul to heal, build strength, and find peace.
- I am healthy and whole.
- I permit myself to heal from the inside out.
- I am ready to give my best. I have prepared well for this.
- I have the perfect body, a brilliant mind, and a tranquil spirit.
- I prioritize and practice self-care daily.

- Each day, as I wake up, I feel grateful for life.
- I am building a strong body to help me live a healthy life.
- Obstacles do not break me. They strengthen me.
- I choose to focus on my mental wellness.
- My mental health diagnosis does not define who I am as a person.
- I believe everything heals with time.
- Everything happens for a good reason, always.
- I have compassion and kindness for everyone.
- I know the right person is going to enter my life soon.
- My health is getting better each day.
- I choose to be happy.
- I can manifest joy and healing.
- Peace and appreciation flow through my mind like a clear stream.
- My external beauty does not define me. Instead, it's the purity of my heart that matters the most.
- Everything is alright in my realm.
- I'm slowly healing from all the losses, heartbreaks, and disappointments.

- I'm patient – I give myself enough time and let go of things that I can't control.

- I create space in my current life to heal my sadness and let go of the past.

- I'm sure that I can endure bad days.

- The more I let go of my past, the more I can focus on moving forward and enjoying life.

- I'm not a victim and do not fear anyone.

- I'm not inferior to anyone. My weaknesses are my strengths.

- I have a positive mindset. If I fall back, I'm not going to be stuck forever.

- I am learning and growing every moment.

- Nothing hampers my optimism and self-control.

- I have perfect health.

- All the care and affection I need is within me.

- I don't hold resentment against the people who have hurt me in the past. I prefer to let go and focus on what I want.

- Pain is the best teacher, and I'm using it to learn how to meet life's challenges.

- I am healthy.

- It is my track record that I am 100 percent successful in letting go of negativity. Yes, I am capable of doing this as well.

- I release all emotional blocks that prevent me from healing and enjoying peace of mind.

- I have a healthy and pain-free back.

- I welcome blessings to rain over me.

- I am vibrant and resilient.

- I am always kind.

- I am a lot more energetic than my wounds and sickness.

- I have decided to open my heart to love again.

- I hope to feel the precious innocence and eternal warmth of deep love.

- I am anxious, but so what? I can handle it.

- Life is God's beautiful gift.

- I deserve a life filled with love and happiness.

- I trust and respect my body's wisdom.

- I am in charge of healing and understanding the needs of my body.

- I know my limitations. I am independent and respect my boundaries.

- I am creating better mental health each day.

- No matter how hard the situation becomes, I'm going to win in the end.

- I prefer my inner peace more than false hopes and temporary satisfactions.

- I always aim to surround myself with positive people and things.

- I take in relaxation and release all the tension out of my body.

- I prioritize what I think about myself more than what others think of me.

- Love is my priority, not the loss.

- I am ready to conquer the hearts of everyone with my work.

- I have the power to heal myself, and I'm getting healthier every day.

- I love everything that has shaped me into who I am.

- Stress cannot take control of my life because a divine force protects me.

- I am not afraid to share my true feelings.

- My past doesn't define my present and future.

- My motto in life is to forgive myself and those who hurt me.

- I am worthy, talented, deserving, and healthy.

- I heal by replacing my negative thoughts with positive ones.

- I feel loved and can live in peace.

- I have a soul full of energy and pure love.

- I'm in the process of healing my mental health.

- I will cure my wounds, soul, mind and see things differently.
- I will discover the purpose of my existence and own my truth.
- There is confidence, hope, and vigor all around me.
- I am in great shape and thankful to my body for healing.
- I am a warrior who celebrates my tenacity.
- I cultivate peace, energy, and love in my spirits.
- I am okay.
- I am flowing and adaptable.
- Calmness and poise have stepped into my life.
- I have no time for drama and pessimism in my life.
- I heal faster when I focus on self-love instead of self-criticism.
- I want to fly free, so I've given up on everything that weighs me down.
- I meditate to free my mind from negative thoughts.
- I am mentally well and stable.
- My body is in harmony with the Universe.
- I aim for peace daily, no matter how difficult it is.
- I am ready to heal and accept miracles beyond my expectations.
- I am healthy and happy.

- I give my body the care and attention it deserves.

- I'm always looking for new methods and ways to improve my health.

- I am lean, fit, and fabulous!

- I am thankful for my strong bones and good health.

- My body is clean and free from any sicknesses and diseases.

- My body is ready to get in shape.

- I love my body, and I'm kind to myself. This love and kindness transform into a healthy me.

- I choose nutritious and healing foods to maintain good health.

- My body receives all the essential vitamins and nutrients it needs to survive.

- I love to smile. It's my gift to the world.

- I choose health and well-being because I'm worth it.

- I'm free of diabetes, blood pressure problems, and all life-threatening diseases.

- I love my body for all the amazing things it can do!

- My body functions exactly as it is supposed to.

- I am grateful to be healthy at every age.

- I take good care of myself as I want to enter old age as a healthy person.

- I am creating new and healthy beliefs and perceptions about aging.
- I am aging gracefully.
- I love my skin and appreciate how youthful it looks.
- Every day, my skin is becoming healthier.
- I am learning new ways to improve my skin health.
- I consume healthy food that nourishes my skin and enhances my overall beauty.
- My skin is smooth, soft, and radiant.
- My skin is naturally healthy and unblemished.
- My pores are healthy.
- Everyone envies my clear and firm skin.
- I admire my glowing, vibrant and gorgeous skin.
- I am grateful for my healthy skin and how beautiful my face looks.
- I embrace the wisdom of my body.
- My body knows what is best for it. So, I listen to my body, and that keeps me healthy.
- I love my healthy routine since it is good for me and helps to inspire my friends.
- I am full of energy.

- I drink enough water to hydrate my body.
- I have chosen good health for my entire life.
- Since I exercise, I know my body will repay me with extra years of good health.
- I am grateful for my body.
- I treat my body with utmost love and respect.
- With each repetition, my body builds itself.
- Each time I exercise, my body grows stronger!
- I love feeling strong and fit.
- I can run 5 miles without a break!
- My body stays in perfect health all the time.
- I keep my body in ideal shape for myself and my family.
- I crush all my fitness goals!
- I treat my body like a temple.
- I invest plenty of time taking care of my body.
- My body is one of the most valuable gifts I will ever receive.
- My body deserves the best treatment. So, I exercise daily and feed it nourishing food.
- My health is my highly treasured wealth.
- I am powerful, confident, and motivated.

- I radiate confidence, joy, and health.

- I am pain-free and disease-free as I avoid extremities in life and live in moderation.

- I radiate positive energy and vitality.

- I love accomplishing things.

- My mind is clear and focused.

- Since my mind is healthy, I can easily focus on finishing my tasks.

- I'm motivated to have a productive day.

- I'm motivated to work hard today.

- I'm alive, well, and healthy.

- Everything is working well for me.

- My mind is calm and at peace.

- Happy and pleasant thoughts contribute to my healthy body.

- I release emotions that create unhealthy habits.

- I always think about my wellness, and these healthy thoughts result in my good health.

- I am motivated to get more done.

- I have the energy to finish my tasks.

- I am on my path to becoming a healthier person.

- I have strong willpower.

- I love having healthy drinks.

- I choose to be healthy.

- I choose to eat well and work out regularly to energize myself.

- My body is in great shape.

- I am slim, sassy, and I feel great!

- I pay attention to my body.

- I look and feel youthful.

- I charge my body with nutrient-rich fruits and vegetables, thus having a ton of energy for my workouts.

- I take care of my body.

- My body is my best friend.

- I work out to honor the strength and grit of my body.

- Finding new ways to eat healthily empowers me and puts me in control.

- My immune system is healthy and robust.

- Every day, I take care of myself physically, mentally, and spiritually.

- My body and mind are healthy and vibrant.

- I deserve to feel healthy and vibrant.

- I believe in blessing and helping others. Such a mentality makes me stress-free and keeps away diseases.
- I send positive and loving thoughts to all parts of my body, and my body responds by remaining healthy.
- I focus on releasing all the tension in my muscles and notice how much easier and lighter I feel.
- I accept every situation as it is.
- I am mentally strong.
- I am healthy and thriving.
- I give equal priority to my mental and physical well-being.
- I take mental health breaks to recharge.
- I permit myself to take some rest without feeling guilty about it.
- I am worthy of love and healthy choices.
- I lovingly do everything I can to help my body stay healthy.
- I feel confident in my ability to better my health today.
- I nourish my mind with healthy and wholesome thoughts about my body.
- My body is a kick-ass machine!
- My body and mind vibrate with good energy and good health.
- My health challenges make me a warrior.
- I have enough energy for all the daily activities in my life.

- Work, rest, and play – all are equally important to me. However, I maintain a balance among the three, and that keeps me fit.

Chapter 13

Affirmations for Weight Loss

In terms of health, affirmations are useful resources to put yourself in an ideal position. Weight reduction claims can only be an acknowledgment and acceptance of something you tell yourself if you are tempted to eat to lose weight. It doesn't lead you back into your old habits but helps you progress toward this target.

It could be a slogan, a mantra, or whatever you want to call it. The trick is to give the brain positive signals to match any desire. This helps you to lose weight further. It should be something you have confidence in and will keep you on track.

According to Barbara Hoberman Levine, the mind and body come together to make a conscientious effort to focus on something. Every day, people who want to lose weight face a battle against cravings and temptation. This is when declarations come in. As a personal motto, this person would "own" statements not borrowed from another person. You can think of words like "I'm on a health journey" or "I love what I do today.
Many people believe that saying the affirmation words is enough to melt the pounds without effort, but the words themselves are powerless. The sound is the most significant part of the declaration.

Consider the meaning of what you want to do for a moment. The rule of attraction is caused by the dominant focus on universal feelings, beliefs, and expectations. This dominant focus stimulates corresponding feelings, helping you know what sort of result you are getting.

When you've got an overarching thought such as:

- I hate my body.
- I hate being obese.
- I hate to feel self-aware.
- I hate to feel insecure about my body.
- I hate these extra pounds.

To present a slim, healthy body, you must select thoughts that make you feel like you have a slender, healthy body.

One conventional approach to declarations is to say that they are valid:

"I weigh 125 pounds. I'm slim, athletic, and safe."

Only when you make those comments will you understand that they won't work for everybody automatically. You know that in the back of your mind, they're wrong so you feel a little resistance.

This opposition serves to delay the campaign. This resistance can be resolved by reciting the sentence repeatedly tens of times a day. Over time, you can gradually eliminate the resistance and start resonating with that frequency.

For weight loss and smoking cessation, I repeat every day how the love of self is essential to find one's way. Indeed, when we arrive at our first hypnosis session to lose weight, we have often tried many diets. It is even very likely that a kind of "internal war" has taken hold. The positive affirmations for losing weight are therefore daily support and easy to set up, allowing one to continue the work done in the session. They allow you to work yourself both self-esteem and self-confidence, which are essential to move on the path to weight loss.

- Life is beautiful, and I enjoy it by staying fit and maintaining my ideal weight.

- I have a dieting and weight loss plan, and I will continue to stick to it.

- I have the potential to transform my life with the decisions I make every day.
- Every day, I am steadily approaching my ideal weight.
- I love being physically fit.
- I love exercising and working out daily as it helps me maintain my weight.
- The more I exercise, the better role model I can be for others!
- I am motivated to do exercise daily.
- Motivation for exercise comes easily to me.
- I am committed to finishing my exercises.
- I strive to set goals that are realistic to attain.
- I never miss a workout.
- I can't wait to hit the gym.
- I am going to have an excellent workout.
- I have a lot of fun going to the gym regularly.
- I am ready to work out because I am full of energy.
- I am ready to push myself to reach new limits.
- I am ready to give my 100% in my workout.
- I am getting the body I always wanted.
- I take deep breaths so that my metabolism is at its perfect rate.

- Each physical movement that I make burns the extra fat in my body and helps me maintain my ideal body weight.

- I love myself unconditionally.

- I release all mental and emotional blocks to losing weight and becoming fit. I deserve to be healthy.

- Losing weight comes naturally to me. I do it at will, whenever necessary.

- I easily attain and maintain my ideal weight. The excess weight falls off me readily.

- My deep breathing exercises increase my metabolism and facilitate my weight loss.

- My metabolism rate is at its optimum levels.

- I love to eat healthy food, and it helps me reach my ideal weight.

- I show respect toward my body by feeding it well.

- I take time to chew the food I eat to digest it properly.

- I am a disciplined eater.

- I am highly conscious of the food I eat.

- I am in control of all my choices and actions.

- I eat nutritious food.

- I always eat balanced meals.

- My body and mind are well-nourished.

- Everything I eat strengthens me.
- I am now dissolving all my desires for unhealthy food. My love and appreciation for healthy food are now growing.
- I have a healthy relationship with food.
- Food is not my enemy.
- Every day, I make good eating choices.
- I prefer nutritious food over junk food.
- I realize junk food is an addiction.
- I no longer crave junk foods.
- I only crave healthy and nutritious meals.
- I live healthily and plan my diet.
- I eat moderately.
- I eat small healthy meals.
- I am in control of my cravings.
- I only eat when I am hungry.
- I eat timely and work enthusiastically.
- I do not snack at night.
- I eat just enough food to nourish myself.
- I always stop eating when my stomach feels full.

- I delight in healthy delicacies.
- My skin is fresh with more fruits and vegetables.
- I enjoy feeling light and clean.
- I take extra care in nourishing my body with vitamin-rich foods.
- I only desire healthy food items such as lean protein and healthy fats.
- The food items I eat are increasing my metabolism.
- I only eat meals that give my body the fuel it needs to thrive.
- I no longer eat for comfort but health and vitality.
- I eat what my body needs.
- I now eat only healthy food to maintain fitness.
- I forgive myself for any error I may have committed in the past regarding food.
- Every day, I make conscious efforts to choose the proper meals to eat.
- I am 100% committed to losing the extra weight.
- I will not give up on my diet goals and will persevere until the end.
- As my body and mind are healthy, I lose weight regularly.
- I am shedding my excess weight right now.
- I have a beautifully toned body.

- I am improving my shape every day.
- Every day, I am getting slimmer and fitter.
- I am a physically active person.
- I am fit and attractive.
- I see a "fitter" person looking back at me when checking myself in the mirror.
- My weight does not define me.
- I am a thin person.
- I am slim and lean.
- My tummy is flat and toned.
- Every day, my body is getting thinner.
- I have a fit and toned body.
- I am in control of my thoughts.
- I am in control of my choices.
- I am in control of my entire life, and that gives me more confidence.
- I am thrilled to break a sweat and burn some calories.
- I am 100% committed to creating a healthy lifestyle for myself.
- Each cell in my body is fit and healthy, and so am I.

- I easily keep my weight under control through a combination of healthy eating and exercising.

- My body is a sacred temple.

- Everything I eat nourishes and rejuvenates my body and mind.

- It is becoming easier to make small changes in my life. I am enjoying the feeling of well-being these changes are giving me.

- I do not aim for perfection. I accept all my mistakes and learn from them.

- I accept my past and know that the future will be bright and happy.

- I'm not afraid to say no when I need to.

- I have transcended my impulsive habits regarding food. I now eat only healthy meals in limited quantities.

- I exercise daily to enjoy a healthy, toned body. I love the feeling exercise gives me.

- I take immense pride in all my hard work.

- I let go of all the negativity that rests in my body and mind. I choose to be positive and to surround myself with positive people.

- It does not matter what others say or do. What matters more is how I choose to react and what I choose to believe about myself.

- I believe in my capability to lose weight successfully.

- I'm fully confident that my weight loss plan will work, and my weight will stay at a fixed point from now on.
- I take care of myself and it makes me feel good
- I feel better and better
- I am proud not to give in to gluttony, bad for my health
- Each day brings me a little closer to my goal
- I have a healthy life and I eliminate my bad habits
- I lose weight because I love myself (not because I don't like my body)
- I have earned the right to be joyful and to have self-confidence.
- I can do it.

Chapter 14

Affirmations for Spirituality

White supremacy manifests itself in several ways and through a range of tactics. It has led to the birth of the notion of race, and the othering, subjugation, enslavement, and colonization of a whole continent's worth of human beings. There isn't a single nook or cranny of the earth that has been left unaffected by the consequences. A fundamental belief behind it all is the idea that there is only one right way to do things, and that there is only one kind of person who should be emulated.

As opposed to religious freedom , it's possible that the United States was founded on the notion of religious freedom for colonies such as the Quakers, Shakers, Puritans, and Protestants who wanted to believe and practice in a way that differed from what the monarchy mandated. This so-called freedom was unfortunately enjoyed at the expense of other people's liberties. This was tragic.

Everything, however, was not lost in the process. On a broad scale, attempts were made to deprive black people of their language, religion, culture, and customs, as well as their history and heritage. We were never able to entirely renounce the religious and spiritual practices that kept us connected to our source, despite our best efforts.

This tradition offered food and security to the black community during all the hardships we faced, even when they had to be buried, changed, and syncretized with the religion of our oppressor.

Modern evidence may be seen in the flexibility of black spiritual traditions, and also in the many methods by which we have used them to get through some of the most difficult eras in our history. For centuries, prior to the development of wellness and mental health, there was always "the black church," which served as a beacon of the hope for people in difficult times. Whether one believes in God or not, religion and spirituality have been shown to have good impacts on one's mental health.

It has been shown that spirituality, as well as healthy activities for the mind and body, may have a major influence on mental health and emotional well-being, according to the National Alliance on Mental Illness. According to all the recent findings of a recent study published in the Journal of Religion and Health, author Archie Smith Jr. believes that religion and spirituality are key aspects of the black identity.

When it comes to mental health, Smith writes, "to dismiss the religious character of human beings while striving to restore them to psychological health would not only belittle a significant mental health resource in the black experience," but it would also be "a belittlement of a significant mental health resource in the black experience." Specifically, the study states that it "would further alienate black people from a knowledge of the creative and spiritual depths in which their humanity participates and upon which their ultimate well-being ultimately depends."

Many blacks, and certainly those who have gone before them, hold the belief that one's total well-being is contingent on one's participation in spiritual practice and the performance of its rites. This means that spiritual well-being is intimately linked to mental well-being, and the two activities should be employed in tandem rather than separately.

- I believe I am a spirit living inside a body and on the road to enlightenment.

- I'm a magnet for miracles.

- I have access to the unlimited abundance of the Universe.

- I let rest, security, and love wash over me.
- I am a beautiful soul.
- I surrender to God. He is always with me. I do only his bidding.
- I am one with the Universe.
- I am complete because I am a Divine creation, a part of the Infinite Intelligence.
- My body and mind are always in alignment with the Universe.
- I do all things through God, who strengthens me.
- I respectfully and patiently ask for Divine guidance on everything.
- My life is a blessing.
- The Universe shines its pure light on me.
- Finding enlightenment comes naturally and effortlessly to me.
- I am free.
- I can tap into the source energy at any time.
- The Universe guides me on anything and everything divinely.
- I am a channel for inspiration.
- I am pure.
- Today, I am closer to the Universe.
- I am on the path to enlightenment.

- I breathe in the light of God.
- I am responsible for my spiritual growth.
- I acknowledge God in every creation.
- I am kind to all living things.
- I have faith in the divine plan of the Universe.
- I am an eternal and infinite being here on Earth to learn my lessons.
- Spirit is always guiding me.
- I release all the blocks to my spiritual connection and embark on my journey to self-realization.
- I am grateful for all the incredible blessings in my life.
- I let go of fear so that I'm ready to realign.
- I know that the Universe has my best interests in mind, and I am receiving all I need to succeed.
- The wisdom and knowledge of the Universe live inside me.
- I am a divine being.
- I am far more than my thoughts and feelings.
- I know the Universe is guiding me toward the highest good.
- I feel secure in the arms of God.
- God's love is flowing through me now and always.

- I am a divine expression of God.
- Positive energy flows to and from me.
- My spirit is whole.
- I am the light in all situations.
- I am love.
- The power of God moves my spirit.
- I beg for forgiveness from those whom I may have wronged and forgive all those who have wronged me.
- I am His, and He is mine.
- When I love others, I receive even more love from them in return.
- I unlock my heart and mind to the perfect love of the Universe.
- My spirit is at peace.
- I view my obstacles as opportunities to get closer to God.
- All my thoughts, actions, and words are guided by divine power.
- I derive happiness from the Universe.
- All is well in my life. I am immensely blessed.
- I'm ready for the Universe to lead me.
- I am connected to the Universe.
- I am holy.

- I allow the Universe to function through me.
- My spirit is enlightened.
- I am in sync with my inner guide.
- I am rooted in Mother Earth's energy.
- I always listen to my inner compass.
- I'm willing to learn through love.
- I emanate peace and love.
- I share my joy and love with those who thirst for peace.
- Everything happens at the right time, and I'm happy to live this journey.
- I am with God, and God is with me.
- The Divine Spirit is present all around me and guides me at every step.
- My life is full of gratitude and compassion for God.
- My energy is in tune with the Universe.
- My heart is tranquil.
- Divine light permeates every particle of my being.
- The Universe provides for all my needs.
- I believe everything in my life is working for my highest good, and I'm receiving all that I'm meant to have.

- I am a spiritual entity having a human experience.
- I take a step back and let the Universe lead the way.
- I unlock my mind and heart to the guidance of God.
- This world is my classroom, and the people are my assignments.
- My true strength lies in the present moment.
- I feel the power of divine love.
- I shine my light on those around me.
- I am made of the light of the Universe.
- My spirit and courage are unwavering.
- I'm ready to lift the veil of the spiritual realm.
- I believe religion to be a way of life. It is a way of living an ethical life.
- I am aligned with my higher purpose.
- I am a kind, loving, and spiritual person.
- I let go of fear and pain.
- I live in love.
- I am an extension of the Universe.
- I embrace the bond I share with all life forms on this Earth.
- The healing power of the Universe flows through all the cells of my body.

- The Universe has my back, always.
- I am sacred.
- I always let love lead the way.
- I am connected to the wisdom of the Universe.
- I trust my intuition.
- I live in nirvana.
- I share my knowledge with the world.
- My intuition is my superpower.
- Love flows through me.
- I allow God to guide me in everything I do.

Chapter 15

Affirmations for Achieving Goals

Another major problem that individuals who have poor self-esteem suffer from is a lack of drive to pursue their dreams, which is compounded by an array of negative ideas that tell them they aren't worth anything. They tell themselves that there's no point in going out and trying to become something because they know they're going to fail. This causes them never to set goals for themselves or lookout for people to mentor them or act as role models. Over time, this can manifest in the person feeling purposeless and lonely, leading to other mental health issues such as depression.

Setting goals are a great way to keep your head above water and give yourself something to work toward. If you achieve a goal you have set for yourself, you will feel a mental boost in confidence, and everything you previously felt you were unable to accomplish will suddenly become a possibility for you to pursue. If completed many times over any given period of time, it can change your life in ways you never thought possible. As a consequence of your efforts, you will convert yourself into a new person who is more confident in their abilities, happier with what they have accomplished, and mentally better as a result.

Before going on about the kind of goals you can set and how you can slowly work toward them, you need to know what you want out of life and visualize it. What do you want to look like? Where do you want to live? What kind of car do you want to drive?

The point of visualization is to give yourself an image of what you're working toward. You don't want to worry about the journey; just focus on the destination for now. Typically speaking, the more specific you are with visualizing, the better. Setting goals is part and parcel of our daily lives, and every person has to take part in it if they are to achieve anything worthwhile. We have to set goals in all areas of our lives, including our finances, careers, health, relationships, and even our spirituality. We are more and more influenced to aim for what comes next. The goals you set can be either of a personal or professional nature, or even both at the same time.

Setting goals means selecting a certain target important to you and asking how to achieve it, whether big or small. The most essential thing to consider when creating goals is knowing what you want to achieve and how much of your time and resources you are prepared to devote to achieving those objectives.

Set goals that you are passionate about. Let your goals align with your dreams, and you will be able to enjoy seeking them. Doing what you care for means you do it for more than just the financial rewards. You do it because it has meaning to your life. This will help you, especially during the bumpy times, to keep your head focused because you truly care for what you have set out to accomplish.

Remember that procrastination can be crippling, and, therefore, you should never entertain it. When you set your goals, do not file them away to be done another day. No. Get started here and now. Most of the time, procrastination comes because we fear the path we are about to follow and the unknown which lies ahead.

To maintain your resilience and positivity as you work on your goals, come up with ways that have meaning to you and for which you can reward yourself. Set your goals and once you have achieved something, maybe after a step toward the ultimate goal, reward your accomplishment. Treat yourself to something wonderful like a night out, your favorite food, or a little shopping.

You can plan out several goals, but the two main ones are short-term and long-term goals. Before looking into the ins and outs of setting them, it's important to know how to properly structure a goal. Luckily, there is an acronym that does just this: SMART. It stands for:

Specific - The goal is specific.

Measurable - You're able to measure when you've accomplished your goal. This stops you from aimlessly working towards something without an end goal in sight.

Achievable - You can accomplish the goal you're setting out to do.

Relevant - What you're doing is relevant to where you see yourself by the end of the goal.

Time-Based - You're able to set a deadline with this goal.

SMART goals are great because they are simple. They allow you to organize and set out many goals at once rather than sitting there, planning them out in your head, only to realize a month later that it isn't realistic and you don't have a deadline.

Following your grasp of the fundamental structure of a good goal, it's time to analyze one of the two key kinds of goals: long-term aims and short-term objectives.

Long-term goals are the "bigger picture" goals. The point is to give you a huge benchmark to strive for. They usually take months and years to accomplish and require a lot of work and dedication for them to work out. Goals should be written in the same SMART style as the ones that were just discussed, and they should be able to be broken down into smaller, more manageable chunks.

An example of a long-term goal can be, "I want to have $1,000,000 in my savings account by Christmas." You can easily work with this and break it down into smaller financial goals and benchmarks you must meet to have that much money successfully.

Note: Long-term goals should be something that you're always working toward. Other examples can include learning a language, completing a degree or certificate through school, traveling a continent, building a house, or assembling a car. Now that you understand what a long-term goal is, it's time to look at the second of the two goals: short-term goals.

Identify short-term goals that you want to achieve in a short amount of time and set them for yourself. (This is usually anytime in between 1 day and 2 weeks.) In order to better manage your time and energy, it is necessary to break down a large target into smaller, more achievable milestones that you can use to track your progress and better manage your resources over time.

An example of a short-term goal can be, "I want to have $250,000 in my savings account by April 1st." Assuming this goal is tied to the long-term goal mentioned beforehand, this would be a great way to take the larger $1,000,000 goal and break it down into something smaller and more attainable.

From here, you can choose to break it down into something smaller and say, "I want to have $75,000 in my savings account by February 1st." You can keep on repeating this until you've broken the goal all the way down to a weekly money goal. The more short-term goals you have, the better.

Don't be afraid to have many short-term goals working at once. Like how you can have many long-term goals to work towards at once, you can have even more short-term goals to work towards.

- My future is bright.
- I am dedicated to achieving my goals.
- The best is yet to come.

- I am taking immediate action to achieve my objectives in order to live the lifestyle I want.

- I will reach my goals.

- It will all be figured out.

- I am open to all possibilities that lead to a greater purpose.

- There is hope.

- My dreams matter.

- I'm going to work hard.

- I can. I will - end of story.

- I am free to create my reality.

- I won't compare my behind-the-scenes to someone else's highlight reel.

- I am almost there.

- It might be difficult out there, but I am destined for greatness because of my design.

- My possibilities are endless.

- I will allow myself to evolve.

- The very fact that I exist in this world has the potential to make a difference.

- I will trust my process and applaud myself for my progress.

- I won't give up.

- I won't get stuck.

- My future is a perfect representation of what I see myself to be right now.

Chapter 16

Affirmations for Overcoming Obstacles

As long as history, black women have been held to a higher standard than their white counterparts when it comes to obtaining the same accomplishments. As single moms in need of government aid, we were portrayed in this way. In addition, we are women who have children without the presence of a father.

Today's culture portrays black women in a similar light: as young moms who are sluggish and thirsty for male attention, and who couldn't care less about themselves than they do about the men in their lives. Our hair is scrutinized at our places of employment, with our bosses describing it as "unprofessional" if we don't keep it up. People identify us as being angry when we express our thoughts and disagree with others. We don't receive nearly enough credit and acknowledgment for what we've done to benefit society.

We are confronted with a never-ending cycle of difficulties and setbacks. However, even if they seem to be subtle in nature, they are real and have the capacity to make a difference in our daily lives. If we get into the practice of speaking affirmations to ourselves on a daily basis, we notice that our attitudes and actions will begin to shift in a good direction.

These affirmations will provide you with the insight and understanding you need to get through difficult circumstances. All the lessons that might be taught during times when things aren't going your way will become more apparent to you as time passes.

- At this point, I realize I have conquered 100% of the hard things I thought I'd never overcome.

- I'm strong.

- I'm fit.

- I'm tough.

- I'm bold.

- I'm incredible.

- I can do this.

- I'm appreciative of misfortune since it permits me to develop.

- There is an advantage and a benefit in each experience I have.

- My solidarity is more prominent than any battle.

- All encounters I experience shape me to be the most noteworthy form of me.

- I trust and accept that everything is turning out for my good.

- I develop profound fortitude and empathy inside my mind, body, and soul.

- Everything is unfurling at the right time. I release stress and decide to trust in myself.

- The universe gives me what I need at the ideal opportunity.

- What's mine is already mine now. I'm actually where I'm intended to be.

- My energy isn't reserved for stress. I use my energy to trust, accept, and have confidence.

- In any event, when something doesn't occur how I needed, I know I'm on the correct path.

- I give up my opposition and permit the universe to give me what I need.

- I can discover confident and idealistic approaches to look at setbacks and challenges.

- At the point when I'm feeling overpowered, I give myself space to pause and relax.

- I have the strength and knowledge to deal with anything that comes my direction.

- My capacity to conquer my difficulties is boundless. My capability to succeed is endless.

- I'm unafraid to fall flat. I acknowledge the personal development that comes from these encounters.

- I'm ready to release negative feelings and thoughts that don't serve me.

- I'm willing to accept that things will work out, even when it doesn't seem like it.

- I can't generally control the outer world, but I can handle my responses to it.

- I let go of stresses that deplete my energy.

- Rather than zeroing in on what's turning out bad, I center my energy around what's going right.

- Outside powers can't stop my strong spirit.

- I trust my instincts even in the face of unpredictability.

- I might stagger; but I never stay on the ground.

- I might make errors, yet I won't stop.

- I'm benevolent and empathetic toward myself when I make an error.

- Mistakes don't equal failure.

- Mistakes don't characterize me. I'm permitted the grace of making mistakes.

- I'm ready to discover lessons in my misfortunes.

- I use disappointment as a stepping stone to progress.

- The entirety of my issues have solutions.

- Challenges are the basis of my success.

- I rise despite the difficulty.

- Regardless of what occurs, I remain aligned with confidence, trust, and love.

- The universe has me covered.

- I can do hard things.

- I won't ever surrender.

- I can defeat each challenge in my life.
- These difficulties are intended to make me more grounded.
- I have the unyielding confidence of steel.
- These difficulties are for me to turn out to be better.
- I will never bend before the difficulties.
- I have all that's needed to become successful.
- I can get over this trouble.
- I'm grateful that the universe is attempting to teach me with the help of this difficulty.
- An elevated degree of challenges in life implies more accomplishment throughout my life.
- I can oversee everything.
- I have the capacity to conquer everything without exception.
- Nothing will stand in the way of my achieving my life objectives.
- I'm a couple of steps from my goals.
- I'm free from any and all harm regardless of the circumstances.
- Difficulties are new opportunities that will assist me with developing.
- I can get across everything.
- I'm open to every one of the difficulties in life.

- I'm becoming more grounded as the days pass.
- I'm learning new methods to conquer difficulties day by day.
- I'm upheld by my family in the entirety of my struggles.
- These hardships will assist me with drawing nearer to my accomplishments.
- These difficulties are building my determination.
- These difficulties are intended for my improvement.
- I have compelling emotional support.
- I have every one of the abilities to conquer these challenges.
- This difficulty will end very soon.
- The best version of myself is just a few of successes away from being a reality for me.
- These misfortunes are intended to make me a superior individual.
- I'm developing and learning.
- I don't fight my problems. Instead, they are opportunities to learn.
- I practice positivity that assists me with solving everyday issues.
- These are minor issues in my day-to-day life.
- Strength and development will come to me after nonstop efforts.

- I am wired such that I realize how to get over every one of the torments in my day-to-day life.

- Supernatural occurrences are conceivable in the event that I overcome this struggle.

- Some stunning things are going to occur after this difficulty.

- I value every one of the happy moments which give me the power to defeat affliction in life.

- The prize will taste great when I have overcome a battle.

- The products of my work are sweet.

- I'm prepared to endure now and live like a hero.

- The remaining part of my life will be loaded with bliss and extravagance.

- I will give my best today to appreciate tomorrow.

- I'm chasing after my purpose. I will not allow any difficulty to prevent me from understanding that.

- I'm thankful to every individual who didn't help me because now I have figured out how to do it without anyone's help.

- I've realized how to get over this misfortune all alone.

- I have the energy to fight this battle.

- The universe is in support of me.

- The harder I battle today, the greater my triumph will be.

- I'm ready for the triumph that is going to come in my direction.

- I'm ready for change.
- I'm prepared for the thrill ride of my life.
- I will become more knowledgeable after this challenge.
- I'm hanging around for the ultimate success.
- I'm here to battle and become successful.
- I'm prepared to take life head-on.
- In the case of nothing going right, I am ready to make it right.
- Things will turn out to be better with time.
- I will turn out to be better at making decisions with time.
- In my most trying period, the universe will guide me in the right direction.
- I'm good to go and do the ideal goal of my life.
- I'm striving hard to fight the circumstances in my life, and I will arise.
- Life is showing me lessons that I would have dismissed.
- I accept that there are no restrictions to my life.
- I'm here to inspire others through my obstacles.
- Regardless of what the issues are, I generally feel honored.
- The more prominent the obstruction, the greater the prize.

- I realize that these troublesome pathways will lead me to my goal.

- These challenges are vital to mold the personality of an individual.

- I'm not here to abandon my aspirations no matter what comes my direction.

- I'm making my future.

- I'm developing because I am struggling and learning.

- At the core of this hardship lies that once in a lifetime chance that will take my life to the next level.

- I won't surrender in the hours of challenges and will keep on persisting.

- I won't submit to these afflictions in my day-to-day life.

- I will adapt to meet the situations in my day-to-day life.

- I will raise my bar and become the best.

- I'm smart, and I love to learn.

- I can change the world.

- I can defeat challenges; challenges assist me with developing.

- I will be alright regardless.

- I have the ability to make my life what I need it to be.

- I improve every day and make it better than yesterday.

- I'm imaginative and ground-breaking thoughts come to me.
- I can learn anything when I am quiet.
- I'm patient with myself.
- I'm a problem solver.
- I'm a champion.
- I'm pleased with who I am.
- I will zero in on how honored I am and not how stressed I am.
- Even within the sight of affliction, I embrace new challenges.
- These difficulties are building my strength.
- I see reasons to have hope.
- I'm content with all that has occurred, is going on and will occur.
- I need to acknowledge whatever comes my direction that I will try to meet it the best way I can.
- I have what I need to get past this.
- I've realized that whatever in life I go through, I develop from.
- I will take in what I need to from today, which will make me a more grounded individual.
- Regardless of what the issues are, I generally feel honored.
- I'm ready for the triumph that is going to come in my direction.
- I'm free from any and all harm, regardless of the circumstances.

- Life is filled with consistent change. My pain, however small, won't be as intense forever.

- I'm learning new methods to defeat difficulties every day.

- I can count on others for help. I have a good support system.

- Things will turn out to be better with time.

- I'm loaded up with joy and without any difficulty at this moment.

- I'm in charge of how I think, feel, and act.

- My feeling of timelessness is reinforced.

- I have the ability to change the parts of my life that I don't care for the slightest bit.

- I'm adaptable and can adjust when life doesn't work out as expected.

- I'm not a disappointment, but rather a survivor.

- My endeavors are being upheld by the universe; my dreams become reality before my eyes.

- I'm getting more grounded.

- I'm pleased with my capacity to recuperate from difficulties.

- I won't give in to fear or pessimistic situations.

- I will get back up. Again, and again. The quicker I recuperate from difficulties, the quicker I'll get to where I'm going in life.

- I am capable of overcoming every obstacle that life throws at me.

- I'm ready for change.

- The battle is real. So is my determination.

- I can get over this trouble.

- I'm a solid and skilled individual.

- Setbacks are essentially alternate routes to an option that could be superior to what I had planned!

- These challenges towards my big dream are intended to shape me for the purpose.

- This is only one part of my biography.

- My negative thoughts will not last forever.

- Whenever I face misfortune, I ask myself what is there in the present situation that brings a more noteworthy comprehension of my life, who I am, and why I am here?

- I will use my current difficulties to develop and fulfill my place in this life.

- I realize that I am fit for conquering every one of the afflictions of my life.

- I know when to continue in a particular direction and when to give up and shift direction.

- I push through the most troublesome challenges. I focus on what the outcome will resemble.

- I emanate magnificence, appeal, and elegance.

- My apprehensions about tomorrow are liquefying away.

- I seek the assistance of people around me, so we can confront the difficulties together.

- Even in affliction, I succeed, and I flourish!

- Every bad situation must come to an end.

- Disappointment is essential for me to progress.

- I can decide to be thankful regardless of what my conditions are.

- My misfortune is my fuel!

- Although these situations are troublesome, they are for a short period in life.

- I use my positive perspective to stir up excitement in others to defy affliction. This makes us a more grounded and relentless group.

- When conditions change, I will feel even more appreciative for what I have.

- Whining will not change the situation, only an uplifting outlook will.

- I'm greater than my misfortune!

- I can oversee everything.

- I will never lose balance before difficulties.

- The products of my work are sweet.

- Everything is great in my life.
- I discharge what no longer serves me.
- Everything bad must come to an end.
- Obstructions make me more grounded, and I should have an appreciation for the test.
- I transform my impediments into opportunities.
- I understand that excruciating encounters are steppingstones to the right course.
- Sometimes fortitude means hanging on despite the situation.
- Obstacles in my way are not barriers to achieving my dreams, they are hurdles to be surmounted on the journey to my dreams.
- I rid myself of all emotional blocks that can get in the way of my peace of mind.
- I promise myself to get back up with even more determination if I stumble on the way to success.
- This is the confirmation I have been waiting for to get up from my defeat and try again.
- No challenge is too intimidating for me to back down.
- Every setback I experience is nothing but another lesson in my success story.
- My mind is protected from all negative blockers that may try to deter me from forging ahead achieving my vision.

- I refuse to allow the setbacks of today define the possibilities of tomorrow.

- I defy all odds set against me by overcoming pitfalls constructed by society for women like me.

- I push back against any adversary that chooses to stand in my way.

- External factors cannot quench the fire of my resilience.

- Obstacles in my way will fall to my feet as stepping stones to my destination.

- Hard times will not define me, instead, the story will be told of how I conquered my fears and overcame my hardships.

- I am equipped with everything I need to weather storm on the horizon.

- Nothing is strong enough to keep me from achieving my goals.

- I am a survivor and no obstacle can keep me under.

- No matter what comes my way, I continue to persevere along the path of success.

- I begin to overcome all the obstacles that have knocked me down in the past.

- I believe in my ability to stand strong even in the face of adversity.

- Despite the numerous obstacles in my way, I will leave a legacy of determination and courage behind.

- I confidently confront new inhibitions with the courage to overthrow them.

- I am adequately inspired and motivated to always forge ahead in my pursuits.

- I cultivate courage and resilience in my mind and body as a take on new challenges in my journey through life.

- I will not be tempted to quit just because others around me are throwing in the towel.

- My strong determination for success will be a source of inspiration to others struggling with thoughts of giving up.

- I see all my challenges as potential victories.

- I refuse to let fear cripple my mind from clearly seeing the opportunities I have to overcome the obstacles in my way.

- Even in the presence of fear, my courage will endure.

- I am sensitive enough to recognize when to retreat in order to gather more strength and create better strategies for solving my problems.

- I take my goals seriously and I am committed to achieving every single one of them with sheer determination and faith in myself.

- I let go of every negative habit or attitude that may stand in the way of my progress in life. I refuse to be an obstacle in my own life.

- I let go of relationships that may hinder my growth and progress in life.

- I develop the intelligence to maneuver through obstacles.

- I take active steps to sharpen my problem-solving skills.

- I take charge or my will and my emotions to subdue outbursts that may cloud my judgment.

- I learn from past mistakes and I face my challenges with newfound zeal and lessons learnt from past attempts.

- I mute the voices of discouragement in my head and instead I begin to think thoughts and speak words of encouragement over my life.

- I begin to see and address myself as an overcomer.

- I am constantly working on myself and therefore the challenges I face are met with a newer and better improved version of myself.

- I am unafraid of any and all scenarios that may arise in my life.

- My resolve to succeed remains unyielding even in the face of adversity.

- My body responds with tenacity to everything my mind wills it to do.

- I refuse to be inhibited by any social construct because they do not define me. I decide I far I go on my journey.

- The greater the obstacle, the greater my celebration when I overcome it.

- The only obstacle powerful enough to crush my dreams is my inability to try harder therefore I refuse to be my own biggest enemy.

- Sometimes brilliant opportunities are disguised as impossible situations, I take advantage of every situation and I am rewarded with life changing opportunities.

- It is my choice not to whine about challenging circumstances; instead, I choose to boost my spirit by concentrating on how to make the most of any scenario in which I find myself.

- I am a strong, independent and grown, I am capable enough to take care of myself and handle my business.

- Today I will take the leap of faith to try something I have always been scared to try.

- I will endure my battles and I will reap the benefits of my endurance.

- I am equipped with everything I need to go through my experiences with grace and dignity.

- The obstacles I face today are not big enough to drown my future in discouragement.

- I will continue to build my resilience to tackle every challenge that comes my way.

- I will be patient with myself through the process of solving and overcoming my problems.

- I trust in my abilities and determination to carry me over the obstacles in my way.

- My challenges are not as difficult as they seem, I will not be intimidated by their appearance.

- I am an overcomer and my experiences in life will bear witness to that fact.

- I am tougher than I seem and my life will reflect that there is more to me than meets the eye.

- My mind is brilliant and it offers me brilliant solutions to overcome whatever obstacle may stand in my way.

- I give myself space to relax and breathe whenever I feel overwhelmed with anxiety.

- My mind and body work together to assist me in gaining victory over all of life's trials and disappointments.

- With faith in myself, my ability to conquer my challenges is limitless.

- I will pick myself up and face the fears that have defeated me in the past.

- Regardless of the obstacles that lie in the path of my aim, I will not be deterred from achieving my objective.

- I have set out to conquer my fears and fulfil my destiny, I will not return discouraged and defeated.

- I do not need to be anybody else to make my dreams a reality, I have everything I need within me.

- Though life's challenges may be tempting, I will not compromise my principles or boundaries.

- I will not give into the pressure of coveting other people's achievement, instead I will focus my energy on my own success story in the making.

- I am able to take my mind off the immediate problem to visualize the bigger picture of success.

- I possess the grace to surmount even the most difficult hurdles in life that others have tried and fail.

- The goal is to succeed at everything that I endeavor, failure is not an option.

- I might make mistakes but I will never quit.

- I use my past mistakes to my advantage.

- I trust that in everything that I do, I have a support system that has my back.

- Being a woman of color neither makes me too weak nor underqualified to accomplish my goals.

- I have faith that even the obstacles that I face are there to develop my character and teach me endurance because everything works together for my good.

- I can do all things because I draw my strength from an endless supply.

- I do not struggle blindly, I run my race with dexterity and a sound mind.

- As gold is purified by going through the fire, I will go through my adversity and come out stronger and better.

- I have the ability to conquer all things through persistence and a positive mind set.

- I will be continually strengthened through my efforts and resolve to never give up on myself.

- I am strong enough to take whatever life throws at me and I am resourceful enough to use them to my advantage.

- I have the courage to walk out of the unfavorable conditions that surround me, and I dare to make a better life for myself.

- I refuse to let impatience rob me of the benefits of all my hard work, I will continue to press on.

- My little victories are worth celebrating, they prepare me for the bigger ones ahead.

- Even though good things hardly come easy, I will give whatever it takes to get the best of things in my life.

- My mistakes make me more familiar with my adversity and I discover how to defeat it by learning from my mistakes.

- All of my problems have solutions and that means they are not impossible to for me to overcome.

- I am not a failure, my challenges do not define me.

- I will patiently endure my pain in order to enjoy the gain that comes with it.

- My difficult journey will lead me to a place of beauty and rest.

- I let go of hesitation and I find my way through, around, over or under all obstacles that try to hinder my progress.

- I shake off all doubts about myself and my journey as I step decidedly into action to accomplish my biggest dreams.

- I may restart my journey as many times as I need to in order refocus and readjust, but I will never give up.

- I possess a brilliant mind capable of breaking down complex situations into simplicities that can easily be overcome.

- I have a dynamic personality that can approach any challenge from different angles in order to find the best solution for solving it.

- Whenever fear tries to overwhelm me, I look deep within to find strength and I transform my fears into the energy that propels me forward on my journey.

Chapter 17

Affirmations for Happiness and Gratitude

We know that happiness is a very difficult emotion to define precisely (especially as it tends to be very subjective and varies from person to person). Some experts describe happiness as "the perception of being satisfied with one's life and the degree to which positive emotions prevail over negative ones", but this is a definition a bit far from what we feel when we feel in seventh heaven ...

According to one of the fathers of Positive Psychology, Martin Seligman, happiness can be broken down into three basic tendencies.

Pleasant life - happiness as a search for positive emotions, enjoyment and hedonistic pleasure.

The rewarding life - being happy through rewarding activities and commitments such as work, being with family, or cultivating social relationships.

Meaningful life - the tendency to pursue happiness by directing one's strength towards a greater purpose, felt to be important.

If you combine all three factors, you will find that the amount of enjoyment is at its maximum. That is to say, a full life is one in which the sum is greater than the parts: pleasure, gratification, combined with a meaningful personal experience, together determine the way we describe our existence in the long run.

The secret of happiness, therefore, seems to lie in the quality of social relations. In this sense, our psychic balance depends, in large part, on the experiences we share with others, on the possibility of having intimate and sincere conversations with trusted friends, on the feeling of having someone you can rely on in times of difficulty.

The virtual hyperconnection of modern times often gives us the illusion of being surrounded by infinite social connections. But although social networks are able to "quantify" the number of friends, likes, comments and views, at the same time, we know how far this is from the true bond that unites us to each of those people. The truth is that cultivating authentic social relationships takes time and energy, encouraging you to get involved and experiment with different contexts and situations in which you can get in touch with the other and, last but not least, requiring a good dose of commitment and motivation.

Yet satisfying social contacts accentuate positive feelings, lower cortisol levels and stimulate immune function, even protecting us from the risk of contracting diseases, as shown by the famous study by psychologist Sheldon Cohen, in which, people with a low percentage of relationships were 4.3 times more exposed to cold contagion: loneliness is therefore riskier than smoking, concluded Cohen.

If you are having trouble cultivating positive relationships, are going through a period of conflict or loneliness, ask for a psychological consultation.

Happiness levels also vary depending on what stage of life we are in. The longitudinal study conducted by the Universities of Warwick and Melbourne highlighted how each phase of life involves a natural oscillation in the levels of emotional well-being. This curvilinear trend presents several peaks and phases of decrease:

Around the age of 20, there is a "peak of happiness". This a phase of life full of stimuli, confidence and optimism toward the future and good physical shape. Between the ages of 30-40, responsibilities increase and perceived happiness decreases a little, but the greater autonomy and maturity gained in this phase of life compensate for the stress associated with the need for stability and job fulfillment.

According to the study, the "midlife crisis", the one included in the period between 40-50, is the most difficult period of life. There is a significant reduction in perceived happiness. We begin to evaluate the objectives achieved and those that will inevitably have to be renounced. But we don't get discouraged because after the age of 50, life tends to improve. The 50 to 70 age bracket is characterized by a renewed peak of happiness! This phase of life, in fact, has been renamed the "period of serenity", a moment in which to concentrate on the present and finally enjoy some relaxation!

The American writer and activist, Jonathan Rauch explains in his book, "The Curve of Happiness", why life improves after age 50. Of course, happiness is not an emotion that can be taught or imparted from the outside; it depends on the path of life undertaken by each of us. There are, however, ways to promote your emotional well-being and increase the perception of immediate positive feelings.

- I am happy to be alive and experience this beautiful world with all of my senses.

- I permit myself to be black and happy.

- No matter how I feel or look, I always choose to be a happy black lady.

- I am perfectly content with my life at this moment.

- I am worthy of feeling happy.

- I deserve to live a happy life.

- I experience joy in everything I do.

- My life is overflowing with happiness, peace, and love.//
- Even in difficult times, I choose to see the good in life.
- I create my happiness by accepting every aspect of myself with unconditional love.
- Being grateful leads to happiness.
- I am thankful for all the beautiful things in my life.
- I am willing to be happy now.
- I am happy, healthy, and grateful.
- I build the life I want with my positive thoughts.
- I allow myself to feel good.
- I am happy, and I know it.
- I enjoy a life of comfort, health, and harmony.
- I am emotionally stable.
- My happiness is a gift to my friends and my family.
- I am tolerant and live peacefully with people.
- Today, I promise to surround myself with happy thoughts and feelings.
- Today, I will attract only happy people around me.
- I always choose to walk in happiness and love.
- Every day, I attract circumstances that fill me with joy.

- I find ways to bring happiness to other people.

- The positive energy around me nourishes my body and helps me radiate joy to others.

- When I focus on the positives in my life, I am naturally happy.

- My inner joy is the origin of all the blessings in my life.

- I commit to living a happy and productive life.

- I choose the happiness of this moment and not the pain of the past.

- The world deserves my authentic, happy self.

- Life's simple pleasures bring me great joy.

- My choice to be happy keeps me healthy.

- The Universe is conspiring with all of its ability to bring me complete happiness.

- I only attract happy and positive people into my life.

- I naturally gravitate to people and situations that support my happiness and peace.

- Happiness is my birthright.

- I choose to be happy irrespective of my circumstances.

- Happiness is one of my priorities, and each decision I make brings me to a state of complete bliss.

- Every day, I choose happiness over any other emotion.

- Even if I am feeling sad, I instantly choose to be positive and happy.

- I have absolute control over my emotions, including my level of happiness.

- Happiness is my true nature, and that is something I remind myself of daily.

- No one dictates my level of happiness.

- I am entirely responsible for my levels of happiness.

- I am happy with the person I've become and accept myself for my flaws and mistakes.

- I only allow positive and happy thoughts in my mind.

- I am full of optimism and positive energy.

- Wherever I am, I only see smiles and happiness in the people around me.

- My positivity inspires people and lifts their spirits. And seeing them happy makes me feel great too.

- The more I spend time with friends and family, the happier I feel.

- The more I love, the happier I become. Therefore, I choose to love each day.

- Optimism and happiness flow through my veins.

- God supports me in my pursuit of happiness.

- The more I work on myself and seek self-improvement, the happier I become.

- Happiness does not originate from outside but from within me.

- I pray for happiness, so I receive more of it.

- Wherever I go, happiness follows.

- I only live once, so any moment I spend not being happy is time wasted.

- No matter what others say about me, I always stay happy and love myself.

- Happiness and love are the major driving forces in my life.

- I define what happiness means to me, not anyone else.

- Each morning I wake up, I express gratitude to the people I love, thus making me happy.

- I forgive others and don't hold grudges since I know such negative emotions get in the way of my happiness.

- I only focus on things that are beneficial to my happiness.

- I enjoy being a happy black woman and never feel guilty about it.

- I let go of thoughts that get in the way of my happiness.

- I reflect on my past to learn from my mistakes and not to beat myself up. This habit helps me stay balanced.

- No matter what mistakes I've made in the past, I deserve to be happy.

- I'm not a reflection of my circumstances; I'm a reflection of how I react to them. When I choose reactions that are healthy and generate happiness, my life becomes better and more meaningful.

- My purpose in life is to be happy, and I remind myself of this fact daily.

- I keep meeting people who want me to be happy.

- I pursue my passions since it makes me happier.

- I engage in self-care routines that help me find peace and regenerate.

- I cannot tolerate negative people in my life.

- If anyone gets in the way of my happiness, they fall out of my life with ease.

- The only things I seek in life are happiness and love. Everything else is irrelevant to me.

- I'm not scared of anything because I have the power to overcome my fear with the strength of happiness and love.

- I have the potential to bring more happiness into my life whenever I want.

- Blissful thoughts pop up in my head with ease.

- Every single minute of my day is something I look forward to.

- I feel lighthearted about things that used to cause me distress.
- I am the one in charge of my life, and that makes me feel powerful and happy.
- I am always in a complete state of bliss.
- Life is a classroom where I'm constantly learning new ways to be happy.
- The more I realize how content I am, the more I want to pursue it for a lifetime.
- People remember me for the happy memories I give them.
- Happiness doesn't lie in what I get but rather in who I become.
- I always choose to look at things from a positive perspective.
- One thing that cheers me up is the journey. I try to embrace it to its fullest extent, and this makes me much happier.
- I have everything I need to be happy.
- I live a life that is consistent with my values, which makes me feel good and content.
- I maximize my happiness by detoxifying my mind and body.
- I try not to stay in a negative state for long. Instead, I allow myself time to process and work on being happy again.
- I encourage others to be happy.
- I smile at strangers because it makes both of us happy.

- I am always looking for new reasons and opportunities to be happy.
- My intuition tells me the things I need to do more to stay happy.
- I am gifted and unique, and this makes me feel happy.
- I am grateful that I'm alive.
- I eagerly wait for each new day with gratitude.
- I appreciate every facet of my life.
- I am thankful for myself.
- I am thankful for the beautiful life I lead.
- I'm thankful for all that I have and look forward to what's in store.
- I am grateful for my persistent attitude since it helps me find success and abundance in the harshest of situations.
- I'm lucky to live the life of my dreams.
- I thank the Universe for shaping me into who I am and providing me with what I have.
- Every day, I have more aspects of my life for which I'm grateful.
- I am grateful that I'm able to live in this incredible world.
- I am grateful that I'm able to do what I love.
- I am grateful that I can witness the goodness and beauty in everything around me.

- I thank the Universe for all the blessings in my life.

- I am thankful to have a safe, secure home to return to at the end of the day.

- I am thankful for each individual who, in some way, is a part of my life.

- I feel fortunate to have a beautiful family, and I am proud of them.

- My family has been with me through it all. I am grateful for them and don't take them for granted.

- I am thankful for my parents, who love me and have taught me everything I needed to know. I know they did their best to make sure I was healthy and happy.

- I feel grateful to have found a partner who understands me completely.

- My kids give me the ability to practice patience, kindness, and playfulness. I am so thankful for them!

- I consider myself lucky that my friends and family care for my well-being and want to see me happy.

- I'm so happy to have my friends in my life – they make me feel like the luckiest person alive.

- I refuse to take my best friend for granted. So instead, I focus on all the reasons why I'm grateful they are in my life.

- I am grateful for the love I'm capable of giving and receiving.

- I am lucky that so many people in my life love me and bless me with their good wishes.

- I am thankful to the Universe for helping me find love and happiness in my life.

- I might not always say it, but I sincerely appreciate the love I receive. I try to share most of it and am thankful for more love coming my way in the future.

- I appreciate all those who helped in my life's journey.

- I appreciate every person who makes it possible to get food on my table every day.

- Every day, I meet people who share their knowledge and insights. I appreciate all the guidance they've been able to provide and am genuinely thankful for them.

- I will be eternally grateful to every teacher who has helped me in my learning journey and made me into the individual I am today.

- I see and appreciate the positivity in everyone, including myself.

- I feel fortunate to have access to nutritious food and clean water.

- I am grateful for all the things my body can do!

- I feel thankful that I am healthy and can enjoy every day to the fullest.

- I appreciate the beautiful nature around me.

- I wake up every day appreciating the beauty that I see in my surroundings.

- I appreciate the light that I see the first thing in the morning. It gives me energy and empowers me to be the person I know I can be.

- I love spending time outside every day and seeing the magic of nature that is all around me.

- I treat all animals as sacred because they share countless benefits with us daily.

- I always remind myself that my life is a gift.

- I am thankful for the lessons I learn from each experience.

- Although I may have made mistakes in the past, I am grateful for them because they have made me wiser and helped me grow.

- I feel thankful for my friendly co-workers.

- I am thankful for the money I am earning.

- I am thankful that I can spend my money on things that bring me happiness.

- I am grateful for my past experiences since those experiences make me a better person and improve my life on some level.

- I am grateful for all the new experiences that I'll have in the future.

- I feel grateful for everything that I have right now.

- I am thankful to have a relaxing bath before sleep, brush my teeth, and put on my favorite pajamas.

- I am thankful that I can lie down in a cozy bed.

- I am thankful for all the blessings I have at the moment.

- I am thankful for my night's sleep and all the benefits my body and mind get from it.

- I always express my deep gratitude to God and everybody in my life. I'm aware that I'm incomplete without them, so I thank them for coming into my life.

- I feel grateful to the Universe for helping me realize that everything happens in life for a purpose.

- I feel grateful to the Universe for making me who I am and giving me what I have.

- I feel grateful to the Universe for manifesting all the beautiful things in my life so far.

- My goal is to live a grateful and fulfilling life.

- I appreciate the unwavering support from the Universe in everything I do.

- I am thankful to the Universe for manifesting all the beautiful things in my life so far.

- I appreciate every blessing, no matter how small or big it is.

- I am grateful that the Universe has bestowed me with wealth.

- I feel blessed that money is constantly flowing into my life through finances and other means.

- I am fortunate that I can do what I love and make a lot of money doing it.

- I'm grateful to work in a job that pays well and provides me with a sense of fulfillment by the end of the day.

- I am thankful that I can learn new things and thus develop and grow in the process.

- I am thankful for the dreams I had yesterday because they are the reality of today.

- I've been lucky enough to become successful and want to share that success with others.

- I am grateful for every opportunity that I get to do something good and help others.

- I am grateful that I can solve others' problems and help them out through my innovative ideas and skills.

- I feel lucky that I am mentally and physically strong and can do anything if I set my mind.

- I am certain that my efforts will be rewarded, and for this, I am grateful.

- I am lucky because my dreams and desires manifest in everything I do.

- I am grateful for the willpower that gives me the strength to survive against all odds.

- I thank the Universe is teaching me vital lessons through my life experiences.

- I'm grateful for the obstacles I've faced because they have allowed me to prove myself.

- I appreciate the Universe for helping me realize that everything in life happens for a purpose. Even unpleasant situations can have a silver lining.

- Even though some days might be challenging, I am consciously seeking peace in my life. I trust that the Universe will always take care of my well-being.

- Obstacles are growth opportunities. Hence, I choose to see every obstacle as another chapter in my life and stay positive throughout everything. Thank you, Universe, for helping me evolve.

- I am thankful I've grown more determined and resilient over the years and am confident that I can survive anything, no matter what.

- I ensure that I make an effort to express my appreciation since my experiences have shaped me into who I am today.

- I know that when I focus on something, I'm more likely to achieve it. That's why I appreciate the results and value the work I put in every day.

- I reside in a world of abundance and feel grateful to be alive!

- I give thanks to the Universe for helping me find joy and abundance.

- I appreciate each of the opportunities the Universe presents before me.

- I always express thanks for what I have, even when everything seems to be going wrong.

- The more I focus on the things working in my favor, the happier I become and the better my life gets.

- I always remind myself to look for something good, even in the darkest of days, because there is so much for which I should be grateful.

- From today onwards, I will make a brief stop to appreciate the beauty of life and enjoy every second of it.

- I'm fortunate to be living a fulfilling and happy life and have no complaints about it.

- I feel grateful for my heart that pumps fresh blood throughout my body.

- I am grateful for my lungs that breathe in the fresh air.

- I am grateful for my healthy bones and muscles.

- I am grateful for my healthy and beautiful skin.

- I am grateful for my robust immune system.

- I am grateful for my ability to taste delicious food.

- I am thankful for my healthy body. Every organ of my body is precisely working as it is supposed to be.

- I am thankful for my wonderful smile.

- I appreciate the wisdom that helps me extract valuable learnings from every situation of my life.

- I appreciate that things are always working in my favor.

- I am grateful for my ideas.
- I am grateful for being balanced in every area of my life.
- I am grateful to helpful souls who guide me in my life journey.
- I am thankful that I can replenish and rejuvenate myself.
- I am thankful that I can make the right choices for myself.
- I am thankful that I can be my authentic self.
- I am thankful that I can manage several aspects of my life with ease.
- I am grateful for my inner peace.
- I am grateful that I can find positive lessons from my experiences.
- I am thankful that I can sleep peacefully.
- I feel fortunate that I can do my best each day.
- I feel grateful to the higher power for protecting me and keeping me safe.
- I feel grateful to the higher power that supports me with unconditional love.
- I am grateful that I have the habit of appreciating more and expecting less.
- I am grateful to have more than I need.
- I am thankful for having a job.

- All I have now is this moment, and I am grateful for it.

- I take responsibility for my present because I am its creator. I am thankful for everything so far and vow to wake up every day expressing this gratitude.

- I appreciate that the future is looking brighter every day.

- I strive every day to live with a greater sense of appreciation.

- I'm grateful to the Universe for providing me with all the energy I need to be successful.

- No matter what I want and desire, I am lucky that the Universe supports me and gives me what I need.

- I am thankful for the abundance pouring into my life.

- I am thankful for the smooth ride that life has been on, setting me up for success.

- I want to thank the Universe because life has given me so many precious gifts and opportunities over the years.

- I am happy with what I do as it brings me a lot of joy.

- I am grateful that I can find the positive side of any situation.

- I am grateful for both my blessings and burdens. I make the best of both by looking at my obligations as my blessings.

- I am grateful that I consider challenges as stepping stones to growth and success.

- I am grateful I have so much to appreciate in life.

- I ensure that I pause every day to express my deepest gratitude for everything I have in my life.

- There are many ways that the Universe rewards me every day, and although I might not realize it, I am grateful for all of them.

- I appreciate every beautiful moment I have had on this planet.

- I refuse to take any minute for granted and will embrace each day as new and with a sense of gratitude.

- Every day, I wake up and know that there will be many challenges to face. Yet, I'm determined to keep going and do my best to become a better person than the day before.

- I'm grateful for all the fantastic growth opportunities that have come my way.

- I am amazed by the world around me. Each new day provides a unique opportunity and a new gift for which I am grateful.

- I am thankful for this feeling of gratitude – I know it leads to joy, mental peace, and the life of my dreams.

- My sense of gratitude expands my perspective and helps me appreciate all the different ways of living, thereby leading to my happiness.

- I live a life of gratitude and am always thankful for the help and support from those who have cheered me along the way.

- I am grateful for the positive things in my life.

- I am grateful for the abundance that I have and the abundance that's on its way.

- I understand how lucky I am to have so many people who care about and admire me.

- I am grateful for my patience.

- I am grateful to the Universe for always putting me in the right place at the right time.

- I feel grateful for my ability to manifest my dreams.

- I feel fortunate to have multiple sources of passive income.

- I feel fortunate for all the luxuries that surround me.

- I feel thankful for my unlimited financial abundance.

- I feel thankful for the fantastic opportunities that have come my way.

- I am thankful for the enormous success that I am constantly achieving.

- I am thankful for my past experiences, as they have helped me evolve as a person.

- I feel thankful for all the positive and loving people in my life.

- I am grateful for the love I receive every day from everybody.

- I am grateful for my relationships.

- I feel thankful for my supportive family.

- I feel thankful for my unique friends.

- I feel thankful for my caring spouse.

- I feel thankful for my respectful children.
- I am thankful for my mental strength and courage that help me maintain my composure in challenging situations.
- I am thankful for getting another chance to make my life better today.
- I am thankful for being able to love myself and others.
- I am grateful for my wonderful life that is overflowing with so many blessings.
- I am grateful for the infinite opportunities that are opening up for me.
- I am thankful for all the things that are going right for me at this moment.
- I feel lucky that I can take care of myself and others.
- I feel grateful that the Universe is always working for my highest good.
- I appreciate the skills and knowledge I possess.
- I continuously thank people for being a part of my life.
- I feel thankful for the chance to be a better person each day.
- I am thankful for my confidence in my capabilities.
- I feel happy and fortunate for the life I have.
- I feel grateful for my strong body, and it helps me get through life effortlessly.

- Every day brings me more reasons to be thankful for the blessings I have received.

- My friends have made a significant difference in my life, and I am grateful to each and every one of them.

- The fact that I live in a safe and secure environment makes me grateful.

- I am appreciative for the knowledge and experience that I have gained from everyone I have met.

- I am overwhelmed by the riches that surrounds me, and I consider myself quite fortunate.

- I live in the present moment, mindful of my surroundings and grateful for what I have.

- I am grateful for all of the things that my amazing physique enables me to do.

- I am so grateful to be alive.

- I love and appreciate my beautiful family.

- I appreciate my strength and resilience.

- I am thankful for the consistent flow of money that has occurred in my life.

- Gratitude in challenging times helps me grow.

- For everything wonderful that has happened in my life thus far, I am grateful to the Universe.

- For all of the love in my life – both given and received – I am eternally thankful.

- I give thanks for each exquisite moment.

- I am aware of the possibilities that the universe provides, and I express gratitude for each and every one of them.

- Thank you for the lessons that each event has brought me. I am thankful for each one.

- Every day, I am filled with appreciation and excitement.

- My gratitude goes out to those who have the potential to learn, develop, and grow.

- I am grateful for my errors since they have helped me to become a better person.

- Gratitude makes me feel positive and hopeful.

- Gratitude is the magnet that attracts all my desires and manifestations.

- Life is all about appreciating our blessings, and I strive to do that every day.

- I have numerous reasons for which I am happy and grateful.

- I feel fortunate to live in a safe neighborhood.

- I feel fortunate for my home where I can rest in safety.

- I am grateful for the continuous supply of fresh air around me.

- I feel grateful for my ability to create abundance and prosperity in my life.

- I feel grateful for my ability to visualize the life I want.

- I feel grateful for my financial security.

- I am grateful for my accomplishments as a black female entrepreneur.

- I am quite grateful that I have access to nutritious food and clean drinking water.

- I find gratitude in every experience.

- I notice and appreciate the light in everyone, including myself, and I encourage others to do the same.

- Because I have the ability to bring my aspirations to fruition, I am glad.

- I am grateful for what I have.

- I am grateful for every blessing, no matter how little.

- My perspective on the world has changed since I have been filled with thanksgiving and gratitude. Every day is a fresh start, as well as a new opportunity.

- Today, I am grateful.

- I will take deep breaths.

- I am thankful for everything in my life.

- I am grateful for another day to grow on my journey.

- I am proud of myself.
- My life is beautiful.
- I appreciate the good things in my life.
- I am grateful for all I have.
- God has blessing me with an amazing family.
- I am grateful for who I am as a person.
- I am so grateful to be alive.
- I am grateful for my black body.
- I am thankful for my blessings.
- I am loving.
- I am filled with gratitude.
- I am thankful for my parent's sacrifices.
- I am grateful for this wonderful human life that has been given to me.
- Today and every day, I am blessed.
- I am grateful for all the people in my life
- I have everything I need right now.
- I am grateful to be alive at this moment.
- I am grateful that I can enjoy all the little things in my life.

- I am grateful for the gifts of Mother Nature and my ability to access them freely.

- I am grateful that I can live in this divine female body.

- Practicing gratitude makes me happier.

- Gratitude is the best attitude to have.

- Gratitude increases my awareness and mindfulness.

- I am always in a state of thankfulness.

- I welcome the opportunity to do something meaningful today.

- I pause every day to express gratitude for everything that I have in my life.

- I start every day with a grateful heart.

- I am full of happiness and gratitude.

- My life becomes a blessing when I express gratitude for even the simplest things in life.

- I am a magnet for blessings.

- I am thankful for today.

- Nature, in all of her splendor, has a special place in my heart, and I cherish the opportunities to interact with her on a daily basis.

- I am grateful for who I am.

- I can live in the moment.

- I invite gratitude into my heart

- I am appreciative for everything my family has done for me throughout the years.

- I love that I love what I love.

Chapter 18

Affirmations for Friends and Family

Y ou are doing more harm to the connection when you are afraid to reach out to or connect with your black friends concerning race out of fear of ruining the relationship. What if you spoke out and expressed yourself honestly about your thoughts? Racism is something that people in the United States have to deal with on a daily basis in their regular lives; this is particularly true in metropolitan areas. If you refuse to even bring up the subject with others in your immediate vicinity, it is probable that you may be seen as self-centered and uninformed.

To show that you care about someone, you should be deeply interested in the topics that are important to both you and them. Truly lasting relationships can only be formed when both sides are willing to engage in challenging conversations about their own lives and experiences.

The fact that you avoid bringing up the subject of racism with your friends and family creates the appearance that you are disinterested in their lives and their perspectives on racism. This is analogous to turning your back on the elephant in the room and allowing it to take up important real estate between you and your partner.

Despite the fact that discussing race might be difficult, it is through these more in-depth discussions that people are able to connect with one another at some of their most difficult times in life. As Desmond Tutu, the Dalai Lama's close partner and friend, memorably observed, "When faced with injustice, it is easier to sympathize with the oppressor than it is to stand up against it."

Do not convey the attitude that a friend's or family member's lived experience has no value and should not be regarded authentic or deserving of respect. Listen and engage in a discussion with those who may feel belittled and disrespected. Others who want to make a long-term commitment to anti-racism must be ready to engage in challenging discussions with those who have different viewpoints.

Make it plain to your Black friends and family that you are prepared to give them space if they request it on a regular basis. Being realistic about the fact that being a black person in the United States in this time period is challenging is important for survival. We are faced on a daily basis with the prevalence of racial violence in our country, which we find both uncomfortable and sad. The coronavirus outbreak that occurred in the United States caused a disproportionate amount of injuries to individuals of color, as well as to the general population.

- I respect others.
- I always obey my parent's instructions.
- I can see love and affection in the eyes of my family members.
- I am friendly.
- My parents will always take care of my needs.
- I bring out the good in others.
- My parents' support allows me to achieve anything in life.
- I like to help my family.
- My family is always willing to provide a hand.
- I am surrounded by love.

- I am protected.
- I care about others.
- I will never abandon my family.
- Nothing else on my wish list is more important to me than the safety and security of my family members.
- I can talk about and share my feelings.
- I will never say NO to any reasonable demands from my family members.
- We all take care of each other's needs.
- I am helpful.
- My family members never fail to make me happy.
- I will make time for my family.
- I am my family's strength.
- I share an unconditional love for them.
- I am forgiving.
- I trust my family members with everything.
- I accept compliments from others.
- I will treat others the way I want to be treated.
- I am an important part of my family.

- I am only in control of my own actions. I cannot control others.
- I get inspiration from my family.
- I am never alone.
- I will always make sure that my family is doing okay.
- I support others with love and kindness.
- I make an effort to recognize the good in people.
- I will never let my family down because of my behavior.
- I am one of the reasons my family is happy.
- I am considerate of other people's feelings.
- I make like-minded friends easily and naturally.
- I am a good friend.
- I receive love from my family.
- I am surrounded by individuals that adore and respect me.
- I don't try to tear down other people.
- I am a wonderful friend.
- I include others.
- My family is looking out for my best interests.
- I make other people feel better.

- I always share.
- I treat others with compassion.
- I do not have to keep secrets from my family members because I know they will understand.
- I am honored to have a family like mine.
- I will take care of my family.
- I am generous.
- I have no harsh emotions for anyone.
- I am comfortable communicating with my family members.
- I give daily love to all the members in my family.
- I will respect other people's boundaries and I will tell others to respect mine.
- My family loves me so much!
- I am happy when they are happy.
- I take my family's criticisms positively.
- I will respect all the emotions in my family.
- I am everyone's friend.
- I can forgive others.
- I love my family and friends.
- I let my family have their personal space.

- I am an asset to my community.

- I love to watch my family doing well.

- I am gentle with myself and others.

- My family is always there for one another.

- I behave in a manner that demonstrates respect for my children.

- My children will feel accepted and loved unconditionally by me.

- The more I let go, the more I fall in love.

- We stay fit and love to exercise.

- When anything is out of balance, I look for answers and am directed to ideas that make a difference in the situation.

- I do what it takes to give the best to my family.

- Life is good in my family.

- We have a great time together.

- I listen to understand.

- I am my children's rock.

- I respect my children; I respect myself.

- Everyone is willing to contribute to the upkeep of the order and proper functioning of our home environment.

- Whenever possible, I approach disciplinary tasks with a calm, honoring tone of voice and manner that is considerate of my child's feelings.

- My love becomes stronger as I give it more of myself.

- Dinner is a pleasant event that we all look forward to each night.

- I recognize the pleasure I get from spending my days educating and loving my children.

- I validate my child's feelings.

- I am learning a lot from my children.

- All of my children have a sense of security and dignity because of me.

- I am a good listener.

- When anything is out of balance, I am able to discover solutions.

- I am unwavering in my love for my children.

- I am my children's safe space.

- Our family goes out of its way to get along with one another and to be good friends to one another.

- Though these times are difficult, they are only a short phase of life. This too shall pass.

- My love for my children is unconditional.

- I say "tell me more" frequently.

- My relationship with my family is becoming stronger, deeper, and more stable each day.

- My children look up to me and recognize my worth.

- There is tremendous harmony in our family.

- I realize that discipline is a tool that may be used to assist modify behavior when it is not in accordance with what is best for the individual.

- My love and connection helps my child above all else.

- I have good communication skills.

- I assist them in learning how to maximize their genuine selves via the application of proper discipline.

- I embrace and value the bond that exists between me and my children.

- I have patience.

- What I like about our family is the traditions that help to make our everyday and holiday experiences more enjoyable and memorable.

- I am a loving and caring friend.

- In all of my connections, I shall express my appreciation.

- I bring out the best in others.

- I appreciate all of my relationships.

- I deserve the best, and I accept the best now.

- When my intuition tells me to say no, I allow myself to do so.

- I welcome other women of color into my life with open arms.

- I am deserving of respect.

- I practice kindness, and I cultivate love towards others.

- I have more than enough to contribute to the world's well-being.

- I am a beautiful black lady who is deserving of love and respect.

- I respect everyone's journey.

- I am the energy I want to attract.

- I will not allow people to prevent me from accomplishing what I want to achieve in the future.

- I am free to evolve and release anything that takes away from my growth.

- I am respectful of others.

- I spread light to those around me.

- They choose me for a reason.

- I know I can be successful and still root for my peers.

- I am attracted to useful energy, and it excites me.

- I am an asset to my community.
- I am going to stop comparing.
- I have made the decision not to wait to be picked.
- Instead of condemning others, I evaluate myself to see whether I am performing at my highest level.
- I am a good effect on those around me, and I surround myself with like-minded individuals.
- I understand everyone else's issues are not mine.
- I will surround myself with positive people.
- I am ok as I am.
- I am interested in understanding the ideas of people without passing judgment on them.
- It's not their job to like me; it's mine.
- I am lovable.

Chapter 19

Affirmations for Health and Fitness

After getting out of bed, jot down three things for which you are grateful each morning. It's time to do something different. If you usually sit quietly in a team meeting, barely speak to the coffee barista that serves you coffee, or you stand quietly in the playground away from the other parents, try something new. Speak! Say hello, comment about the weather, say something interesting or contribute to the team meeting and state your opinion or idea. This can make you feel happy and even proud of yourself.

Spend some time every day on yourself. Taking care of yourself is important, and even if it's something like reading, going for a walk, going for a coffee with your friend, or taking a long bath, it's important for your health and happiness.

Do something kind or help another person. Taking time away from ourselves and doing something for another can help us to focus. Just taking some time to focus on something can help us move away from our negative thinking patterns.

Walk away, breathe, and take a few moments to collect your thoughts. Sometimes we can be a little irrational when we aren't feeling confident as those anxious feelings become too much. Sometimes a brisk walk, a chat with a friend or just some air can make a wealth of difference.

Now for the secret:

From this moment on, behave as the self-confident person you want to be; whatever you do, wherever you go, whoever you encounter, live like and be the person you want to be, the self-confident man you expect to be. Over time, you're going to grow into and become this reality. After all, it's who you're already— you're just peeling off the layers to get to your self-confident self.

When it comes to taking good extra care of you and your physical health, there are three important components to consider: eating properly, exercising consistently, and getting enough sleep. As you work on these areas, be sure to seek out the help of professionals when needed and keep on top of things like medical appointments to ensure your overall physical wellbeing.

What you put into your body sends important messages about how much you value yourself and prioritize leading a healthy life. This subject can fill a book on its own. Essentially, you want to consider your current eating habits and strive to make changes to eat right consciously. This includes eating balanced, regularly scheduled meals, including healthy and nutritious foods, eating in moderation, listening to your body signals and hunger cues when you are hungry or full, and avoiding pitfalls like emotional eating or fad diets that set the stage for failure. If you struggle with eating issues, seek out your health care provider's help or, better yet, a qualified nutritionist who can help you find balance in this area.

Look at your relationship with exercise and think about what physical activities you currently do and their reasons. Exercise also plays a role in our level of self-esteem. Did you know that exercise releases hormones that create the same neurological effects as antidepressant medication? Exercise can be highly effective in decreasing depressive moods that can aggravate low self-esteem. I can't emphasize this enough: make some form of physical activity a regular part of your life. Standing is better than sitting; five minutes spent moving is better than nothing—the point is, every bit helps. Seek out activities and routines that allow you to stay consistent and find enjoyment, with enough variety to stay interested.

Your body does important work while you sleep; this is when it restores and repairs itself! To feel at your best, ensure you are consistently getting enough restful sleep. Poor sleep can leave you feeling irritable and thus more vulnerable to the anxious and negative self-talk messages that chip away at self-esteem. If you ever have trouble sleeping, it might be beneficial to establish a disciplined nighttime ritual for yourself. Turn off all of your devices an hour or two before bedtime, sip some chamomile tea, and spray a few drops of lavender on your pillow to help you fall asleep faster. Instead of falling asleep to the television, offer yourself gentler options like a light read or a meditation.

Know what you can bring to the table. Are you a good negotiator? Are you a good passer? Are you a good songwriter? Are you a good teacher?

Whatever your skills are, nurture them and show them to the world. Everyone or each of us has always something to offer the world's well-being, and we can all make a difference in some way. For some, it'll be solving the water crisis; for some, it'll be as simple as being a mango farmer. One doesn't have to be "bigger" than the other. We're all unique with our own set of gifts. Our job is to use that gift in the best way possible.

Value your body before anyone else does. As you begin reflecting on the things you like and dislike about your body and appearance and simultaneously begin paying more attention to society and the media's impact on your self-image, see if you can try to shift your whole focus from trying to measure up to impossible standards to appreciating how amazing your body truly is. Rather than focusing on looks, think about all of the things your body does and the ways that the different parts help you achieve your goals. What are some things you can be appreciative of about your body?

Research has found that body dissatisfaction and self-esteem are closely linked. As one increases, the other decreases, so it's important to begin paying attention to society's messages that impact body image and consider how you feel about yours. Having an appreciation for your body and general contentedness with your appearance is both parts of self-esteem; however, having a good and realistic body image doesn't always ensure high self-esteem. It's simply one piece of the puzzle.

- Although my ancestors and forefathers may not have used affirmations as a therapy to heal, I will.
- I will look for the emotional well-being treatment I need and deserve. How I recuperate is my decision.
- Each time I work out, I in a real sense feel my body developing further!
- With every repetitive exercise, my body grows itself.
- As I work out, my body will repay me with more years of good wellbeing.
- I'm ready to run 5 miles without a break!
- I achieved all my wellness objectives!
- I stay fit for myself and for my family.
- By working out, I am an astounding good example for other people.
- My body moves, and it feels astounding!
- My body functions as it should.
- My metabolism works like a machine!
- I'm lean, fit, and marvelous!
- My body is in amazing health.

- My body is sound and solid.
- I deal with my body like a sanctuary.
- I have the right to feel amazing and lively.
- I love my body for everything astounding it can do!
- I'm thin, cheeky, and feeling extraordinary!
- I'm prepared to do any physical activity I wish to do!
- I work out to respect my body and its solidarity.
- I drink water for the duration of the day to hydrate my body and brain.
- I feed my body with nutritious food varieties and my body is appreciative!
- Every day, my body develops further.
- I am youthful.
- I am more youthful.
- Individuals appreciate how energetic I am.
- Nutrients flow around my body.
- I have energy and excitement forever.
- I'm determined.
- My skin is smooth.
- My skin is glowing.

- My skin is delicate.
- My skin gets a lot of nourishment and energy.
- Nutrients are bountiful all around my body.
- I feel more energetic.
- I'm active and positive.
- I'm youthful on a fundamental level.
- My body's natural defense system is strong.
- I'm channeling my energy to recuperate my body.
- My immune system is impervious.
- I will recover from the cold.
- I will recover from any diseases.
- I'm sending nutrients around my body.
- I send energy to my internal organs to work on their wellbeing.
- I direct essential materials around my body to remain healthy.
- My wellbeing improves.
- My recuperation rate is amazing.
- I'm generally sound.
- My wellbeing is generally at the top.

- I'm a quick healer.
- My body recovers at a quick rate.
- My body is sound.
- I generally feel my best.
- My blood pressure is at a low and healthy level.
- My blood pressure is now becoming lower.
- I appreciate working out.
- Exercise helps me feel good about my general health.
- I eat healthy food sources.
- Junk food doesn't interest me anymore.
- Eating whole foods is something that comes easily to me.
- I realize that I am a resilient individual and I can succeed.
- I'm certain about the changes in my way of life.
- I am better each day.
- I am not overwhelmed at work.
- It's not difficult for me to resist the urge to panic.
- Stress and tension are not difficult to control.
- I love my new self-perception.

- I am fit and great.
- I'm bringing down my blood pressure with my positive thoughts.
- My actual body is unwinding.
- My tensions are easing away.
- My negative thoughts are easing off.
- My mind is becoming quieter.
- My mind is clear and quiet.
- I'm always easing up.
- Unwinding is simple for me.
- I keep a quiet tone and stance.
- I generally set aside a few minutes for unwinding.
- I appreciate relaxing.
- I don't find it difficult to unwind.
- I'm sound, vivacious, and hopeful.
- My body, brain, and soul cooperate to keep me sound.
- I'm thankful for my life's power and energy.
- My immune system is solid and manages any microbes, germs, or infections.
- I like each cell in my body.

- I love everything about my body.
- My body is lovely and attractive.
- I feel attractive and alluring.
- I like my body's special attributes.
- People think that I'm hot and alluring.
- I'm thankful I am at this weight.
- I'm excited when I look in the mirror.
- I send love and healing to each organ of my body.
- I get better and more fit.
- I focus on what my body needs for wellbeing and imperatives.
- All that I think, say, and do make me better.
- I keep a record of the status of my health.
- I'm encircled by individuals who empower and support healthy decisions.
- I inhale deeply, workout often, and feed my body nutritious food.
- I seek healthy, nutritious food varieties.
- I love the flavor of leafy vegetables and fruits.
- I enjoy working out and building my muscles.

- I let go of pressure in my body with each exhaled breath.
- I rest well and calmly.
- I'm free from agony and my body is invigorated.
- I long for new, healthy opportunities.
- Each cell in my body vibrates with health, energy, love, and healing.
- I'm alive and well mentally and physically.
- I do everything to keep up with my health.
- I have positive thoughts.
- I'm improving inside and out, and I'm getting better.
- I'm at my ideal weight.
- I eat those food varieties that I need to keep up with my ideal health status and energy.
- I start every day feeling great and buzzing with energy.
- I am energized for the duration of the day.
- I'm overflowing with health and energy.
- I see youthfulness in myself when I look in the mirror.
- Each stress I feel is a sign to loosen up and let go.
- I expect to be healthy.

- I generally have a high amount of energy to do all that I like to do.

- All around, I'm improving and getting better and better.

- Each cell in my body cooperates in ideal harmony to create wonderful health.

- I pay attention to my body's needs.

- When I put out great energy, the universe will favor me with positive

- wellbeing and health.

- I change my mindset and denounce the negative thoughts in my mind.

- I'm able to recover once more.

- I trust the healing process and assume responsibility for my way to recuperation.

- I will increase my confidence by healing my whole body.

- I stay fixed on accomplishing my wellbeing objectives.

- Cooking healthy foods is a delight.

- Hi, kitchen, you are my sustenance place. I like you!

- I have all I need to assist me with planning tasty, nutritious food.

- I am so appreciative to pick food that upholds my best health.

- I can make a nutritious, tasty meal.
- I love investing energy in the kitchen!
- I merit the time and cash I put into my wellbeing.
- I'm learning new things that mend my body slowly and carefully.
- I'm willing to set aside the effort to care for myself.
- I am so appreciative of this awesome food.
- I'm very much nourished in anticipation of the day ahead of me.
- My body recuperates and fortifies with each bite I take.
- I shower love on this meal as well as on my body.
- This food is healing me.
- My taste buds are changing each day.
- At this point, I don't want food sources that don't support me.
- I radiate boldness, magnificence, and elegance.
- I pick wellbeing and health over restrictive eating regimens and extreme exercises.
- I feel incredible when I take care of myself.
- I give and get love.
- A total feeling of prosperity engulfs my life.

- All parts of my being are essential and alive.
- All I have are ideas that create abundance and enhance health.
- Every one of the cells in my body is getting back to their ideal state.
- Every one of the cells in my body resonates in amazing harmony.
- Being healthy is one of my primary interests, and I put this desire into action on a regular basis.
- Breathing lifts my mindset and stimulates my body.
- From the inside out, I am developing and becoming better as time progresses.
- Divine life moves through each cell in my body.
- Each move I make moves me towards further improving wellbeing.
- Each cell in my body is renewing, repairing, and restoring itself.
- Each cell in my body vibrates with well-being.
- I commend my excellent health.
- I reward myself with improved wellbeing.
- Each atom of my being reverberates at wonderful speed.
- I'm alive and well.

- I permit myself to be healthy.
- I alone have the ability to control my wellbeing.
- I'm an ideal illustration of wellness and wellbeing.
- I'm generally healthy. Ailments never visit me.
- I'm honored with strength and completeness.
- I'm resistant to the common cold.
- I'm in tune with internal harmony, imperatives, and happiness.
- I'm currently claiming the wellbeing and prosperity that is mine.
- I'm the healthiest I have ever been.
- I control my wellbeing by the force of my positive thoughts.
- I guarantee myself the best health by the healthy decisions I make.
- I have the heavenly ability to recuperate my body.
- I realize that bountiful wellbeing and health are my inheritance.
- I realize that genuine joy brings perfect well-being.
- I only take part in exercises which are healthy and life-upgrading.
- I only think sound, enriching thoughts.

- I intend to live to be 100 years of age.
- I rest my dedicated eyes.
- I take phenomenal consideration of myself since I am awesome.
- I take steps towards a better way of life.
- The hereditary coding of my body is getting back to its unique wonderful state.
- The extra time that elapses, the more prominent I feel.
- There is a limitless stream of wellbeing in the universe, and it streams towards me.
- There is no restriction to how great I can feel.
- Today, my main concern is my own prosperity.
- Today, I am available for the regular progression of health.
- Today, I favor myself with endless health.
- Today, I feel more magnificent than yesterday.
- All-inclusive energy moves through each cell in my body.
- An all-inclusive soul is in each iota of my being. And with my appreciation, it re-establishes me to prosperity.
- With each breath I take, I am bringing more prosperity into my life.
- I'm deserving of excellent health.

- I'm open to seeing all that is not serving me, and I will see everything with love.

- I acknowledge where I am, and I'm prepared to take advantage of this opportunity to develop.

- I center around positive advancements.

- I'm upheld and adored during this journey.

- I make my health great by discussing and pondering my health.

- Despite the fact that there is inconvenience within me, I adore and endorse myself.

- I'm in charge of the mental environment I make. My ideas can change, and the positive ones I pick are helping me recuperate.

- I'm allowed to be new at this moment.

- I discharge all cynicism, since it's not who I am. I clear a path for affection since that is who I am.

- I'm a companion to my body. I pardon my body and treat it with a similar adoration I want to get.

- Regardless of what has been or will be, my internal light can't be dimmed.

- I deal with my uneasiness and agony like I would an innocent kid. I care for my body with unrestricted sympathy and care.

- I'm doing all that I can to assist my body with being well as fast as I can.

- I pick thoughts that set a healthy atmosphere inside and around me.

- I'm a willing member in my own health plan.

- Each decision I make, I make it with care and affection for life.

- I'm alive.

- I'm on the path of continuous learning and expanding. I respect the journey even when I don't get it.

- I am so appreciative to be alive. I appreciate being here.

- I'm willing to be with the entirety of my ideas and feelings without reprimanding them. Rather than dismissing them, I remain and comprehend them.

- I'm searching for approaches to communicate love. I'm searching for excellence right now. I'm searching for encouraging signs wherever I go.

- I am ready to take the final step necessary to begin my healing process.

- Today I will meet others with kindness and sympathy as a reflection of a healthy inner self.

- I am patient with myself as I give myself time to heal from past hurt and disappointments.

- I release myself from the bondage of negative words spoken against me which have shaped the way I see myself.

- I let go of all the pain and anger I have bottled up inside, I rid myself of all the bitterness that has eaten away at my heart and mind for too long.

- I forgive myself of past mistakes, I forgive myself in advance all the mistakes of the future and I use them as lessons to propel me forward on my journey through life.

- My failures will not define me, my disappointments will not discourage me, I refuse to let these cage me.

- I decide today that I will let old wounds heal, no more ripping off the scabs to relive my pain.

- Whatever is left of my old wounds can no longer hurt me. Instead I begin to see them as battle scars that declare the victories of battles that I have fought and overcome.

- I refuse to feed the fear that prevents me from working through my pain. I am fierce enough to face whatever is left of my pain and I am brave enough to move on.

- I am mature enough to acknowledge my mistakes and I am humble enough to ask for forgiveness from those I have hurt.

- I am brave enough to show compassion and forgive those who have hurt me, whether they deserve it or not.

- I feel my pain and I feel my anger but I refuse to let them consume me, instead I process them and I use them to my advantage.

- I learn to accept things that are out of my control and I give my mind over to peace and tranquility.

- I put my health - mental, physical and spiritual - above all else as I strive for a healthier life.

- I entrust myself with the duty to take good care of myself and to maintain a healthy and balanced life.

- I commit myself to the gradual but effective completion of my healing process.

- I gather strength from within to endure all the momentary pain I have to endure in order to heal.

- My body, mind and soul function together in a way that supports a healthy daily living and the actualization of my goals.

- Letting go of what is behind me, I look forward to a brighter future filled with love and happiness.

- I step out of the dark closet I was forced into by heartbreaks from the past and I courageously open my heart to love and trust again.

- I am ok.

- I constantly meditate on positivity to rid my mind of all negative thoughts.

- I restrain myself from projecting the offenses committed against me on others around me who mean well.

- I am grateful for the gift of life as each new day provides a fresh slate to begin again.

- I eliminate every form of negative energy around me and I create a safe space for myself where I can heal and thrive.

- I embrace the kind of lifestyle that supports wellbeing of my mind, body and soul and I begin to make choices that guarantee growth in every area of my life.

- Every time I meditate of healing, my body responds in kind.

- I trade all my frustrations, anger and failures for hope, peace and determination.

- I turn the page on sorrow and pain as I begin a new chapter in my life.

- My determination is geared towards getting healthier and happier day after day.

- I set my heart free from the prison of unforgiveness.

- I release my attachment to any and everything that keeps me stuck in my painful past.

- I am willing to forgive myself even if others withhold forgiveness from me.

- I am full of vitality and strength, I refuse to let anything drain me of my energy.

- I refuse to be affected by any external negativity that tries to throw me off balance, I am at peace with myself.

- In order for my emotions to heal and become vulnerable again, I am committed to provide an atmosphere for them to do so.

- My mind is free from anxiety and my heart is free from worry.

- I refuse to let depression overwhelm me, my happiness comes from within and it radiates all around me.

- I am a beneficiary of divine health, sickness will not overpower me.

- Every cell and organ in my body function as they should to support a healthy lifestyle free of infirmity.

- I have the strength to let go of every habit that can potentially sabotage my health and quality of life.

- I choose to adopt a healthier lifestyle and I make choices that prioritize my wellbeing above all else.

- I possess a healthy mind, healthy emotions, healthy body, healthy hair and healthy skin. My whole life is in great shape.

- My new experiences will be better and they will outnumber the painful experiences from my past.

- I refuse to drag any negative piece of my past into my future, I leave what is past in the past and I focus on moving into a future that will compensate me for my past losses.

- I give my body and mind all they need to flourish.

- I forego resentment and I embrace love and peace with all men.
- I live a healthy life in a healthy body.
- I choose thoughts of complete wellness.
- I create an environment for myself where my health can thrive.
- I block all channels of illness in my life.
- My mind and body respond positively to nature.
- Every time I lay down to rest, my body receives all the rejuvenation it needs. When I wake up I am revitalized and reenergized for the day ahead.
- I say yes to all things that support a whole lifestyle.
- I receive strength in my mind, body and soul.
- I have no control over my past therefore cease to condemn myself over past deeds.
- As I go through my healing process, I look forward to a future where I will be whole.
- I will let it hurt, I will let it bleed and I will let it go for my healing process to be complete.
- I may not be able to undo the wound, but I have the responsibility to let myself heal.
- For my healing to begin, I need to stop touching my wounds. I let go and I let healing take its full course.

- My body is my temple, and I vow to take care of it every day.
- I eat great food that makes me feel good.
- I drink plenty of water every day.
- I sleep well at night.
- I can recover quickly from illnesses.
- I am strong.
- I am a survivor.
- I am full of energy.
- I am in good health.
- I am free from disease.
- I enjoy my life.
- I am alive.
- I love my body.
- I am in control of my health.
- My body is in extraordinary shape.
- My heart is beating steadily.
- My blood sugar levels are normal.
- My body is at the perfect weight.

- My cells are healthy and multiplying.
- My immune system is functioning correctly and fighting off germs.
- All cells in my body are healthy and working to keep me alive.
- Every day, my body gets healthier.
- I am grateful to every organ, bone, muscle, and other parts of my body.
- I believe that good health comes from love and appreciation.
- I feel perfect physically and emotionally.
- I ensure that I maintain my body at optimum health.
- I am totally in sync with life.
- I am open and receptive to any healing energies from the Universe.
- I believe every cell in my body has a certain level of intelligence and knows how to maintain and heal itself.
- I strive to keep my body and mind healthy by exercising and choosing healthy, wholesome food.
- I have the support of the Universe within me, which is why I can live without pain.
- I am grateful that my cells tirelessly fulfill their duties and keep me alive and healthy.

- I regularly massage my hands, legs, and body with love to thank the cells for what they have done. I love them.

- Healing is compassionately caring for my body, soul, and spirit.

- Being healthy is crucial for all facets of life. It affects what I do, how I feel, and what others see and think about me.

- I feel healthy when I have a dynamic balance in my life.

- I feel at peace with all aspects of my mental and physical well-being.

- Healing has brought me inner peace and restored the natural order of my body.

- My body is my own wellness house. Every day I adopt habits that bring wellness into my life.

- Healing does happen! I try to turn my thoughts off and let the healing power of my body naturally do its work.

- My healthy body is my best asset, and I love staying in good shape.

- I do all I can to look after my body's health.

- I am open to all the positive and healing energies that are out there.

- My body is always trying to maintain perfect health by optimizing its natural defense systems.

- My diet is something I put a lot of time and effort into since I want to feed my body nourishing food that will help me thrive.

- I monitor my thought process and remind myself only to think healthy thoughts.

- I clear all thoughts of fear, anger, hatred, jealousy, shame, self-pity, and guilt from my mind.

- Healing my mind changes how I treat my body, affects the environment around me, and opens doors to new opportunities.

- My body is a perfect healing device because God made me that way.

- When I am overflowing with love, I naturally enter a state of health and healing.

- The more I love myself and others, the healthier I become.

- A healthy mind is necessary for a healthy body.

- My goal today is to turn every negative thought in my mind into a positive one.

- I am worthy of being happy, healthy, and prosperous.

- Becoming healthier is more than just losing weight. It also includes improving the quality of my life.

- I'm going to control myself and not give in every time I have a craving.

- I don't need to compete with anyone. Instead, I'll live my life at my own pace.

- I'm proud of myself because I can turn down things that aren't healthy for me.

- I will invest in myself because I'm worth it.

- I reject toxicity in all its forms.

- I'm committing to a healthier lifestyle.

- My motivation behind losing weight is to feel happier, healthier, and look better in clothes.

- I promise to do my best every day.

- Taking care of my body and mind is not selfish; it is a healthy choice.

- I am ready to take better care of myself.

- Exercising, eating good foods, and being around great people are simple yet effective ways to practice self-care.

- I will create a healthy environment to grow in.

- I am grateful for the health, wealth, and happiness that surrounds me every day.

- I am a magnet that attracts health, happiness, love, wealth, and wisdom from the Universe.

- I have everything required to heal completely.

- As my positivity grows, so does the health of my mind and body.

- My skin is clean, soft, and healthy.

- I can easily digest food and drinks.

- I can comfortably tolerate different weather conditions.

- My body gets healed quickly.

- My spine is healthy and elastic.

- My muscles are well built.

- My vision is perfect, and I do not need lenses and glasses.

- My hair is dense and healthy.

- I am full of energy.

- Whatever I eat or drink, my body absorbs only the most valuable materials for my optimal development.

- I'm eating healthy.

- My immune system is robust.

- I feel perfect in my body.

- Self-care is difficult but necessary if I want to stay healthy.

- I am taking care of my body and mind with healthy foods because I have a lot of respect for myself.

- I enjoy foods that are the best for my body.
- I love every cell of my body.
- I always make healthy choices.
- I love myself and therefore take care of my body by exercising and eating healthy.
- I like to exercise and eat nutritious meals because I feel good, and my body stays strong.
- I have self-discipline, which helps me control what I eat.
- I am cultivating healthy eating and exercise habits that I'll have for the rest of my life.
- I will never lose my motivation to eat healthy food and exercise.
- I will only eat healthy foods.
- I know I will eventually reach my health goals by making small changes every day.
- I believe that any healthy choice I make today will help me in the long run.
- I am ready to embrace a healthy lifestyle.
- My body is mine. It belongs to me.
- I am a goddess.
- My body is bold and brave.
- I focus on positive progress.

- My body is strong.

- I am so grateful to be alive. I cherish being here.

- By talking about and thinking about my health, I am able to maintain excellent health.

- The only way out of misery is to be in the midst of it. The only way out of discomfort is to get uncomfortable first.

- I know my power.

- My body is beautiful.

- I am purpose.

- My body is conscious of its own requirements and aspirations.

- My body is in the best form and size that it can possibly be at this time.

- My body is celestial.

- I am healthy and strong.

- I am a survivor.

- In order to assist my body recover as rapidly as possible, I am putting out all of my efforts.

- Positive improvements in my life are deserving of my efforts.

- I consider myself to be a friend to my body. Forgiveness is mine, and I treat my body with the same loving love that I would want to receive in return.

- I feed my spirit. I train my body. I focus my mind. It's my time.

- I look for ways to express love towards my body.

- I am worthy of good health.

- The things that make me different are what make me special.

- I feel comfortable in my skin.

- I choose positive thoughts that help me heal.

- I am willing to look at anything that is no longer beneficial to me.

- I am on a road of growth and am always learning new things.

- My body is bursting with feelings of love and acceptance.

- My value is not determined by my physical appearance.

- I am willing to be honest with myself about my ideas and emotions.

- I am open to exploring new avenues for enhancing my health.

- I am at peace with where I am and am eager to take advantage of this newfound chance to progress.

- My body has the ability to cure itself.

- I surrender to the intellect of my body in order to improve my health.

Chapter 20

Affirmations for Better Sleep

We are all aware that sleep is critical to health, both in terms of duration and quality. But how crucial is sleep for our health? Poor sleep has a detrimental influence on our day-to-day activities as well as our general health. It may affect our physical appearance, work performance, and social relationships, as well as overall health.

Insomniacs report feeling fatigued on a daily basis, and many also experience cognitive issues such as attention deficit, concentration and memory deficit, increased irritability, or emotional lability, which in rare circumstances may even result in anxious or depressed moods.

We can therefore affirm that the importance of sleep is central to health, yet it is a very widespread phenomenon in the population. What can we do in our daily life to help find adequate sleep? Good sleep is essential for many functions: it helps to improve the immune response, cardiovascular protection and also tissue repair, through cellular restructuring, which occurs massively during the night.

The well-being of our skin, in fact, is involved in the lack of a good sleep, many will have happened to wake up after a short and disturbed sleep and find the visible signs on the face, with drier skin and more marked wrinkle signs. It is no coincidence that in America they coined the term beauty sleep: demonstrating that sleep and skin quality go hand in hand. After all, women know this well, because the appearance of their skin is intimately linked to the time dedicated to rest. In particular, around the period of menopause this phenomenon can be accentuated; hormonal imbalances very often induce insomnia problems also linked to nocturnal "hot flashes".

A good remedy can be to introduce a greater quantity of antioxidants, which contribute positively to the reparative processes of the skin such as, for example, polyphenols thanks to their antioxidant and anti-inflammatory power. Polyphenols are found in many foods, such as grape seeds, but generally in fruits and vegetables, green tea, black tea, red wine, coffee, chocolate, olives and extra virgin olive oil.

Sleeping is not just a pleasant and relaxing activity: it serves our body to regenerate and recover physically and mentally. In short, we need sleep. Not only that, we need quality sleep. Taking the right time to rest is very important. An adult should sleep between 7 and 9 hours a night to have positive effects on health, mood and, in general, on their well-being.

Normally during the night, you go through three different phases that are easily distinguishable during sleep monitoring: light sleep, deep sleep and REM (Rapid Eye Movement) phase. These stages are crucial for proper rest and recuperation, and Garmin wearables can identify which of the three phases you are now in, as well as how long you have been in each of the phases.

Light sleep

In the light sleep phase, eye movements and muscle activity slowly begin to slow down. This phase helps us relax and prepares the body to enter the deep sleep phase.

Deep sleep

In the next phase of deep sleep, eye movements and muscle activity stop altogether, while heart rate and breathing slow down. The body enters a phase of recovery and physical recovery, the bones and muscles are strengthened and the immune system is strengthened.

REM phase

The REM phase is the last stage of the sleep cycle, characterized by rapid eye movements that go from small pulses to larger pulses as you exit the deep sleep period. In this phase, dream activity is recorded: your brain is almost as active as when you are awake. The REM phase is important for creating memories and processing information.

Women need more sleep: their sleep is more fragile than that of men, and they are subject to more environmental stresses. New research points to women's greater difficulties in sleeping. According to Jim Horne, a sleep neuroscientist and director of Loughborough According to the University's Sleep Research Center, women tend to utilize their brains more than males, requiring a greater amount of sleep to recuperate.

The latest data also confirms that insomnia is widespread especially among women and often goes hand in hand with anxiety and depression. In general, women's sleep is better than men's in their youth, but over time, including factors such as pregnancy and menopause, it tends to get worse.

- I am grateful for the persons I came into contact with today.

- I am pleased with my development and want to continue on this path.

- I am committed to the kind of life I envision.

- I attract miracles into my life.

- I create a life I love and am proud of.

- I release whatever fears or concerns I may have and turn them over to Spirit.

- I believe in my intuition and pay attention to my inner voice.

- I choose peace.
- I am better than I was yesterday.
- Today, I did my best. And tomorrow is another day.
- I use this opportunity to appreciate the beauty that surrounds me.
- Today, I became a little bit wiser.
- I am centered and focused.
- I create a life I enjoy living.
- I'm proud of my culture, background, and experiences since they helped shape who I am now.
- I am God's masterpiece.
- I release today.
- Everything that worked today stays with me, and everything else goes.
- I am self-assured in all I do.
- I welcome and embrace the lessons I learned today.
- I have chosen to accept and embrace the mystery of life.
- I believe in me.
- I inhale confidence and exhale doubt.
- I forgive it all.

- Everything that is happening done right now is taking place for the sole purpose of benefiting me in the end.

- I am loved.

- Tomorrow is a fresh start with a fresh start.

Chapter 21

Affirmations for Career, Success, and Wealth

- I'm successful.

- My capacity to overcome my difficulties is boundless. My capability to succeed is endless.

- Others' opinion about me doesn't make any difference, for I know who I am.

- I'm an incredible maker. I make the life I need and appreciate it.

- I have decided to think and make an awesome and fruitful life for myself.

- Each challenge I face is a chance to develop and improve.

- I'm energetic and useful.

- I have complete power over my life. I can create all the success and prosperity I want.

- I am letting go of any shackles, preconceived notions, or old beliefs that have held me back. It's time for new growth, and I'm willing to bet on myself to get there.

- I'm open to new ideas and not resistant to change.

- I will be successful and achieve all that life has to offer because I deserve it.

- I know I can succeed.

- I am thankful for all the skills and talents that life has bestowed upon me.

- I am excited to go to work today and feel hopeful for the future.

- The Universe is full of opportunities for me and my career.

- I am fortunate to be surrounded by people who make me feel great and believe in my capabilities.

- I recognize opportunities when they come to me and take advantage of them when I can.

- I find innovative and creative ways to be successful every day.

- Whenever I need help, I find the best resources and solutions.

- Everywhere I look, I see the many steps that lead to my success.

- I know how to use my time wisely.

- I will always put in the effort to achieve success in every part of my life.

- I am passionate about my work, and it is a massive part of my journey to success.

- I'm proud of my goals and my values are in line with them.

- I work with an inspiring team that shares the same enthusiasm as me.

- By being successful, I am creating opportunities for others too.
- As I tackle new challenges, I feel confident and empowered.
- I am a born problem-solver – I naturally come up with solutions for problems.
- I always attract people who encourage me and are successful in their own right.
- I see each new challenge as a unique opportunity.
- When I achieve a goal, I celebrate with joy and gratitude.
- The more I succeed, the more confident I feel.
- I feel blessed for all the abundance flowing into my life.
- I value my intuition and can make educated decisions.
- I stay committed to my vision and continue to do my work with passion.
- Every day, I have new ideas that inspire and motivate me.
- I effortlessly achieve success in every task I undertake.
- I always expect good results, and good things keep happening to me.
- I am proud to make valuable contributions to the world.
- I learn from brilliant mentors who constantly share their knowledge, wisdom, and guidance.
- With more abundance entering my life, I open myself up to more opportunities.

- I thrive under pressure and am stress-free.

- I'm always happy to think of new ideas that make me more successful.

- I have cleared all limiting beliefs that were previously stopping me from succeeding.

- I dress every day as the best version of myself – both physically and mentally.

- I dream big without inhibitions.

- I am proud of myself and naturally attract other people who see me as unique.

- I am creating a positive mindset that leads to abundance and happiness.

- I am successfully achieving my full potential and doing beautiful and inspiring things.

- I am doing my best to make the world a better place by being confident and assertive.

- I am thankful to be successful financially.

- I am living my dream of a successful life!

- My success results from persistent hard work, and no one else can take credit for it.

- Opportunities follow me everywhere. All I need to do is grab onto them.

- I always focus my thoughts and efforts in one place to achieve maximum success.

- I only remember my accomplishments when I look at my past. I do not dwell on my failures.

- Success isn't so much found when I get an award or receive a prize or promotion. Instead, I find it in the journey leading up to that day.

- Success is a reality that I live in daily.

- I am willing to work hard for everything I want since no one will hand me success for free.

- My success is unique. Hence, the more I share it with others, the more successful I become.

- When I hear negative comments, I put a positive spin on them to focus on the bright side and continue my journey toward success.

- I always think positive as positivity leads to success.

- If I think about an idea and am committed to it, all the work I need to do will become easier.

- I am successful in all aspects of my life.

- Success follows me everywhere.

- I want to work on and succeed in numerous things in my life.

- I never let yesterday's stress overwhelm me today.

- Stress only hampers my success if I let it.

- My life is solely about balancing success and being humble.

- I follow successful individuals to reach my personal goals.

- My success is most useful when shared.

- Success and happiness are interdependent, and I am thankful to have found both in life.

- I will address every possible work task today that I have been delaying.

- I am successful in the workplace due to my hard work and determination.

- Today, I will interact with one of my coworkers and get to know them better since good teamwork leads to successful companies.

- I am the senior director of success in my life and career.

- Every day, I help my coworkers and motivate them to reach greater heights in life.

- When something disturbing happens at work, I remind myself that success comes to those who know how to overcome challenges.

- I can achieve any level of success in my career.

- I am confident I will have even more success in the future because no one can ever take away my motivation to succeed.

- I have attained success in many avenues of my personal life.

- My journey to success will begin within the walls of my own home.

- When life is hard at home, I only have to remember my success in other areas.

- I can independently take care of myself and my own home, which I consider an accomplishment.

- I am a successful parent who is only getting better.

- I am a source of inspiration in the eyes of my children.

- The way I raise my children brings success in all aspects of my life.

- I am truly successful when I can see my children achieving their goals and dreams.

- Encouraging my children to pursue their ambitions is the most loving thing I can do for them.

- I will not let my past failures impact the accomplishments my children see today.

- My successful parenting rituals start in the morning when I wake up and continue throughout the day.

- Every day, I get the chance to lead by example in front of my children, and that makes me feel accomplished and successful.

- Through my actions, my children learn the attitudes and behaviors of a winner.

- My success story will motivate others to follow.

- The only success I will ever experience is found within myself.
- No one can copy my success because I genuinely am unique from everyone else.
- Life did not hand me my success – I worked hard to get it.
- I can attain success in all areas of my personal life if I allow it.
- I am talented and unique, and I've learned that I can be happy and prosperous just by using my talents.
- I am on the path to becoming the best version of myself since I am well aware of my hidden talents.
- When I look within myself, I can see how successful I am.
- When times are tough, it is my successes that make it easier to keep going.
- I have the personal qualities and skills to succeed in anything I do.
- I will not let any negative thoughts that cross my mind hinder my success.
- I'm an epitome of inspiration, bliss and love.
- I drive myself to learn and develop in all areas of my life. It brings me satisfaction, opportunity, and reason.
- I have decided to think positively and make a brilliant life for myself.
- I can make sound decisions and take actions.

- I find it easy to prevail at all that I do.
- People stare at me and can't stop thinking about how I draw in success.
- I'm appreciative of my success.
- I have courage.
- My aspirations are manifesting in front of me.
- I'm strong, tenacious and committed.
- My contemplation and thoughts are the seedlings of my prosperity.
- My life is filled with wealth and success.
- I'm educated about business and stay up to date with the world.
- I'm making an astonishing life.
- I can show monetary plenitude.
- I'm motivated to accomplish my work objectives.
- I'm drawing joy and accomplishment into my life.
- I'm changing myself into a more fruitful individual.
- I have a game plan to complete my dreams.
- I would meet my desires and dreams.
- I am destined to be fruitful; it is normal for me.

- The power is inside me. I gain from my mistakes, live in the now, and plan for what's to come.

- All difficulties in my day-to-day existence are openings for development.

- I love that the opportunities to be fruitful are surrounding me.

- Breaking old standards of conducting myself permits me to develop and move to the next level.

- I realize that my contemplation affects my existence, so I focus on the things I need for myself.

- It is clear to me what I want to do in the future, and I am satisfied with where I am right now.

- I'm a success magnet, and I draw in success in whatever I do.

- I think only of my achievements.

- I use all moral channels to become fruitful. I investigate every possibility to meet success.

- I'm searching for new opportunities and new doors to open for me.

- Success for me is a continuous cycle. After one achievement, I focus on another one.

- I see success in all that I do. Little victories develop into enormous accomplishments for me.

- I'm making monetary security with my abilities.

- I imagine myself encompassed by progress.

- I assume responsibility for my prosperity.

- I have certainty and fortitude that I am a successful person.

- I'm allowed to change the objectives that don't serve me.

- I love to put resources into my future because I am worth it.

- I can take the necessary steps to take care of business without any problem.

- My days are filled with motivation and love.

- I'm certain and good at what I do.

- I feel fruitful in my life at this moment, even as I run after future successes.

- I'm aware of what I need to do in order to achieve progress.

- As I permit more plenitude into my life, more opportunities open for me.

- Where I focus my mind is the place where I will focus my endeavors.

- I'm thankful for every one of my abilities and gifts that serve me so well.

- Today I am successful. Tomorrow I will be successful. Every day I am successful.

- I have the potential and capabilities to maintain my own business.

- I will be better today than yesterday.

- I pay attention to my instinct and trust my internal guide.

- My self-worth and confidence are expanding every day.

- Positivity prompts achievement in many ways than I will ever comprehend.

- I'm enjoying my work today and am idealistic about the coming days.

- I believe in myself and have tolerance to bear the tough situations.

- I put my energy into things that make a difference to me.

- Understanding my own triumphs begins with understanding myself.

- My business fulfills me and others.

- If I think about it, I believe it. On the off chance that I have confidence in it, I will invest the energy to make it genuine.

- I make an extraordinary manager because I care for my workers as well as the organization.

- This moment isn't the opportunity to wish I had accomplished more. Now is an ideal opportunity to do more.

- I can care for myself and my own home, and that in itself is an interesting point to consider a triumph.

- I'm ready to pay attention to others' recommendations and analysis, learn from them, and incorporate them into my life.

- I'm on the right professional path.

- Nobody is better at my work than I am.
- I'm keen, sharp and driven.
- I know when I put my everything into my work, I am compensated.
- I'm positive about my abilities to get to the top of my career.
- Being successful at work is simple for me.
- Love, wellbeing, and success get drawn to me.
- I encapsulate relentless confidence within me.
- Life feels incredible.
- There is a way if I commit myself.
- I am so energized in light of the fact that all my plans are working out as expected.
- Extraordinary things come my direction.
- I'm a cheerful individual.
- Openings appear to fall right onto my lap.
- I'm ready for business and life.
- I'm a decent individual who merits achievement and joy.
- I love myself for who I am.
- Everything turns out well for me.
- I'm energetic and useful.

- I use positive intuition to show a positive life.
- I have decided to think positively and make a great life for myself.
- It's not difficult to prevail at all, that I do.
- I prepare to stun the world.
- The universe accommodates me.
- I have a particularly astonishing life.
- I am so fortunate. Life is working in my favor.
- My objectives and dreams work out.
- I'm passionate about being better and more fruitful.
- Some way or another, the universe assists me with accomplishing my objectives.
- The universe is flowing in my life, and I'm overwhelmed with prosperity.
- Money wants me.
- I'm motivated, driven, and tenacious.
- I find it simple to be realistic.
- When I go after what I need, it comes to me.
- My brain is a magnet for every beneficial thing.
- I have achieved a lot in all aspects of my life.

- I'm thankful that I am so healthy, glad, and fruitful.
- All that I do brings about incredible achievement.
- I can never come up short, for all that happens adds to me being better.
- The seeds of my greatness lie within me.
- I am love, healthy, and rich.
- My affirmations for success prove to be fruitful.
- I upgrade all aspects of my life.
- My life continues to improve and gets better.
- I merit success.
- I see joy and achievement in any place I go.
- There isn't anything I can't do.
- It is so natural for me to succeed, even in the face of criticism.
- I can inspire myself with the snap of my fingers.
- I can get myself from the right perspective and in a moment.
- Nothing and no one will keep me little. I claim my power from this day forward.
- My prosperity isn't for anything to decide.
- I go first and forge ahead. I'm my own hero.
- The world anticipates me.

- I am my number one example of overcoming adversity.

- I don't rush my success. It is a way of life.

- I planted the seeds today, realizing I will get what I hope for.

- The best investment I make is in myself.

- Life picked me for a reason. I benefit as much as possible from it.

- I give myself full consent to pursue my dreams, regardless of whether I remain alone or not.

- Success is mine. Not from a shallow perspective, but rather a rich, prosperous existence.

- I can have everything. Life is to be enjoyed.

- I have done the practices. Today, I will perform at my best.

- I am made of a similar energy as the sun.

- My present reality doesn't restrict my ability to imagine what I am able to do.

- I run after other things, not just money. I'm experiencing my fantasies

- I discovered joy today. This is my mystery to prosperity.

- I invest in what I do because it reflects who I am.

- I don't think twice about the significant stuff. I realize I am deserving of the best.

- I work to my qualities, and things come my way without any problem.
- My worth isn't related to my victories.
- Self-discovery is the greatest achievement.
- I find myself chasing after my qualities, not in pursuing momentary successes.
- I act with trustworthiness, which ensures success.
- Life is too valuable to even consider wasting pursuing status.
- I cleanse thoughts that enter my brain and cause me to be uncertain about my capabilities.
- Perceived limits are not reality. They are just thoughts.
- Life isn't to be conquered. It is to be lived.
- I am patient and wait for things to occur at the right time.
- The brain plays tricks and would make me question my capabilities. I won't give in to it.
- I invest my energy on earth well.
- Fears are part of life, but I realize that they are rarely true.
- My success and my luck increase.
- Success isn't something that happens. It starts from the little things we do today.
- I deal with myself like royalty, and my aspirations follow.

- I plan out my objectives to accomplish them.
- My pay increases every single month.
- I no longer self-harm.
- My days are filled with motivation and love.
- Nobody else will choose how I feel.
- I'm an inventive person.
- My life is filled with affection and appreciation.
- My mind is not rigid. It changes and adjusts as needed.
- I can solve every challenge I encounter because I am solution-oriented.
- Nobody can get me to act out of character because I am in control of my emotions.
- Change starts from me.
- I'm not a product of my circumstances but my decisions.
- We all have different purposes in life, and I will not compare mine with others.
- I will not quit because I haven't discovered other possibilities.
- The better I feel, the better I attract.
- I decide to continue to attempt, even when I am discouraged.
- I acknowledge that things aren't always simple, but I will do them anyway.

- I become more skilled as I gain skill.

- I have conquered obstacles before, and I will this time, as well.

- I investigate every possibility to be effective.

- I'm seeking after my own meaning of success.

- Success isn't always discovered on the day I get an award, receive a trophy, or improve in my career. It is discovered on the path that leads up to that day.

- I have more things in my day-to-day life that I need to work on, so I can be fruitful in them.

- I'm appreciative of individuals I have watched become successful. They have guided my own success.

- My accomplishments are best when shared.

- Success and love are connected. They are both crucial to my existence.

- Understanding my own triumphs begins with understanding myself.

- I'm always ready. So, luck favors me.

- I have deserted my old, incapable habits and embraced new ones that breed success.

- I defeat my limits by persistence. Attempting is my mantra for progress.

- I am a strong and successful black woman.

- I love being a strong and successful black woman.
- I am capable of accomplishing great things.
- My role is to create, and it's the most important job I do.
- I spend my time concentrating on the job at hand.
- Success and money come to me effortlessly.
- I achieve more by doing less.
- I understand that the more challenging the task, the more important my work is.
- I am becoming more of me.
- People recognize me as a leader.
- I own all the resources I need to face any obstacles that come my way.
- I am a millionaire.
- I am ready.
- I naturally attract success and prosperity.
- I am heading towards the finish line without getting off my route.
- I believe in my skills and talent.
- A negative attitude towards life can never bring me success.
- I am talented.

- I choose to be happy.
- My colleagues respect me for my ideas.
- I make an impact.
- I make strategic moves to reach my goals.
- Each day, I take the necessary actions to take me where I want to go.
- I know everything I'm looking for is available to me at this time.
- I never wait for the right time to start creating the future I want – I do it now!
- I strongly believe in my abilities.
- I trust in the process.
- The simple approach is often the best.
- Every day, I wake up early and work on my goals.
- I always do better than what I did yesterday.
- I am ready to complete all the tasks that come to me.
- I finish my tasks one by one by breaking them down into small chunks.
- My decisions and actions bring me success.
- I'm motivated and determined to reach my goals.
- I will become the successful person I know I can be.

- I am more powerful than I appear to be.
- I can accomplish anything if I set my mind.
- I am 100% committed to becoming the individual I need to be.
- I commit to creating a self-sufficient black female-owned business.
- I am building a successful business every day.
- I am obsessed with my customers' success.
- Today, I will move my business forward.
- I am getting closer to my vision.
- As a black female entrepreneur, my business helps me fulfill my life purpose.
- My business changes lives.
- My business is expanding and impacting more lives each day.
- My business is a huge success.
- I can and will build financial wealth.
- My creative ideas create a positive impact on the world.
- I pride myself on trying my best to move up in the world.
- I believe in hard work and using my talents to get ahead.
- I always put myself out there.
- I value my success and want to do as much as I can for it.

- It all starts with me.

- I am the one who is in control of my destiny, and I'm the only one who can make something happen.

- I am in the process of creating the most extraordinary life I can imagine.

- I have committed myself to my goals and doing what is right.

- I feel strong, excited, passionate, and powerful.

- I have all of the time and resources I need to do the tasks that are important to me.

- Now is my time!

- I am rich in every way.

- My goals are possible.

- I invest my time and energy toward creating new opportunities for my future.

- I let go of the things that no longer serve me to create space for what inspires me.

- I am responsible for living my life to the fullest and set an example for my black sisters, daughters, and everyone around me.

- I welcome more discipline in my life.

- It's my mission to pursue and achieve my goals, despite all odds.

- I will not live by how others define success or being a "good person".

- I have a never-ending desire to become the best that I can be.

- I was born with an insatiable achievement drive that refuses to settle for anything average.

- I have the freedom and the capability to create the life of my dreams.

- I am doing great.

- I deserve to have wealth.

- Obstacles and challenges strengthen me.

- I'm getting stronger every day.

- My work makes a difference.

- I make excellent use of my time.

- I believe I can achieve greatness.

- I believe in my innate abilities and always try to utilize them in the best possible ways.

- I am committed to doubling my earnings in the next 12 months to provide financial security and experiences for my family.

- I know I can achieve even more success. Thus, I won't settle for anything less.

- I can no longer accept less than the best for myself.

- There are no boundaries to what I am capable of doing.

- I'm confident in myself and my ability to succeed.
- My knowledge and hard work make me an expert in my profession.
- My career is always thriving.
- I am grateful for everything I have.
- I learn and grow every day.
- Attracting more success comes quickly and effortlessly to me.
- I am an outstanding leader who leads my team with confidence.
- I create my definition of success.
- I can change the world.
- My ideas are worth millions.
- I love what I do!
- I enjoy searching for my purpose.
- My passion and purpose motivate me to strive for success.
- I am thankful for each person who has contributed to my success.
- I focus on what I do because I am aware of the importance of my job.
- I have the emotional and mental strength to do hard work.
- This year, I will make all my dreams come true.

- I can, and I will do this! Nothing can stop me!
- It is in my destiny to be wealthy.
- I love how easy and natural it is for me to be prosperous in life.
- Being and staying wealthy is my second nature, and thus I am always rich.
- My purpose is to live an abundant, successful life.
- Every day in my life is a wealthy day.
- I never fail to amass wealth, no matter what I do – be it a hobby or work.
- I have a dream job that pays me a handsome salary.
- I am confident that I can meet my financial goals.
- I feel optimistic about wealth.
- My mind constantly visualizes money and thus attracts more wealth into my life.
- I believe in all the positive aspects of money, wealth, abundance, and prosperity and let go of all the negative ones.
- My life is constantly flowing with wealth. I've never faced any obstructions when it comes to getting rich.
- I want to become wealthy – and that's okay.
- I welcome wealth with open arms.
- I am happy to see my wealth grow with every passing day.

- Life makes it easy for me to get new opportunities to create wealth.

- I earn enormous amounts of wealth doing what I love.

- Every day, in every possible way, I become more affluent and more prosperous in every domain of my life, including financially!

- I know that the Universe provides me with limitless opportunities to achieve my goals and become wealthy.

- I have decided to let go of all inhibitions and open my mind to receive all the wealth my heart desires.

- I focus on positive thinking, abundance, and prosperity, which allows me to live a rich, wealthy life.

- The wealth of the Universe comes to me, and I receive it in avalanches of abundance and prosperity.

- Attracting prosperity is my natural state of being.

- Prosperity pushes me to do my best.

- I can visualize my bank balance and wallet overflowing with money from all the hard work I put in.

- I'm living my life of luxury and wealth.

- Wealth, freedom, and contentment are my reality.

- I have amassed a massive fortune and have more money than I ever thought would be possible.

- I'm happy and feel great about my life, health, and wealth.

- I live a financially independent lifestyle with multiple streams of income.

- I continue to make millions while I travel and explore the world.

- I make money in my sleep.

- My earnings grow every month, more than doubling in some cases.

- Every day, I get notifications regarding cash deposits toward my bank account.

- My wallet always has plenty of cash.

- As a wealthy person, I have the freedom to do whatever I want. It's amazing how liberating that feels!

- I can buy absolutely anything in the world.

- My unlimited wealth lets me travel first-class, live extravagantly, and have life's luxuries.

- I now live in this beautiful home that I can afford without any problem.

- I can now travel the world and visit the most stunning and fascinating destinations.

- I enjoy myself with my friends and family during my free time.

- I am the master of my financial future.

- My actions create endless prosperity.

- I often receive wealth in expected and unexpected ways.

- I have plenty of financial security.
- I have shifted from scarcity thinking to abundance thinking.
- I am always enthusiastic about the wealth life has to offer.
- New income streams are always welcome.
- I'm very passionate about becoming wealthy and earning an unlimited income.
- I am in alignment with the energy of wealth and abundance.
- I am at peace with all the money I have.
- Every day, I am becoming richer.
- One of my favorite engagements is to create wealth, prosperity, and abundance.
- I'm wealthy. I live like it, think like it, and act like it every day.
- Wealth is pouring into my life.
- Good fortune is attracted to me like a magnet!
- I realize I can do a lot of good for the people by maintaining my wealth.
- I use my wealth as a tool to do something unique and fantastic for the world.
- I am a wealthy and successful entrepreneur who dares to live life on my terms.

- I am a skilled professional who can create products and services that will improve my financial situation and undeniably make me rich.

- I am a wealth-creating machine.

- I was born to create wealth and constantly focus on my business.

- My business is flourishing and growing fast – it is attracting several loyal, paying customers.

- As I continue to grow my wealth, I will provide employment opportunities and growth for everybody around me.

- The Universe wants me to be wealthy to use my accumulated abundance and help those in need.

- I'm getting richer as I give more of myself to my community.

- I have decided to remain wealthy to do a lot of charity work.

- I always give back to those who have less.

- I use my wealth to help those in need.

- Everywhere I look, I feel an overwhelming abundance that I can use to help everyone.

- I use my wealth to support myself and help others.

- It is an honor that, with wealth and privilege, I can make a massive difference in the lives of my fellow human beings.

- The more I give back to society, the wealthier I become.

- People shower me with their blessings for helping the community.

- I earn and donate my wealth to maintain an equilibrium, and a healthy balance is always good for the soul.

- Everything I give away always returns to me, multiplied by an infinite amount.

- I am the embodiment of wealth, abundance, and prosperity.

- I'm grateful for all the wealth in my life at the moment. It is a reminder of the potential I have within me.

- I vow to fulfill my financial dreams despite all odds.

- I can conquer any financial hurdles that are in my path.

- I am passionate and driven, which inspires me to stay on track with my goals.

- Every decision of mine, whether it's conscious or unconscious, creates wealth.

- I am so focused on my wealth-creation ideas that I think about them all the time.

- At the core of me is a wealth-driven person who knows what they want and isn't afraid to get it.

- I was born with a multimillionaire mindset. Hence, I think, act, and feel like a millionaire – I am a millionaire.

- I am an extremely wealthy person.

- I know how to create unlimited wealth – and am rightfully doing so!

- I am open to all the wealth the Universe wants to bless me with now.

- Living a life of luxury is so much easier compared to living in poverty.

- I have built my wealth by being honest in all aspects of my work.

- Being wealthy and happy is my birthright.

- Whatever decisions I take in life, it always helps me accumulate more wealth and brings me one step closer to financial freedom.

- Being wealthy brings me happiness and peace of mind. It's something that everyone should experience.

- Wealth is positive energy – an indication that symbolizes the divine.

- I promise to stay wealthy so that I can help other people in their times of need.

- I am starting to get used to the fact that I am a millionaire.

- My financial situation is improving at a rate that is beyond my wildest dreams.

- My lifestyle is brimming with over-the-top luxury.

- I have successfully aligned my energy with the vibration of infinite wealth.

- I'm proud to declare that I am the first person in my family to make a million dollars – I am the first to become a millionaire.

- Every day, my wealth is increasing.

- I'm rich, and wealth is my identity – we're inseparable.

- I have the ability to turn my thoughts into reality.

- I have the ability to make the intangible become tangible.

- I always do my best and it always pays off.

- My positivity coupled with my work ethic are the key reasons for my success.

- Things get easier and easier for me every day.

- I am becoming more and more efficient every day.

- I am becoming more and more wealthy every day.

- I am on a constant road to improvement.

- With my hard work and positive mindset, success is inevitable for me.

- I will achieve my goals, it is only a matter of time.

- I will achieve success no matter what it takes.

- I have a habit of excellence that shows up in everything that I do.

- Quitting is not an option for me.

- With hard work, I know that I can make my thoughts into reality.

- I do something every day to help me reach my goals.

- My daily habits will lead up to the achievement of my goals.

- I know that good things are always coming to me.

- I trust that good things are always coming to me.

- I believe that good things are always coming to me.

- I expect positive outcomes from the work that I put in towards reaching my goals.

- Success is my new normal.

- When I think about the things I have accomplished, I well up with pride.

- Every day, I learn more and more to help me reach my goals.

- Being wealthy is something that is for me, not just for others.

- My success is inevitable.

- I remain flexible, knowing that it is possible for solutions to come to me in ways I may not expect.

- I am climbing to new levels and new heights every day.

- Excellent opportunities are always falling directly into my lap.

- Success will happen to me, not just to other people.

- I have a clear conscience about the way that I make my money.

- I know that it is possible to make a lot of money and still be ethical at the same time.

- I believe that it is possible to be rich and still be a good person.

- I believe it is possible to have integrity and wealth, and I have both.

- I am grateful that I remain humble despite my financial success.

- I feel guilt free about my desire to make money and be wealthy.

- Striving for wealth is a noble goal that will help both me and my loved ones.

- I am grateful for the opportunity to change lives with the money that I make.

- I believe it is possible for me to be rich despite my past circumstances.

- I shamelessly admit to my desire to be wealthy.

- I am able to be responsible with large amounts of money.

- I am surrounded by lucrative opportunities to increase my net worth.

- I am flexible, knowing that success can come to me in ways I do not expect.

- I have a natural intuition for identifying opportunities for success.

- I pursue success, and success pursues me.

- All of my daily habits are in support of my mental health.
- All of my daily habits are in support of my emotional health.
- All of my daily habits are in support of my physical health.
- I have the ability to form good habits with ease.
- I have the ability to break bad habits with ease.
- Success is in my future, even it wasn't in my past.
- All of my positive thinking habits are backed up with hard work.
- All of my actions always result in creating wealth for me.
- Everything that I touch turns to gold.
- It is okay for me to make wealth generation a priority for me.
- Every opportunity that I pursue is successful for me.
- I only have positive thoughts and positive energy when it comes to money.
- I am successfully able to manage large amounts of money.
- I am constantly being presented with ways to grow my wealth.
- I maintain my humility despite my massive success.
- Money positively impacts my life and the lives of others.
- I have a healthy relationship with money.
- I consciously release all guilt tied to my own success and wealth.

- I have power over money, but money does not have power over me.

- It is okay for money to be important to me.

- I feel like a success on the inside.

- I think as successful people think, and act as successful people act.

- My mind is filled of images of success.

- I am mentally, emotionally, and physically conditioned to achieve success in everything I do.

- I am bursting with positive energy and self-assurance.

- I have enough courage to take on my goals and achieve my dreams.

- I am happy today, tomorrow, and every day of my life.

- No situations, life circumstances, or challenges can bring me down.

- Yes, today is my day.

- I love myself with everything I've got.

- I wear my uniqueness as a badge.

- There are no hurdles that I can't cross.

- Every day is an opportunity to do it better, an opportunity to become a better version of myself.

- I am a strong black woman.

- I am a beautiful black woman, and I embrace respect, love, and kindness.

- I deserve all the good things that show up in my life.

- My self-worth doesn't depend on society's definition of me.

- Life is an exciting journey for me.

- My hair texture is perfect and beautiful, just the way it is.

- I esteem myself as invaluable

- My self-worth does not need the validation of people outside my body.

- When I look at myself, beauty is all I see.

- Today is another day to live the incredible life I desire.

- I have complete control over my feelings and happiness.

- Every day I get better than I was the previous day.

- I have the power to create all the change I want to see.

- I am successful at attracting the correct individuals into my life.

- I surround myself with people that contribute to my growth and the advancement of my dreams.

- I hold the keys to my happiness.

- The universe will conspire to ensure that everything happens precisely as planned.

- What they think of me is irrelevant; the only important thing is what I think of myself.

- I am beautiful, courageous, and daring.

- I am made of the strength of ten thousand moons.

- Life's tough, but I'm tougher.

- I inhale positive energy and get rid of every negative energy.

- I am proud of who I am - limitless, beautiful, and wonderful.

- I let go of all anxiety, depression, and attachments.

- I let go of unforgiveness, grudges, and malice.

- I am worthy of all the happiness in the world.

- I am full of happiness.

- I am getting stronger and bigger than every limitation.

- I win by staying true to myself.

Chapter 22

Affirmations for Gaining Confidence

Self-confidence is an emotion, but it is a feeling that may have an impact on who we are as people and how we think, act, and interact with others. It's the way we feel about ourselves and about ourselves; it varies from individual to individual. Another way to say it is that if you are self-assured, you have confidence in your own abilities, characteristics, judgments, and religious views. It is possible that you will have insufficient self-confidence and will begin to question your own ability, which would have a negative impact on your decisions and actions throughout your whole life.

In other words, when we accomplish anything, we question whether or not we did it properly or efficiently. We often believe that we will fail, and this lack of confidence may have an adverse effect on our performance or our capacity to deal with certain circumstances. It may also have an influence on how we feel, which can have an impact on how we conduct our life because we cease making changes and taking risks.

Our sense of self-worth has an impact on our moods and actions. It may have an effect on many aspects of our lives, including our careers, relationships, and even our family lives. Those who lack confidence may suffer anxiety and may be compelled to engage in activities they would not want to because they are too self-conscious or embarrassed to say no to their peers. They may be passed over for that promotion because they are too timid to stand out for what they believe in.

They are self-doubting and make unfounded assumptions about their skills. People who are self-assured stand out from the crowd. People may be able to rely on them since they are certain that they will get an honest answer. The fact that they believe in themselves is evident in everything they do, and it serves as an inspiration to others to believe in themselves. People who lack confidence don't know how to deal with their emotions and thoughts, and as a result, they aren't in command of their own destiny or their own achievements. Because they see themselves to be beaten before to beginning, they accept loss and, as a result, make it more difficult for other people to defeat them. Even while it is easy to become trapped in a rut of self-doubt, only those who take action to develop and work on themselves will be able to climb out and thrive.

When one has confidence in oneself, it is a profound and reasonable belief in one's own talents and potential. This involves being aware of one's own shortcomings as well as being aware of one's own abilities. It is a positive attitude that leads to the belief that one has the essential resources to react positively to the problems of life.

The degree to which you have confidence in the product reflects your self-perception. Your appearance has an influence on the way men see you. People's interactions with one another and their reactions to you are a reflection of how they perceive the way you think. As a result, if you don't have a strong sense of self-worth, it will be difficult for others to put their faith in your abilities.

The degree to which you can trust someone is a function of how you see yourself. Your appearance has an influence on the way men see you. Furthermore, if you don't have a strong sense of self-worth, it's likely that others may find it difficult to embrace your abilities.

Low self-esteem is a commodity too reliant on your bad features and the things you do incorrectly. In other words, you are the most dangerous foe you can imagine! Individuals who radiate self-assurance are not necessary reliant on the approval of others to succeed. They pay attention to and appreciate the views of others; nevertheless, at the end of the day, they evaluate themselves.

Optimistic people, like the majority of people, set reasonable goals, adhere to defined objectives, and pursue their aspirations. We are likewise confronted with difficulties. So, what do self-assured persons do when things don't turn out the way they expect them to? Convinced individuals take a step back to assess the circumstance and seek out the most advantageous solutions accessible.

During these endeavors, if things do not turn out as they want them to, they reach a point when they realize that they will not always be able to do what they set out to accomplish. When we go on from this point, we bring with us the lessons learned from earlier practice sessions. We are looking forward to establishing new goals and accomplishing new dreams in the future. Although they are now older, more informed, and better equipped with experience, their strong conviction in their abilities has not altered.

As opposed to their male counterparts, women are often the gender that seems to be the more concerned or that looks to be more negatively affected by little setbacks, according to research. They also typically suffer from low self-esteem and a lack of confidence. Several studies have shown that when women are under pressure to project self-assurance, their reactions and behaviors are different from those when they are not. Let's face it: we don't live in the 1920s anymore, and you are just as capable as your male counterparts and possess just as much skill (and in some circumstances, even more aptitude) as they do.

There are some factors that each and every woman should be aware of; these elements may have a significant influence on their confidence and capacity to tackle any barrier and develop a strategy that they would be willing to stick to in order to accomplish their goals and be successful in the future.

The amount or lack of confidence is irrelevant; hormones have a critical effect on how you feel about your appearance. As a result of their naturally occurring testosterone production, men have the edge in this case. Tests have demonstrated that testosterone decreases cortisol levels in the body, which in turn lowers stress levels in the individual tested. It is easy to see why men appear calm in situations that might leave women feeling harried and agitated when they are, in fact feeling the same way. Guys have around 100 percent more testosterone in their bodies than females under certain scenarios.

In general, women have a more harder time digesting serotonin, the feel-good chemical released by our brains when we are pleased with ourselves. Serotonin also aids in the feeling of being more comfortable in one's own skin. Despite the fact that sugar intake delivers an instant boost of feel-good power, the long-term benefits of physical exercise are achieved via constant participation. Enhance your energy levels, ladies, and you'll be ready to face your next encounter with a good feeling coursing through your body.

According to study findings, women worry and show signs of anxiety around three to four times more often than men, which may lead to their lower levels of self-confidence. A larger portion of the female brain governs worry and concern compared to men; in fact, this portion is twice as big as the male portion.

Women are famously cautious and wary of taking risks because they are afraid of being disappointed. But when women overcome their fears and confront their difficulties head-on, they show that they're quite competent, if not more so, than the males in their respective sectors. Males, on the other hand, prefer not to accept it, despite the fact that women do sometimes outperform them in certain scenarios.

It is necessary to have faith in one's own talents before engaging in any activity. Our self-assurance empowers us to put our ideas into action and make them a reality. A high level of self-confidence allows you to evaluate your abilities at a higher level than you would if you lacked self-confidence. Women often underestimate their abilities as a consequence of a range of factors, and women are more likely than men to take less chances in their careers.

An increase in self-assurance will always result in an increase in performance.

Now you have proof that you are as capable and possess similarly outstanding talents to males of same age and gender, take advantage of this opportunity! Make no assumptions about your identity, your talents, or your achievements on the basis of scientific or social norms; instead, challenge yourself to prove yourself. Make all of your efforts to boost your self-confidence and get your head in the game by committing to it. It is only through believing in themselves that women can achieve the same levels of success as men.

Despite their differences, women are equal in every way, and it is past time for them to acknowledge this and emerge out of the shadows. Get on that horse and ride out into the distance by yourself, rather than sitting around waiting for your prince to come to your rescue. You are not needed to sit side-saddle, and you are not compelled to do so.

- I am aware of my potential

- I am evolving into a more positive version of myself.

- I am worthy of having what I want

- I accept compliments easily

- As I allow myself to let go, I see a marked improvement in my state of mind.

- I am strong

- I have complete confidence in all of my life choices.

- I am accepted.

- I love and respect myself.

- I am enough.
- I am a winner. I believe that everything is going to work out for me.
- I possess the tools that I need to succeed.
- I have faith in my ability to socialize.
- My strength is bigger and stronger than my struggle.
- Fear does not live within me.
- Every day, I am getting stronger.
- I can do this.
- I do not give up.
- This is who I want to be.
- I am not able to be made inferior by anyone.
- I am fierce.
- I am invaluable.
- I am an inspiration to others.
- I am the fire.
- I will be driven by success.
- I'm not envious of other people's success since I'm certain that my own is on its way to being realized.
- I am confident and self-assured when I speak.

- I will say no when I need to.
- No one can defeat me except me.
- I am not afraid to be different.
- I can achieve my every desire.
- I am comfortable in my skin.
- If I fail, I know that I will not chatter.
- My confidence is limitless.
- I am worthy of love.
- Other people do not define my happiness.
- I choose hope.
- I choose to be positive.
- I will not listen to other people's negativity.
- The only commitment that I need to make it to myself.
- I believe who I am.
- By acknowledging my self-worth and my confidence, I accept that I will succeed.
- My mistakes do not define me.
- I love myself unconditionally.
- I am pleased with who I am and with what I have done thus far.

- Today, I will choose me.
- I am grateful to see another day.
- I have the knowledge and potential to achieve everything I want.
- Today, I will do something great.
- I only have positive thoughts.
- Today, I will have a kind heart.
- I got this.
- I will speak positive words today.
- I will make decisions for my happiness.
- I will spend dedicated time on myself.
- I know that I am on the earth for a purpose.
- A higher power creates me, and I know the woman I am.
- I am opened to opportunities.
- I am filled with positive energy.
- I choose to do amazing things.
- I will not apologize for being myself.
- Today is a productive day.
- I choose my path to happiness.
- I am filled with confidence.

- It is a new day.
- I welcome positive vibes into my life.
- I will conquer all of my goals for the day.
- I know I am smart and capable.
- Today, I will have awesome ideas.
- I control my success.
- Nothing is stopping me.
- As a result of doing something I have never done before, I will create a good chance today.
- I am a force of nature.
- I do not sweat the small stuff.
- I can choose how I feel, and today I have chosen happy.
- I am prepared to demonstrate to the world who I am and what I have to give them. My feminine energy exudes beauty and confidence.
- I am beautifully me.
- My hair is perfect just the way it is.
- My authentic self is extremely attractive.
- I am beautiful inside and out.
- I am proud of myself.

- There is beauty, love, and vibrance in my imperfections.
- I love and accept my skin.
- My skin complexion is amazing.
- My beauty and intellect are exceptional.
- I adore my skin.
- I hold the key to my happiness.
- The fact that I have a body and that it can do so many things for me makes me glad.
- I accept my body unconditionally.
- I am a sincere, authentic woman.
- My beauty radiates from inside me.
- I enjoy nourishing my body and mind.
- I choose to be happy.
- I choose to love myself today.
- I am whole, just as I am.
- My life is abundant.
- My body is sexy and gorgeous.
- I am bold, beautiful, and brilliant.
- I am the Queen I was born to be.

- I am aware of my potential.
- I'm working on being a more improved version of myself.
- I am worthy of having what I want.
- I accept compliments easily.
- I am strong.
- I have complete confidence in all of my life choices.
- I am accepted.
- I love and respect myself.
- I am enough.
- I hold the characteristics necessary for complete happiness.
- I am more than enough.
- I work hard to become the best version of myself.
- My life is just beginning.
- I am doing an amazing job.
- I am willing to learn and grow.
- I have great ideas.
- I am going to take a chance.
- When I go beyond of my comfort zone, my self-confidence increases.

- I have faith in myself.
- I stand up for my beliefs.
- I have many unique gifts and talents.
- I am brave.
- With every breath, I feel stronger.
- I can do hard things.
- I am capable.
- I stand up for things I believe in.
- I am courageous even when things are unknown to me.
- I have arrived precisely where I'm supposed to be.
- I embrace change.
- I am confident.
- I listen to my inner wisdom.
- I can handle this.
- I have the courage to be myself.
- My choices are my own.
- I have everything I need.
- There is nothing I am not able to overcome.
- No matter how difficult the task is, I am capable of doing it.

- I trust myself.
- I am awesome.
- I understand that obstacles provide a chance to learn and improve.
- I can make good choices.
- I believe in myself.
- I can totally do this.
- I am a hard worker.
- I can be a leader.
- I have the words I need to express myself.
- I stand up for myself.
- I am not intimidated by the prospect of taking on significant challenges.
- I can say no.
- I will get through this.
- I can do anything.
- I am strong and determined.
- I have courage in everything that I do.
- Even if it is difficult, I am capable of completing the task.
- I can achieve my dreams.

- I can, and I will.
- Being true to myself is what matters.
- My hair creates the ideal halo around my face.
- My voice is powerful.
- I love myself.
- My skin is gorgeous.
- I have inner beauty.
- I am important.
- I am whole and complete.
- I am worthy of love.
- I am healthy and am growing up well.
- My body is beautifully perfect.
- There is no one better to be in my place than me.
- I get better every single day.
- I am truthful.
- I am an amazing person.
- I deserve to be loved.
- I strive to be the greatest version of myself that I can be.
- I believe in myself and my abilities.

- I matter.

- I don't want to be seen as someone other than myself.

- I won't compare myself to others. Everyone is on their own path.

- I am strong inside and out.

- I am whole.

- I accept myself for who I am.

- I don't need to be perfect.

- How others see me does not characterize me

- I am focused on achieving my goals

- I am allowed to make my OWN existence I have options in all circumstances Nothing remains among me and my most noteworthy great

- I am not terrified of the obscure on the grounds that I realize I can beat every one of the difficulties that come my direction

- I am better than negative considerations and low activities

- I can, I will End of story

- I merit the best and I acknowledge the best at this point

- I exercise my body every day effortlessly and am stunned at the manners in which it can twist, move, stretch, and posture.

- I have full trust in myself.

- I love difficulties since they draw out the most incredible aspect of me.

- I arrive at any objective I set my heart to If I dream it, I can do it. No objective is far off.

- I'm happy for my lifestyle, adolescence, and experiences; they made me who I am.

- My difficult work, modesty, and tirelessness will take care of things. None of my work will be squandered.

- Play is important and helpful.

- I'm structure a steady organization that supports and inspires me.

- I permit my confidence to control me the correct way.

- I am honored and ensured by my local area.

- I am enabled to develop each day.

- I am content with my development at this time.

- I am bringing up God-dreading kids who will change the world.

- I can achieve any thought I consider.

- I have an exceptionally certain self-personality.

- I pay attention to my body when it needs rest.

- I regard myself and am meriting regard from others.

- I trust myself and my abilities.

- I will show my kids the world.

- I'm agreeable inside my own skin.

- My kids matter.

- My contemplations and feelings matter actually like anyone else's.

- Today is another day to start once more .

- By recognizing my internal identity, I am one bit nearer to mending.

- I permit myself to be available to new freedoms and conceivable outcomes I am liberated from accepting that my choices are restricted.

- I am delightful and deserving of each wonderful thing.

- I am making the existence I need.

- I am in charge of my fate.

- I am spilling over with restored certainty consistently. I proceed to develop and turn into a further person for me and for individuals around me.

- I will pardon. Forgiving myself as well as other people lets frees me from the agony of the past. I excuse and I am free.

- I decide to relinquish the OLD so I can at long last beginning gaining ground with the NEW way I need to take in my life.

- I don't need to delay until I feel prepared to follow up on my objectives. The circumstance won't ever be correct. I'm prepared at this point.

Chapter 23

Affirmations for Leadership

Because of the persistent concerns of discrimination and sexism in the workplace, it may be difficult for black women to advance to the top of the corporate ladder. The difficulty in accepting leadership responsibilities stems from the fact that we do not get the support and connections we need from top leaders. According to reports, black women are undervalued in the promotion and wage rise procedures. As black women, we have a more difficult and terrifying experience than any other group of people when it comes to ascending the corporate ladder. Instead, we're overrepresented in the lowest-paying positions, but we're also the least likely to be recruited and promoted.

Leadership is not about our physical power and drive for us black women. It all comes down to how trustworthy we look and how hard we battle for the common good. When black women take the initiative, we succeed. This is true regardless of whether black women are working to close the wealth gap, campaigning for a free and fair election, or preparing to take on the most powerful position in the nation.

Using these affirmations may aid leaders in visualizing and concentrating their behavior on serving their followers. They provide support for what may already be taking place and provide you the ability to establish better practices.

- I bring new points of view and thoughts that are good and are unique to my experience.

- I make decisions that increase my capacity to be my true self at work. Whether expressing myself through my appearance or my language, I am responsible for those choices.

- I will continue to maintain my integrity by being aware of how I lead, and how I use my position to inspire others.

- I choose to not allow people's uncertainty of my potential to be a good leader make me feel insecure. I learn from constructive criticism and others' insights, but I don't allow them to restrict my leadership potential.

- I choose to look for help from my colleagues in making my workplace more inclusive.

- I realize that as my qualities and talents increase, I can be an asset to my organization. I will capitalize on these attributes to increase my visibility and opportunities in my workplace.

- I will create my own opportunities when the way ahead isn't clear. I have profound creativity. I realize that I can build comprehensive and high-performing associations in which I can prosper.

- I was born to lead

- I let go of the urge to have complete control over everything in my working environment.

- I embrace change with appreciation and good faith.

- I think every day about my encounters, recognizing and incorporating the lessons I have learned.

- I motivate others through my weakness, permitting them to see me as a human.

- I offer thanks every day for the endowment of leading others.

- I adjust my authority to the individual, understanding that everybody's requirements are unique.

- I release all suppositions, investigating only with interest and a desire to comprehend.

- I embrace change in its entirety, knowing that it offers the blessing of learning and development.

- I have a reasonable vision of the sort of leader I need to be, and I make a purposeful move every day to work toward this.

- I request input, acknowledge it, and make a decision on what I learn.

- I'm roused by adoration in everything I do.

- I lead with good energy. I care for myself physically, so I can be awesome for those I lead.

- I'm sure about my gifts and capacities.

- How others see me is an immediate impression of how I see myself. I hold my head high and talk with lucidity and certainty.

- I stay present and positive since I realize my ideas today make my future.

- I get strength from building profound associations with others.

- I tap into and influence the innovative power of my group.

- I face challenges, realizing this is the manner by which we develop.

- I release fear, the sensation of lack, outrage and stress, knowing that these are my problems that can hinder me from becoming the leader I want to be.

- I've realized that disappointment is a human development. I need to become acquainted with it.

- I help other people see and understand their actual potential.

- My actual reason as a leader is to further develop the beneficial experience of others.

- I try to live at the moment, for the present is all I can handle.

- I release judgment and criticism.

- I invite unique and contradicting opinions, understanding that we are more grounded when we hear all voices.

- I'm grateful for my group and partners for all they have shown me and are yet to teach me.

- I talk honestly.

- I trust others, accepting they have genuine motives.

- I'm accessible as a leader, as I realize that my best commitment as a leader is in those I lead.

- I generally cater to everyone's benefit and to the needs of the larger society.

- I can handle my group!

- My team needs a leader like me!

- I have the energy to do this!
- I know I can do this!
- My direction will help the group's confidence!
- I will give them my best oversight!
- I won't fail my instructors who trust I can do this!
- I am qualified to carry out this task!
- I will be fair in making my decisions.
- I am honored with a solid and authoritative voice!
- I have a leadership quality!
- I can't flop in this new section!
- I'm not a rigid person, so I know I am fit for being a leader.
- I have the capability to fill in as an inconceivable officer.
- I will learn new things in this pathway to becoming a leader.
- I am dependable and reasonable enough to be a leader.
- I have fostered a ton of abilities to be a decent leader.
- My orders and choices will be agreeable to my group and not me.
- I won't permit my group members to go down due to my inadequacy.

- I will not lose focus- this can be a resource to become a decent leader.
- I am pleased with my capabilities.
- My team needs a strong and committed leader like me.
- No one except for me can lead myself.
- I can adjust and resolve any new emergency.
- I don't fall powerless in difficult situations. This must be the most important part of a leader.
- I am already a leader.
- People will gain so much from me.
- I am brave to be a leader.
- I can feel a leader inside me.
- I am not impressionable.
- Under my authority, the group will thrive.
- I can run the world.
- I have every one of the qualities of a leader.
- I have the authoritative abilities.
- I can cause people to follow my orders.
- I don't arrive at resolutions without paying attention to everybody.

- I know how to unite the group.
- My characteristics can be of incredible help to others.
- I don't get affected by what individuals need to say.
- I know how to stand my ground in troublesome and uncomfortable times.
- I am sharp and intense enough to not get deceived by humans- this can make me a decent leader.
- I don't lose my control when things don't go according to the arrangement.
- Nothing can stop me.
- I like to face challenges.
- People will see other qualities about me: my leadership potential.
- I can keep my group inspired and focused during difficult stretches.
- I like to challenge and take challenges from my opponents.
- I learn from each downfall.
- I won't allow my colleagues to struggle in isolation.
- I generally make sure to give the acknowledgment for the success to the whole group and not me.
- I am ready with a back-up plan for the group.
- I don't make everything look like I am doing it alone.

- I am prepared to take up any difficulties.
- I don't allow the cooperation to stop.
- I don't ease off from my obligations and responsibility.
- I have a strong will!
- I don't find anything troublesome.
- I can deal with any circumstance.
- My abilities will be of incredible use.
- I can oversee everything all alone without permitting my group to stress over it.
- I generally arise as a victor.
- I keep my fight on despite the fact that every other person has lost hope.
- I am not drawn off-track from my goal.
- I can take the group to a higher level with my stunts and plans.
- I won't let any other individual disparage my capabilities.
- I know what my motivation is.
- I am dedicated to my obligations.
- I don't need to ask individuals to take care of me.
- I can discover my direction without any problem.

- I realize nothing can be accomplished if I don't make an effort to get them done.

- I don't mislead myself.

- I have strong feelings in regard to life and the approach to manage things.

- I couldn't care less regarding people snickering or passing judgment on me if I realize that I am doing the right thing.

- I don't allow pessimism to defeat my energy.

- I am not a doubter or a hopeful person. I am sensible, and this is the thing needed in a leader.

- I can construct options for myself and the organization.

- I'm certain and ready to deal with any snag tossed before me.

- My presence is powerful.

- I have the ability to make positive change.

- My capacity to vanquish my difficulties is boundless. My capability to succeed is limitless.

- I'm appreciative to gain from new encounters, regardless of whether I struggle.

- I'm engaged and steady.

- I'm pleased with myself and all that I have achieved.

- I generally motivate others towards their aspirations.

- I lead others by being a positive role model.

- I'm an incredible visionary.
- I'm an insightful individual and try to move others with my words.
- I'm liberal with applause and praise.
- I'm an inspiration to others.
- I draw out the best in others.
- I have an attractive character.
- I help other people to zero in on the best parts of themselves.
- I realize that I can only lead others to where I have been.
- I make sure to thank people.
- I set precedents that others follow.
- Today, I became the dominant focal point.
- I help other people to zero in on the best parts of themselves.
- I'm approached to assume responsibility for a circumstance.
- I convey what I expect of others.
- I draw in others to collaborate with me to achieve a specific goal.
- I'm ready to start to lead my group.
- I will keep on fostering my standing as a leader.
- Every day it becomes simpler to step up and begin to lead.

- My relational abilities are strong.
- I get things going.
- I can never be happy with living beneath my potential.
- I make choices and I keep my strategies adjustable.
- I'm a social butterfly.
- I act according to what is morally correct.
- I take risks more than others might suspect is safe.
- I do good unto others.
- I'm proactive.
- When I am approached to assume responsibility for tough spots, I get good results by building a culture of collaboration.
- Others seek me for incredible counsel and results because I settle on significant choices that benefit the individuals around me.
- Relational abilities come easily to me. I'm eager to acknowledge new demands and figure out how to get things going.
- I will make a world that is more impartial.
- I take good care of myself so that I can also provide care to others.
- My personality has made an extraordinary viewpoint and I live every day sharing it.
- My seat at the top is set; it's waiting for me to claim it.

- I'm enhanced and satisfied by my connections, which develop further every day.

- I have a spot in a team aimed to create equity, and it is more grounded because I am included.

- As I settle on choices that benefit my community, I generally guarantee fairness will be the number one priority.

- I'm destroying the frameworks that create imbalance piece by piece.

- I'm a powerful articulation of leadership.

Chapter 24

Affirmations for Love and Relationships

Are you okay? Don't worry, you will be, but first, take a deep breath, find a safe space, and take a seat. Release the tension in your shoulders. Roll your shoulders back, keep your head up, and just breathe. Never doubt your beauty, ability, courage, or even your dreams due to your skin color.

Release the anxiety and tension in your mind. You may want to disconnect from social media and reconnect with yourself. A journal is an open book to the mind; explore it. Reconnect with the people who love you. They will remind you how precious you indeed are. Connect with your faith. You can always find strength, courage, and guidance there.

Do you know that you matter? Your life matters, you are beautiful precious, and you are loved. Whenever you feel down, come back to the safe space. The people who fought to get you here. For all the things that you still want to do and accomplish, remember to take a deep breath, keep your head up straight, and whenever you're ready, come back to this safe space.

Stop worrying about what everyone's thinking about. For example, say you're walking and see a group of girls laughing. Stop thinking about what everyone is talking about or that something is wrong about you. In reality, they may just be laughing at something that has absolutely nothing to do with you. They may be admiring your beauty, thinking, "she's gorgeous." Don't take people talking while looking at you the wrong way. They may be talking about how good your hair looks. People don't have the right to tell you their opinion of you constantly.

If all black women started a self-love journey, we could heal generations. Did you know that you can heal? Did you know that you can cry and surrender to the tears falling form your eyes? Did you know that the trauma and pain you've experienced aren't essentially normal; they've just been normalized? Did you know that you don't always have to be strong, push through, and carry on? But most importantly, did you know that you are not alone?

It is okay not to be okay. You can cry and be vulnerable, and neither makes you weak. You don't always have to have it together. The whole idea of the strong black woman may seem like a character in a folk tale to you. The ways of a strong black woman were never directly taught to you; it was shown to you through the behavior and actions of mothers, grandmothers, and family.

The strong black woman trope hurts black women more than it helps them; it tells them they should be strong and resilient. It doesn't allow them to engage in the behaviors needed to preserve their strength and resilience.

If all black women started a self-love journey, we could heal generations, you may be thinking to yourself. How can something so simple as self-love potentially heal black women and possibly even their culture? The answer lies in the definition itself. Self-love is the will to protect, nurture, preserve and celebrate one's emotional, physical, spiritual, and mental health. Self-love goes against all that the strong black woman is supposed to be.

Where the strong black woman trope says to be selfless, self-love says to be selfish. Where the strong black woman trope says show no emotion, self-love says explore them. The strong black woman trope says we don't have time for mental health; self-love says to make time. Self-love follows the hierarchy of cognition.

Reconstructing your thoughts will influence how you feel, which will then affect how you behave. Eventually, it will change the way that you treat yourself. For black women, this is essentially simple because the only thing that the strong black woman is allowed to be is strong. She is expected to push things under the rug, hide her trauma, suffer in silence, but this isn't simple. There is so much that you have to learn and so much more that you have to unlearn.

Successful individuals use a variety of strategies to develop solid and long-lasting connections. Here are some:

1. *They state the objective of the relationship at the onset.*

One of the things that might bring sorrow is having an anticipation that has been postponed. They claim that the relationship between expectations and disappointments is inversely proportional: the more your expectations, the greater the amount of disappointment you will experience if those expectations are not satisfied. Consequently, in any kind of relationship, it is critical to understand what to anticipate from a person and what the other person might expect from you as well.

2. *Have open communication.*

You must be able to say honestly what you feel, and you must be willing to listen to what your partner is saying.

3. *Give generously and don't wait for the favor to be returned.*

When you give, do it with your whole heart and don't expect something in return. Successful people don't keep a list of what's in it for them, or what they can get out of people or situations. The sincere offering of one's time, money, energy, or knowledge can be ultimately rewarding.

- I am more than worthy of love.
- I am beautiful without effort.

- I am an extraordinary person.
- I have a charming, sexy, feminine energy that will attract a loving relationship.
- I am good enough.
- I deserve and will receive a fulfilling romantic relationship.
- I love myself unconditionally.
- I will attract a happy and healthy relationship.
- My past relationships will not predict my future relationships.
- I am capable of receiving love from my partner.
- Being single does not diminish my worth as a vibrant, strong and sexy woman.
- There are more than enough good partners out there.
- My heart is open to attracting a trusting and loving relationship.
- I attract healthy relationships.
- Successful relationships do exist.
- I will not accept less than what I deserve in a relationship.
- The right person will come at the right time.
- I have time for a relationship.
- I can trust my partner.
- I am hopeful and can find love.

- The boundaries I set in my life will attract a loving and respectful partner.

- My marriage grows stronger every day.

- I am the prize in a relationship.

- I am loved.

- To be around me is a fun experience.

- I approach others without fear.

- I speak only with love and honesty.

- My future is filled with passion, romance, and love.

- I deserve real friendship and unconditional love.

- My perfect match is waiting for me.

- I have a natural charm.

- People are naturally happy around me.

- The affection and respect that I deserve are due to me.

- I deserve love, and I receive love.

- I am attracting infinite and true love.

- I am attracting a loyal and caring partner into my life.

- The right person for me is entering into my life right now.

- I am so happy to have a kind, loving, understanding, and supportive partner.

- It is so fulfilling and fun to be with my partner.
- Love is abundant in my life.
- I have a healthy and loving relationship.
- My love for my partner is unconditional.
- Separation is an illusion; my partner and I are one.
- I always treat my partner the way I want them to treat me.
- My partner is loving, generous, and kind.
- I exactly attract what I need and want in my relationship.
- There is absolutely nothing my partner can do to make me stop loving them.
- I express love in various ways.
- I am open to love in all its forms.
- I am honest, unbiased, and independent.
- My partner loves and appreciates me.
- When I'm with my lover, I feel secure and protected.
- I see my partner through my eyes of love.
- I have a twinkle in my eyes for my partner.
- I concentrate on the good in everything.
- No one is perfect, including me.

- I express gratitude daily and thank my partner for their gifts to the world (and me).

- I strive to put the best foot forward in my relationship.

- I have faith in my relationship.

- I listen with a receptive heart and a loving ear.

- I have found a partner who loves me very much, and I love them.

- I have found the right person, and we are getting married now.

- Every day, I experience love and warmth in my marriage.

- I am happy to be in the company of my loved ones.

- I have a passionate and satisfying relationship with my spouse.

- I have found my loving life partner.

- My partner accepts me and loves me as I am.

- Marriage is now a reality in my life.

- There is love in my married life.

- I am married happily to the person of my dreams.

- I feel blessed to have a wonderful and loving spouse.

- I feel blessed to have the most incredible and romantic married life.

- My spouse and I share the same interests.

- My spouse and I enjoy each other's company.

- My partner is a reflection of me.
- Love and happiness are continually flowing into my married life.
- The Universe is showering love upon my married life.
- I am a loving and supportive partner.
- I am thankful to have a loving and supportive family.
- There is love and peace in my family.
- My life is overflowing with love, happiness, and satisfaction.
- I have excellent relationships with my spouse and children.
- I am understanding.
- My goal is to create balance and clarity in my married life.
- I listen so that I can understand and not because I want to "win."
- No one ever wins in an argument.
- I practice patience with grace and ease.
- I communicate in peace and with compassion.
- I am responsible for the foundation on which I have developed my relationship.
- I remain in balance with my emotions.
- I do the best I can.
- I am flexible.

- I'm either destroying or creating in every moment.
- I am reliable, trustworthy, and truthful.
- I support my partner's dreams.
- I encourage my partner to aim for the stars.
- I accept my partner's flaws and leave room for growth.
- I set an example of what I want to see in my partner with every action I take.
- I only speak kind words about my partner.
- I leave the door open for affection.
- I avoid blaming and pointing fingers.
- I never complain.
- I state my needs clearly and honestly.
- I express my truth without putting blame or shame.
- I always leave room for improvement.
- I never give my spouse the cold shoulder and constantly leave space for change.
- I release all grudges and resentment.
- My energy modifies conflict into oneness and unity.
- I never bring up old wounds (unless to heal them).

- I establish the tempo and tone for the expression of love to take place.

- Happiness starts from within me.

- I can't change anyone else; I can only change myself.

- I am content and happy alone, and my partner only adds to the existing good feelings.

- I create a safe and loving place in my home that is always inviting to my partner.

- Love radiates from my very being and affects everyone around me.

- Loving my partner is equivalent to loving myself.

- I stand firm and grounded in love.

- I am a warrior for love.

- No one has the power to hurt me, for I am the only one who can hurt myself.

- Through intention, I achieve my ideal relationship.

- I think positively of my partner.

- With love and support, my partner can be the best version of themselves.

- Everyone likes me and wants to be my friend.

- I have many good friends who love my company, and I enjoy theirs.

- People feel at ease when they are in my presence.
- My colleagues like me and respect me.
- I radiate love and affection toward the people I love.
- There is harmony and respect at my workplace.
- I look inward to find the answers to my problems.
- I accept responsibility for my actions and try to rectify my wrongs.
- I am forgiving.
- I will never give up on love.
- Energy spent loving is never a loss.
- I am glad for the positive connections that I have in all aspects of my life, including my work.
- Thanks to my family and friends for their love and support, I have been able to achieve my goals.
- I am constantly connecting with people who help me advance in my career.
- My relationships with my loved ones grow deeper and deeper every day.
- I am grateful for the bonding time I get with the people I love.
- I constantly attract high quality people effortlessly.
- I am fully comfortable being myself around my friends and loved ones.

- I am constantly learning and growing thanks to the amazing people around me.
- I freely give and receive love.
- I enjoy giving and receiving love in all my relationships.
- I meet exceptional people all the time.
- I am deserving of finding love in my life.
- I am grateful to be loved for who I am.
- The person who I love is fully committed to me.
- My life is better because of the amazing people in it.
- My relationships energize me and make me feel light.
- Everyone around me enjoys my company.
- My platonic relationships are happy and healthy.
- My romantic relationships are happy and healthy.
- I am surrounded by great friends who genuinely care about me.
- I have ample free time to spend quality time with my loved ones.
- My romantic partner is loving, supportive, and generous to me.
- I am surrounded by loyal people who love me unconditionally.
- I am grateful for the free time I have to create lasting memories with the people I love.
- I have an encouraging and exceptional life partner.

- I am loved and accepted by my partner for who I am.

- I always attract wonderful people into my life.

- My quality of life is improved by the people around me.

- I am a better person as a result of the relationships I have with the individuals in my life.

- I have excellent working connections with everyone with whom I come into contact.

- In my life, my family has been a continual source of love, joy, and support.

- The more love I give, the more I receive.

- No matter the circumstances, I can always be my true self around the people I love.

- I easily attract healthy relationships with mentally and emotionally healthy people.

- I am happy to be surrounded by positive and optimistic people.

- I am grateful for the overflow of love in my life.

- I am forgiving of others and they are in turn forgiving of me.

- I am grateful for the lessons that my relationships teach me.

- In loving my partner, I grow to love myself more and more each day.

- Everywhere I go, I am met with compassion and kindness from others.

- I am open with receiving love.
- My relationships are full of joyful surprises.
- My relationships are a source of self-discovery and self-improvement for me.
- No matter who I am with, or where I go, I am met with love.
- I am grateful to be in relationships based on mutual love and respect.
- My relationship with my partner is based on honesty and loyalty.
- My partner and I bring out the best in each other.
- In all of my relationships, we make each other become the best versions of ourselves.
- I am open with giving love.
- I am just as happy in my time alone as I am in my time with loved ones.
- My partner and I love each other unconditionally.
- I am fully emotionally available to the people I love who love me.
- I express love openly and freely to all people.
- I feel love in my heart for all people.
- I am empathetic to others.
- I always express my appreciation for my loved ones.

- My loved ones always express their appreciation for me.

- I cherish my time with my loved ones and am grateful for every moment together.

- I am fully present when spending quality time with my loved ones.

- I feel fully accepted by everyone around me.

- I am grateful for the unconditional love I feel from my loved ones.

- I am grateful to be surrounded by successful people who show me what is possible for me.

- I am happy that my family and friends believe in me.

- I am happy that my romantic partner builds me up and has full faith in me.

- I am grateful for the opportunity to inspire my loved ones to improve their lives.

- I am happy that I encourage my loved ones to be the best versions of themselves.

- My living example of resilience, ambition, and success serves as inspiration to everyone around me.

- The right teachers and mentors for my life goals always find their way to me.

- I am thankful for the mentors that have come into my life to guide me.

- I am glad to have had mentors in my life who encouraged me to go farther.
- I am fortunate to have had mentors in my life who have given me positive feedback.
- I have a wonderful intimate relationship with my partner.
- My partner and I have a passionate, healthy sex life.
- I radiate love to everyone around me.
- I love the feeling of being in love.
- I attract love easily.
- Everybody loves me because I am a good person.
- I give unconditional love to everyone.
- Love is the foundation of all my relationships.
- I radiate pure, unconditional love.
- I am in a loving, supportive relationship.
- I am worthy of being loved.
- I welcome love with open arms.
- I am a magnet for my perfect, love match.
- Love is flowing to me and through me at all times.
- I am attracting magnificent, life-long friends into my life.

- Because of the wonderful individuals in my life, I have become a better person.

Chapter 25

Affirmations for Work and School

- My brain is powerful.
- I love to solve problems!
- I am smart.
- I don't know everything and that is ok!
- I express my ideas easily.
- Doing my best is enough.
- Every problem has an answer.
- I am capable.
- I am open to new ideas.
- I am always learning.
- I am capable of doing everything I set my mind to.
- I work hard.
- Changing my mind is a strength, not a weakness
- I am open and ready to learn.
- I trust my intuition.

- I enjoy absorbing knowledge.
- I am intelligent.
- I manage my time well.
- I have confidence in my abilities to resolve challenges.
- I like being punctual.
- I am creative.
- It's okay to not know everything.
- I think before I react.
- I can ask for help when I need it.
- Learning is fun and exciting.
- I make errors from time to time, but I choose to learn from them.
- Every day, I accomplish all of my schoolwork on schedule.
- I give myself permission to make mistakes.
- Every day, I aim to be the best version of myself.
- I'm prepared to succeed.
- I listen to my intuition.
- I am able to effectively manage all of my obligations and tasks.
- I am capable of so much.

- I am expanding my mind every day.
- The more I study, the more I will advance in my career.
- I am a great listener.
- I always act responsibly.
- Today, I excel in my work spaces.
- I attract wonderful contracts with good pay.
- I am large enough to contain all of the things I seek.
- I have an active brain that can conjure up the best business ideas.
- I am an overflowing well of intelligence.
- I do not falter in my pursuit for business excellence.
- My black excellence precedes me and no workspace can steal that from me.
- I welcome good jobs and offers into my life.
- Toxic workspaces would flee at the sight of me.
- I am too big to accommodate small minds.
- My business blooms despite all hurdles and discouragement.
- I am the queen in my kingdom and nothing on earth can bring me down.
- I am in control of my businesses.

- The market conditions would tilt towards helping me fulfil my goals.

- I am made for so much more.

- I am a breathing body of excellence.

- I am worthy of the best working conditions.

- I wine and dine with the best people in my industry.

- I seal the best business deals with grace and ease.

- I'll not be broken by my quest for better opportunities.

- I don't write business applications in vain.

- I am ready to take over my industry with my intelligence and business sense.

Chapter 26

Affirmations for Black Parents to Become a Confident Parent

- I rely on the assistance that is available to me, in whatever shape it may take.

- I am valuable to my family.

- I constantly make sure that my family has everything they need.

- I am a badass black mom!

- Motherhood reveals my strengths to me.

- I am powerful and strong.

- Being a mother has shown to me how resilient I am.

- Comparisons do not serve me

- My children are fortunate to have a mother who is so concerned and dedicated to them.

- I radiate grace, confidence, and care.

- Today I am strong and healthy.

- I am brave and courageous.

- I am raising world changers.

- I will make the most of today.

- I am powerful beyond measure.

- I am exactly what my kid needs. Worrying about what other people think just serves to divert my attention away from being the parent I need to be.

- Because of every struggle that I overcome, I become a stronger black mother.

- Some of my fellow moms come to me for guidance and inspiration.

- It takes bravery for me to expose my children's vulnerabilities.

- The most effective mothers are those who are most challenged. It demonstrates that they are concerned enough to do better.

- My kid sees me as a good mother in his or her eyes, thoughts, and heart.

- I am a kind lady that offers a wonderful example for her children to follow.

- In my parenting position, I am increasing in confidence and competence.

- My abilities are limitless if I trust what I am told to be true and act on my beliefs and emotions.

- My children need me in their life.

- My spouse and I agree on healthy parenting approaches.

- Only good lies before me.
- I am a great mother.
- With each passing day, I grow in my ability to be a confident mother.
- I am bold and gutsy for attempting something even when I believe I am unable to do it.
- My self-worth has been acknowledged, and my self-confidence has skyrocketed.
- In the eyes of my children, I am the ideal mother.
- I am capable of raising my kids.
- I make good decisions for my children.
- I am self-assured and brave, and I advocate for myself.
- I exude strength, grace, and flexibility.
- As a mother, I put forth my best effort at all times.
- It takes strength to be a good mother, and today I'm feeling particularly bold.
- I am doing a good job.
- I am brave.
- I will be the type of person I would like my children to become.
- I am admired.
- I exhibit the characteristics necessary for complete happiness.

- I am important in the lives of my children.
- I listen to the spirit and I am guided.
- I am more than enough.
- I'm working hard to become the best version of myself.
- I constantly remember to provide a good example for my children by acting in the same manner.
- I urge others to make the same choice that I did.
- I am raising individuals who will make positive contributions to the well-being of society.
- Being a mother makes me feel beautiful.
- It is more vital to me to love my children than it is to love every minute of motherhood.
- I am a good role model to my children on how to take care of my body.
- My children are taught to be confident in their appearance, including their hair, skin tone, and physical traits.
- 'Just a mom' does not exist in the real world.
- I will show my children the world.
- I am the kind of mom that my kid needs in order to flourish.
- My superpower is that I am a black mother.
- I am raising black professionals, politicians, and leaders.

- I enjoy food preparation and can even find resources to support me when I need a break.

- My life is just beginning.

- I am doing an amazing job.

- I love being a parent.

- Having quality time with my children is essential to me.

- I teach my children how to be polite, generous, and loving in their interactions with others.

- I am conscious of the nature of my kid and encourage him or her to live their own truth.

- I want to demonstrate to my children what it is to take care of oneself.

- I teach my kids to be authentic.

- I am willing to learn and grow.

- I stand up for my children.

- I provide a safe atmosphere for my children in all aspects of their lives: physically, emotionally, psychologically, spiritually, and elsewhere.

- I am a leader to my children.

- There's value in showing my kids my vulnerability.

- I am black girl magic.

- Time and attention are more essential to me than material items when it comes to my children's development.

- While I am teaching my children today, I will also be receptive to the lessons they may have to share with me.

- My children have blossomed because I am the precise mother they need; thus I have no need to compare myself to other moms.

- I instill in my black children the importance of being tough and fearless.

- I am my child's lifelong teacher.

- I take the necessary precautions to guarantee that I am contributing to their health and well-being.

- I instill in my children a love and respect for their physical selves.

- I am everything to my children.

- I am healthy and vibrant.

- My children matter.

- Every day, I set an example for my children.

- I am building wealth to leave my children an inheritance.

- Set high expectations for myself and my children, and they will learn that everything is possible for them as well.

- I love how much joy this role gives me.

- My decisions benefit my children.

- In my life, I have been called to parenting, which is the most powerful calling on the planet.

- In my home, I am raising God-fearing children who will make a difference in the world.

- I demonstrate to my children how to attain their objectives by reaching my own objectives.

- Motherhood has revealed my strengths and I am becoming a better version of myself.

- I want to teach my children how to be advocates for compassion and fairness in the world.

- I am a great parent.

- When change is the best choice, I am not averse to making adjustments.

- Only I can provide my children with a contented mother.

- As a father, I serve as a role model, a mentor, and a friend to my children.

- Instead of being defined by a single success or failure, motherhood is comprised of the sum of my parenting decisions.

Chapter 27

Affirmations for Self-Worth and Self-Love

In reality, the determination to provide your family with a clean, caring, and secure home is part of your motivation to aspire relentlessly to "do more and cram more into your day." What I mean is you have to put the brakes on, look in the mirror and ask, "what about me, what do I want?" and turn the light of love to satisfy your desires and rock your inner core.

In many cases, the better it becomes to view life through the lens of self-love and your happiness without feeling guilty and "selfish" to place yourself first, the more you practice self-love. The need of self-love and acceptance is emphasized across all spiritual teachings and ideologies, and this is true at the end of a day.

There are self-love activities to make you love yourself more today:

#1 Write self-love quotes, affirmations, and inspirations: "I am the apple of my eye, the light of motivation I pursue", "Every day I love myself more and more" and "The more I respect and appreciate myself, the more I develop within". Build your affirmations or choose the three above, write them down. You can sneak your affirmations into your handbag as an extra treat to yourself or write them out on your phone and read them to yourself during the day, especially when you feel anxious. You will immediately relax into your being's more caring side.

#2 Pray and show gratitude for your health and wellness: If you're not Christian, you may be confused by the thought of meditation. As I went through a phase of challenging "Jesus and all that sacred stuff," as my brother and cousin passed away, I understand that that brought me to a more meaningful and soulful link with life over the years. Over the years, though, I now appreciate the importance of spending a few minutes in quiet contemplation and prayer.

If you're waiting quietly, I've composed a prayer of thanks that I'm happy to share with you. Take a moment and utter the prayer below:

Dear Divine Mother,

Thank you for the grace that runs from my heart openly, for the love and devotion that I now offer to myself, for the emergence of boundless energy and rivers of goodwill. Thank you, Mother Earth, for the many streams of life that float into my head now and then endlessly enriching my existence and filling me up till I overflow; for the feeling of peace and peaceful heart; and for the sensation of peace and peaceful heart. I am purely awful and hope for ever more streaming creation. Thank you, Holy God, for granting me the reason to value myself.

#3 Meditate: If you're doing meditation, you know it's one of the best gifts. There are plenty of meditations out there, and you will come across different techniques and insights during your self-love path. As a novice, studying and acquiring yoga from an experienced teacher is always better.

Here's a guided self-love meditation for you to practice:

- after you've spoken your 3 daily affirmations, made your morning teacup, and said your daily Gratitude Prayer, find a quiet space.
- put your phone on a 3-minute timer to make yourself comfortable.

- take a few steady breaths in and out of your nose, lower your shoulders and read the following passage to yourself loudly.
- Sit in silence after reading it and take a couple more minutes remaining still before re-engaging with your day as the timer stops.

Guided self-love meditation

I breathe in calm. I breathe out love. I breathe in warmth. I breathe out pleasure, breathe in forgiveness; I let go of the pain and sorrow I breathe in love and happiness, I let go of the misery I breathe in life and groove in sync with my core rhythms.

Closing thoughts and call to action.

I urge you to set aside 15 minutes to follow these clear self-care habits as you wake up for the next 5 days. When you begin your day, you will feel refreshed, energized, and, the best of all, cherished and nurtured. I would love to know how you're getting on.

It's the mystery we're both posing as we recover and rebuild broken self-esteem. We want to respect ourselves more thoroughly and enjoy ourselves. We certainly know the anguish of creeping into those old feelings of worthlessness. They learn even how we are most "sensitive" and self-critical.

But how do we get to the feelings of self-love from these wincing, self-denying feelings on earth? How do we value ourselves when we don't so clearly respect ourselves in many ways? Do not be depressed if you feel this annoyance. It will often seem like "you can't get there from here" in finding your way to self-love. This obvious impasse is to be anticipated.

And this is why. We must first feel full and nourished to feel happy and feel a positive sense of self. Of course, the issue is that these self-negative feelings discourage us from being satisfied and filled properly.

This is especially true as our sense of self, self-image, and entire personality falls heavily into these hurt emotions. Since we "tell" ourselves that this injury is not enough (not adequately great, not sufficiently small, not sufficiently achieved, not sufficiently "complete," etc.), we rob ourselves of that essential, continuous nourishment we need to encounter more.

So, our double-binding is there. We can't see our worthiness to be filled and to see our worthiness. We can't fill ourselves. So how are we supposed to get here? Thankfully, the Bridge to Self-Love is an intermediate step, a "condition" that bridges the gap between that self-rejection deficiency state and the normal sense of self-love. It's a place that allows us to keep getting nourished, given the self-negative feelings, so we can restore and reawaken the inherent sense of being all right and necessary.

And the middle position is self-acceptance and respect for oneself. Unlike that mystical, distant land of self-love, it's remarkably easy to find this intermediate place - and incredibly strong.

Self-acceptance and kindness are not about trying to convince yourself that you are good or effective (or whatever) at the moment when your damaged emotions warn you that you are not. It's not about having to kill yourself and correct what's "wrong" with you so you can fulfill the intense, perfectionist vision. Neither of these responses gives you much.

Getting into this middle position requires nothing more than handling oneself in reaction to these painful feelings and stressful times with patience and compassion. Let's be clear about this. These wounded feelings you don't deny. You don't doubt it's hard. You simply respond in a different way to these painful feelings.

Serving yourself instead of the wounded feelings means that you're taking a different role. You're taking a step backward and realizing that as intense as these wounded feelings sound, they're just that: wounded feelings. They are feelings that a wounded place creates. In fact, they don't give you accurate information about your dignity. They only warn you of a hurt, wounded position.

And you choose to be compassionate, caring then healing with yourself in the first place in reaction to that hurt position.

Note the difference again. You choose to handle yourself with dignity, care, and compassion rather than crumble into these fake, self-negative feelings-instead of believing them, viewing yourself as a corrupt person, and driving yourself even harder. By adding kindness and understanding to this painful place, you react to this painful signal.

It is not about "fixing" yourself to regain your self-esteem. It's about self-FEEDING. Your task is not to please oneself or your life's "wounded" perception. Your task is to fix the wound at the heart of it: to feed the poor, judging spot. And you do this by coming to this position with patience and compassion rather than harshness.

In reality, a sign of your bruised self-esteem is the determination and toughness to repair yourself. A strict response is a continuation of the bite, refusing behavior. So, if you choose to treat yourself calmly and compassionately instead, you break that self-hardened pattern. Despite terms of what you "know" is wrong with you, when you can step back to continue to be compassionate and embrace yourself, the real sense within you continues to be nourished.

It's waking up. Your positive sense of self becomes stronger and stronger when you pursue this strategy. And just to be sure about that, self-acceptance doesn't discourage you from taking positive steps for your growth and progress or make the necessary changes in your life. These efforts actually require you to be particularly supportive, patient, and self-approving. This is the same strength you need to recover, improve, and push on.

The more these positions become sensitive, so unpleasant, the more caring, gentle, and cautious you need to be with yourself. The challenge we encounter in learning to love ourselves is that the particularly painful emotions correlated with damaged self-esteem have the unpleasant capacity to "erase" our sense of self-esteem and self-worth altogether... and, in essence, we can't find love for ourselves.

We have to be prepared for this very "natural" answer to our wounds. And consider it with sympathy. Patience and patience, thankfully, are expressions of kindness. Especially when they are directed at you, and this little move will start to bring you back to you immediately: back to fullness and back to life.

Are you enjoying yourself?

Symptoms that give you a self-love deficiency

"Will you see yourself as valuable?" may appear to be a silly question at first glance. However, it is a highly important subject that demands a thorough response. Does it make you smile when you hear this question, or does it make you cringe a little? This would be your first sign of the above issue, based on your response. If you respect yourself, when you are confronted with this problem, you should feel good. Check out below the 3 indicators that will alert you whether you lack self-love or not.

First, ask yourself if you believe that self-love is an act of selfishness? Most people believe it's self-love or it's selfish. It's not real. Have you ever heard of what the saying, "If you don't respect yourself, nobody else can love you?" That assertion has so much validity because; knowing oneself provides an awareness of how to live.

Second, do you need other people around you to praise? If you are constantly searching for approval, this is also a good indicator of lacking self-love. It's a must to know how to create internal self-love.

Third, do you need to make others happy about yourself feeling happy? If you're trying to make someone happier for yourself, only having a little joy, then it's time to ask yourself, why? It's okay to enjoy doing things that make others happy, but if it's not balanced with your happiness, it might be another sign that you lack self-love.

Don't hesitate if you lack self-love. It's easy to create. The first move is to realize that you need it.

- The person that I am now is not the person the world perceives or believes I am; rather, I am an incarnation of perfection, and I am beginning to exhibit excellence in everything that I do.

- My body is a sacred temple that is intricately designed and I begin to treat it with the love and acceptance it deserves.

- My skin is beautiful and it glows with a radiance that causes me to stand out everywhere I go.

- I am a strong woman, I walk with a confident spring in my step and my head is held high with dignity.

- I embrace the peculiarities that make me who I am.

- I am not a misfit, I am uniquely built in the reflection of my heritage.

- I exist therefore I matter.

- I speak positive things into my life, I think positive thoughts about myself and I begin to attract positivity all around me.

- My will is empowered to walk away from all forms of negative influences around me.

- I am worthy of love and therefore I allow myself to be vulnerable enough to receive love.

- I am wholly beautiful, mind body and soul.
- I advance each day on my journey to self-love and self-discovery.
- I find peace, comfort and acceptance within myself.
- My life is worth living, tomorrow is worth waiting for.
- I will be kind to myself, I will nurture my mind, feed my spirit and pamper my body.
- When I realize that I am the creator of my own narrative, I begin to change its script in order to portray a more compelling tale of bravery, fortitude, and self-actualization.
- Even if it doesn't look like it, all things are working together to benefit me in the end.
- I refuse to depend on others for my validation, I define my own self-worth.
- I begin to set healthy boundaries and I receive the strength to adhere to them.
- I learn from my past as I move on from it, I take charge of my present and I prepare myself for a glorious future.
- I am priceless, of inestimable value and not everyone deserves access to my personal space.
- I am not buried under, I am planted and I begin to nurture myself for fruitful growth and expansion.
- It is okay to decline without creating excuses or trying too hard to explain myself.

- I am dedicated to learning how to love myself better.

- I stand out like a shining light and I refuse to dim my light for anyone.

- I come from a history of survivors, I am a descendant of strength and I reach deep within myself to find the resilience planted in my genes.

- I celebrate myself and I take pride even in the little victories.

- I step out of the fear and self-doubt that has held me captive and I begin to share my beauty with the world.

- People come and people go, some remain a part of my life while others may wish to leave. Through all of this, my self-worth remains the same.

- I have the power to change whatever I am not comfortable with around me and within me.

- I am grateful for the girl I left behind and I am proud of the woman I am becoming.

- I love my body and I am thankful for how it was created and what it can do.

- This day is a gift with limitless possibilities and I as I step out into it, I seize all the opportunities it has to offer me.

- As I attract positivity in my life, I choose to withhold negativity from others. I exude the positivity that I attract.

- I look into the mirror and the person I see is a goddess who gets better with each day.

- My strength and confidence are renewed daily, my self-esteem is boosted daily and I begin to see myself for the amazon that I am.

- I am an asset to myself, those around me and the world at large.

- My hair is a lustrous crown that signifies the royal blood that runs through my veins.

- There is strength in my fragility, wonder in my delicate frame and power in my softness.

- I am proud of my culture and how my experiences have shaped me into a phenomenal black woman of excellence.

- When self-doubt threatens to pull me under, I will look within and remind myself of my true worth, then I will rise above the demons of insecurity.

- I am beautiful, from the kink and curl in my hair to the graceful stride in my steps.

- I am confident enough to take off the mask I have been wearing while pretending to be someone else and I will unapologetically exist as who I am.

- I am intentional about investing in the positive things that bring me joy.

- I am intentional about blocking all channels that give negativity access to my life.

- I'm not going to let my frustrations get the best of me.

- I begin to attract like-minded people to form healthy and respectful relationships where I can thrive and find support.

- I let go of the bitter people in my life to create space for better people to come into my life.

- I starve my weaknesses and I feed my strengths.

- I deserve better and I refuse to let my insecurities intimidate me into settling for less.

- I resist the urge to form an inferiority complex by comparing myself with other people.

- My happiness comes from deep inside me and it cannot be hampered by factors external to me.

- I do not live for the validation of people and therefore their criticism cannot kill me.

- I allow myself to have fun and enjoy life to the fullest.

- I am at ease with myself and I refuse to be too hard on myself.

- I fall more in love with the person I am becoming daily.

- I love and appreciate every contour, curve or bulge on my body for its unique beauty.

- My lips, my nose, my hips and everything about my body is appropriately proportional to my bold and vivacious personality.

- I am a living, breathing reflection of the beauty and excellence that my heritage embodies.

- Instead of wallowing in self-pity, I choose to turn my losses into wins worth celebrating.

- I am not a cheap knockoff, I am an original work of art.

- My opinion of myself carries more weight than the negative opinions of others about me.

- I will learn how to love myself unconditionally.

- I am loved, I am chosen and I am cherished.

- I treat myself with the love and grace that I give to others.

- I will endure disrespect and humiliation, I will communicate how I would rather be treated.

- I will not criticize myself for not being who I think I should be, instead I will learn to love who I am.

- Bad days do not make me an incompetent person: they make me human.

- I free myself from the need for perfect and I strive instead for self-improvement.

- I will begin to root for myself the way I would support and encourage a dear friend.

- I intentionally begin to think positive thoughts about myself first thing when I wake up and last thing before I go to bed.

- I cultivate the habit of feeling proud of myself.

- I am deserving of love and I will not beg to be loved.

- I will not shrink myself for others to feel good about themselves, I will blossom the way I was created to.

- I am grateful that I was created this way, I am wonderfully and beautifully made.

- I will not let my mind be a bully to my body.

- I am secure with myself because my self-esteem keeps growing daily.

- I am creating a beautiful life.

- My choices are inspired by wisdom from within and they aid me on my journey through life.

- I am precisely who I need to be and where I need to be in this moment.

- My whole life radiates the beauty that my soul is made of from within.

- My life attracts everything good and it gives everything good in return.

- I am cocooned in self-care and self-appreciation.

- My self confidence remains unshaken even in the face of disappointment.

- I do not need external factors to complete me, I was created whole and I am enough.

- My life is amazing and it can only get better from here.

- I feel comfortable speaking my mind and expressing my feelings.

- I am not unworthy or all the wonderful things I desire, I deserve all the amazing things my heart desires.

- I am comfortable in this glowing skin.

- I will no longer downplay my achievements, I am worthy of every compliment that I receive.

- I am a valuable addition to society, my life makes a difference.

- I am courageous and outgoing, my life is an adventure full of surprises.

- I do my best every day and today's efforts are better than yesterday's efforts.

- My feminine energy exudes beauty and confidence.

- I am beautifully me.

- My hair is perfect just the way it is.

- My authentic self is extremely attractive.

- I am beautiful inside and out.

- I am proud of myself.

- There is beauty, love and vibrance in my imperfections.

- I find beauty in my surroundings.

- I love and accept my skin.

- My skin complexion is amazing.

- My beauty and intellect is exceptional.

- I adore my skin.
- I hold the key to my happiness.
- The fact that I have a body and that it can do so many things for me makes me glad.
- I accept my body unconditionally.
- I am a sincere, authentic woman.
- My beauty radiates from inside me.
- I enjoy nourishing my body and mind.
- I choose to be happy.
- I choose to love myself today.
- I am whole just as I am.
- My life is abundant.
- My body is sexy and gorgeous.
- I am bold, beautiful and brilliant.
- I am the Queen I was born to be.
- The love I've for myself increases my capacity to love others.
- I'm always headed in the right direction.
- By shining my light.
- I don't have to earn my worth.

- I belong in any space I walk into.
- I concentrate on what gives me energy. My energy serves as my compass.
- Being me is how I win.
- I'm my stylish source of alleviation.
- I'm loved and supported.
- My tone-worth is high.
- I'm the stylish interpretation of myself just as I am.
- I always find new ways to come home to myself each day.
- I'm unconditionally good.
- I'm gentle with myself through all transitions.
- Of the outgrowth, I'm supported.
- My passions are valid, and I recognize them all.
- I always allow myself to feel so I can heal.
- My magic speaks for itself.
- I have the ability to choose how I feel, and today I have chosen happy.
- I am content with myself, and my mind is clear.
- I am lovely in my flaws.
- I'm comfortable in my own skin.

- I am confident
- I am deserving of love and admiration.
- I'm grateful.
- Self-care is a self-loving deed.
- It's enough for me to be who I am.
- I'm a goddess, believe it or not.
- I'm overflowing with delight, joy, and love.
- I am a beautiful woman of color.
- Difficult times pass.
- I am not superior to anyone.
- I am a strong person of color who deserves all of the good things that come my way.
- I am the best, and I am proud of who I am.
- I am grateful for the peace of mind that possessing money can provide if I manage it properly.
- Financial stability gives me peace of mind.
- All of my resistance to wealth is cheerfully surrendered.
- I am a strong black woman.
- I love being a strong black woman.
- I love being an independent black woman.

- Black is beautiful.
- Being black makes me strong.
- I speak kindly to myself.
- I am proud of my culture.
- I am more than my surroundings.
- I believe that every dream I have can and will be accomplished.
- I am a walking example of black success.
- I set clear boundaries in my life, and only attract people that respect these boundaries.
- I welcome abundance into my life.
- I am open to receiving without guilt.
- It is important to speak my truth.
- I am a prosperous black woman with endless opportunities.
- My brown skin is a blessing.
- I am grateful for my uniqueness.
- I am a great person, I love being me.
- I am not my surroundings, I am my own beautiful soul. I create what I want.
- I am brave, brilliant, and beautiful.
- I choose to live a long prosperous life.

- I feel an inner smile when I think about how far I've come.
- I am a woman of action, I permit my actions to speak for me.
- Today will be an abundant day.
- My possibilities are unlimited.
- I enjoy being a strong black woman.
- I am a magnet to positive people and circumstances.
- I treat my body with respect.
- I treat my body with dignity.
- I am a strong black queen with the power to change the world.
- I remind myself every day that black truly is beautiful.
- I love the woman I see when I look in the mirror.
- I have limitless potential.
- My beautiful brown skin is a blessing that I would not change.
- I embrace my culture.
- I am committed to being responsible for my life.
- Black is greatness.
- I am filled with gratitude for my beautiful brown skin.
- I allow myself to fulfill my potential.
- I choose to see the beauty in who I am.

- I am a force to be reckoned with.

- I enjoy being loved.

- I give positive energy a great home within me and release any negative energy from knowing that it does not serve me.

- I embrace being me.

- I am successful.

- I am stronger than my previous experiences.

- I understand that being black does not limit my options in life. I create my life with intention and action.

- I only share my time and energy with people worthy of my presence.

- I do what is best for me and those that I love.

- I believe in myself.

- I move on quickly from failure, knowing that it is only a true failure if I allow it to stop me.

- I am purposeful with my actions and always keep my goals in mind.

- I am open to receiving love in abundance.

- I have a positive attitude towards others.

- Being black is beautiful.

- I love all that I am and all that I am becoming.

- I never settle for less than I deserve.
- I am an independent thinker. I make decisions with confidence and intention.
- I am talented.
- I am worthy of love.
- I am worthy of being celebrated.
- I have inherited strength through my black heritage.
- I love my natural beauty. I don't need to change for anyone.
- If I choose to change anything about me, it is out of self-love, not shame.
- Anything is possible for me.
- There are so many strong black females in the world, and I am one of them.
- I release all preconceived ideas of who I am or what I am supposed to be. I am my own woman.
- I am filled with gratitude for my perfect imperfections.
- I am glorious.
- I am thankful for my black heritage and those that paved the way.
- I am a queen.
- I release any desire to appease other peoples' opinions and expectations.

- I am worthy of success.
- I am brave.
- I avoid instant gratification and seek what's best for my long-term benefit.
- I love feeling the freedom that comes with being myself and being true to who I am.
- I know that overcoming hardships is a part of life. I have the presence of mind to know that hardships do not last.
- The color of my skin instills me with strength.
- I am unique, and I will not change to please people or fit the opinions and expectations of others.
- I am blessed with a resilient soul.
- My ambitions are achievable.
- It feels so good being a black woman.
- I love myself unconditionally.
- I am loved.
- I am deserving of my desires.
- I release all individuals that don't accept me for who I am.
- I don't need acceptance and validation from others.
- I love overcoming challenges and becoming stronger.
- The color of my skin is a gift.

- I am a positive influence on those around me.

- I express my truth without fear of judgment.

- I am beautiful inside and out.

- I stand up for myself, protect my values, and defend my happiness.

- As a black woman, I am worthy of receiving unconditional life, just like everyone else is.

- I put myself first in life, for that is the foundation to helping others.

- I only allow loving souls to enter into my life.

- I treat myself like the queen I am.

- I recognize that challenges create growth and opportunity.

- I feel protected and loved by the people I allow into my life.

- I can achieve anything, and I know this is true.

- I am beautiful.

- I am my own responsibility, and this is a responsibility I treat with the greatest respect.

- I am growing greater every day.

- I am committed to loving myself.

- I am more than my past.

- I enjoy being black and blessed.

- I accept abundance into my life.
- I love my curls and perfect frame.
- I was created exactly how I was intended to be.
- I live by my own rules.
- I am committed to sharing my true self with others, without shame, fear, or guilt.
- My black heritage is one of strength.
- I feel proud and privileged to be black.
- I am a powerful, successful black woman.
- I am excited to see all that I can achieve.
- I plan for my future by making decisions with thought and intent, not in search of instant gratification.
- I am in command of my life, no one else.
- I love myself.
- I am a living, breathing example of black excellence.
- I love being an abundantly successful black woman.
- I effortlessly drop negative people and behaviors from my life.
- I welcome success into my life.
- I embrace my differences knowing that they make me unique.
- I choose how I feel, I don't let others determine this for me.

- I am kind to myself and to others.
- I choose to celebrate how amazing I am.
- Damn it feels good to be me!
- I am deliberate and fearless with my actions.
- It is okay to be seen, I choose to express who I am without fear of judgment.
- I can live my best life.
- I enjoy being black and abundant.
- I am unwavering in pursuit of my best life.
- Being black is a blessing.
- I am unapologetically me.
- I choose to love myself.
- I am not limited by the color of my skin, being black is a gift.
- I know that every obstacle and challenge I overcome in life makes my story greater.
- I speak my mind freely and fearlessly.
- I am confident.
- I am worthy of respect.
- I feel deep gratitude for the sacrifices made by my ancestors and appreciate how blessed my life truly is.

- I permit myself to live without seeking the approval of others.
- I am forgiving of myself and others.
- I release all blame, knowing that it does not serve my future.
- I am a vibrant soul, free to express myself without fear.
- My skin is not a barrier to my success, and it is a gift that gives me the strength and courage to succeed abundantly.
- I am my only limit.
- I am worthy of abundance.
- I can achieve anything I give my all to.
- I am deserving of abundance.
- I am committed to growing as a person every single day.
- My beautiful black skin makes me feel like I'm glowing. I am beautiful.
- It is important to live true to myself, who I am, and what I believe in.
- It is okay to experience difficulty, as this creates my growth.
- I love my black skin, and it is a blessing.
- I am black and successful.
- It feels so good being me.
- I have the willpower to create all that I desire.

- I am a phenomenal black woman.

- I am a courageous, bold black woman.

- I only share my energy with souls that make me feel loved.

- My thoughts and feelings are valid.

- I bring my dreams into reality.

- I choose the path that leads to my greatest success in life, not the path that is easiest.

- The color of my skin does not limit me in life.

- I am worthy of attracting positive, uplifting, and ambitious souls into my life.

- Being black is amazing.

- I feel amazing when I am being true to myself.

- I release all negative beliefs that may hinder my success and abundance.

- I am open to becoming better than I am today to align myself with better influences, opportunities, and a greater quality of life.

- I know that it is safe to put my feelings first.

- I get excited when I think about how much I can still grow as a person.

- I am worthy of greatness.

- I welcome love into my life.

- I attract blessings just by being me.
- I love and appreciate my black heritage.
- I create black wealth that lasts beyond my lifetime.
- I am committed to bringing my dreams into reality.
- I live for me, not for the opinions of others.
- It feels so good being black and abundant.
- I release blame towards others knowing that I am in control of my life and destiny.
- I am capable of greatness.
- I am filled with gratitude for the blessings already present in my life.
- I love my voice, and how I speak. I will never change my natural tonality to fit the expectations of others.
- I always live my truth.
- I know my worth.
- My body is with me for life; therefore I choose to treat my body with care.
- The strong woman I see when I look in the mirror is all I need.
- I accomplish whatever I set my mind to.
- I permit myself to put myself first.
- I only share my energy with souls that make me feel safe.

- I am committed to being a source of positive energy.
- I choose to find beauty in my struggles, knowing that it is making me stronger.
- I am blessed.
- I choose to feel gratitude, knowing that I am truly blessed.
- I am proud to be black.
- I embrace my greatness.
- I love the woman I see in the mirror.
- I am grateful for all that I am.
- It is safe for me to release toxic people from my life.
- I dream big knowing that I am capable of anything.
- I am free to be myself without guilt.
- I am confident in my ideas and beliefs.
- I am not defined by stereotypes of who I should be, I am my own woman.
- I release any grudges or ill-feeling towards people that have wronged me, I choose not to harbor negative energy.
- I truly believe that black is beautiful.
- I feel blessed to be black.
- All that I need is within me, and my inner abundance creates a blessed life.

- I am a confident black woman.
- I cherish being me.
- I am intelligent.
- I am filled with gratitude for the challenges and obstacles I overcome, for they make me a more resilient person.
- Being black adds to my being, it does not take from being.
- I choose to see opportunities everywhere.
- I give my everything into achieving my goals knowing that being black is not a limit to my success.
- I love who I am.
- I am capable of whatever I put my mind to.
- I release all stereotypes, I am my own woman.
- I am worthy of peace.
- I am grateful for my black heritage.
- I am a beautiful black woman.
- I do not have to hold onto anyone who does not positively impact my life.
- My heritage gives me strength.
- I am growing stronger with every challenge I overcome.
- There is nothing I cannot achieve if I am willing to work and grow.

- My blackness makes me stronger.
- I speak confidently, my voice is heard.
- I embrace my femininity and love who I am.
- I can accomplish all that I desire.
- I treat myself with respect.
- I am free to be myself.
- I accept myself.
- I release all previous thoughts and emotions about being black that do not serve me.
- I love every inch of my body.
- I am committed to achieving my goals.
- I remind myself every day that life itself is a gift; therefore, I truly am lucky and blessed.
- I choose courage over doubt.
- I trust myself.
- I don't need permission to live my best life.
- The struggles I experience make me stronger.
- I share my uniqueness openly and unapologetically.
- I express gratitude for who I am.
- My beautiful black soul makes me feel empowered.

- I am constantly improving and growing as a person.
- I welcome peace into my life.
- I accept that I will not always have the answers, but I am always willing to find them.
- I take time to work on myself.
- I am worthy of appreciation and respect.
- I do not hide from challenges, I believe in my ability to overcome them.
- I love being free from drama and negative influences.
- I am strong.
- I feel comfortable in my own skin.
- I only surround myself with other ambitions like-minded individuals.
- I forgive myself for making mistakes, as this is a part of being human.
- I am a fearless black woman.
- My heritage is full of strong black women.
- I only share my goals, dreams, and intentions with loving souls.
- I am grateful for all of my imperfections.
- I know that self-discipline is self-love.

- I am remembered for the actions I take being myself, I do not change who I am to receive recognition from others.
- I can change the world.
- I am a positive influence on my community.
- I release guilt for I know it does not serve me.
- I am always seeking the next challenge in life.
- I am a leader.
- I forgive my past and stride towards an abundant future.
- I am more than society's expectations of me.
- I am writing my own success story.
- I receive love just by being me.
- I am worthy of a wonderful life.
- As a black woman, I can create success and abundance just like anyone else can.
- I celebrate who I am and who I am becoming.
- I inspire the next generation of black success.
- I surround myself with positive influences to better myself.
- I have an aura of confidence in everything that I do.
- I am healed of all negative thoughts and emotions.
- My thoughts and feelings matter.

- I welcome joy into my life.

- I am born from a long lineage that chose to overcome, this makes me powerful beyond imagination.

- I am the author of my destiny.

- If I could be born again, I wouldn't change a thing about me.

- I cherish my black heritage knowing that it has given me strength.

- I always choose growth over comfort.

- I release all generational trauma. I am my own person.

- I am an unstoppable black woman.

- I only share my energy with souls that love me for who I am.

- I am lovingly made.

- I am a creator of circumstance, not a creature of circumstance.

- Black is abundant.

- I am thankful for the pain of my past and choose to move on.

- I am important, I am significant, I am remembered.

- I celebrate my individuality.

- I nourish my soul by speaking kindly to myself.

- I am enough.

- Being a strong black woman makes me feel unstoppable.

- I am a beautiful black lady who deserves to receive love, respect, and kindness.

- I love myself.

- I admire my body.

- I adore my skin.

- My body is a gift from God.

- There is beauty, love, and vibrance in my imperfections.

- I am fit and highly energetic.

- My body is sexy and gorgeous.

- I have unique qualities and talents.

- My beauty radiates from inside me.

- I understand the importance of the female cycles that my body experiences.

- I persevere. I am relentless. I keep going.

- I am a loving and caring daughter, mother, sister, partner, and friend.

- I feel comfortable in my skin.

- My feminine energy exudes grace and confidence.

- My body is my responsibility. Hence, I actively do what's best for me.

- My beauty and intellect are exceptional.

- I have a positive body image.
- I respect my body.
- I allow love to fill every aspect of my life and embrace the warmth this love gives me.
- If my body needs healing, I will take joy in doing so.
- I always treat my body with the love, care, and appreciation it deserves.
- I feel the presence of peace, harmony, and positive energy all around me.
- I empower myself and all the black women in the world.
- I eat tasty and nutritious foods that keep me as healthy as possible.
- I feel blessed to have excellent physical health.
- My authentic self is charming and attractive.
- I love the way my body looks.
- I am attractive and dress amazingly.
- My hair is perfect just the way it is.
- My curls are gorgeous and unique.
- I can wear whatever hairstyle I want.
- My hair is beautiful, whether it's short, medium length, or long.

- There is nothing such as a bad hair day for me – my hair is always great!

- I deserve to feel safe, confident, and comfortable in my body.

- I love and accept my skin.

- My skin complexion is fantastic.

- I am confident in my sexuality.

- I am worthy of happiness and success.

- I deserve a healthy body.

- I feel grateful for my body's power and strength.

- I combine femininity and intelligence elegantly.

- I love my divine female body.

- I feel thankful to be living in this divine female body.

- My body is an extraordinary gift, and I treat it with love and kindness.

- My body is perfect and beautiful the way it is.

- My body tells me everything it needs in perfect time.

- I am grateful for my body.

- I am a sincere, authentic woman.

Chapter 28

Affirmations to Motivate Yourself Daily

Every human motive is driven by motivation. The outcome of that "motive" is what the general populace tags to be achievement or failure. Therefore, motivation is the confidence of one's consciousness towards attaining a set goal: this goal could either be negative or positive but is driven by the force of action called "motivation."

Most people have lost their sanity because they lack motivation. They blame their predicaments on lousy governance, family, religion, environment, society, etc. No doubt, all of these factors have in a way influenced one's action, which alternatively gives birth to the unfavorable or favorable result gotten by the individual.

Use of the mind:

The mind has proven scientifically and biologically to be the driving force of the human configuration. The brain does most of the arithmetic, culminating reasoning, strategic planning, and analysis, brainstorming, conferring, surmising, forecasting, estimating, assessing, suggesting, etc. But the "mind" is likened to the beast, "lion," ready and determined to make a move regarding the consequence. "If I succumb I perish, but if I aim and succeed then my joy is complete," says the lion. Thus, the application and usage of the mind are crucial to increased motivation.

Take positive risk:

Success is a product of the consistent and repeated inspection of progress. Success is like farmland. You vacate the grass and wheat, you clear and refuse to water the ground for the freshness of seeds, you attract dryness and rotten seed produce, you fail to employ time and season, and you attract more adversity for yourself. Consequently, the only way to plow your way to success is talking about positive risk to avoid insufficiency. So positive risk-taking has never been sacrilegious for those who want to increase motivation; instead, it is the boost that projects and flowers you into the aura of success.

Learning:

Learning is life; learning gives existence; learning gives vitality, energy, courage, self-worth, confidence, etc. One can never stop learning unless they are overdue. The principle of learning is the key that widens the mind's horizon to take a positive risk that can shift one from a position of "mediocrity to celebrity": a degree of a lower class to an upper class. No matter how mindful a person is, they can still be limited. Take, for instance, a knowledgeable driver; if he is not a mechanic, he'll still need to visit the mechanic to fix his car when a fault is detected (even if it's mild).

So, learning gives you the momentum to seek more knowledge, providing you with the courage to attempt numerous issues in life irrespective of your status quo, career, family background, nation, environment, culture, gender, race, etc.

The mind is the chief executive in the architecture of humans. The head creates the operational environment while the mind drives the body to execute. Therefore, every human being - big or small, young or old, male or female - possesses the proficiency and capacity to increase motivation. It all boils down to the individual's readiness to "clench the bull by the horn" since nobody other than "you" can motivate you to push the limit. As a confident black woman, you will encounter many people who want to tear you down, validate your dreams and the goals you set for yourself. They will find flaws in almost everything you do and will strategize in so many ways to deter you from moving forward with the things you want to do as an intelligent black woman.

This group of people will deprive you of specific resources or limit your access in the hopes that you don't win the race. The truth is, if you know you have a light, let it shine. If you look in the mirror every day, you will see a reason to pursue what makes you happy.

Don't let anyone sway you as a black woman. Sometimes they think you want to be better than somebody else. They don't even want to believe that you are as clever, intelligent, and intellectual as you are. They will do what they can to belittle, isolate, and put you in such a place where you second-guess yourself. You have to build yourself up every day and be secure with who you are because if you are not, it will be effortless for them to coerce you into changing your path.

People expect you to fail, but it doesn't mean that we don't need to rise above it just because there is an expectation. We need to set examples for young black girls who want to dream just as much as others do. We have to break down the doors to ensure that we have just as much success and power as the next person.

As a confident black woman, there are a million and one reasons why you shouldn't do what you need to do. Still, if you find one explanation for why you need to keep going, you find one, you better keep going. Find another way: there's an alternative to everything, and there's more than one way to do one thing. For that reason, you will persevere. Where there's a will, there's away. If you conceive it, then you can do it. There is no reason you need outside justification for things you believe can change a world.

We need to be in a realm where we get down with the best of them to be just as intelligent and intellectual. You must start to forget about your Women Crush Wednesday. What is your Woman Crush Wednesday doing for you? Are they doing things that help benefit you in your community? You have to get your priorities together as a confident black woman.

This piece is for that black woman who struggles with her confidence and security. It helps her find her purpose in a world where people continuously want her not to prevail. You have to keep going. If there is something you do well, do it well. Do it and teach the next person, but be selective with whom you share your craft because there are people who will learn and take from you. They will have you think you have not contributed to the world we live in because your name isn't on it. That doesn't mean you don't have a claim to success, and they just took it out of greed.

Because people don't want to see a black face, they don't want to believe that you can have that much charisma and intelligence. If you definitely have a goal, believe in it and put forth the effort necessary to achieve it.

If you are a confident black woman, you don't have to wear it. You don't have to compromise your integrity. You don't have to look for outside validation. You are good enough as a confident black woman. In the face of adversity, you must smile. It would be best if you never let them see you sweat.

A dream is only a dream if you don't put it into action. Making it a year of change and a year of endless possibilities. Make it a trend to have young black women be as successful as they want even though their counterparts may wish otherwise, and they may seek your demise.

Hopefully, you love yourself as the young black woman you can become. If somebody cannot see your worth, that is on them, not you. If somebody does not know the value of something, they will always misuse it.

Know that with whatever skin color you have, whatever hair type you have - curly, kinky, straight, silky tight curls, loose curls, big hair, thin hair – does not matter. You are gorgeous, and you are beautiful. Whatever your weight and whether you want to be smaller doesn't matter. Suppose you want a little chunkier. Anything you want to be, know that it can happen.

It doesn't mean that you don't value yourself. At this very moment, right now, as you are with no adjustments and no changes, you are amazing. You're so beautiful just the way that you are. Know your standards. You have to know what is beautiful to you because what's attractive may not be beautiful to others.

I want you to realize that this world is one big head game, and once you learn to play the mother head game, it's no longer a game anymore. You can start living; what stands between us and where we want to go is never what we think it is. It is not the economy, not the president. It's not that somebody already dominated the health food industry or dominated Facebook advertising or dominated TV advertising, and there's no room left.

It's always the story we tell ourselves as to why we can't achieve something. If you want to be successful, write down why because many people say, I want to do it for money or I want to do it for passion. Therefore, it will determine the steps you have to put in place to be successful because if you do it for love or a chair, you need to bring people on board to help you.

You can try to be what you want, but you have to make adjustments to achieve your goal. If you're not happy at work, you need to know where you're going in life.

People make a mistake in their goals. They have too many insurmountable steps. Even a plan doesn't allow them to reach success quickly enough. If you're willing to chase your dream, your goal needs to change, and your level of sacrifice needs to change as well. Every period of your life creates a choice. How do you want to spend that moment? Who do you want to be? Don't opt for B plan. If you know what you want to do, commit to it.

I have to take this real.

I have to push myself out to do the work.

I have to suffer to achieve success; otherwise, I'll never be that woman I wanted to be.

Do you gain knowledge through suffering? Hell is a world that very few have ever seen? It is a beautiful world when you view yourself as the weakest person on earth after finding yourself.

That's where the hard part is, making your dream a reality; that's where the hard work comes in. That's where people know why you keep crying every day. Mental toughness is standing up in the morning and doing the same thing again and again.

Take whatever the goal is: by doing it, you become the best.

For anyone out there is dealing with and insecurities, the first step is getting rid of the shame because the guilt is what traps insecurity.

Outcomes in life are frequently a lagging measure of one's habits; we think the thing that needs to change is our bank account, or the test score, or the number on the scale. The thing that you need to change are the habits that precede these outcomes. Rather than making the goal a default, the thing you focus on almost exclusively, make the system the default and only check on the goal occasionally to see if you are moving in the right direction.

Achieving a goal only alters your life for the moment; it's not the thing you are looking for. We think of the results of the thing that needs to change. Still, it's the process behind the results that counts - like if you have a messy room. You don't need a clean room. It would be best if you had better cleaning habits and your room would always be clean. Another example: you do not need to lose some pounds; you need better eating habits and then your weight will always be around where you want it to be. You don't need more money; you need better financial habits and then you'll always have enough money to manage the things that come up.

Once you have adopted that mindset, you are not even pursuing behavior change anymore. You are just acting in line with the type of person you already see yourself to be. It is like correct behavior changes real identity. Once you have changed that internal story, it is way easier to show up each day. You are not even motivating yourself that much to do it.

The cost of your good habit is in the present, and your bad habit is of the future. The final form of total satisfaction is a reaffirmation of your desired personality. Suppose your desired identity is to be the type of person who doesn't miss workouts or is an athlete. Every time you do a set of squats and are in the middle of the rep, you're already getting gratified because you're acting in alignment with the type of person you want to be. Now it takes a little while to get to that point.

Imagine that somebody goes to the gym for the first week or the first month, and they don't quite identify that way yet because they haven't spent enough time there.

When you walk into the gym for the first time you feel very uncertain. It is not your territory; you don't feel like it is your terrain. But once you show up again for a week, a month, or a year, at some point, you cross an invisible threshold where it starts to feel like "this is for me" or "I belong here". Once you have crossed that phase, it becomes more likely that you can will a reaffirmation of your identity and start to feel gratified instantly.

You can do other things in the short term to feel more gratified while working on these habits.

- I'm going to have a good day.

- Every morning, I greet the world with a grin.
- Today is a fresh start.
- I am ready for this day.
- I am well rested.
- Today is going to be my day.
- I will be a good listener today.
- I can be anything I want to be
- I am in control of my emotions.
- Today I will spread positivity.
- I'm choosing to have an amazing day.
- Today I am a leader.
- Right now, I have everything I need to be a successful entrepreneur.
- Today I am going to shine.
- I am energized.
- Today is a new beginning.
- I feel healthy and strong today.
- I am pleased and comfortable with the way my life is going.
- I have everything I need to make today a great day.

- I am resilient.

- I declare my day a blessing.

- Today, I choose joy and laughter. I'll laugh loudly and be joyful until the end.

- I excel beyond doubts today.

- I am in control of my day.

- I'll not let anything steal my joy nor rob me of my peace.

- I shine brilliantly like the sun.

- Today is my day of rising, and I'll rise with so much elegance that the sun would become jealous of me.

- My day is full of excellence and unparalleled success.

- I thrive everywhere.

- I blossom like the morning sun.

- I step away from every distraction that would ruin my day.

- I perform beyond my expectations today.

- Today, I choose myself.

- I am a very beautiful work in progress.

- I attract positivity today.

- I know no bleakness today.

- I am courageous enough to move away from the things that no longer serve me.

- I start my day with joy and end with joy.

- I connect with people who are instrumental to the achievement of my goals.

- I dream big dreams today and they come to pass.

- I do not struggle today.

- I stand out with ease and elegance.

- I live my biggest dreams.

- I sing my best songs in the most sonorous of voices.

- I am loved fully.

- I am not overwhelmed by the activities of the day.

- I have enough strength to help me get through my day.

- I rid my day of stagnation.

- I move forward in ease.

- I reach my destinations safely.

- I do not get into embarrassing situations.

- I work with my head held high.

- I do not cower to defeat.

- I rise above obstacles.

- I thrive in every place.
- I am blessed in big measures.
- I take advantage of opportunities.
- I create my happiness.
- I am aware of myself and the power I possess.
- I give no one the power to toss me about.
- I am aware that I am more than enough.
- I show myself as much care as I need.
- I am independent and whole.
- I do not stay in places that shrink me.
- I have value to offer.
- I'm so valuable that mediocrity hides at the sight of me.
- I speak boldly and wisely.
- I stand up for myself when the need arises.
- I do not keep mum in uncomfortable situations.
- My mental health is safe and healthy.
- I am a big body of blessings.
- My life is full of ease.
- I know no difficulty.

- I shine effortlessly.
- I believe so much in myself.
- I am no home to failure.
- I am the Queen of my territory, and I am a queen with pride.
- I win.
- I am better than I was yesterday.
- I have all that I need to have a perfect day.
- Today is a blessing.
- Today is full of productivity.
- I am happy to be alive.
- I'll smile big smiles today.
- I am open to learning new things.
- I am the most wonderful person there is.
- I know my worth.
- I do not allow myself to be trampled upon.
- I am in control.
- Nothing can stop me from smashing today's goals.
- I smash my goals with ease.
- I am ready for today's success.

- Today is a wonderful day.
- I am positive about today.
- I'll grow in new dimensions today.
- I am elegance in human form.
- I am full of peace.
- Nothing can stop me.
- I cheer myself into excellence.
- I am full of intelligence and brilliant ideas.
- I am super strong.
- I am deserving of greatness.
- I do not live in regrets.
- I step into this day with new energy and warmth.
- I do not focus on yesterday's failures.
- Today is the best day of my life.
- Today is a great day to try again.
- I am strengthened enough to face today.
- I will have a fulfilling day.
- I live this day with power and strength.
- I find joy in the small things. I'm going to make today count.

- Today I will work through my fears.
- Every day and in every aspect, I'm improving and becoming better.
- All is well in the world.
- I woke up today feeling empowered.
- Today, I will be present in the moment.
- I feel awake and alert.
- Today I choose to think positive.
- I can accomplish anything today.
- I woke up today for a purpose.
- I choose my own attitude every day.
- Today I will be confident.
- Today will be great.
- I am excited for this day.
- To be joyful, today is the best possible day.
- Every day brings new opportunities.
- Thank you for this new day.
- I'm starting a new chapter today.
- Today I will choose me.

- I am grateful to see another day.
- I didn't get out of bed this morning with the purpose of being ordinary.
- I have the knowledge and potential to achieve everything I want.
- I intend to be the change I desire to see in the world.
- Today I will do something great.
- I only have positive thoughts.
- Today I will have a kind heart.
- I got this.
- I will speak positive words today.
- I manifest the great day I want to have.
- I have a beautiful day ahead of me.
- I will make decisions for my happiness.
- I will spend dedicated time on myself.
- I know that I am on the earth for a purpose.
- A higher power creates me, and I know the woman I am.
- I will be open to opportunities.
- I am filled with positive energy.
- I choose to do amazing things.

- I will not apologize for being myself.
- Today will be a productive day.
- In recent years, I've come to grips with the notion that I am more than my circumstances.
- I choose my path to happiness.
- I am filled with confidence.
- Setting limits and adhering to them are things I feel comfortable doing.
- It's a new day.
- I welcome positive vibes into my life.
- I want to have pleasure in every second of every moment.
- I will conquer all of my goals for the day.
- Today is a fresh day, and it is past time to get things started over again.
- I know I am smart and capable.
- Today I will have awesome ideas.
- I control my success.
- I am comfortable saying "no" as a complete sentence.
- Nothing is stopping me.
- I'm going to make a positive difference today by doing something I've never done before.

- I am a force of nature.

- I don't sweat the small stuff.

- I have the ability to choose how I feel, and today I have chosen happy.

- I am ready to demonstrate to the rest of the world who I am and what I can give.

- I am a strong black woman.

- I am a bold black woman.

- I am a capable black woman.

- I am a patient black woman.

- I am bursting with potential.

- I embrace my truth every day.

- I am an affectionate black woman.

- I am an agreeable black woman.

- I am a creative black woman.

- I am a responsible black woman.

- I love my natural hair.

- I am a charming black woman.

- My fears and insecurities never stop me from achieving my dreams.

- I am an energetic black woman.

Chapter 29

Affirmations for Black Women that will Change Their Lives

- I'm better than I was yesterday.
- I have the qualities necessary for success.
- I'm building a powerful organization that energizes and propels me forward.
- My ability to overcome obstacles is infinite.
- I have an optimistic attitude toward myself.
- I accept responsibility for my happiness and growth.
- My creative energy will inspire me to come up with outstanding and novel ideas.
- I'm moving forward with my goals now so that I can live the life I want.
- I have everything I need to make the most of my opportunities.
- I'm moving forward with my goals now so that I can live the life I want.
- My accomplishments are limitless.

- I am deserving of joy and prosperity.

- I'm always on the lookout for new passive income streams that allow me to make money even while I'm asleep.

- I enjoy seeing some of the world's most beautiful and intriguing locations.

- I enjoy going on vacations with my friends and family.

- I can afford whatever I desire.

- Every day, I observe how my world is improving.

- I am extremely grateful for my healthy health.

- I have the ability to effect change.

- I am mentally, physically, and spiritually powerful.

- I'm making the life I want.

- I'm open to fresh ideas, inspiration, and prospects for generating additional revenue sources.

- While looking in the mirror, I am struck by the might and force of the divine-human who looks back at me.

- My inspired actions have brought about prosperity in my life.

- My birthright is wealth. I have wealth within of me.

- I am brimming with positive, loving energy.

- Everything works out perfectly for me. I am creating my dream life.

- Every day, I feel better.

- I'm sowing the seed of my desire and watching it grow into a full-fledged desire.

- Enough is enough for me.

- I am bringing value to the world by functioning as a beneficial presence!

- Every day I am moving towards my best life.

- Everyone's journey is respected by me.

- I get to pick how I want to live my life.

- I am exuding a warm and pleasant aura.

- Within me, I sense a bright and healthy energy.

- I am fortunate to have found the ideal job that allows me to look forward to each day.

- I see myself as attractive, loving, and powerful.

- My universe was created by me.

- My earnings are steadily increasing.

- I'm going to devote some time to investing in myself.

- I attract blessings like a magnet.

- I invite love and happiness into my life.

- In my imagination, I am able to experience my materialized consequence.

- I'm discovering my passion and purpose and pursuing it with enthusiasm every day.

- I'm going to have a good day today.

- My muscles are becoming stronger every time I exercise.

- I'm comfortable in my own skin.

- I am fit and healthy.

- I'm going to some fantastic dinners at some of the greatest restaurants in town.

- I'm confident that I can be successful while still supporting my classmates.

- I am intelligent, resourceful, and driven. I only accept yes as a response.

- I'm full of self-assurance.

- When I consider myself, I perceive a strong and capable individual.

- To me, money comes easily.

- Considering my talents, I am entitled of a substantial quantity of money.

- My spouse shows me deep and passionate love every day.

- I believe in my own greatness.

- In my life, I would welcome an endless supply of money and fortune.

- In my life, there is always more than enough money.
- I am committed to exploring all options that lead to a higher goal.
- My body has done incredible things and will continue to do so. It's quite lovely.
- I give out an aura of infinite, unconditional love.
- Every day, my business improves further.
- I open my home to others as a haven of love and comfort.
- The more appreciative I am, the more amazing things appear in my life for me to be grateful for.
- Every encounter has taught me something.
- My black is a thing of beauty.
- I will not allow the opinions of others to define who I am or what I believe in.
- I appreciate the fluidity and power of my vehicle, and I can feel myself driving it.
- I have a strong drive to make my intentions a reality in my life.
- With the career that I am enthusiastic about, I am well compensated.
- I will complete all of my daily objectives.
- I'm manifesting the life of my dreams!
- I love my home because it is huge, gorgeous, and well-designed.

- I know how to make wise choices.
- Every day, I feel healthier and healthier.
- I adore the fact that I am now residing in the home of my dreams.
- As a complete sentence, I am at ease stating, "no."
- I enjoy attending various events with folks I enjoy.
- As I approach closer to my eyes, I push outside of my comfort zone to reach my goals and discover comfort in change and new settings.
- Love comes freely and naturally to me.
- I'm grateful for another day.
- Whatever the situation, I will utter pleasant words and think happy thoughts.
- My soul is eager to go on the adventure of a lifetime.
- I am a stunning black woman.
- I trust my inner guide and heed to my instincts.
- Every dollar I spend and donate is multiplied by a factor of ten.
- I'm quite peaceful and serene, yet I'm also very inspired.
- I am content, healthy, and powerful.
- I enjoy creating my inner life and watching it develop to its full potential.

- I totally and boldly accept love into my life.
- I am vibrating at the highest level of love.

Chapter 30

Don't Reflect it

Today's wisdom: If it is not your name, don't answer or react to it.

Affirmation: I am not the stereotype, and I define who I am.

Encouragement:

A stereotype is a generalized view held by others about a group of people, an ethnicity, or a race. This perspective is mostly based on the observations of a relatively small proportion of such people, and these observations are then used to characterize the whole group of individuals. What's unfortunate about categorizing individuals is that the purpose of the observer influences what they will pay attention to. In the majority of cases, the observer's aim is typically wicked, as will be their views.

When individuals stereotype something, they pay little attention to the positive characteristics of the people they are characterizing because stereotyping is a kind of social control. Slavery and the period of acute black oppression were justified via the employment of stereotypes, which were used to justify tyranny, immorality, and evil perpetrated against blacks. In this way, categorizing a group of people serves to expose them to widespread contempt while also making it impossible for them to break away from their oppressors' control.

Do you recall the old adage that says something: If you want to hang a dog, don't you first have to give it a terrible reputation? This is exactly what stereotyping attempts to do. They hunt for a derogatory term and attach it to a group of people to justify their oppression or mistreatment of those who are different from themselves. This is why you and I must reject any and all negative stereotypes that have been imposed on our race or ethnicity.

They use derogatory language and label us with several bad labels to excuse their inhumane treatment of us. If you're a black woman and want to express yourself or stand up for yourself, people will label you as proud, angry, loud, and other derogatory terms. If you're a black guy and display your dominant personality, people will feel intimidated and label you as a thug, aggressive, drug peddler, or anything else they choose.

It is because they are so afraid of us that they have adopted a contemporary method of subjugation: they label us based on stereotypes in order to continue to legitimize their cruelty. When a police officer unjustly shoots and kills a young black man, do you notice that the officer immediately labels him a thug and searches his past for a misdemeanor that can justify their evil act - even if the misdemeanor has nothing to do with the event that led to the officer's unlawful shooting? And have you also observed that as soon as they do, everyone begins to exonerate the cop of his wrongdoing and begins to place the blame on the individual who was unfairly fired at?

All of this constitutes the consequences of stereotyping a group of individuals. In order to oppose these wicked labels imposed on us by refusing to reflect them, we must all take a stance and refuse to be reflected in them. Our guys are neither thugs, thieves, crackheads, or any other kind of criminal. And our ladies are not enraged, prostitutes, welfare moms, or anything like that. We must begin to define ourselves and refrain from providing justifications for continuing our persecution.

We must be mindful of our behavior and the manner in which we conduct our lives. We must begin to reflect who we are for the rest of the world to perceive us, and we must convince them that they were wrong to label us with such demeaning tags. Given that we are not stereotypes, we should not enable someone to psychologically influence our behaviors and actions via the use of nasty preconceptions.

Don't allow someone to have such authority over you. Don't give someone the right to oppress or treat you unfairly by providing them with a reason. If you don't reflect or behave in accordance with stereotypes, they will have nothing on you and will be unable to deny you the benefits you so well deserve.

What anybody says about you is meaningless if you don't do something about it. Some of our brothers and sisters are still following the script and falling prey to negative preconceptions, which is a sad state of affairs. We must be sensible and begin the process of creating a new identity for ourselves. Neither are you an addict nor a pimp nor a thug nor an aggressive person, nor are any of the negative stereotypes being used to control us and throw us at the mercy of those who want to take advantage of us. Remember that you are in none of these categories.

That isn't who you are in the first place. Stop getting worked up every time someone attempts to get under your skin by labeling you as something. You are not a stereotype, so don't behave as if you are. Demonstrate your uniqueness by living a diverse lifestyle. Make them realize that so many of us are not who they are portraying us to be, and that we deserve to be treated fairly and with respect.

Our society is not characterized by baggy jeans, sagging trousers, violence, wild sex, or irresponsibility, among other things. The richness of our culture must be conveyed so that they realize that it is not what it is erroneously presented to be.

Assume that someone or something is going to modify our story. If that's the case, it's just you and me. Let us project a positive image of ourselves and disappoint anyone expecting us to adhere to their negative story about us. We are not stereotypes, so let's stop behaving as if we are, and let's refuse to provide them with any justification for continuing to carry out their cruel agenda against us.

Declare these words aloud to yourself:

I am not what you say I am.

I am not who you say I am.

I am not a stereotype and I refuse to conform to what you want me to be and keep giving you a reason to oppress me.

I am not the stereotypes and I will never reflect what I am not.

Chapter 31

Understand What You Present

Today's wisdom: A woman's confidence is in his/her understanding of who he/she his and the enormous strength and power at his/her disposal. When you know who you are, what you stand for, what you represent and the enormous power at your disposal, you stop thinking lowly of yourself.

Affirmation:

I am strong and powerful

I am bold and courageous

I am tough and resilient

I am fierce and fearless; I am full of life and blossoming.

I am fruitful and bountiful.

I am rich and resourceful.

I am black and beautiful.

Encouragement:

Some of us feel self-conscious about our looks because we think there is something wrong with being black, brown, or whatever other adjective you want to use to describe us. This group of people has a difficult time embracing who they have been created to be because they have an incorrect perception about the nature of their blackness and the consequences of that perception.

The color black is seen by some individuals to be a symbol of evil, as well as anything bad; and as a consequence, they think they are wrong for being black. Individuals who attempt to conceal their blackness by bleaching their skin fail to grasp that being black is about more than just skin color; it is also about identity as a person, which they do not understand. It is a naturally occurring component of your blood and genetic structure. The ability to bleach your skin may allow you to disguise your blackness, but the ability to bleach your blood to modify your genetic composition is questionable. No. When it comes to your identity as a person of color, you will never be able to change who you are as a result of your ethnicity. Therefore, you must first admit that this is a fact.

The third and last point I want to make is that some of us have erroneous perceptions of what it means to be black, which is why we aren't proud of our identities as individuals. Did you know that the color black symbolizes power, authority, and authority in several cultures? Did you know that the color black symbolizes perseverance, originality, and refinement, among other things? When someone tells you that we are present in their company and they are terrified, did you take notice? It wouldn't have seemed to you that despite the fact that our presence may be dreadful, the vast majority of people tremble when we are in the presence of someone they are close to?

If you don't recognize how much power and influence you have, you place yourself in a situation where anybody may simply trample over your rights. Given that we are still standing strong and moving ahead in the face of the horrendous oppression, hardship, and exploitation we have faced, it should provide you with some sense of how powerful we — that is, you and I — really are.

Currently, we have the power, authority, and influence to bring about significant changes in our communities, our country, and the whole world. As a result, they are very terrified of us and trying all they can to keep us under control. Is it possible that you have never stopped to think about why we are the minority group that is most despised and persecuted in the United States? Have you ever wondered why we are the most blackmailed species on the face of the planet? Have you ever thought about it?

I want to inform you that, at one point in time, we were denigrated by the mainstream media based on the color of our skin and the physical look of our bodies, designating us as dirty and unsightly. Are you aware, on the other hand, that this similar physique is something that most other races are prepared to pay a large price for and risk their lives in order to have an artificial fix via surgery? If I told you that a large number of people with fair skin are darkening their skin to make it a deeper shade of brown, would you believe me?

We should be proud of what we have naturally and this includes our physical appearance. Skin has a relatively slow rate of aging as compared to other organs of the body and can endure exposure to a wide range of environmental conditions. Our skin is thick and healthy-looking, and it reflects our unique personalities. We need to learn to be thankful for what we already have in our lives. We must be absolutely clear on who we are as a group and what we stand for to function properly as a group.

As opposed to this, your gloom reflects something beneficial rather than anything bad. For it is only in the darkness that we are able to tell the tale of our trip and how far we have come. In terms of visual expression, your blackness acts as a visual representation of your power and influence. Your blackness reflects the strength you possess. People shudder every time they see you because they realize who you are; they understand that you are a powerful person - and this is why they tremble.

However, it is regrettable that so many of us are still unaware of our own identities. We're defining ourselves in terms of how other people see us and what we're capable of doing. As a result, we accept their claims that black is terrible, unpleasant, uncultured, and so on since we are oblivious of our own selves as people.

Because you are not wicked, don't allow any negative image of your blackness to lead you to lose sight of your identity and your value in the world. Nobody else except you has the ability to define who you are. As a result, stop paying attention to what other people think of you.

Recognize who you are and what you are attempting to achieve in your life. You are characterized by the characteristics of power, strength, resilience, influence, and authority. You're a person of amazing worth, and I appreciate everything about you. Recognize your own identity and retain your composure. You're black, therefore don't be concerned about what you represent or how you seem to others.

Declare these words aloud to yourself:

I understand who I am.

I also do understand who God created me to be and what I stand for.

I am a boy/girl of power.

I am a boy/girl of great strength, a boy/girl with significant influence, and I must make my life count.

Chapter 32

The Only Obstacle That Can Stop You in Life

Today's wisdom: Your greatest obstacle in life will not be the tough challenges that come your way or the negative people that speak or work against you; your greatest obstacle in life is yourself. The man/woman who can overcome himself/herself can overcome anything.

Affirmation:

No matter what or how tough things get, I will never give up on myself.

I must attain my life's ambitions no matter what happens.

Encouragement:

People may be harsh, greedy, and evil. People can be exploitative and oppressive. People can be racist. People can be discriminatory against you for no good reason. But you know what? People can also be kind, compassionate, and forgiving. If you don't stop yourself, none of the above-mentioned groups of individuals will be able to prevent you from accomplishing your goals, desires, or life mission.

The greatest obstacle you will encounter in your life is not the people who will be mean to you and work against you, but yourself. You're the driver of your life and only you can decide when you're going to stop or what/who can stop you.

A dumb and reckless action is to prevent yourself from doing the things you like doing or leaving an activity afraid to try it again because you have failed in your past efforts or because some people laughed at you.

You are the driver of your life, so you alone should determine your destination. If someone is able to influence you to stop at a destination that isn't your intended one and you oblige, then you never understood why you were heading to that destination in the first place.

If the destination is important to you and you know why you are going there, you will confidently stand and resist anyone who would want to stop you halfway to your desired destination.

The fact is that there are many circumstances and people in life who will actively come in your way in an effort to stop you, disturb your aim, or whatever it is that you are striving to achieve; whether or not they succeed is totally in your control.

No obstacle in life can defeat you if you don't give up on yourself and stop the chase. Other's aim will be to discourage you in whatever way possible and make you doubt yourself and the dream you're chasing, but if you can keep your head up and never give up, they will get fed up and let you be.

So, if you want to get them off your back and put them to shame, please, never ever-ever give up on yourself - no matter what. You may take a hit and fall, and you may make some losses or make some mistakes here and there, but please never let any of these to stop you from moving forward.

Let the hit be an avenue for you to build your resistance, let the fall be an avenue for you to regain your strength, strategize, and be more conscious of your path and steps, let the mistakes and failures be an opportunity for you to find out the better way to succeed at what you want to accomplish, and let their rudeness, discrimination and oppression be your motivation for wanting to make it - no matter what.

You can have that thing you desire, you can face that fear and overcome it, you can accomplish that plan, you can bring to materialization that dream, and you can give yourself the life you desire, if and only if you make up your mind to never allow anything or anyone make you stop halfway to your dream destination.

You're unstoppable, so I plead with you never to be the obstacle that will bring your life to a stop. If you don't stop, there's nothing that can stop you.

Declare these words aloud to yourself:

So many things would want to stop me in life, so many people would want to stop me from doing what I love, expressing my strength and reaching my goals, but I refuse to allow that happen. I will never-ever allow anything or anybody to prevent me from doing what I love or from achieving my goals. I will always maintain my integrity and will always speak up for myself, my future, and my life. I will never give up. I am unstoppable in my pursuit of my goals.

Chapter 33

Nobody is Useless – be a Blessing and Not a Curse

Today's wisdom: If I'm asked to give you just one piece advice with respect to relationships, it would be: if you can't ease anyone's pain, try as much as you can to not make it worse or be the cause. We're not in life to hurt one another but to build or assist one another in any way we can.

Affirmation: I am a blessing to myself, my family, my friends, my community, my state, my nation and my world. I will make myself useful.

Encouragement:

There is no such thing as a useless person in this world of ours. It is our collective responsibility to make a tangible and substantial difference in the lives of the individuals in our immediate vicinity, as well as those across the globe. All of the things you see around you are the product of the efforts of individuals like you and me. The small acts that each of us performs on a daily basis, no matter how insignificant, all add up to shape the world as it will be decades from now. The people who reside in your local vicinity have contributed to the development of the environment in which you live.

Individuals in your immediate surroundings are accountable if the immediate environment is hostile and insecure. Conversely, if your immediate environment is welcoming, pleasant, peaceful, loving, and secure, the people in that area are responsible. A mirror of what is going on in the minds of the people who live in your area, town, or society is what is occurring in your neighborhood, town, or society.

As a species, we are causing more problems for ourselves and our environment than we should; rather, we should be providing gifts to it. Take a peek at some of our neighborhoods made uninhabitable due to gangs. Throughout our black communities, our black brothers and sisters are turning against one another and sowing seeds of dissension. Our ability to adapt and rise up against our oppressors will be severely hindered if we continue to torture ourselves.

It is because of our own egos, pride, intolerance, and struggle for survival that we are turning ourselves into a curse upon our fellow African-Americans and our communities, as well as on our own progress. Do you believe it will be like this for a long time? Working together and being tolerant of one another are important if we are to be successful in our fight against our oppressors, and we must start doing it immediately.

Come on, let us stop killing one another, disclosing information, and causing ourselves pain and misery. Instead of seeing one another as rivals, let us band together to work for the common good of our families and communities. Ending gang warfare and killings, as well as the backstabbing are all necessary steps to be taken now. We are becoming our own bottleneck.

It will cost us very little money if we are willing to put out the effort. Believe it or not, the smile you decided to put on someone else's face wasn't just for show. It will not be in vain if you decide to donate a bit of assistance or support to someone in desperate need. It is not in vain when you choose to do an act of compassion for someone who may not have merited it in the first place.

To establish a chain of compassion that runs across the globe and makes the world a lot better place for everyone, all it takes is for one person to do something kind for another, and then another does something nice for another, and so on.

Depending upon how we look at it, every action adds to the betterment or destruction of our environment. It should be noted that your universe starts with the family or group of people of whom you are a part. In your life, it is possible to judge whether or not you are operating as a blessing or a burden based on your interactions with people and how useful you make yourself.

Every one of us already has the characteristics or talents to be of service to our planet; nevertheless, we must make a decision, and the outcome of that decision will be shown by your actions in the future. Your actions should be evaluated in terms of whether they are supporting and contributing positively to your family and immediate community, or if they are inflicting damage on those around you, even those who concerned about your well-being.

Every now and then I come across young people who take joy in destroying public property and causing difficulty to others. That is not the appropriate way for someone who has received a blessing to behave. One should endeavor to consistently grow and provide value to the world if blessed with such abilities. Always seek to learn and contribute to the betterment of your family, community, school, and any other setting in which you are found.

You are a gift to your community because you are there to make a positive contribution to its well-being. Show the world your value, make your impact felt, no matter how little, be among those who are not afraid to be nice and kind to others, be that person who people will notice, feel comfortable and safe around, and encourage others to do the same.

You are not on this planet to cause others sorrow or to make their lives more difficult; rather, you are here to be of service to others and offer them happiness. In fact, being a pain in other people's buttocks will not get you a medal, but people will never forget the person who makes them smile or does a little act of kindness on their behalf.

I urge you to share a little portion of your blessings with others in your near neighborhood, regardless of where you happen to be. This will be a benefit rather than a burden to your surroundings.

Declare these words aloud to yourself:

I am a blessing.

I am not a curse.

I am useful.

I am not useless.

I am a builder, not a destroyer.

My life will be a plus, it will never be a minus.

I will make positive impact in this life!

Chapter 34

Know Who You Are

Today's wisdom: Your worth in life is determined by no one but you yourself, and this worth determines how seriously you'll take life and yourself.

Affirmation: I am a star, I am a rare gem and I have an inestimable worth. I will never devalue myself.

Encouragement:

Only you can degrade or devalue yourself; no one else can. Our images were formed when we were much younger through experiences with the people around us and the feelings we had about ourselves as a result, but this should no longer be the case.

Nothing other people have said or done to you has the ability to define who you are or how you should conduct yourself in the future. To be exploited in this manner is inappropriate for your position of importance. People have always said negative things about us because they were jealous - some because they were irritated - and they never meant it. Some saw us as competitors and began attacking us in order to gain an advantage; and on rare occasions, people have said things to us out of frustration or anger that they did not intend. In addition, some of us have made the mistake of using these terrible events to define ourselves and form negative self-images.

Listen pal, you're not what anyone says about you. Any negative name anyone calls you is not who you are. You are who you think and say you are. You are an individual of inestimable worth; you're a star and blessing to the world. You're not the sum of your experiences, so never define yourself by them.

Whatever anyone has called you is not who you are. Stop addressing yourself by the negative tags that others place on you. If you don't agree with them, discard immediately whatever negative name they've called you and do not allow it to bother you because that is not who you are.

Even if you are unable to control what other people say or do, you have the ability to influence how you react to what they have said or done to you in the future. And the easiest way for you to control your reaction to what anyone says or does is to create your own positive definition and use it to counter any negative image that anyone wants to shove down your throat.

If you know who you are, you would pay no attention to anything negative that anyone may do or say to you. Consider yourself through the eyes of your creator and bask in the glory of the exquisite piece of art that you have been transformed into.

You have been wonderfully made, you're a rare gem - a star - and you're a man/woman/boy/girl of inestimable worth. Be proud of yourself and never ever allow anyone to devalue you with his/her words or actions. You also should never ever devalue yourself because you are priceless.

Declare these words aloud to yourself:

I refuse to judge myself by people's opinion of me.

I refuse to allow the negative things that people say to get to me and make me devalue myself.

My self-worth will never be diminished by anybody else's opinion of me.

I am a woman/girl of inestimable worth, and I will always hold myself in high esteem.

Chapter 35

Take Responsibility for Your Life

Today's wisdom: When you fail to do what you're supposed to do to make your life better, you're making the decision to settle for less than you deserve.

Affirmation: I refuse to settle for less.

Encouragement:

Settling for less is living less than you're truly worth. And the majority of us are settling for less. We are living far less than we truly worth. Why? Because we've made ourselves believe that we can't actually have what we deserve. We have gotten fed up trying without making any headway.

I see so many black kids dropping out of school and refusing to learn a skill. I'm wondering about the type of life they desire for themselves and their children. Our girls are doing odd jobs and turning into strippers. One can't help but wonder about the quality of life that such girls will live with odd jobs. What about our men/young men? Many of them are turning to drugs, crime, and all sort of negative lifestyles. We are wondering why things ain't getting better for us.

After all, nothing will work out for you unless and until you are prepared to put up the required effort. You will not observe any genuine good growth or change in your life unless you are the one who initiates and facilitates authentic good development or change. For those of us concerned about not being provided with chances and that we are being excluded from our country's economic potential, allow me to pose the following question: if an opportunity presented itself right now, would you be in a position to take advantage of it? Do you think you are employable in your current position? Do you wish to make a career change? Do you have a talent in great demand? If so, contact us. Possessing a bachelor's or master's in business administration is highly desirable. In such a case, what assets do you have to put to good use to make a reasonable income and provide for yourself?

In life, everything is structured so it can only take place at a certain time of year and during a specific season. Remove yourself from the situation for a moment and ask if what you're doing now will keep you going for the amount of time you want it to. Will it give you with comfort in your life. If you haven't done so, this is a terrific moment to start. Determine whether or not the things you're doing right now make you feel good about yourself and happy in your accomplishments. take stock of your present position. It is important to ask yourself this question, regardless of whether you are happy in your life or just trying to get by (survive) from day to day.

Your life is the result of the choices you make. Your decisions and actions today determine the quality of life you will live tomorrow. Most of us are making the decision to settle for less by choosing to do nothing about our future. We're placing ourselves in tight corners, where people can easily use us.

Maybe some of us lack support; maybe the system is in some way working against us; maybe our communities or neighborhoods are not inspiring us enough; maybe your color is making you to be discriminated against, etc. I don't care what your excuse is for not aiming and exerting enough effort to improve yourself; I simply want you to know that "you don't have an excuse!"

If you make wonderful decisions and engage in extraordinary activities, it is impossible to live a life that is not pleasant as a consequence of your efforts. Because we picked the easy way out of a tough circumstance, rather than the result of lacking better options or running out of better alternatives, "less" has become the defining characteristic of our lives. As a consequence, we are making justifications for not putting out the work required to live the life we want.

As a result, we begin to place the blame for our arduous existence of struggle and agony on everyone and everything else, rather than on ourselves. Because of your low social status, you will continue to suffer as a consequence of your failure to accept responsibility for your actions. You have a duty to live your life in the manner you feel is best for you and your circumstances. When it comes to achieving success as an entrepreneur, you have ultimate control over the result of your endeavors. Understanding your life's pieces and sewing them together into a coherent whole is your own personal duty.

You have to make a full and total commitment to yourself in every way; there is no one absolutely committed to you. This is about your ability to seize opportunities presented by the crumbs that will fall from the banquet table of life if you do not act promptly.

It follows that you have total control over your circumstances; you have the ability to design a life that is absolutely beautiful....As a result, I'd like to put forth following question: "Are you content doing what everyone else is doing, or are you motivated to achieve the highest possible level of quality?"

Declare these words aloud to yourself:

- My comfort in life is in my hands.
- I can make my life as comfortable as I want it to be.
- I choose to make the best decisions and perform the actions that will give me an edge in life.
- I choose to take responsibility for my life.
- I refuse to settle for less.

Chapter 36

Self-Image, Mindset, and Results

It seems likely that black women's perception of themselves as superheroes is the result of their high degree of self-confidence and determination to give up easily, rather than the result of their real superpowers themselves. In today's culture, a great number of black women occupy crucial leadership positions, filling gaps all over the place and taking advantage of opportunities to demonstrate their talents and characteristics.

A black woman's contribution is undervalued in many parts of the world. She seeks anything that will help her reprogram her mind to think in a different way and recognizes aspects of herself that she hadn't previously recognized. This is especially important in a world where many devalue a black woman's contribution. The only thing she needs is something that will help her reprogram her mind to think in a different manner and allow her to see elements of herself she has never seen before. She is on the hunt for anything that can fulfill both requirements.

In terms of reprogramming and altering your subconscious mind, positive affirmations are very effective and efficient tools. Individuals may be able to assist you in attaining any objectives you have set for yourself in the future. In order to make a difference, every woman must change her way of thinking since the cosmos was created to treat women differently than their male counterparts.

The great majority of women report feeling inadequate. As a consequence of social conditioning, females eventually begin to believe they are unimportant and have a lower social position than their male counterparts. Insofar as you use affirmations for black women as a technique, you will be able to effectively cope with and conquer all your difficulties.

Words of affirmation for black women are a powerful mental tool that should modify your viewpoint and help you experience the transformation you want on an in-depth level.

A person's confidence is defined as the capacity to keep an emphasis on their abilities and strengths rather than their inadequacies. Placing attention on your shortcomings might drain your energy and leave you feeling overwhelmed; but when you intentionally choose to put your attention on your strengths, your self-esteem will soar as a consequence of the increase in self-esteem.

To achieve their maximum potential, black women must learn to be confident in their talents, skills, and everything else going for them in their lives. Words of encouragement have the ability to reprogram your brain, enhancing your feeling of confidence while simultaneously decreasing worry.

It would be best to devote time to building your mental state as a woman if you desire to be more fruitful in life. Be regular with these words of affirmations and record your advancement as you do it.

A black woman needs to get this into her mind: no matter, she is beautiful just the way she is. Many black women have been battling low self-esteem because they either do not believe they are pretty or have heard more about their weaknesses and ugliness than their beauty. It often results in depression and a lack of confidence.

You need to dedicate your time to building your mindset as a black woman if you desire to be more productive in life. Be consistent with your words of affirmations and measure your success as you do it.

The wrong belief system sponsors the limitations we see in many women today, especially black women. A limiting belief system has made them remain in the position they are in. It comes from their self-identity: an identity formed by what society has made them believe about themselves. It came from past ugly experiences, the harsh words often spoken to them, and other unpleasant things they were exposed to during their childhood.

Your self-identity sponsors your success or failure. Many black women have created a self-image that supports failure and setbacks. These women have been conditioned to see themselves as failures, which is why they can't rise beyond that level. They can change their mindsets and reprogram them, but they keep sabotaging themselves. They keep missing great opportunities to make them great because of their low level of confidence, low self-esteem, and shallow-mindedness.

I remember seeing a clip, where someone was abusing a black woman physically. This type of thing often makes black women weak. But the reality is that while you may not be able to choose how people treat you, you have that power to decide how to respond. You may not be able to select the kind of treatment society gives you, but you can choose the outcome of your life.

Many great women who have made themselves examples to inspire others didn't get where they are by chance. They labored on reprogramming their minds, changing their self-identities, and getting rid of the self-sabotaging belief that often keeps black women low. As I have said, many of these women have sustained this mindset or belief system for decades: it's what society has made them believe.

There are many ways to deal with a wrong belief, mindset, or limiting belief system, and one of those effective methods is affirmations. Affirmations are very potent, and many people still do not know it.

Many people have heard about affirmations, but they haven't engaged in the practice simply because they don't understand the mechanism involved or think it doesn't give immediate results. Affirmations are potent when dealing with limiting belief systems if you engage in it with understanding.

Your mind is like a compartment. It houses thoughts that have been formed over the years. These thoughts enter your conscious mind and affect your actions and habits. Let us just say that you are the sum total of your mindset.

One knows what is in their mind by just checking the results, habits, and actions. This is not further from the truth. This school of thought has proven it over and over again. You look like your mindset, or your belief system. Whatever you believe is what will come to you.

If you don't believe you can be great, then forget about greatness because it will never come to pass. It is what you house in your mind that determines your outcomes. We have said before that self-image affects a mindset, and your mindset affects your thoughts, thereby determining what you get in life, including marriage, business, leadership, etc.

Many people tell me that affirmations don't work because they feel the results don't come easily. This is because you don't form a self-image in a day. One's self-image is created in one's childhood days through several experiences, as explained earlier; and there is always a mindset attached to the self-image you have acquired. Dr. Matlz did a fantastic job on the issue of self-image and getting results in his book, "Emotions Free Trade."

He vividly explained how this works and how we can conquer this belief system, further emphasizing the work on affirmations in breaking down the wrong belief system and reprogramming one's mind to change life's results.

Affirmations work in such a way that they revamp your mind. It will be difficult for someone to trace where you are coming from. As a totality, they act as a hammer to break down the wrong mindset, change your self-image, and help you release old habits that are destructive to your life. But if affirmations are to work, there are certain principles you must apply.

Many people don't understand these principles before they write affirmations, and they end up not getting results. Everyone has a unique self-image and mindset that bring results; it means if you must change your results through affirmations, you can't just write the .

The words of affirmation for black women help to change the wrong beliefs you hold about yourself, and you start to see the deposits inside that can change your position in life. They help boost your confidence.

The affirmation's words will help you dispel those erroneous notions and prepare your mind to begin appreciating your genuine beauty and the things that are wonderful about you.

In today's society, you may inquire of any successful black woman about how she came to be in the position she now occupies. You will come to the awareness that no one can attain the pinnacle of their vocation, career, or potentials unless they accept personal responsibility for working toward their life objectives. Career women, company entrepreneurs, and individuals who want to make a difference in the world are taking personal responsibility for their lives on their shoulders. These individuals make purposeful judgments that propel them in the direction toward which they should be moving.

You will benefit from reading this words of affirmation for black women because they will assist you in shifting your perspective and motivating you to take steps that will propel you to success and greatness in your personal and professional pursuits.

There is no correlation between a person's capacity to achieve and their gender. It was not intended just for guys, but rather for people of all genders and sexual orientations. In response to what they have heard and the way their brains have been conditioned, many women have developed an attitude that they should focus their efforts on countering and overcoming.

Conclusion

Prejudice and intolerance will be encountered on a frequent basis in our society; yet this does not reduce our ability to rise above it and accomplish whatever goals we set for ourselves during our lives. Without your explicit written approval, no one has the ability to hold you back, limit your potential, or prevent you from being the person you were intended to be. A formal authorization from you will be necessary before anybody who will be representing you in court can begin working on your behalf.

You may get this authorization here. Your legal representation in court will need a copy of this written authorization, which you should give to them as soon as possible after completing the application.

There is no other place on the planet, where you earn the ability to have an impact on the events that occur in your life, and there is no other place on the planet where you have the ability to command the events that occur in your life. You must begin with yourself if you want to make an influence on the events in your life. Everything about your self-image and the feelings about yourself, as well as your actions and triumphs, may be controlled entirely by your thoughts and feelings. This is a well-known reality in the waste industry because no one will be ready to provide you with garbage as an alternative if you refuse to accept trash. Why is this a well-known fact in the waste industry? In the event that you make a conscious decision to stop from participating in dishonest conduct, there is a greater likelihood that the next time dishonest activity is seen, it will not be aimed at you.

There is no one else in the world who has a realistic chance of attaining the degree of achievement that you have the capacity to achieve in your lifetime, except you. You are one-of-a-kind. The ability to reach any goal you set for yourself in life is within your grasp. With the advancement of communication technologies, it is now possible to speak with anyone at any time from any location across the globe. Provided you have the necessary abilities and resources, you will be able to complete, or at the very least partly complete, whatever it is that you set out to do.

It is possible to demonstrate self-love in a variety of ways, including being calm in the face of hardship, persuading yourself that you deserve more, and then taking every step possible to give yourself more. Also indicative of this characteristic is the capacity to enjoy life to the greatest degree feasible.

Clearly, you have the knowledge, abilities, and skills to carry out your tasks! Congratulations! Congratulations! Congratulations! Regardless of the circumstances, I have high confidence in your ability to attend the meeting on the scheduled day. Please join us for a visit and spend some time with us. In the event that you consistently put up your finest effort, you will realize excellent benefits as a result of your perseverance and commitment.

Your abilities and potential are well-known to everyone, and no one can dispute that you are a person of extraordinary skill and promise. It was ultimately determined that declining to take advantage of the opportunity to allow such natural magnificence to break out into the world and become apparent to everyone was not a viable choice.

Affirmations for Men

Life-Changing Affirmations for Success, Confidence, Health & Wealth That Will Drastically Boost Your Mindset and Increase Your Happiness

Willie Brown

Introduction

We both know that being a fearless, successful man in this competitive world and doing it while black is one of the hardest things in life. You will always be judged and cast off as if you are not equal to what society says. You are continuously belittled as if your thoughts and ideas aren't good enough.

You are ridiculed, criticized, and laughed at behind your back because you are simply never the best or as good as you know you are. The world may not say this, but it's how we feel deep inside. I've been there. My question is, how can we get through our days as if it does not bother us? As if it has no impact on the true potential we have inside us. It feels as though we don't have an answer. I am here to tell you, we do.

You are meant to shine bright, brother, in this world as if your spark of light is the centerpiece to your purpose. Because it is. Today is when you let go of all the insecurities, fears, and inhibitions that have held onto you for dear life and let the masterful power of your true inner man guide your way. Remember that you are a successful black man; you are smart, you are likeable, you are compatible, and you are a good looking person that any reasonable woman would want to be with.

You will never want for anything. You will never be jealous of anyone who has more than you because you already have more than you even know. I will teach you how to use your mind and heart to amplify every fiber of your soul.

Remember that you are a black man. Wealth and prosperity are bestowed upon your inner self. I call this affirmation because it's a reminder of who you are, and who you can be. It reminds you that all you are and meant to be creates your future. You are the limitless version of yourself. You are a black man surrounded by hate from those who will never understand you. Anger and hatred are not your attributes. As a black man, turn your back on hate.

You will not turn your back on love because love is your greatest strength; it's in your heart and in your soul. Learn to appreciate life, brother. Embrace love. Be a loving, kind, and patient person. Be what the world needs from you. Hold those feelings of anger and hate very close to your heart and squeeze it tight, until it's no longer a problem. Unlock the gate inside you to the empowering power you were designed to be.

Stop looking outside yourself to find who you are; you're going to be put yourself under intense pressure should you attempt it. You can never see your true self from the perspective of someone else - only through your own inner vision.

Look within. You're the only one who can define you. the perception you have of yourself comes from within you to make you feel loved and valuable and spur you to aspire to become the best you can be in life.

You're the only one who holds the key to the lock that contains your happiness and self-satisfaction. You can only find that key by looking inside yourself rather than around you. As you look within and at yourself after going through this book, you will see a different, positive and new version of you. You'll see the need to lavish love on yourself daily because you know you greatly deserve it.

Chapter 1
Positive Affirmations

Law of Attraction and the Power of Your Belief

You've definitely heard of the notion of a half-full or half-empty glass and how simple it is to identify someone who is optimistic or pessimistic when they use that concept to their advantage. Take note, however, that whether the individual is an optimist or a pessimist, he or she is successfully altering reality depending upon his or her temperament. Essentially, this implies that the optimist will only see water while the pessimist only sees nothingness, yet they are both true in a certain way.

The law of attraction operates in a similar manner: your thoughts have the ability to distort reality, and if you have a pessimistic outlook on life, you are more likely to draw terrible occurrences into your world. Take note of how many negative people are trapped in a cycle where they are unable to maintain a positive disposition any longer as a result of the numerous negative events that continue to occur in their lives. But the reason for the numerous negative events continuing to occur in their lives is that they are unable to maintain a positive disposition.

The law of attraction is based on the concept of "polarity," which is the idea that everything in the universe contains either a positive or a negative kind of energy. It states that everything, from the food you eat to the people you talk to, to the things you say, to the things you think contains either a positive or a negative energy, depending upon your perspective. It's important to note that being around individuals who moan or yell a lot may make you feel lousy even if you're not directly experiencing what they're going through — this is the law of attraction at work.

When you put your attention on the bad, more negative events will occur in your life. When you put your attention on the good, on the other hand, more of the same will come your way in the future.

Fortunately, there is a method to influence the law of attraction and make it work in your favor: altering your thoughts via the use of positive affirmation and the power of manifestation. Positive affirmations provide you with a new set of eyes through which to see the world, and as a result, they give you the confidence to do many things you never imagined were possible.

How to Use Affirmation Effectively

Believe it or not, some affirmations may cause more harm than good. For example, have you ever told a friend not to be nervous and ended up making him twice as nervous as he already was? The mind is clever, and it won't give up its disposition without a fight, so here's what we do to make effective affirmations:

- **Turn declarative affirmations into interrogative affirmations** – One of the most recent findings in behavioral psychology is that people are more willing to admit defeat in an argument if asked questions instead of being attacked by argumentative statements. For example, if you're nervous about giving a company presentation, you tell yourself, "I'm going to do great! I've practiced all night and I've done this man times before," Instead, ask yourself, "Last time I've presented, people were amazed at how entertaining and informative my slides were. What can I do to make this presentation even better?" By giving yourself concrete questions to answer, the brain doesn't think it needs to defend itself. Use this tip whenever positive declarative affirmations don't seem to work.

- **Be specific with your affirmations** – In order for your brain and the Universe to collaborate properly, you have to be clear about what you want. A lot of people have problems identifying exactly what they want but have no trouble identifying what they hate. If you're one of those people who notice the negatives more than the positives, don't fret; a simple workaround is to find the opposite of the things that you hate. For example, find a song you really hate to the point that you cringe and squirm whenever it plays on the radio. Now find what you believe is the opposite of that song in terms of how it makes you feel. In most cases, the opposite is your favorite song. In short, if you know something that makes you unhappy, then chances are, the opposite of that will make you happy.

Here are step-by-step instructions on probing areas of your life that need positive affirmations:

1. Write down your regular daily routine

2. Separate the things you experience into three columns:

    A. Events you enjoy experiencing

    B. Events you don't enjoy experiencing

    C. Events that don't really evoke a strong emotional response.

3. For column B, look for the complete opposite of that event and list it in column A. For example, if column B contains a statement like "never getting a good night's sleep and always waking up groggy and tired," it should be converted to something like "having a restful sleep and waking up feeling refreshed, alert, and ready to face the day!" and placed in column A.

4. For column C, look for the positive version of that event and list it in column A. For example, if column C contains a statement like "eating breakfast," it could be converted to something like

"eating a healthy, delicious breakfast that'll keep me energized throughout the day" and placed in column A.

5. Column A should now contain specific events in your life that you can use as a starting point for positive affirmations!

- **Be consistent with your affirmations** – a phenomenon has been observed where people who use their goals and dreams as passwords to accounts they access everyday end up achieving those goals and dreams. This has everything to do with the fact that people are compelled to write these objectives and desires again and over again, causing them to soak into the darkest recesses of their subconscious minds. By consistently affirming yourself at least thrice a day, your mind will eventually learn to accept a better form of a reality you've crafted.

- **Believe your affirmations** – Telling yourself that you are calm and relaxed before an interview doesn't mean you're going to deny that you're nervous. On the contrary, you're actually acknowledging your nervousness and then positively affirming to overcome it. If you notice that you're reacting in a very strong and negative manner when you try to affirm yourself, try to apply the tip regarding converting declarative affirmations into interrogative affirmations. It's extremely important to believe what you're telling yourself; otherwise you'll be subconsciously affirming the opposite.

- **Imagine your affirmations** – Humans are visual creatures, which means we absorb information better when in a form that we can visualize. If you're affirming the financial aspect of your life, imagine performing the required steps in achieving that goal. Imagine waking up early, talking to more clients, doing some additional studying, etc. Then imagine reaching that goal and how your life will be changed by your actions and sacrifices. This should be repeated many times until you no longer feel disconnected from the scenario you're in. Do this until it feels too real to let go.

Benefits of Positive Affirmation

Positive affirmation isn't just the act of trying to "fake it 'til you make it." Rather, positive affirmation is the act of focusing on positive values, making you more resilient to stress and other gunk you don't need in your life. If that alone doesn't convince you, here are some more benefits of positive affirmation:

- Positive affirmation lets you see the water in the half-filled glass. Going back to the analogy of the pessimist and the optimist, the optimist will be able to water a wilting plant, quench someone's thirst, clean something, etc. with the water he sees. The pessimist, on the other hand, sees nothing but a lack of water to fill the cup and does nothing until the remaining amount of water completely evaporates. Using the power of affirmation you open up worlds of possibilities you never thought existed, which will definitely give you more opportunities to do the things that make you happy.

- Positive affirmation gives you control. By practicing positive affirmation, you will have much better control over different aspects of your life simply because you're more aware of the events that hurt you and those that help you. In fact, you are consciously making an effort to choose the latter.

- Positive affirmation doesn't have to be a mundane ritual; positive affirmation isn't just to help you make great company presentations or helping you overcome stress. Positive affirmation is also to help you achieve new goals and dreams! You can positively affirm yourself with a power chant or even a power stance to enforce your ideas. In a sense, positive affirmation is already a positive event in your daily routine!

The Power of Repeated Words and Thoughts

REMEMBER how you would repeatedly say a phrase or a sentence in order to remember it for a test? In most cases, repeated words and ideas have the tendency to become permanent when done over a period of time. By repeating your affirmations over and over again, your subconscious will gradually accept and believe what you're saying to yourself.

Reprogramming the Subconscious Mind

The subconscious mind is the most powerful portion of the brain, but it's also the hardest to manage since it's always changing. Everything you really want in life is stored in your subconscious mind, including your aspirations, goals, anxieties, and nightmares.

Because the subconscious mind has not been persuaded, certain affirmations will not function because the subconscious will continue to attract bad experiences. In order for your affirmations to begin to have an impact on your life, you must first fool your subconscious mind into embracing your affirmations.

Here are some tips to help your affirmations get through to your subconscious mind:

- **Find the balance between ambitious and realistic** – a lot of people go overboard with their affirmations. Some people who are earning very little and are buried in debt might say, "I am rich and I earn $100,000 per month." Of course, the subconscious mind knows right away that this isn't true. One way to fix this is not necessarily to tone down the dream, but to add more realism into it, e.g., "I have the strength and determination to free myself from debts and work harder to earn $100,000 per month."

- **Give your subconscious mind proof that your affirmations are true** – affirmation alone won't change your life; you have to mix in action as well. Affirmations like "I have a muscular physique" are useless if not combined with proper exercise, rest, and nutrition. A better version of the previous affirmation would be, "I choose to work out at least three times for a week, get at least seven hours of sleep, and eat healthy meals in order to keep my strong physique."

- **Create affirmations that evoke strong emotions** – notice how a lot of people remember quite easily events that made them cry, laugh, etc. Make sure that when you create affirmations, you include adjectives that evoke happy, inspiring, and motivational thoughts. Instead of saying, "I choose to wake up early every morning," say, "I choose to wake up early every morning feeling recharged, refreshed, and ready to take on the day!"

- **Make sure your affirmation targets you** – tailor your affirmations especially for yourself. For example, an affirmation like "my boss will give me a promotion" is rather weak because that affirmation targets your boss and not you, i.e., you do not have any control over your boss. Instead, opt for something like "I choose to feel that I always get quality work turned in and therefore deserve a promotion."

Using Positive Affirmations to Change Your Life

The human brain hates change; it tries its best to remain in a state where it spends minimal energy, which translates to being lazy and unsuccessful. Positive affirmations trick the brain into thinking that you're already living the life you want, and therefore it more readily accepts the necessary changes that have to happen in your life.

What would you actually do if you happen to wake from a very long sleep and were told that you are an astronaut, a soldier, or a doctor, etc.? You'd probably act differently. You'd talk more confidently, you'd walk more confidently, and basically, you'd be a completely different person. You'd easily surpass your previously self-imposed limits because you believe that you've already overcome them. Like the half-filled glass, you now see your body's capabilities instead of its limitations. By leveraging the power of positive affirmations, you'll be able to tap into your subconscious mind and reprogram it to give you the life you've always wanted.

Chapter 2
The Power of Affirmations

Affirmations have real self-motivating power. You may or may not be good to yourself or accept yourself. You may be confident or, on the other hand, not sure of yourself. You may be positive or negative, happy or unhappy, depending upon what you say to yourself.

Whenever a situation causes nervousness or worry, declaring these statements will help you overcome the difficulties and initiate the changes you want to see in your body. For these changes to be positive and lasting, you must treat yourself with love and kindness, that is to say, as you would treat a friend.

When you start losing weight, whether for health or aesthetic reasons, it is not always easy to stay the course in the long term. Thanks to positive affirmations, you will be able to gain motivation and self-esteem to continue on.

What are Positive Affirmations?

To make positive affirmations is to speak positive words to yourself out loud (preferably when alone!). There is a personal development technique used to retrain your brain to think more optimistically. You may make positive comments regarding your health, your job, or even your self-confidence, relationships, and other aspects of your life.

The goal is to attract happiness by pronouncing it! At first, one does not believe frankly in what one says. The lyrics are even the opposite of what we think but by dint of saying it, the brain will believe it, and so will we! This is how they will have a real impact on our lives.

Examples of statements to lose weight

- I take care of myself and it makes me feel good
- I feel better and better
- I am proud not to give in to gluttony, bad for my health
- Each day brings me a little closer to my goal
- I have a healthy life and I eliminate my bad habits
- I lose weight because I love myself (not because I don't like my body)
- I can do it

How to Create a Powerful Positive Affirmation?

The start of a new year allows us to take stock and set inspiring goals. Have you thought about what you want to do, get, achieve and become in 2022? We suggest you create powerful positive affirmations for each of your goals.

Experience the Magic of Performance

Affirmations will help you identify those aspects that are most important to you. You can test your goals with the "12 questions from the coach." This will ensure that each goal is inspiring and truly beneficial for you. These questions will help you, for example, to identify the internal conflicts that can sometimes block the achievement of your goals. Here are some guidelines before you start creating a positive affirmation. Make sure your goal isn't causing you unwanted los.

Avoid the goals that force you to say, for example, "But if I do that, I won't have time to see my friends anymore."

The affirmation grows stronger each time it is repeated. You have to repeat it out loud with as much emotion as you possible can. The best times to repeat your affirmation are in the morning (waking up) and before going to bed.

We are now ready to begin. Complete the following table for each of your goals, following the guidelines. State the objective clearly and precisely.

Example: I would not like to be overweight

Your objective: put the statement in the first person singular.

Example: I do not want excess weight

Your objective: The affirmation must be positive.

You have to say what you want rather than what you don't want.

Example: I want to lose weight

Your objective: Add adjectives and superlatives

Example: I want to be super slim, have a healthy, athletic, and balanced body.

Your objective: Add numbers and details.

You have to say when, how much, why, etc.

Example: I want to lose 10 kg before the end of February, be super slim, have a healthy, athletic, and balanced body

Your objective: Associate a gesture with the affirmation. The gesture must give strength and motivation.

Example: Clenching your fist with a smile.

Your objective: Add "or even better" at the end of the statement.

Example: I want to lose 10 kg before the end of February, be super slim, have a healthy, athletic, and balanced body, or even better.

Your objective: Repeat your affirmation twice a day. The greater the amount of emotion you put into it, the more powerful it is going to be.

Get into the game. Put enthusiasm and determination into it.

Chapter 3
Daily Affirmations for Positive Thoughts

There's actually nothing quite like the sound of a supercharger on a fast automobile or motorbike to get your heart racing. Wouldn't it be so great if you could turn your life into a supercharged machine? You can do it: it all begins with positive affirmations.

When it comes to how you go from one day to the next, affirmations are critical to your success. Even on your toughest days, positive affirmations serve as a gentle reminder to keep going. More significantly, they serve as a gentle reminder that you are deserving of good things in your life, despite of your past sins.

The Affirmations

1. I am a positive person.
2. I like to view things from the bright side.
3. Whenever something happens to me, I pause, reflect on the situation and then react.
4. My life is filled with joy.
5. I am constantly having positive thoughts.
6. I am feeling happy and strong.
7. This day is a fantastic day.

8. I am always super excited to wake up each day and have a productive day.

9. My heart is filled with love, joy and positivity.

10. I feel secure and confident.

11. I am good enough.

12. I reject all negative thoughts and I accept everything positive.

13. I live an interesting life full of adventure and excitement.

14. I am a happy person.

15. I attract positive people into my life.

16. When people think of the most joyful person in their life, they think of me.

17. I spread joy and happiness to everyone.

18. I am feeling lucky and grateful every day for everything I have.

19. Today is going to be a spectacular today.

20. My life is fantastic.

21. I attract pleasant and joyful people into my life.

22. I feel enthusiastic about everything that I pursue.

23. My days are filled with fun activities and laughter.

24. I can self-motivate instantly whenever I need to.

25. Every breath that I take, I breath in happiness.

26. I am in total control of my life and any negative thought that enters my mind, I immediately let it go and move on.

27. I use positive affirmations daily to become a happier person.

28. I'm constantly energized and full of life, which is a great feeling.

29. I am blessed with all the energy I have.

30. I have complete control over all of my emotions, and I am choosing to feel positive and pleasure right now.

31. I take on life with a calm and relaxed attitude.

32. I have deep relationships and feel connected to my close friends and family.

33. I spread love to people and receive even more love back.

34. My life is free of clutter, noise and drama.

35. The possibilities of life are endless and I make sure to make the most of every possibility.

36. I truly believe in myself.

37. I am making a permanent change to become a positive individual.

38. I am brave, strong and confident.

39. Every time that I fall, I get up with ease and try again.

40. I am dedicated and driven to achieve the goals that I have set for myself.

41. I see myself as a very happy person.

42. I am feeling optimistic about life.

43. I let go of things that I cannot control and focus on things that I have control over.

44. I trust myself in making good decisions.

45. My positivity comes within and is not affected by the outside world.

46. I am adding something special to this world.

47. I take every failure as a learning lesson because I know that I will eventually succeed.

48. Having a positive attitude has helped me be a happier person.

49. Other people enjoy being around me because they get to partake in my happiness.

50. I am always feeling amazing and I am grateful for it.

51. Every single day of my existence is filled with anticipation.

52. I attract positive people into my life.

53. I have all that I need and I am deeply grateful for everything I have.

54. I feel fulfilled and satisfied with my life.

55. I take on challenges and grow as a person every day.

56. I always achieve the goals that I set for myself.

57. I always tend to look for the positive aspects of any circumstance.

58. I am always feeling very happy.

59. I fully approve of the person I am.

60. I am loved and appreciated by other people.

61. Every new person I meet has good things to say about me.

62. I am feeling joyful every moment of life.

63. I deserve to live an amazing life.

64. The universe is helping my achieve my dreams.

65. I believe in my talents and skills, and I can achieve any goal I set for myself.

66. My life is a whirlwind of love and pleasure.

67. I am constantly filled with positive energy.

68. I feel inspired and motivated every day.

69. I become more and more positive every day that goes on.

70. I love myself and I love the life I'm living.

71. I receive love and kindness from my friends, family and even strangers.

72. I am living life to the fullest.

73. I always looking for the good in people.

74. I feel a sense of peace at all times.

75. My positive energy is a blessing to the people around me.

76. I feel safe, confident and enthusiastic about life.

77. I am experiencing joy and happiness every day.

78. I deserve love and respect.

79. I help other people become positive by being positive myself.

80. I always feel a surge of happiness at the start of every day.

81. The world is a better and more joyful place with me in it.

82. I have the power to let go of negativity and fill myself with positivity.

83. I feel alive and fresh.

84. Every time that I take a breath in, I feel myself being filled with peaceful energy.

85. I am a masterpiece.

86. I am worthy of feeling happy and being loved.

87. My life is absolutely wonderful and I look forward to each day.

88. I spread positivity at all times.

89. I am eternally thankful for the extraordinary life that I have been blessed with.

90. I am capable of accomplishing everything that I set my mind to.

91. I allow myself to feel happy.

92. I always carry a feeling of inner peace.

93. I am a relaxed person that people enjoy hanging out with.

94. My accomplishments gives a deep feeling of satisfaction.

95. I am living the best life that I can live.

96. Every minute of my incredible existence is one I cherish.

Chapter 4
We Are All Humans and no Human is Inferior

"Nobody can make you feel inferior if you don't think you're inferior."

Affirmation: I am not inferior to anyone.

Listen good: you are not inferior to anyone. Neither is your race inferior to any other race. When God created man, he created just one man and woman, and we all are descendants of that one man and woman. So we are all created equal, and we are all equal.

Race is a distinction created by man for political purposes. They do this to exploit, subjugate, and oppress those with different physical features than their kind. They came up with lots of negative concepts to justify their oppressive tendencies.

Do you know why blacks were singled out for oppression? It was because blacks were discovered to be very tough, strong, skillful, productive, and not easily infected by diseases or broken down. they can quickly adapt to any weather condition. Hence, the oppressors became intimidated by our wonderful traits; and since they have governmental power, the use it to subjugate and oppress us and try to limit us so we wouldn't manifest our true potentials and greatness.

They are intimidated by our toughness, strengths, and abilities. Do you know that we are responsible for the development of the US, the UK, and some of the world's developed nations? Yes, that is a fact! Go and read your history books and discover the truth of your greatness. Our skills and resources were exploited all in the guise of colonialism and slavery.

We built nations because we were skillful, strong, and challenged, and not because we were inferior. Can a qualified person be inferior? Can a tough and strong person be regarded as inferior? Read between the lines. They intended to break us down with their oppression and negative tags, yet we are still standing strong, pushing harder to show them that we cannot be broken.

They may use the law and armed forces to weigh us down, just as they have always done systematically, but we are still pushing harder, trying to let them know that they can never stop us from taking our rightful place.

They are intimidated by us. They are leery of our toughness, scared of our strength, and of what we can achieve should we be given the chance to express ourselves freely without any interference - like every other race. That is their fear and why they are trying all they can to break us and stop us from manifesting our true potential with their unjustifiable hate and oppression.

We always have to keep our heads up and keep moving forward. If they want to break you, please do not allow them to do so. Do not allow them to stop you from dreaming; do not allow them to stop you from reaching to higher heights; and do not allow them to stop you from believing in yourself and working hard to achieve the future you desire.

They have tried all they could, but we are still standing strong. Look at how far we've come. Look at what we have achieved despite the subjugation and oppression. Look at the changes we are making. Our voices are beginning to get heard, and we are on the verge of enthronement. Let's keep our heads up and aim for our goals. The more we climb higher, the more we scare the shit out of them, and the less their grip will be on us.

You are not inferior; you cannot be inferior, and you should never act inferior. God never created any race, and God only created humans – that is, the human race. Don't ever allow any man to judge, discriminate against or oppress you because of the color of your skin. That you are black is who you are, and neither you nor anybody else has the power to alter that.

You're great! You're created for a purpose: you're created to be great and created black. Embrace yourself and be proud of your blackness because you're created complete and excellent, and no one is superior to you.

Declare these words aloud to yourself:

- I am created by God
- I am created for a purpose
- I am created to be awesome
- I am created to be great
- And I am created black
- I am not inferior to anyone

Chapter 5
Why You Should Love Yourself

"The Only Gift You Owe Yourself Daily is Love."

Affirmation: I love everything about myself.

The number one thing you owe yourself each day is acceptance and love. Acceptance is being at peace with who you are, while love is making the most of who you are, that is, giving yourself the best treatment possible and a shot at life. You can't love anything you don't first accept.

I have come across people who never liked themselves, and you can see such self-hate in how they live their lives and their relationships with the people around them. They neither think anything good about themselves nor says anything nice because they see nothing good in themselves.

This is a difficult way to live as such a life has a constant companion sadness, anger, self-hate, worries, anxieties, insecurities, and a continuous feeling of worthlessness. No wonder such people can consciously engage in self-destructive acts and see nothing wrong in them.

If you dig deep into such people's lives to find out why they feel such way about themselves and always look down on themselves, you will discover that such people have great difficulty accepting themselves for who they are; hence, the problem they're having with treating themselves right.

You see them going about seeking validation and putting themselves at the mercy of others to be exploited and mistreated. They don't understand that they are the ones reflecting how others would treat or relate to them.

Let me tell you this: no one can treat or love you better than you treat or love yourself. And you will have great difficulty treating yourself right or loving yourself unless you first accept yourself.

No one will accept you if you don't first accept yourself. People might pretend to accept you, but their main aim for such acceptance is because they want to use or exploit you. True blessing can only come from within. That is the beginning of your accurate self-awareness, discovery, expression, manifestation, and love.

If you're someone who's always struggling to get validation or acceptance from others, then I must tell you that you're putting yourself in a disadvantaged position, and you can never get what you're looking for. One of the ways you identify a man who hasn't yet accepted himself for who he is and giving himself a daily dosage of self-love medication is how he treats and carries himself.

The way you hold yourself and go about your everyday life will be influenced by how highly or poorly you regard yourself and how accepting and loving you are of others. Some people are not nice to themselves, and they fail to carry themselves with pride. Such an attitude is usually due to a lack of self-acceptance and self-love.

You see them trying to please everyone to get validation, but they are always left drained, exploited, and feeling worse about themselves than they were before they embarked on their validation quest.

Let me repeat this again for emphasis' sake: No one can give you what you haven't first given to yourself. Also, no one can treat you better than you're already treating yourself. You can't claim to deserve acceptance, love, respect, and good treatment from others if you're not flooding your life with such goodness.

You are loveable and deserving of love, but in order to get love from others, you first have to love yourself. The love you show yourself will serve to show the people around you how to love you. Besides, how would you even know what love truly feels if you haven't first practicalized it on yourself?

Self-acceptance and self-love are the doorways to self-improvement. Until you accept and love yourself for who you are, you will never see those aspects of your life that need improvement because self-pity and self-regret will prevent you from discovering what you can truly improve on.

People who have great difficulty accepting and loving themselves for who they are most often spend their time trying to change who they are. Only through self-acceptance and self-love can you know the elements of your life that can be changed or improved and the aspects that can't.

Recognize and appreciate your individuality as it pertains to your identity since this is the first step toward living a life that is balanced, enjoyable, and satisfying. Nobody can give you what you haven't first given to yourself, so it would be in your best interest to accept and love who you are because you're all you've got.

Declare these words aloud:

- I accept and love myself for who God made me be
- I accept and love my complexion
- I accept and love my skin
- I accept and love my ethnicity
- I accept and love my race
- I accept and love my personality

- I accept and love my life
- I owe myself a daily dosage of love
- I will never deprive myself of this precious gift
- I accept and love everything about myself

Chapter 6
How to Eliminate the Feeling of "Not Good Enough"

"The commonest cause of insecurity in most people is self-comparison."

Affirmation: I am enough.

Self-comparison is one of the major inhibitors of self-expression. It has made so many people place themselves in the cocoon of self-dissatisfaction that it is making them believe they're not just good enough. It is only when you've understood that you're completely different and you're not anyone else that you'll start living life and enjoying it as you should.

You see people measuring themselves against others saying, why don't I have that? Oh, why is my life not like his? Why am I not that tall? Why is my nose not like his? Why is my skin not like others? Why am I this short? I wish I weren't black; maybe I would've... Oh, I wish I was from that family, maybe... etc.

These people completely take their eyes off themselves and focus on others who they think are better than they are. Listen, the only thing that self-comparison can do is to blind you from seeing who you really are and create the feeling of not being good enough.

Being enough is understanding who you are and accepting the fact that you're made perfect and complete. It is seeing yourself as an individual and embracing everything about your individuality. Nothing is missing in you, and you don't need to look a certain way or have certain things in your life to feel complete. You're already enough.

Some of us have an identity conflict, and we don't seem to know or understand who we are. We accept everything thrown at us by the media and start trying to fit the image the mainstream media are trying to make of us. We are trying to fit into someone else's idea of who we should be because we've allowed them to brainwash us into believing that something is missing in the way we look. We start feeling ashamed.

No one can make you feel complete or enough. Such a feeling stems from within based on your uniqueness as a person. If you have the feeling of not being enough, then you have to look deep within yourself to find what is causing such an awkward feeling in you and address it.

There's nothing as bad as trying to fit into another man's description of who he/she thinks you should for him/her to accept you as okay or complete. That is what conforming is all about; only someone that doesn't truly know and understand who he/she is conforms to other people's opinions.

Allowing anybody or anything to affect your identity or what you believe in is never wise. Not some stranger who knows nothing about you, but only you have the ability to choose what is acceptable and undesirable about yourself. Consider a circumstance in which you want to make modifications or enhancements to your physical appearance or personal characteristics. Such an upgrade or adjustment should be done because you believe it will enable you to enjoy a much better, higher quality of life than you already enjoy and not because you want to appear acceptable or good enough in the eyes of people who aren't concerned about your well-being.

Whatever you do for yourself should not be because you're trying to correct what you think is a defect, but because you know you deserve the best and want to make yourself the best you can be. Be confident and secure in your skin. Accepting, loving, and valuing yourself for who you are is essential. No one can make you feel good enough or adequate' and only you can make yourself feel that way.

There is nothing missing in you. You're complete, you're enough, and you should never entertain any thought or anyone that tells you otherwise. Yes, you are adequate! Yes, you're good enough! And it would be best if you always walked with this consciousness because you're the only one with the power to define who you are and make yourself feel good about yourself.

Declare these words aloud to yourself:

- I am made complete in all aspects
- I am enough in all aspects
- Everything about me is good
- Nothing is lacking or missing in m
- I will never wish to be like anyone else
- I will never allow my feelings or anyone to make me feel ashamed or less of myself
- I will always see and appreciate the awesome qualities in me
- I will never undermine myself in any way
- I know I am made complete
- I am good enough for the good things of life

Chapter 7
Take Responsibility for Your Life

"When you fail to do what you're supposed to do in order to make your life better, you're making the decision to settle for lesser than you deserve."

Affirmation: I refuse to settle for less.

Settling for less is living less than you're truly worth. And the majority of us are settling for less. We are living a life inferior to what we are worth. Why? We've made ourselves believe that we can't actually have what we deserve and have gotten fed up with not making any headway.

I see so many black kids dropping out of school and refusing to learn a skill, and I'm wondering about the type of life they desire for themselves and their children. Our girls are doing odd jobs and turning to stripping; one can't help but wonder the type of quality life that such girls live. What about our men/young men? Many of them are taking to drugs, crimes, and all sorts of harmful lifestyles, and we wonder why things aren't getting better for us.

Nothing is going to even work out until you put up the effort to make it work. If you want to see any genuine good development or change in your life, you must be the one who initiates and facilitates such progress or change. We are complaining that we are not being given opportunities, and we're being excluded from the economic opportunities in our country, but let me ask this: should an opportunity come your way now, will you actually be in a position to grasp it? Are you employable? Do you have a marketable skill? Do you have a degree? What do you have that you can use to earn an honest living and give yourself comfort in life?

Life is designed in a way that everything has its time and season. Have you ever sat down and considered if what you're presently doing can sustain you for as long as you desire and give you comfort in life? Is what you're currently doing making you feel good and proud of yourself? Are you living life or just trying to get by (survive)?

Your life is the product of all your decisions. Today's decisions and actions determine the quality of life you will live tomorrow. And most of us are making the decision to settle for less than we should be getting by choosing to do nothing about our future. We're placing ourselves in tight corners where people and life can easily use us.

Maybe some of us lack support; perhaps the system is in some way working against us; perhaps our community or neighborhoods are not inspiring us enough; maybe your color is making you be discriminated against, etc. Whatever your reason, it is not aspiring you to put in the effort to make yourself better. I just want to let you know that "you don't have an excuse!

There's no way you will make great decisions, take significant actions, and not have a great life. The majority of us are living a life of "less," not because we never had options but because we chose to take the easy way. We are giving ourselves excuses not to work hard for the type of life we truly desire.

We are ending up blaming everyone else for our uneventful life of struggle but ourselves. If you can't take responsibility for your life, you'll keep struggling at the bottom. Your life is your responsibility. Your success or failure is your responsibility. The building up of your life is your responsibility.

Nobody owes you anything: you owe yourself everything. If you really want to live a great life, you have to desire it and work hard for it. Failure means that you're making up your mind to settle for the crumbs that fall off life's table.

Your comfort in life is in your hands, and you have the ability to make your life as comfortable as you want it to be. So I'm asking you, "are you gonna settle and do what everyone else is doing or you're gonna go for the best?"

Declare these words aloud to yourself:

- My comfort in life is in my hands
- I can make my life as comfortable as I want it to be
- So I choose to make the best decisions and actions that will give me an edge in life
- I choose to take responsibility for my life
- I refuse to settle for less

Chapter 8
The Instigator of Confidence

"A man's belief in his/her seal of approval. Whatever you don't believe, you don't approve of, and whatever you don't approve of, you won't give it your all and thus cannot get it done."

Affirmation: I have confidence in my abilities.

One of the reasons some of us don't attain greater heights in life is because we don't believe we can attain such heights. You can never get anything done without considering that you have the ability to get it done. You can never effectively utilize a tool or gift if you don't have the confidence to put into use.

If you can't do something, it's not because you can't actually do it or suck at it, but because you've yet to believe that you have what it takes to do it. The ability to do anything you can imagine in life is within you, but you can never discover such an ability unless you first believe in it.

Your belief enables you to discover your ability and stir in yourself the confidence to do whatever it takes. I will take a moment to ask you this question: "who do you think you are?"

You will be as confident as the perception you have of yourself. What do you think about yourself? Do you think you're beneath others or above them? Do you think you have great talents and abilities? Or do you see yourself an empty vessel with nothing to offer?

Your confidence is the assurance that you have whatever it takes to accomplish what you set your mind on. It comes down to your belief in your abilities and yourself. It is the seal of approval that you are able and capable. It is the force that gets you to stand up and act.

Nobody can achieve anything in life without confidence. Extraordinary abilities or skills without confidence lead to mediocrity. All the great women and men you've heard about gave themselves an opportunity to be heard because they chose to ignore that voice of self-doubt that was preventing them from taking charge of the opportunities before them.

Discover your unique gifts, sharpen your skills, develop yourself, read widely, and equip yourself with all that gives you an incredible edge on the path you've chosen in life. When you know who you are and believe that you're capable of anything you set your mind on, you will never allow fear to silence you from taking action when you need to. Whenever an opportunity shows up to make the world know the stuff you're made of, don't chicken out or allow fear to shut you up. Stand up like the king you are and let the world know what you've got in you.

Be confident in yourself and never allow fear, anyone, or anything ever to stop you from expressing the beautiful gifts, talents, skills, and abilities that God has deposited in you. Only when you display your gifts can the people around you know your worth and feel compelled to give you a shot.

Believe in yourself, think you can get anything done, and activate the ability already deposited in you. Your confidence is in your belief, and when you believe you can, the confidence to make it happen will automatically spring from you.

Declare these words aloud to yourself:

- I will not allow fear to cause me to bottle up my skills, talents, and abilities
- I will not allow anyone stops me from expressing the kinds of stuff that I am made of
- I will be confident in myself

- In order to express myself, I will constantly hunt for opportunities to do so
- I will give myself a shot at life
- I will take my chances
- I believe in myself
- I have confidence in my abilities
- I have confidence in myself

Chapter 9
We all Need Good Counselors

"When you don't listen, the mistake will be inevitable."

Affirmation: I will listen to good counsel and instructions.

Some of the shits we go through in life could have been avoided if we had listened. Still, our pride, stubbornness, and foolishness always get in the way and compel us to resist and rebel against anyone that tries to tell us what's right or counsel us against certain actions we're taking or about to take that may ruin our lives if we don't retrace our steps.

I have seen young women and men that angrily left home because their parent(s) tried to question the sort of risky lifestyle they're choosing to live and tried to direct them on the right path to take. And most of these cases I have seen never end well for the child.

Sometimes, you can only see clearly and better with the eyes of other people: mostly the eyes of those around you that love you and truly got your back. When someone else tells you about your action and tries to counsel you about it, he/she isn't trying to control you or tell you how to live your life; he/she is just trying to make you see what you've been unable to see concerning such activities and it would be in your best interest to give their real concern consideration as no one knows it all.

You put yourself, your future, and your life at risk anytime you resist a counsel that is aimed to make you better or intends to open your eyes to see the danger in whatever it is that you're doing. Yeah, sometimes the counselor's approach may be wrong, but what is important is what they are saying or trying to make you see.

A man that has made costly mistakes in life or seen people around him make costly mistakes, and the grave consequences of such mistakes in the lives of its perpetrators would never want anyone close to him or that he truly cares about to be caught in the web of such same deadly mistakes.

Your parents or guardians are like the signpost that points you in the right direction in life: they can only point or direct you in the right direction, but going in that direction will be your sole decision.

I know that not all parents or guardians are playing their God-given roles in their kids' lives, as some of them are nowhere to be found. But if you're lucky to have parents or guardians that are doing such, you'd better consider yourself lucky; sit yourself down, put aside your stubbornness and pride, and tap from their wisdom.

I need to let you know here that no parent is perfect. Our parents or guardians are humans like us with flaws too. They are not super humans but mere humans like you. But they have experiences and knowledge that would help guide you on the right path in life if you would listen to them and adhere to their good counsel and guidance.

Some of us make the mistake of judging our parents or guardian by their mistakes and refuse to follow their wise counsels and guidance because of such mistakes. Look, you put yourself, your life, and your future in danger when you resist the wise counsel and guidance of your parents, guardians, or anyone that truly have your interest at heart.

You need to understand that the counsels and guidance that you're being given are for your good. These counsels will always come in handy when you need to make your own choices in life.

Love your parents, never challenge their authority over you and pay attention to their good counsel. When your parents act emotional and yell sometimes, or when they try to compel you to do certain things, it's not because they like yelling or they want to prove to you that they have the power to compel you to do their biddings; it's because they're seeing you heading toward a path that will be destructive to you and they want to make you understand that there's destruction lurking around such path.

Your parents love you, and they want the best for you. Listen to their good counsel and follow their guidance. If you turn out to be someone great tomorrow, they will share in the glory, and if you choose to rebel and choose the wrong path, they will also share in the shame.

Sometimes, our parents can get on our nerves, but they are still our parents. So respect and listen to them and ensure that you choose a path in life that makes them proud always to tell anyone that cares to listen, "that is my son!"

Declare these words aloud to yourself:

- I will pay attention to good counsels;

- I will listen to wise instructions; and

- I will choose my paths wisely.

- I will not ever make the mistakes of my parents.

Chapter 10
The True Test of the Value of Your Desire

"The worth of your desire is measured by the obstacles you passed through to have it. If it was just so easy, everyone would have done it or gotten it, but the fact that everyone could not do it or have it should tell you that it is worth something."

Affirmation: I will not give up on myself.

Anything that is important to your wellbeing, your comfort, your future, and your life is worth fighting for. How bad you want it will determine how seriously you will go after it and how eager you will be to have it. You can only lose in life when you choose to give up on yourself, and nobody can make you give up on yourself – only you can.

How does a man that has given up on himself behave?

He would stop trying to make himself better; he would allow what people say or do to him prevent him from striving further; he would allow his challenges to compel him to involve himself in acts that may cost him his freedom or life, he would lose confidence in himself and his abilities; he would start living his life carelessly and without direction, etc.

When you give up on yourself, you will deprive yourself of having a shot at giving yourself the best in life. The road towards one's success is not always a smooth one, and you must be prepared to deal with the bumps, potholes, speed-breakers, and barriers that you will come across on your path.

You will make mistakes, you will fall here and there, people will get in your way and try to prevent you from expressing yourself, some people won't even give you a chance, and some will tell you that you don't have what it takes, etc. All these they would do in a bid to break you down and prevent you from having what you have the ability for and truly deserve.

Don't allow them to break you, and don't be the one to break yourself. Don't believe any lie that anyone will tell you about yourself, and don't give up on yourself. Nothing good comes easy, and anything that is worthwhile is worth fighting for. Believe in your abilities, belief in yourself, and make a resolve to never give up on yourself until you get the change that you seek.

The trial is just temporary. If you will keep your head up, never give up on yourself and resolve in your heart to make your life count, you will certainly overcome it and attain your heart desires.

Declare these words aloud to yourself:

- Regardless of what I go through in life,
- I will never give up on myself until I get the change I seek.
- I will go for what I desire with all that I've got;
- When I fall, I will pick myself up;
- I will face my fears;
- I will fight my battles;
- I will win the war; and
- I will claim my trophy;
- I will never give up.

Chapter 11
Use It to Your Advantage

"The easiest way to get unnoticed is to be like everyone else."

Affirmation: I appreciate my differences and uniqueness.

Being different is a good thing. It makes you easily seen and stand out from the crowd. Imagine someone different from everyone else being exceptional at whatever he does, and such a person will easily get noticed and talked about by everyone.

I think it's high time we start using our differences to our advantage. A situation in which I was one of the very few black students or members of a group would be a wonderful chance for me to work even harder and become one of the top students or members of the group in question. That way, I easily get noticed and talked about.

Some people may feel threatened or intimidated by you and your exceptional performance, but that is a good thing. It's good for you to make them feel threatened and insecure around you with your exceptional performance or personality than for them to make you feel threatened because you think you can't measure up.

I must tell you this: there's a unique way you feel when you're very good at what you do in a place when you're the minority. You command attention and respect easily, and everyone gets scared to mess with you because they know that you're the real deal.

Have you noticed that most people of other races - mostly the racist ones feel very uncomfortable in the presence of a successful black person or a well exposed and educated black person, and they try to comport themselves when around such a black person? Look, you have to understand that your being different is a plus to you. The fact that you are actually in the limelight provides an excellent chance for you to demonstrate your abilities and make others realize that you are the genuine thing by showcasing your individuality and bragging about your achievements.

We should stop holding back and start going all out for what we want in life. Wherever we find ourselves, we should strive to be among the best. Our total liberation is in our excellence. No one can attempt to single us out negatively and talk down on us if they know that they can't measure up to us in anything. Just imagine us owning industries and calling some of the big shots in society. Do you think anyone would want to mess with such people?

We have everything in us to rise above our challenges and make ourselves heard and seen. Our differences have already placed us in an advantaged position, but we have to see them and exploit them. I know they are fighting so hard to ensure that we don't rise and manifest our greatness, but no one can keep a great man that doesn't want to be down on the ground for too long.

Most of our people have risen from obscurity to the limelight even with the many oppression, subjugation, deprivation, and economic alienation that people of our kind are being subjected to. You, too, can do it. You, too, can make a difference. You, too, can get yourself seen and heard – not for something terrible but for something outstanding.

The tide is beginning to change, and more and more opportunities are beginning to be made available for us. So we have to take such chances - not just take them but excel in them and make them understand that we genuinely deserve being given a shot.

You and I are placed in a unique position, and we can use that position to make ourselves seen and heard by choosing to be exceptional. We have it in us, and we shouldn't be scared to manifest the greatness we have in us wherever we find ourselves.

You were not designed to be the same as everyone else, and you were formed in a unique way as well. You were born with the ability to be extraordinary. You were made to be different from the rest of the pack. You were designed to be exceptional and to command respect wherever you are. You are unique! Everything about you is unique and interesting. You're unmatched. Accept your individuality and learn to use it to your advantage.

Be proud of your uniqueness because it is the symbol of your peculiarity. Don't ever wish to be like anyone else or strive to be like anyone else. You lose your uniqueness once you do that. You were created differently, and you were created special. So use your individuality to your advantage.

Declare these words aloud to yourself:

- I was created to be different;
- I was created to be unique;
- I was designed to stand out;
- I was created to be unique, and
- I intend to take use of my individuality to my benefit.

Chapter 12
You Deserve It

"If you don't take it, it may never be given to you. But you may never attempt to take it unless you believe that you truly deserve it. Also, if you believe you deserve it, you would go for it and do everything you can to have it."

Affirmation: I am worthy of every good thing that life has to offer.

Sometimes we take BS from people because we think we don't deserve to be respected or treated nicely. Some of us also settle for mediocrity and never wish to do anything about it because we think that's the level of life that we truly deserve. Listen, brother: no one will give you anything that you don't first think or believe you deserve.

How you go about your life and what you aim for in life is a reflection of what you believe your value is. Value is a personal thing as only you can create it. Your values influence what you accept from people and how you allow them to treat you.

Value is created in your mind. It is your belief of your worth. Your worth is what you think you deserve, and it is shown in your aspirations, words, decisions, and actions. When you know your worth, you don't take shit from people or life or settle; you go for the best.

And man, you are very valuable, and you deserve every good thing that life has to offer. Nobody is more worthy than you or deserves better treatment than you. You deserve the best in life, and you should always go for the best.

Living a good life is not the privilege of any race. Being comfortable in life is not any race's privilege. The top sphere of life is not reserved for any race – rather, it is reserved for the individual that can pay the price to get there.

Life is what you make of it, and you can have the kind of life you wish for if you can equip yourself with the tools, you need to make it possible and go for it with all that you've got in you.

Do all you can to have and give yourself the best in life because you deserve it. Don't ever deprive yourself of any good thing (or treatment) that you desire, and never ever allow anyone to deprive you of something good that you've truly worked for or deserve. You're the best, and you deserve to have the best. So don't ever settle for mediocrity because you're worthy of good treatment and every good thing that life has to offer.

Declare these words aloud to yourself:

- I know I am valuable.
- And I deserve to be respected.
- I deserve good treatment.
- because I am worthy of them all.
- The good things of life are also my privilege, and I will have them and enjoy them.

Chapter 13
The Choice is Yours to Make

"The decisions you make in life determine the quality of life you'll live."

Affirmation: I will choose my path wisely.

Everything you will become in life is tied to what is called "choice." The choice is your ability to choose. Your ability to know what is right, what you want to do with your life, and doing all you can to get it done.

Whether good or bad, right or wrong, education or illiteracy, working or staying idle, freedom or imprisonment, love or hate, crime or law-abiding, responsibility or irresponsibility, failure or success, etc., you're the one that will live with the consequences.

The kind and quality of life you lead will be determined by the quality of the decisions you make now. Where you are presently is a function of your past choices, and where you will be tomorrow or in the future will be a function of your today's choices and subsequent future choices.

Your choices are what determine the direction and outcomes of your life. If you make them wrongly, you're the one that will live with the consequences, and if you make them rightly, you're also the one that will enjoy the benefits. However you choose to make it, you will be the one in the center of it.

Therefore, you must proceed with carefully while making judgments, as they will determine how high you will soar or how far you will plummet in your professional and personal life. Always think through anything you intend to do and consider its pros and cons before carrying it out.

I am telling you this because most times, we are the ones that enslave ourselves with our actions. Getting yourself involved with bad company or engaging in any self-destructive act is a wrong path. Don't just let anybody persuade you to do anything that might jeopardize your freedom, your future, or your life.

Always keep an eye on yourself and keep an eye on your surroundings. Always ask yourself before involving yourself in anything or carrying out any act, "what's at stake?" Never allow anyone to push you into doing anything with serious consequences that may destroy your future or life.

Don't let regret be your companion. So many brothers are in prison, so many have lost their lives, so many have put themselves in tight corners and very difficult situations because of their choices. Don't make yourself one of such brothers.

Watch your steps. Watch your lifestyle. Watch your association. Many black people today are endangering themselves, their future, their freedom, and their lives because of the sort of dangerous lifestyle they're choosing to live. Don't put yourself in a tight situation and make regret your companion. You have an option. Only you can choose the path of your life, and the path you choose is what will be used to judge you by others, so I urge you to choose it wisely.

Declare these words aloud to yourself:

- I will be careful with my decisions;
- I will be careful with my actions;
- I will be careful with my choices;
- I will choose my path wisely;
- I will never gamble with my life.

Chapter 14
Affirmations for Self-Esteem

People who have no self-esteem often think that they will become confident and happy with themselves when their current situation changes. Seeing a beautiful face when you look into the mirror will make you walk with your shoulders high up, having caring parents will make you feel normal and happy, scoring all A's in your exam will enable you to look your classmates in the eye and say whatever you want, your neighbors will respect you when you own a car and that will boost your confidence, getting married will elevate your status and in turn, make you feel less inferior about yourself.

Self-esteem or the lack thereof is related to external circumstances. "If A or B happens, my self-esteem will increase," so they think. While it is possible that you will see yourself in a better light and get a sense of self-worth from achieving great things, that level of highness you feel will most likely not last. Why? Self-esteem is basically a state of mind. Although the current state of your life and other people's opinion of you may have a bearing on your self-esteem, the ultimate determinant of your self-esteem is your thoughts.

Take this scenario, for instance, and Unemployed Miss A thinks Miss B, who is employed, is more intelligent and better than she is. Employed Miss B tells herself that she would have been running her own business by now if only she was as smart and efficient as her entrepreneur friend. Then there is Miss C, who is also unemployed but thinks her situation is not a result of her not being good enough but because she is yet to develop the skills needed for the job.

What differentiates Miss C from both Miss A and Miss B? The way she sees herself. Miss C understands that she doesn't possess the skills that will land her the job she wants but instead of thinking there is something inherently wrong with her, she singles out the problem and separates it from her core being.

Between Miss C and Miss B, who do you think lives a happy life? It's Miss C, of course. As humans, we are aware of our identity: hating the way we look, how we act, or the family we come from automatically cripples our sense of self-worth. Your level of self-esteem usually depends on how much you like and appreciate yourself.

Don't confuse healthy self-esteem with too high or 'overly inflated' self-esteem, though. Thinking you are superior to everybody is just as psychologically unhealthy as seeing yourself as the dust of the earth—the worst being on earth, undeserving of love. You overestimate your abilities, praise yourself too much, and expect others to do the same even when you don't deserve it. Other people are seen through a diminishing lens, and you act as though the world revolves around you.

Having self-esteem that is too high is dangerous and damaging, especially because it prevents you from embracing self-improvement.

Self-esteem is more complicated than the popular 'high vs. low' concept that is often used to describe it. If you say you have high self-esteem, does it mean you never have moments of self-doubt? And for those who think they have low self-esteem, has there never been a time you felt proud or good about yourself? Given the fact that sentiments change, it might be difficult to determine your degree of self-esteem with certainty. One minute you feel so good about yourself, and the next minute, you are plagued with self-doubt.

Being the human that you are, it is normal to experience varying feelings—both positive and negative. In order to fully benefit from this book, measuring your self-esteem by taking the following self-esteem checkup will be extremely helpful. Be honest as you can when answering the questions. The answers you give will help you recognize how you esteem yourself.

Everybody has a measure of self-esteem, and the level of self-esteem you have now has a source. Our childhood, that innocent period when we didn't know our left from our right when we were led by the hands and guided by our parents and other grown-ups in our lives, is usually a major decisive factor of our self-esteem.

You didn't know that touching fire could burn the skin until your parents told you. Talking loudly, eating while you talk, sitting with your legs spread wide in a panties-revealing way as a girl, not combing your hair, not brushing your teeth every morning, mingling with your unruly neighbors, collecting something from a stranger, or running around in the streets are some behaviors your parents probably told you to desist from doing.

Parents who model self-esteem know how to get their kids to do the right thing while also respecting the individuality and opinions of their children. They encourage you, consistently show you, love, back you up when necessary, and make you understand in a clear and reasonable way how they expect you to behave. These types of parents make sure it sinks in that it is your behavior that is bad, not you as a human being.

Authoritarian parents or permissive parents, on the other hand, usually have a poor way of using words as they tend to be less concerned about the feelings or mental growth of their children. "Stop littering the floor, dirty child," they say, or "bad child, you can never do anything right." Each inappropriate behavior you display earns you doses of scolding or spanking. Some parents nowadays even go to the extent of pushing their kids away or denying them something essential to their existence like food or school fees when their children misbehave.

Consciously or unconsciously, you know that your survival depends on your parents as a child. Their approval matters a lot to you as you don't want to lose their support. Automatically, you start thinking of yourself as a bad, useless or lazy person when you find yourself staying till nightfall without brushing your teeth, hanging out with your 'unruly' neighbors, talking loudly, or doing some other thing that you often receive punishment for doing.

All of these feelings seep into your teenage and adulthood, inflicting your self-esteem. You will find yourself constantly struggling to unlearn what you were often told was the best way to behave or the standard form of elegance.

It all reverts back to thoughts, no matter where your self-esteem stems from parents, traumatic experience, or negative peers; one major factor binds all your feelings and your sense of self-worth together: your thoughts. You should put effort towards challenging your debasing, embarrassing, or painful thoughts.

Although, when a child is always told that he or she is ugly, lazy, and stingy, or dull, he or she grows up with a nagging sense of wrongness. It becomes hard to work to be convinced otherwise. Fortunately, building healthy self-esteem can only be difficult, not impossible.

For what reasons should you devote your time and energy to boosting your own self-esteem? Your overall health and performance depend on it. When you judge and reject yourself, you bring pain upon yourself. Life becomes unexciting, and you engage in activities that are harmful to your health. It is not uncommon to find people struggling with their self-esteem abusing alcohol and drugs, eating poorly, becoming promiscuous, enduring abusive relationships, or suffering from psychosomatic illnesses like indigestion, headache, fatigue, and insomnia.

As you think that people will hate you or not want to associate with you, you withdraw from social settings and end up feeling lonely. Anxiety, stress symptoms, and depression are usually the accompanying baggage of poor self-esteem. Your performance at school and work also bears the brunt of your self-esteem. In the absence of healthy self-esteem, fear overshadows the drive to seize and maximize opportunities for growth.

The fear of self-rejection and judgment makes you take fewer academic, career, or social risks. You already believe that you won't succeed, not when people who are better than you are around, so you shy away from job interviews or meeting people.

Living with a negative sense of self-worth prevents you from maximizing your full potential as it limits your ability to ask for help, handle criticism, express yourself, and solve problems. It's like being your own prisoner, you have an idea that you are capable of achieving so much more, but since you are locked behind the gate of unbelief and fear, you remain stagnant.

With healthy self-esteem comes the ability to navigate life with an assertive and positive attitude –to be truly free from the cage of perfectionism, poor perception of self, and self-rejection. You can stop the judgments and change the way you feel about yourself.

The Affirmations

1. I have the ability to accomplish anything that I set my mind to.

2. I believe that my future is bright and that things will work out for the best for me.

3. I believe in myself and my abilities.

4. I triumph over my mistakes.

5. I learn from each experience to improve myself and do better next time.

6. I radiate positive energy, and my unwavering enthusiasm helps benefit others.

7. I have an engaging and warm personality that draws people to want to be around me.

8. I have the conviction to follow through on my beliefs.

9. I celebrate my uniqueness and individuality instead of comparing myself to others.

10. I am confident and secure in myself no matter what others think.

11. I possess the confidence to take charge of my own life.

12. I am generous and giving, and take other people's best interest into consideration.

13. I prioritize my long term happiness over instant gratification.

14. The capacity to make the right decisions is something in which I have great trust and confidence.

15. I am at my best when I think happy thoughts and push negative emotions to the side.

16. When I believe in myself, I perform at my highest level.

17. I am at my best when I persevere to finish the task before me.

18. I motivate and encourage others to believe in themselves.

19. Whenever I see someone who has achieved something that I want, I see it as inspiration and evidence that I can achieve the same.

20. I conquer my fears and turn them into strengths.

21. I deserve happiness and success because I am a good person.

22. Regardless of my ambitions, I pursue my goals with morality and ethics.

23. I value myself as a person because I have strong character traits of honesty and integrity.

24. I participate in activities that I enjoy to bring happiness into my life.

25. I gladly take on challenges to further increase my self-confidence and boost my self-esteem.

26. I confront my personal demons and turn them around with self-awareness and positive action.

27. I love doing kind things for others because it makes us both happier.

28. I treat myself kindly because I know I am worthy of respect.

29. I love and appreciate what my body does for me, so I pay attention to what I feed it.

30. I possess skills and talents that other people could benefit from.

31. I possess the will and the resourcefulness to change things in my life for the better.

32. I am an authentic and genuine person, capable of speaking my mind fearlessly.

33. I treat others with respect and surround myself with people who treat me with respect.

34. I am a beautiful person, and I respect myself by taking care of my body and my mind.

35. I possess the stamina and endurance to persevere in my pursuits.

36. I am confident and assertive at all times regardless of what other people may think.

37. On a continual basis, I am learning more about myself and working to improve my areas of weaker performance.

38. I deserve to feel happy because I'm worth it and I matter.

39. Before I can love others, I must first learn to truly and fully love and appreciate myself.

40. I make it a priority to be kind to myself.

41. I have control over my effort, and always put my best foot forward.

42. I take care of my outer appearance because the confidence that causes makes me feel better on the inside.

43. I have the willpower to take a break from outside influences like social media if I find myself comparison shaming.

44. My opinion matters, even if it is unpopular.

45. I have the courage to speak my mind on subjects that are important to me.

46. The way I see others is a reflection of the way I see myself.

47. I am better because of the tight knit bonds I have with my friends and family.

48. I feel attractive and confident.

49. I walk into every room with a confident posture.

50. I constantly take note of my talents and abilities to remind myself that I am capable of accomplishing anything.

51. I take time to celebrate my achievements and highlight my successes.

52. I am a loyal and genuine person, and anyone would be lucky to have a relationship with me.

53. The capacity to make others laugh and grin is something I have. I have a fantastic sense of humor.

54. I care for my body with consistent physical exercise because it makes me feel positive about myself.

55. I am a selfless and generous person.

56. I take time to volunteer to help those less fortunate than me.

57. I forgive others because the act of forgiveness is empowering.

58. I possess the potential and the drive to succeed, and I am worthy of success.

59. I am the kind of person who is destined for success and greatness.

60. I speak kind words to myself and remind myself that I can do well and succeed.

61. I evaluate my progress and success based on what I am doing, not what other people are doing.

62. I achieve tiny victories every day that I celebrate and commend myself for.

63. I value myself enough to choose to spend time only with people who love me for who I am.

64. I accept myself as I am, with all of my flaws, and I strive to better myself on a daily basis.

65. I channel all negativity and turn it into something positive.

66. I possess the courage to keep trying even if I do not succeed the first time around.

67. I have the self-discipline to deliver on all of my promises.

68. My self-esteem allows me to reflect on my previous triumphs and motivate me towards new accomplishments.

69. I have limitless potential to succeed and become the best version of myself.

70. I always come out a stronger and better person when I face and overcome adversity.

71. I focus on the present and improving myself for the future, rather than dwelling on the past.

72. I always cultivate feelings of gratitude.

73. I stay mindful of all the happiness I have in my life.

74. I wake up excited every morning, grateful to live another day.

75. I am grateful for the opportunity to become my best self and live my best life.

76. The messages my body, mind and stomach are sending me are constantly in sync with each other.

77. I set aside personal time to engage in activities I enjoy because it makes me feel happy.

78. My space is an expression of who I am, and it reflects my individuality, and my cheerful mood.

79. I proudly display personal items and awards in my space that remind me of my accomplishments.

80. I am enthusiastic about life, which fuels my motivation.

81. I am strong in my will, and I am able to overcome any temporary setbacks.

82. I constantly put effort into becoming happy on the inside because I know that turns into success on the outside.

83. I possess strong desire and determination—two key factors in creating success.

84. I confidently and happily invest in myself because I know I have what it takes to succeed.

85. I have a positive and inclusive worldview.

86. I am accepting of all people's differences, choices, and opinions.

87. I am proud of my positive personal attributes.

88. I always keep my past achievements at top of mind to keep myself encouraged.

89. An optimistic attitude is part of my identity.

90. I am brave and determined enough to keep pushing forward, even through difficult times.

91. I deserve the opportunity to have a rich, fulfilling life.

92. I have excellent critical thinking and problem solving abilities that serve me well in my life and work.

93. I take control over transforming my life because I believe in myself.

94. My positive thinking contributes to positive growth.

95. I have the dignity and self-confidence to always be true to myself.

96. I am proud of my individual uniqueness, as that is what defines me and makes me special.

97. I have a gift of finding the bright side in every situation.

98. My sunny disposition constantly attracts people who improve the quality of my life.

99. I am constantly making progress in my emotional control, emotional development, and emotional intelligence.

100. I have the conviction that my dreams are worthwhile and should be pursued.

101. I am dedicated enough to put forth maximum effort until I become successful.

102. I have the self-control to reject any unhealthy impulses.

103. I have the maturity to see people and situations purely for what they are, and not take anything personally.

104. I am a positive role model for myself and others.

105. I am an optimistic person, with an optimistic mind, heart, and spirit.

106. I have the willpower to resist temptations that do not help me become the best version of myself.

107. I only compare myself to myself and not to others.

108. I have the courage to do the right thing in any situation.

109. I have the power to control my own level of happiness.

110. I love and accept myself, and it inspires others around me to do the same.

111. I remain encouraged and persist with a positive attitude in the face of difficulty.

112. I have the courage to take risks and put myself out there.

113. I have the strength of character to let small things go and always be the bigger person.

114. I am the gatekeeper of my own mind, and I only grant access to positivity.

115. I have the will to change my circumstances when things are not going well.

116. When I want something different, I have the willpower to do something different.

117. I deserve to have hopes and dreams to pursue.

118. I am certain that happiness and success are in my future.

119. I have the patience required to make continuous life improvements.

120. I am a good-natured person, and I do not allow negativity to drag me down.

121. I have the self-compassion to not be overly critical of myself.

122. I am comfortable with giving and receiving compliments and praise.

123. I am secure enough to discuss my viewpoints and experiences with my peers without shame or fear of judgment.

124. I have the individuality to make my own decisions and take responsibility for them.

125. I have valuable opinions to contribute, and I share them with others.

126. Success is not something that's just for others, it is for me.

127. Success is within my control and within my grasp.

128. I am worthy and deserving of all the great things life has in store for me.

129. I am fully equipped to create my version of an ideal life.

130. I have talents and abilities that will get me to where I need to go.

131. I can and I will rise to the top.

132. I am just as capable and deserving of success as anyone else is.

133. I choose to give more attention to my strengths than my weaknesses.

134. My high self-esteem allows me to build strong, long-lasting personal and professional relationships.

135. I am at peace with who I am inside and out.

136. I incorporate physical and mental practices into my daily life that promote positivity and combat negativity.

137. I have the resolve to keep growing and bettering myself every day.

138. I am worthy of being loved by people romantically and platonically.

139. I have the willpower to reshape my thoughts into an optimistic outlook.

140. I proudly and boldly create my own unique identity and don't care what other people think about me.

Chapter 15
Affirmations for Self-Love

Y ou are loved. The universe often conspires against you. In many aspects of life, you are despised. Self-hatred is frequently instilled in children at a young age, along with a desire to be someone or something other than who the Lord has created you to be. Despite the fact that hate has attempted to destroy you, you continue to rise. You are cherished by your Creator, black guy. Your moms, sisters, cousins, brothers, and dads all adore you. Perhaps they are unable to do so because they lack the necessary knowledge. Maybe it's because we don't know how to accept true love when it's provided. Even yet, the truth remains that you are dearly loved. And the love you have the ability to give may break through barriers. The love you have the ability to give may offer peace, bridges, and longer tables, as well as healing, joy, and restoration. Give love whenever you can. Model adoration. Your love has the power to dispel a great deal of hatred.

In fact, self-love is the most rewarding sort of love, owing to the fact that it not only helps you to achieve more for yourself (which is both wonderful and powerful), but it also allows you to draw more into your life from other people. Love is a high-vibrational magnetic force, and your shift in energy will attract individuals who have a similar vibrational frequency to you.

Self-love affirmations are only one of the tools you may use to help you feel better about yourself and earn greater self-acceptance. What's the greatest part? They are the most straightforward strategy you can use in your life to foster more self-acceptance!

These affirmations for self-love may be utilized on a daily basis, and with continued usage, you can anticipate to experience increased happiness, confidence, joy, and other positive emotions. You'll increase your self-esteem, recognize that you are deserving of love, let go of negative ideas and welcome in compassion, have more constant positive thoughts, and strengthen your relationships with yourself and others as a result.

The Affirmations

1. I am whole and entire just the way I am.
2. Everything that I need is within me.
3. I am wholly secure in my being my best self.
4. Today, I choose to let go of any negative thoughts, feelings, and impulses that may circulate within me.
5. Today, I am fully committed to choosing the best version of myself.
6. I have unique gifts, talents, and skills.
7. I am enough.
8. From this moment forward, I fully commit to believing in myself and my gifts.
9. I have a unique personality that brings joy to those around me.
10. I have a special divine purpose that only I can fulfill.
11. I love the person that I am currently and the person that I am becoming.
12. My life is a source of love and happiness.
13. I am stepping into abundance in every single area of my life.
14. I am not defined by my mistakes.

15. I am made better by the mistakes I have made in my past.

16. My identity is not defined by my worst moments. Nor is it defined by my best moments.

17. I am far more than the sum of my failures or successes.

18. My identity stems from a source of energy more powerful than I could ever imagine.

19. I hereby choose to totally let go of all of fears in my spirit.

20. I am growing every single day, and for that I am enough.

21. I am learning every single day, and for that, I am enough.

22. I am doing my best to become my best every single day, and for that, I am enough.

23. I am much more than the outward manifestation of my body.

24. My value lies in something much deeper than my outer appearance.

25. What I look like on the outside is not who I am.

26. My image inside radiates outside.

27. I am beautiful outside because I am beautiful inside, not the other way around.

28. I am undeniably worthy of love and peace.

29. I am undeniably worthy of all the great things this life has to offer.

30. My spirit is free and unchained.

31. I hold all of my accomplishments and failures with equal emotion because I am defined by neither.

32. I wholly accept who I am and the person that I am becoming.

33. Mine is the only acceptance and approval that will ever be needed in my life.

34. I radiate positivity and loving energy to all that I come in contact with.

35. I am fully loved by myself and others.

36. I am fully love-able by myself and others even when it doesn't feel like it.

37. I am wonderful, inside and out.

38. I have the inherent freedom to make any choices that I wish.

39. I carry the intellect, wisdom and inner power to freely choose what I believe is best for me.

40. I am open to signs of guidance that come my way because I know I do not know all the answers.

41. I easily accept compliments and just as easily give them to those around me.

42. I choose to never take anything personally.

43. I hereby choose to always do my absolute best.

44. I only speak the very best of myself.

45. I only speak the very best of others.

46. I do not make negative assumptions about those around me.

47. I am wanted and desired.

48. I honor my values in all ways at all times.

49. I refuse to sacrifice my core values in favor of what may feel good at the moment.

50. I am always moving closer to self-mastery.

51. I show love for others as freely as I show love for myself.

52. I am not held back by any shame from my past.

53. I unashamedly share my talents and achievements with others.

54. I will make certain that I achieve and maintain all of my physical objectives since I am deserving of it.

55. I have no constraints or limits on my dreams.

56. I choose to celebrate who I am now and who I am becoming in the future.

57. It is never too late to follow my aspirations, and I believe this to be true.

58. I have everything I need to make my life into what I want it to be.

59. I am a success. Period.

60. I am overflowing with love for others because I have so much love for myself.

61. I am confidently and excitedly moving forward into the next phase of my life.

62. I am worthy of praise and admiration from others.

63. I have the power to heal physically, mentally, and emotionally from anything.

64. The only thing that defines my success is my willingness to persevere and move forward.

65. I am filled with gratitude for my circumstances and blessings.

66. I love myself to bring my authentic being everywhere I go.

67. The best expression of self-love is how I care for my body inside and out.

68. I carry sufficient strength for fighting through any adversity that confronts me.

69. I am a physical incarnation of love and light.

70. I choose to live my life with exuberance and enthusiasm.

71. I give myself the approval that I crave from others.

72. I deserve love the way that I am right now.

73. I show myself how much I love myself by the quality of self-talk I engage in.

74. I choose to tell myself good things because I love myself.

75. I am always getting closer to fulfilling my destiny and becoming the very best that I can be.

76. My personal journey has pushed me towards all of the gifts and joys that are in front of me.

77. I am now loving myself in a deeper way than I have ever loved myself before.

78. I am constantly gaining more and more clarity and peace.

79. What is being impressed within me is beginning to be expressed around me.

80. My best attributes far outweigh my worst.

81. I possess a deep love for myself and my body.

82. There is nothing that can hold me back from being the best expression of my true self.

83. I am connected to the strongest source of power in the universe.

84. My connection to universal power lifts me high above my circumstances.

85. I carry the power to change my circumstances and achieve all of my goals.

86. My mind and body are working together to help me reach my full potential.

87. I have so much in my life that is worthy of celebration and enjoyment.

88. It is now my time to shine.

89. Self-confidence, harmony, and peace of mind come naturally to me.

90. I love everything about my appearance.

91. As I practice self-love, I become more capable of being loved.

92. I live my truth.

93. I live my life unashamed of my weaknesses.

94. Even when I feel weak, I am still strong.

95. My struggles are nothing but opportunities for growth.

96. I am not a prisoner to my circumstances.

97. My heart is healed from the hurt of my past.

98. I love myself enough to step forward and embrace new adventures that will help me to grow.

99. I make strides daily to become a better version of who I am.

100. I let go of past rejections.

101. Rejection does not have a say in who I am.

102. Rejection does not have a say in what I deserve.

103. Rejection does not have a say in what I am capable of.

104. I am capable of communicating with confidence and certainty.

105. My spirit is an infinite ocean of calm.

106. Serenity is embedded deep within me.

107. No matter what, I am at peace with my past.

108. No matter what, I am at peace with my present.

109. No matter what, I am at peace with my future.

110. I will always believe in myself even if no one else does.

111. I love myself and every aspect of who I am.

112. I am proud of the person I want to be and the progress I have made.

113. Day by day, minute by minute, I grow to love more of my life and everything in it.

114. I have the power and confidence to chase my dreams with fervor and passion.

115. I will always be there for myself, regardless of what I go through.

116. I find peace and joy in my moments of solitude because I love my own company.

117. I am far too much a gift for the world to carry any feelings of self-pity.

118. I will never be alone because I will always be there for myself.

119. I have an unshakeable inner strength.

120. There is much more to me than what it seems from the outside.

121. I am excited about my potential and how it will positively influence my future.

122. I am always finding new reasons to appreciate my uniqueness.

123. Each and every day, I choose to be the very best that I can possibly be.

124. I have confidence in my capacity to make choices that will lead to my financial well-being.

125. I embrace every opportunity to grow as a person and maximize everything that I can be.

126. I am whole, I am complete, and I am worthy.

127. I love the process of becoming my best self.

128. I am in love with identifying the areas of myself that I can improve upon.

129. I am worth more than any words I could ever use to describe me.

130. I hold unlimited power inside of me.

131. Wonder exist within me in abundance.

132. Every step I take is taken with courage and love for myself.

133. I celebrate my many victories and expect to have many more.

134. I am a bright, shining beacon of love.

135. I am worthy of compassion and kindness.

136. I am worthy of endless affection from others.

137. Nothing can diminish the love that I have for myself.

138. I am simply wonderful.

139. Happiness is always accessible to me.

140. I can always make the choice to love myself.

141. I make decisions that are in my best interest.

142. All of my decisions reflect the love and respect that I have for myself.

143. I openly acknowledge and share my gifts and talents.

144. Because I love myself, I am open to improving my weaknesses without self-judgment.

145. My love for myself prevents me from succumbing to external pressures.

146. My self-love instills a strong foundation of faith in myself.

147. I am patient with others because I am patient with myself.

148. When confronted with hate, my heart is immediately filled with love.

149. I honor my unique talents by sharing them with the world.

150. I love myself enough to be assertive when needed.

151. I love myself enough to speak my truth at all times.

152. I am centered and grounded in who I am.

153. I am powerful beyond all measure in pursuit of my dreams.

154. I move through life in complete peace and calm.

155. My life is centered on showing love for all people including myself.

156. I consistently do my best, every time.

157. I love myself enough to have a strong motivation within me to succeed.

158. I exercise grace for the benefit of myself and others.

159. I have complete trust in who I am and what I am capable of.

160. I love myself enough to never stop working towards my goals until I achieve them.

161. I always continue pushing forward, even though the worst of storms, because what is on the other side is worth it.

162. My heart is full of love for myself and others.

163. I always stand up for myself.

164. I am worthy of all new and incredible opportunities that life has to offer.

165. I love my past failures because of the lessons they have taught me to make me better.

166. I draw from my past only when it makes my present better.

167. I lovingly embrace my flaws because it is a part of what makes me unique.

168. I lovingly embrace my strengths because it is a part of what makes me unique.

169. I equally embrace my strengths and my weaknesses, as they collectively make up who I am.

170. I have the power to change the parts of myself that I do not like.

171. I practice self-care as a way to enhance my self-love.

172. Taking great care of my body is one of the ways that I show myself love.

173. I approve of who I am.

174. I take pride in my past.

175. I release all thoughts or beliefs that are not aligned with love for myself.

176. I take action on improving the parts of my body that I can control.

177. I lovingly embrace and accept the parts of my body that I cannot control.

178. I take action on improving the parts of my appearance that I can control.

179. I lovingly embrace and accept the parts of my appearance that I cannot control.

180. My view of myself is the only one that truly matters.

181. I have a loving view of myself that cannot be disparaged by external forces.

182. I have a loving view of myself that is strong enough to withstand anything other people might say.

183. Other people don't have to love me in order for me to love myself.

184. I affirm and grow my self-love through repeated positive self-talk.

185. Regardless of what it looks like, my body works the way it should, and for that I am grateful.

186. I fully trust my conscience to show me the right way.

187. I will not be defined by anything negative that was said about me in my past.

188. I determine my value, not others.

189. My self-worth is in my own hands, not in the hands of others.

190. I forgive myself for any past behavior I committed that was not in alignment with self-respect.

191. Every day is a fresh opportunity to progress in my self-acceptance quest.

192. I am always embarking upon new paths of self-exploration and discovery.

193. I am a strong symbol of energy and vitality.

194. I am the one who knows the best way to meet my own requirements.

195. I release all resentment, even for myself.

196. I am caring and loving to both myself and all others that come into contact with me.

197. I end every day with loving acceptance of myself and all that I accomplished that day.

198. I do not dwell on my weaknesses, but I embrace my strengths.

199. Every day is a chance to grow and improve my relationship with myself.

200. I release all past regrets as an expression of the love that I have for myself in the present.

201. I embrace others with love, mercy, and forgiveness, just as I do for myself.

202. Because I love myself, I do not engage in self-sabotaging behavior.

203. Self-pity is a thing of the past.

204. My future is characterized by abundance and confidence.

205. I embrace and boldly declare all of my accomplishments with humility.

206. I am only constructive in my criticism for myself and others.

207. I provide feedback for others and myself with love.

208. I know how to make the very best decisions for me.

209. I have the courage to do what's best for me even if others are doing things differently.

210. I have empathy for my past pain and I work towards channeling it in a positive manner.

211. I am a very special gift to everyone around me.

212. The world is a better place because I am in it.

213. I make a positive impact on everyone I come in contact with.

214. I have total faith in myself at all times.

215. I can count on myself for anything I need.

216. I am dependable to myself and others.

217. I am becoming a much wiser person every single day.

218. My life serves as a great role model for others.

219. Other people are inspired by the way that I love myself.

220. I delight in my uniqueness and celebrate my differences.

221. I am completely worthy of success.

222. I am willing and able to change any part of myself that I believe needs improvement.

223. I have the power to adopt new skills.

224. I can forgive anyone because I have forgiven myself.

225. I am free to live in accordance with my highest self.

226. I choose to be happy because I deeply love myself.

227. Doing my best is all that I require of myself.

228. I never set expectations of myself out of fear.

229. I never set expectations of myself out of pain.

230. I never set expectations of myself out of low self-esteem or poor self-image.

231. I have a plan for my life and I love myself to follow through and execute it.

232. I have no reason to doubt what I can accomplish.

233. I have no reason not to believe in who I am.

234. I always find new reasons for me to keep loving myself.

235. I see myself as a person who succeeds in all areas of life.

236. A single failure does not diminish or negate my successes.

237. Falling short does not diminish my love for who I am.

238. I surrender doubt and worry.

239. Abundance is meant for me.

240. A prosperous life is ahead for me because I will attract with my love for myself.

241. I have the wisdom to know what I can handle at any given time.

242. I am patient with myself and do not demand of myself more than I can handle at any given time.

243. I am gentle and kind with myself when trying new things and exploring new territories.

244. I deeply trust myself in any situation that I encounter.

245. Where there is abundant self-love, there can be no fear or hatred.

246. Right here, just as I am, I am fully accepted.

247. Unconditionally loving myself is the best gift that I can give myself.

248. I do not require perfection in order to fully love myself for who I am.

249. My reach will always exceed my grasp because I will always pursue what I believe I am worthy of— even if it is difficult.

250. I love myself enough to break free from damaging addictions in all forms.

251. I give myself permission to thrive.

252. I have so many valuable gifts to give to the world.

253. I am amazed at what I have overcome to get to where I am today.

254. I am blessed to be in excellent health, and don't take that gift for granted.

255. I am open to receiving help when I need it in all types of relationships.

256. I release worries with calmness, love, and ease.

257. I know how to accept who I am and strive for who I want to be at the same time.

258. I can accomplish whatever it is that I choose to focus my energies and efforts on.

259. I love the feeling of self-love and acceptance.

260. I bring my best self to everything I do because I am worth it.

261. I bring my best into my relationships because I am worthy of having great relationships.

262. Because I love myself and my purpose, I am persistent in the fearless pursuit of my dreams.

263. I know that is normal to feel fear, and I persist forward regardless.

264. Loving myself means taking charge of my life and making it into the best it can possibly be.

265. My body has so much wisdom, and I choose to listen to it when it speaks.

266. I care for myself through daily practice of serenity and self-love.

267. Because I believe in myself, I can accomplish anything that I desire.

268. Everything in my world is well and good.

269. I know that loving myself means putting energy into what I am able to control.

270. I know that loving myself means graciously accepting what I cannot control.

271. I am totally grateful for all I have.

272. I am totally grateful for all I have done.

273. I am totally grateful for all I have become.

274. I wholly embrace changes with acceptance and peace.

275. I only accept circumstances that are worthy of me and my standards.

276. I choose to practice forgiveness to protect my own peace and sanity.

277. I choose to exercise patience to protect my own peace and sanity.

278. I have achieved success in every aspect of my life.

279. I am getting more and more wise through every experience.

280. I choose to protect my peace by living my life with a focused and calm energy.

281. I am gentle with myself as I work through my personal challenges.

282. I am full of love for who I am.

283. I express my ideas with clarity and confidence because I have a valuable perspective that people need to hear.

284. I am appreciative of my innate loving energy.

285. I am always evolving and making the most out of every chance to grow.

286. I welcome every imperfection that I have because I am in love with myself.

287. I have the emotional strength to show my true emotions without judging myself.

288. I am empowered and strong and in control of my life.

289. I do not allow myself to succumb to self-pity.

290. Self-discipline is one of the ways that I show myself true love.

291. I am disciplined in my actions because I believe in my future.

292. I take rest from my work when needed, knowing that my work does not determine my value.

293. Overworking myself is a form of compensating for what I may lack.

294. I have confidence in the goals I choose to pursue, and that is enough for me.

295. I am my biggest cheerleader and biggest fan.

296. I am resistant to the temptation of engaging in negative self-talk.

297. I love myself enough to always chase my dreams.

298. Because I love myself, I am able to better love others.

299. Although I am not what I do, I am proud of what I have done.

300. My self-love allows me to feel hope for my future.

301. I fully allow myself to love others to the degree to which I deserve love.

302. Intimacy with my loved ones flows from the strong love I have for myself.

303. I am completely safe in the comfort of my own body and mind.

304. If I ever feel stuck, I know that I can count on myself to get through it.

305. Everything is coming together for me.

306. I love my life.

307. I have a beautiful life that I am grateful to be living.

308. I am constantly putting in the work to become a better person.

309. I have the self-awareness to make improvements in myself where necessary.

310. Even while making self-improvements, I still love myself through the process.

311. I do not need to be hard on myself because I am capable of dealing with anything.

312. I am delighted in my presented circumstance.

313. I love myself enough to strive to become the best I can be.

314. I am not mentally burdened by any obstacles I may face.

315. I am loved despite what I perceive as my imperfections.

316. I am perfect in my imperfection.

317. What I consider flaws others consider as unique reasons to love me.

318. I am a very optimistic person, filled with life and joy.

319. I will always be more than enough for any endeavor that I pursue.

320. I love myself enough to always focus on seeing the positive.

321. I own my personal power, and no one can take that away from me.

322. I appreciate and love myself for getting me this far in life.

323. I take time out for self-care because I am worth it.

324. I invest in opportunities to treat myself because I am worth it.

325. I look for ways to exercise self-love.

326. I show self-love by pushing forward for another day.

327. Without regard to my achievements or lack thereof, I am deserving of respect and affection.

328. I accept and love myself without any conditions.

329. I have nothing except admiration and admiration for myself.

330. I take good care of myself and am proud of my appearance.

331. My very best is more than enough.

332. My self-confidence is strong enough to eradicate self-doubt.

333. I love myself enough to strive to make my life the best it can possibly be.

334. I believe in myself enough to want to see that I achieve my fullest possible potential.

335. I believe in myself and want to live my greatest life possible.

336. I love myself enough to create my dream life.

337. I easily and courageously step into my destiny.

338. All is moving towards things working out in my life.

339. I consciously choose to replace any negative ideas with good ones.

340. Even though I may not be there yet, I am on track to a greater future.

341. I'm putting forth the effort to become the most complete version of myself that I possibly can be.

342. I look within myself for peace and love.

343. What I do is meaningful and fulfilling.

344. Each of my days starts and ends in exactly the same manner: with an attitude of gratitude.

345. I constantly become mentally healthier by planting positive thoughts in my strong mind.

346. I am now loving myself more than I ever have, and that love will only continue to grow.

347. I let go of all unnecessary drama in my life because my peace is valuable to me.

348. I love the way my life has gone so far because it will lead me towards my best self.

349. I have a right to be healthy, loving and self-confident.

350. The most valuable love I can have is the love for myself.

351. I treat myself the way I expect others to treat me, and that is with love and respect.

Chapter 16
Affirmations for Accepting Yourself

Perhaps you might learn to embrace and respect your history as well as your present, so that negative ideas will no longer have the capacity to do you harm. Stop rejecting yourself for the way you looked or acted in the past. Learn to truly embrace the fact that the external world doesn't add to or take away the worthiness of your core being. You only acted the way you did because of your level of experience at the time. Stop beating up yourself over what you cannot change.

Accept that you are not perfect. It is your desire to be perfect that makes you conscious of yourself, worrying about what others are thinking of you.

The critic is very good at replaying scenes from your past that you find painful or embarrassing. It never forgets the names of people that hurt you in the past or occasions when you did something that made you feel like sinking into the ground with shame. When the critic attacks you with thoughts like this, simply observing and ignoring those thoughts can be very difficult.

Even though you see a beautiful face when you look into the mirror now, walking down the streets, thoughts of the times when you were too thin, pimple-faced and flat-chested cloud your mind. If you were taunted for the way you look, that is all you hear when you meet other people. It can be really hard to challenge or ignore your thoughts because the derogative words are so loud in your mind and the pictures are so clear—they were once your reality for a very long time.

The next crucial step you should practice after acceptance is forgiveness. Learning to love yourself regardless of what you think about yourself or your past memories. You will not be able to move on from the past if you continue to lament your acts and reject yourself.

Practicing the following "nevertheless: technique can help you make peace with your past. Select events or memories that are capable of eroding your self-esteem and respond with a 'nevertheless' statement. For instance, when your inner critic tells you that you can never amount to much, respond with, "I am not perfect, nevertheless I am growing."

Take your self-esteem assignment notebook and write on a fresh sheet, a list of three or more events or memories that always bring you down as you find them embarrassing and hurtful. Fully describe each of the memories or events and the emotional effect they had on you. Then create a perfect "nevertheless" response to each of those statements.

The Affirmations

1. I celebrate my individuality, no matter how others receive it.
2. I speak and think very highly of myself, and my actions reflect that.
3. I am worthy of success and happiness, so I work to achieve both.
4. Even though I strive to enhance myself, I am happy with who I am now.
5. I deserve and accept only the best.
6. I refuse to let anyone else's negative view of me hold me back.
7. I am worth investing time, money, an energy into my happiness and well-being.
8. I am in love with caring for my body, mind, and spirit.
9. I refuse to talk down to myself; I am amazing.
10. I acknowledge my self-worth on a daily basis.

11. I honor my commitments to myself.

12. I am proud of my roots and where I have come from.

13. I am proud of every mistake and misstep from my past, as it's led to who I am today.

14. I am a priority in my life, and I am treating myself as such.

15. I have faith in the kind of person I endeavor to become.

16. I am bursting with courage, strength, compassion, and love; I am enough.

17. I am loveable and worthy of greatness.

18. The only person or thing that can prevent me from living my greatest life is myself.

19. I make myself more and more proud every day.

20. I choose to be aligned with thoughts that heal my past.

21. I am letting go of others' expectations of me to attain my true self.

22. I am a work of art, made of infinite energy and possibility.

23. I love myself wholly and unconditionally; I am enough.

24. I have the power to choose to love myself and others.

25. I choose to think and feel positively about myself.

26. I am radiant and full of potential.

27. I serve as a positive example to others on how to love yourself.

28. I do not need the approval of others to give me permission to live my life.

29. I do not allow other people to get in the way of my self-confidence.

30. It is okay for me to love myself and simultaneously work to improve myself.

31. It is my mission to live my truth while motivating others to do the same.

32. I choose to build a positive image of myself for myself.

33. I am more than my body, and my body is more than its shape and size.

34. I decide how I feel and think, not only about myself, but everything.

35. I honor myself and the decisions I have made; I choose to be happy.

36. I find it easy to love myself.

37. I am giving it my all, and that is sufficient; I am sufficient.

38. I feel safe and confident in the way that I express myself.

39. I am divine, connected, and loved.

40. There is no wrong decision if I speak my truth.

41. It is always okay for me to be myself.

42. I am unique, and that is beautiful.

43. I do not compare myself and my success to others; everyone has a different path.

44. I respect myself and others with word, thought, and deed.

45. Everyone on the planet is different from me, and there is no one else quite like me.

46. I love myself, so I talk to myself like I would talk to someone I love.

47. My flaws do not define me or limit my worth.

48. The things about myself that I find imperfect, others find endearing.

49. I am a wonderful person from the inside out.

50. I allow myself to be myself, regardless of people accepting it.

51. I am committed to finding and fulfilling my purpose in life.

52. I am allowed to enjoy the abundance I deserve.

53. It is my differences that make me wonderful.

54. I am not perfect, and that is perfectly fine.

55. I do not need the approval of others in order to express my creativity.

56. I don't need approval from others in order to feel good about myself.

57. I am confident and proud of my achievements, past and future.

58. Imperfection is what makes me interesting.

59. Imperfection is what gives me reason to grow.

60. I honor my own goals, dreams, and desires.

61. I am uniquely talented, no matter what anyone else believes.

62. I have faith in my own abilities and my potential to achieve.

63. Today, I will love myself and all my flaws.

64. I wholly appreciate who I am and who I am striving to be.

65. My flaws do not make me any less love-able or less worthy of success.

66. I am radiating endless love towards myself and the world.

67. I forgive myself for all of the instances in the past that I haven't shown myself affection.

68. I show others the example of how to love me.

69. I show others the example of how to honor me.

70. I show others the example of how to respect me.

71. I show others the example of how to accept me.

72. I am accountable for my bad choices, but I forgive myself for them.

73. I now eliminate all self-doubt and forgive myself for harboring it in the past.

74. I forgive and accept all of my regrets, mistakes, and failures.

75. I do not sabotage myself with self-pity.

76. I pridefully embrace my accomplishments, results, and work.

77. No one has permission to hurt me, not even myself.

78. No one can make me feel less than, not even myself.

79. I do not need another person to complete me. I am already whole.

80. I find it easy to be myself.

81. I will love myself first so that I can spread love to others.

82. I love myself, what I have become, and who I can still be.

83. I determine my priorities for myself.

84. I recover from mistakes with grace.

85. I show mercy on myself for my missteps.

86. I am becoming wiser each day.

87. I am secure in my value.

88. I delight in sharing the gift of my uniqueness with the world.

89. I express myself freely, in ways that do not harm others.

90. I trade self-hatred for self-love.

91. I trade judgment for understanding.

92. I trust my actions and have faith in my decisions.

93. I practice having a pure perception of myself and others.

94. It is okay for me to change because that means I'm growing.

95. Being kind to myself is the first step to harmony and peace.

96. I am determined, confident, and courageous.

97. I deserve to be treated respectfully by myself and others.

98. I will stop being so hard on myself.

99. I am gentle and forgiving of my mistakes.

100. I am allowed to enjoy the things I have worked hard for.

101. I have total and absolute confidence in my own abilities.

102. Whether people praise me or speak ill of me, it does not affect my happiness.

103. Satisfaction and happiness come from within myself.

104. The only person I compare myself to is who I used to be.

105. It is quite OK for me to not know everything.

106. I respect myself and honor my values.

107. I do what I need to protect my content state of mind.

108. I give myself permission to make my own decisions.

109. All good things start with my ability to love myself first.

110. I admit my faults and allow myself to be corrected.

111. It is not necessary for me to be flawless to be lovable.

112. I tend to my emotional, mental, and spiritual needs.

113. I feel content, while I work to become my best self.

114. Self-acceptance can happen simultaneously with self-improvement.

115. Self-love can happen simultaneously with self-improvement.

116. Self-respect can happen simultaneously with self-improvement.

117. I express myself without inhibition.

118. I speak my mind without inhibition.

119. I treat myself with empathy, respect, and compassion.

120. It is up to me to choose what I believe and experience in my life.

121. I am in control of how I treat myself.

122. With each breath, I appreciate and cherish myself.

123. I do not hold past mistakes over my head.

124. I am worthy of having a peaceful mind.

125. I am proud of myself and all that I have accomplished so far in my life.

126. My self-image is in my own control.

127. I refuse to let other people's opinions of me lessen my self-worth.

128. My imperfections do not make me less worthy consideration from others.

129. I refuse to see myself as inferior; I am worthy of respect.

130. I am allowed to choose myself.

131. I am allowed to put myself first.

132. I can count on myself.

133. I reframe all my self-talk into positivity.

134. I deserve the very best.

135. I do not lower my standards to make others happy or more comfortable.

136. I choose to accept myself, while still working toward my betterment.

137. I choose to make love a part of my story.

138. Others accept me because I accept myself.

139. Others love me because I love myself.

140. Others respect me because I respect myself.

141. I do not judge myself for my fear, but I will not let it stop me from succeeding.

142. I commend myself for the progress I have made up until now.

143. I am fair to myself and others while working towards my goals.

144. I am allowed to feel emotions and express them without harming others.

145. I forgive myself for the times I did not give myself the respect I deserved.

146. I forgive myself for how I chose to survive in the past.

147. I forgive myself for indulging in things that do not fulfill me.

148. I forgive myself for all of the instances in which I was unable to offer value to the lives of others.

149. I forgive myself for not extending forgiveness to myself earlier.

150. I am a person of amazing character.

151. I appreciate all the positive traits I possess.

152. Every day, I learn to appreciate and love myself more and more.

153. I am friendly, reliable, and kind.

154. I have discovered that my happiness is independent of other people's opinions.

155. I will not feel guilty when others do not approve of what I say or do.

156. It is more important to grow from admitting a mistake than it is to be right.

157. I respect and love myself unconditionally.

158. I allow myself permission to be human and to make mistakes in my life.

159. I feel worthy of the love and success I deserve.

160. I will work towards understanding and improving my shortcomings.

161. Being authentic attracts more abundance than being perfect.

162. The transformation of my mind will take time, and there is nothing wrong with that.

163. I discard all fears of not being perfect.

164. What I am, have, or do is enough.

165. I will not hide my imperfections or be ashamed of them.

166. It is not necessary to accomplish perfection to feel appreciated.

167. I act positively towards others so I can act positively towards myself.

168. My imperfections do not make me flawed—they make me human.

Chapter 17
Affirmations for Controlling Yourself and Your Surroundings

When one's consciousness is focused on the present moment, while calmly noticing and accepting one's emotions, thoughts, and body sensations (mindfulness), one can attain a state of mind called mindfulness.

It is exhausting constantly judging ourselves, judging others, and judging everything happening around us. It takes away from the enjoyment of our own lives, and the constant need for perfection nicks away at our self-esteem because we always inevitably find ourselves unable to live up to what is in reality an impossible standard.

Wouldn't it be great to just be grateful? To fully experience the magic in everyday moments? To love and accept yourself fully despite being on a personal growth journey? To not feel like time is whizzing by as you collapse under the weight of a constant barrage of worries and responsibilities and time commitments?

There are so many responsibilities pulling us in a million different ways such that it's really easy to lose sight of what thing truly matters and get caught up in living in the future, never taking a minute to really appreciate what is in front of our eyes. I's easy to get the impression that every person or circumstance we come across is to be held accountable.

Everything is not about "black" or "white" or "right" or "wrong," although in the world of comparison traps we live in, it's easy to feel this way. Can you find value in the right now? Can what is ever be enough? It's going to have to be if you are ever going to be happy.

Accepting the way things are is not to be confused with settling or giving up all effort to attain growth and advancement. There is nothing wrong with becoming the best you possibly can be. In fact, you should. But acceptance is the place from which you can create the right emotional state to get there and become your highest self and live your greatest life.

So how do we cultivate acceptance? Sometimes a mental reset is just what we need to remind ourselves to slow down, stop judging ourselves, everyone, and everything so harshly, and be grateful. This produces just the mental clarity needed to get back to a mentally, emotionally, and spiritually healthy position from which life can actually be both enjoyed and advanced.

The use of affirmations is a highly efficient method of doing this. Affirmations can quite literally rewire your mind, by physically affecting the neural pathways in your brain. Affirmations, when spoken coupled with the feeling one would feel if they honestly believed them to be true, can be extremely powerful tools in improving and changing your life.

The Affirmations

1. I decide how I feel today.

2. My thoughts have the power to affect my reality, so I choose my thoughts wisely.

3. The most powerful tool I have is my freedom of choice.

4. I only put energy into positive thoughts that benefit my progress.

5. I am able to create a life full of happiness and abundance, and I choose to do so for myself.

6. I do not sweat the small things.

7. I take right actions and make right decisions for myself.

8. I do not allow my emotions to force me into impulsive decisions.

9. I attract the same energy that I put out into the world.

10. I will not stress over things I am unable to alter.

11. I can make the right decisions easily because I am clear on my priorities.

12. I choose to heal from the pains of my past.

13. I will exhaust all avenues in the pursuit of my goals.

14. I make my own happiness a priority.

15. I am not responsible for other people's beliefs, actions, or mistakes.

16. I make the deliberate choice to welcome new opportunities in my life.

17. I have infinite strategies to make my dreams come true.

18. I take responsibility for my life; I am the only one in charge of how my life turns out.

19. I choose to be motivated every day.

20. I turn my thoughts and ideas into action every day.

21. I am in control of my future, and I will continue to focus on the positive aspects of my life.

22. I choose to drop all excuses and make choices that contribute to my betterment.

23. It is okay for me to put myself first sometimes.

24. I thrive in adversity, which strengthens my character.

25. Every day, I am able to connect with myself on a deeper way.

26. I choose to be aligned with thoughts that promote a positive future.

27. I am always working to be my best self.

28. My strength is more powerful than any struggle.

29. I remove myself from any toxic environment that does not serve me.

30. I focus on achieving peace for myself.

31. I am at harmony with my environment.

32. I am not responsible for the responsibilities of others.

33. I speak up for my desires and ask for what I need.

34. I can guide myself in the correct direction.

35. I am always working on the improvement of my attitude.

36. I love myself enough to stick to the boundaries I have set.

37. I make choices that lead to happiness and joy.

38. Good things come to me from unexpected places.

39. I do not need to be saved. I am my own superhero.

40. I can say no with no problem, and I think for myself.

41. Giving in to self-doubt is not an option.

42. I walk away from any relationship that does not contribute to my well-being.

43. Where I feel weak, I hone resilience.

44. Only I can control my actions, reactions, and responses.

45. I refuse to let others make me forget what I deserve from life.

46. I practice self-discipline and self-awareness to attain my highest self.

47. My success, prosperity, and abundance are inevitable.

48. I am relentless, I persevere, and I keep going.

49. I am mentally strong and emotionally fit.

50. I refuse to wait for anyone else to make my dreams a reality.

51. I free myself of all bitterness and anger from the past, so I can be more receptive to the positive possibilities of the future.

52. I love myself enough to set and stick to boundaries.

53. I am allowed to change the direction of my life without anyone else's approval or validation.

54. I take responsibility for my mistakes.

55. I choose not to be afraid, but if I am, I move forward anyway.

56. I am allowed to say no to things that aren't best for me without feeling guilty.

57. I have infinite choices because opportunities are everywhere.

58. I am a powerful person, and I can change anything in my life that does not work for my greater good.

59. I acknowledge thoughts that do not serve me and let them go.

60. I do not make time for those who do not support my highest self.

61. I have the ability to exert control over my thoughts if I so choose.

62. I do not owe anyone an explanation for my choices.

63. I release my fears of imperfection because I am enough.

64. I have complete command of my thoughts and emotions.

65. I overcome my fears by taking action in the direction I want to go.

66. I abandon other people's expectations of me, freeing myself to live the life I want.

67. I create the life I desire.

68. I manage and control how I spend my time according to my priorities.

69. I do not compare myself to others.

70. I surrender my need to control others.

71. I control situations easily, with grace and confidence.

72. I cast away all things that do not help my personal or spiritual growth.

73. I do not waste my time being angry—I choose the peace of letting go.

74. I plan my work and follow through on my plans.

75. I choose freedom, liberating myself from things that block an open path.

76. Only I can control my life and govern my decision-making.

77. The judgments of others does not dictate my choices.

78. I move through my day with confidence.

79. I choose to heal my own life, taking responsibility for what I have done and for what I have allowed others to do to me.

80. I am independent, reliable, and capable of determining my own success.

81. In this moment, I take my power back.

82. I am balanced, connected, and at peace with myself.

83. I choose to be calm in my mind.

84. I commit only to things that support my dreams.

85. I acknowledge fear, but I do not give it the power to control me.

86. I am powerful and capable of anything.

87. I only project what I want out of life—infinite positivity.

88. I control my reactions; situations do not dictate how I respond.

89. I do all things with good intent and purpose.

90. I am not afraid of not knowing, because I am capable of learning.

91. I am capable of choosing how I feel about the things around me, and I always choose happiness and gratitude.

92. I make all decisions with confidence.

93. I will not settle for "good enough" when I know I am capable of greater.

94. If it is not true, I will not say it; if it is not right, I will not do it.

95. I focus my energy on building new things instead of lamenting over the demise of old things.

96. I will not let my emotions overpower my mental strength and intelligence.

97. I only accept positive vibes.

98. If I fear the unknown, I continue anyway. I let nothing stop me.

99. I do not seek revenge on anyone who has wronged me; I am at peace.

100. I create my own future and stand behind what I say and do with confidence.

101. I was not born to give up; I will persevere.

102. Fear is just an emotion; I forbid it to diminish my power.

103. I am letting go so that I can grow.

104. I will not let regret over my past keep me from the success of my future.

105. All that I do today will lead to a better tomorrow.

106. I trust and believe that what I seek is also seeking me.

107. I am in control of my actions and my reactions.

108. I do not hold anyone else responsible for my own happiness.

109. My discipline gives way to happiness.

110. I deal with stressful situations calmly.

111. I reject all habits, actions, and people that do not empower me.

112. The power to realize my dreams is within me.

113. I accept my situation so that I can change it.

114. I am naturally calm, cool, and collected.

115. Today, I will strive to make positive changes.

116. I am able to acknowledge my emotions without letting them control me.

117. I am powerful enough to determine my own future, regardless of other people's opinions.

118. I deal with challenging emotions in a positive and productive way.

119. I think logically and clearly, even in high pressure situations.

120. I have no control over the acts of other people, but I do have control over my own actions.

121. Sometimes, I need to relinquish control, and that's alright.

122. I will accomplish great things, and nothing can stand in my way.

123. My happiness relies not on who I am or what I have, but what I think.

124. Each and every day, I am choosing, not waiting to be chosen.

125. I have control over my thoughts; I have control over my life.

126. I live my life impressing myself, not others.

127. I have all the energy and time I need to accomplish my goals because I create it.

128. I am shaped by my thoughts. I become what I think. So I choose my thoughts wisely.

129. I do not make decisions just to impress others.

130. Moderating and managing my emotions comes naturally to me.

131. I may bend, but I do not ever break.

132. I am the source of my inner peace in the midst of outside chaos.

133. I trust my inner voice and its ability to show me the way.

134. I stick to my values, no matter what other people think.

135. I extract the lesson out of every apparent loss.

136. I can save myself; I do not need to be saved.

137. My efforts have value, even if the outcome is unexpected.

138. I work to understand those who have done me wrong, so I can forgive them and protect my personal peace.

139. Success will come to me through my courage and determination.

140. I make a choice, daily, to radiate positivity and optimism.

141. I do not alter my ideas for the sake of fitting other people's opinions.

142. No one else can achieve success for me; it is my responsibility.

143. Nothing will make me satisfied unless I choose to be happy.

144. I stay true to my personal decisions and life choices.

145. I make my own decisions, undeterred by the opinions of others.

146. I stand by my decisions with confidence and pride.

147. I reap the benefits from being in control of my emotions.

148. I have the ability to be better and will always strive to do so.

149. Those who are likewise on a personal development and improvement journey are the only people with whom I associate.

150. I recognize that individuals perceive the world in a variety of ways, but I stay committed to my own set of principles.

151. My happiness does not come to me; it comes from me.

152. It is my responsibility to solve my own problems.

153. I am intentional in what I do, hear, experience, and see.

154. I challenge my past bad decisions and learn from them.

155. I have a productive, enjoyable daily routine that breeds my success.

156. I do not allow others to take advantage of me, nor do I take advantage of others.

157. I do not always have to be right, but I am always gracious and kind.

158. I do not settle where I am if I know I can do far better.

159. I am disciplined and self-aware.

160. I choose to create a healthy environment for myself that fosters my growth and productivity.

161. I effortlessly embody humility and compassion.

162. I lead my life with self-awareness and self-correction.

163. I am my own source of validation.

164. I do not let the past control my present and future actions.

165. I accept that the past is unchangeable and resolve any anger or hurt associated with it.

166. I stand by my decisions with conviction.

167. I take consistent intentional action towards my dreams to ensure my success.

168. My personal peace is my priority.

169. I choose to manifest greatness in my life in this moment and the next.

170. Other people's needs are equally as essential as mine, and vice versa.

171. I cannot control other people's thoughts about me; I think of myself positively regardless.

172. Even though I face obstacles, I will persevere.

173. I choose not to make excuses, no matter what.

174. I love the feeling of working hard for my goals and seeing the rewards of my efforts.

175. If it is to be done, it is up to me.

176. I am up for the task of creating my best life.

177. I remain calm within no matter what is going on outside of me.

178. Self-control and self-discipline come easily to me.

179. I choose to make myself and others happy.

180. I choose to make forgiveness a part of my narrative.

181. I choose to be productive, taking consistent steps toward fulfilling my goals.

182. I am kind to others, and unbothered by outside opinions.

183. My dedication to my goals is unshakeable.

184. Peace is a natural, effortless part of who I am.

185. I am committed to reaching all of my objectives.

186. I choose to make happiness a part of my story.

187. I have chosen to concentrate on the things that are important to me in life.

188. My self-discipline helps me reach my goals.

189. I surround myself with individuals that are always striving to improve themselves.

190. I choose to fail forward, using every mistake as an opportunity to improve.

191. My self-discipline comes naturally.

192. Opportunities are everywhere, so I have unlimited choices.

193. I have an abundant amount of willpower.

194. I cultivate habits that help me achieve my goals and dreams.

195. I choose to see the lessons in my mistakes.

196. No one can do for me what I won't do for myself.

197. I make gratitude and joy my emotional habits.

198. Today, I choose to take one step further than I did yesterday.

199. I do not live by chance. I live by choice.

200. I have made the decision to accept responsibility for my actions.

201. No matter how high the mountain is, I will climb it.

202. I attract things and people that encourage my growth.

203. Being positive is a choice I commit to every day.

204. I always keep my calm and stay in control of my emotions so I can stay in control of myself.

205. I can and I will, and that's all there is to it.

206. I train my body, feed my spirit, and focus my mind.

207. The past, present, and future will not be changed by my overthinking.

208. I acknowledge guilt as a feeling and not a fact.

209. I believe in what I want so much that it has no choice but to materialize.

210. I choose to get rid of my old habits that do not serve my goals.

211. I accept full responsibility for the decisions I have made.

212. I separate myself from unhelpful obsessive thoughts.

213. I choose to be a priority in my life.

214. What I am is the result of how I think of myself, so my thoughts will be positive.

215. I am responsible for the energy that I release into the world, so I will only emanate positivity.

216. Today, I am focused on my goals, and I will do what I can to achieve them.

217. I can change my life and experience whenever I want.

218. I choose not to give my power to anyone else.

219. My body is a representation of everything I put into it, physically and mentally.

220. I choose to be in a positive environment where I can be my best self.

221. I always have a choice; it is up to me to make the best one.

222. I feel empowered by taking inspired action.

223. Today, I choose presence over regret.

224. I have the strength and willpower to work around any challenges I may face.

225. I cannot control the world, but I can control how I respond to challenges against peace.

226. I alone am in full control of how I choose to live my life.

227. I have the power to choose success and prosperity.

Chapter 18
Affirmations for Relationships and Supporting Others

Ever been around people who walk into a room and instantly brighten it with their presence, drawing people to them and making them feel welcome for reasons they can't quite put their finger on? Have you ever been in a place when someone comes in and the tone quickly dips and shifts in a manner that is both physical and difficult to articulate? Isn't it interesting how some individuals appear to be happy all of the time, no matter what is going on around them? Do you actually know someone who is always in a state of crisis, where something is always going wrong or falling apart in their life, and where everyone and everything seems to be conspiring against them? Do you know someone like this?

For those of you who actually have had the opportunity to tour the globe, you are well aware that a number of the world's most poor people, living in the most difficult of conditions, are blissfully happy. Yet, close to home, you might witness wealthy individuals who seem to have it everything, yet are terribly unhappy. Happiness has nothing to do with what occurs outside of yourself. It all comes down to what is going on inside of you.

It is your frame of mind that makes all the difference. Disempowering ideas may make you feel powerless and hopeless, and they can be difficult to overcome. And since these negative beliefs are often anchored in our subconscious, we are often unaware of the psychological harm we cause ourselves. In contrast, instructing your brain to be cheerful and optimistic while anticipating favorable outcomes for yourself and others may make the difference between experiencing success and experiencing failure.

A successful life is a happy life, and vice versa. And a happy life is a successful life—whatever way you choose to define success is up to you. But it all just really starts (and ends) with the mind, with molding and training it to think in the manner in which you choose.

The use of affirmations is a highly efficient method of doing this. Affirmations have the ability to essentially rewire your brain by physically altering the neuronal connections in your brain, according to research. As long as they are stated in conjunction with the emotion one would have if one really thought what they are saying to be true, affirmations may be incredibly effective tools for improving and transforming one's life.

The habit of pleasant thoughts and a cheerful temperament will make it simple for you to be happy whatever or no matter what your circumstances, and it will be easy for you to bounce back from times of difficulty if you cultivate these habits. You'll also notice that the happier you get, the more that positive events will occur in your life. Moreover, without cultivating a habit of happiness and optimism, you will discover that happiness will constantly evade you no matter how favorable your life circumstances seem to be at any one point in time. Furthermore, the more negatively you see the world around you, the worse things will become for you.

Life is a gift that should be loved and enjoyed every day; instead, the majority of people walk through existence merely waiting for the day to finish, as if life itself is a weight to be carried. Happiness does not come easy to everyone in every situation. Happiness is a learned behavior. Happiness is something that may be chosen. What happens to us is not always under our control, but we have the ability to select our behavior in response to what occurs. Furthermore, optimism and pleasure are always preferable to pessimism and sorrow.

Get your mental peace back, your pleasure back, and the great things you want to bring into your life by doing so. Get the rock solid foundation in place now so that you may look at life with a half-full perspective in the future.

The Affirmations

1. I foster supportive, loving relationships which increase my long-term happiness.

2. My optimistic attitude allows me to build good relationships and strong friendships.

3. I attract healthy and happy personal relationships by projecting a positive attitude.

4. I make others around me happier through my positive attitude.

5. I use empathy and sympathy to support others in their times of need.

6. My positive outlook contributes to my success in my relationships and my overall life.

7. I have an infectious laugh and smile that improves the moods of people around me.

8. I have a network of successful, inspiring people who motivate me to succeed.

9. My friends and I push each other to become the best versions of ourselves.

10. When I need them, my buddies are always there for me, no matter what.

11. I always make room for quality time with my loved ones.

12. I am in relationships that are emotionally supportive and fulfilling.

13. My relationships both comfort me and challenge me.

14. I have mentors and models in every area of my life who inspire me to become better.

15. My significant other and I bring out the best in each other.

16. I possess willpower and self-control, which positively benefits my romantic and social relationships.

17. I surprise strangers and the people in my life with random acts of kindness to brighten their day.

18. I encourage my family and friends to do well because I want to see them at their best.

19. I am respectful of viewpoints and opinions that are different from my own.

20. My agreeable and happy disposition strengthen my connections with others.

21. I grow more and more empathetic every day.

22. My positive outlook attracts positive friends and contributes to further happiness.

23. I am fortunate to have close personal and professional relationships that make me happy.

24. I openly share my thoughts and feelings with my loved ones.

25. My openness with my feelings relieves stress and makes me feel stronger emotionally.

26. I am able to remain positive and optimistic no matter who I am around.

27. I am encouraging to others when they are in need of a mood boost.

28. I am easily able to be patient with my friends, family, and partner.

29. The patience I possess strengthens the emotional bonds in my relationships.

30. My positive attitude is contagious to all who come in contact with me.

31. I support my significant other, friends and family whenever I can because it makes them happy to know I care.

32. I treat people in the same manner in which I would want to be treated.

33. I am happier when I have stronger social connections and familial bonds.

34. My positive relationships with friends and family positively contribute to my self-confidence.

35. I value the quality of my relationships with my partner, friends, and family.

36. I provide support and unconditional love to myself and to those around me.

37. All of my relationships with friends, family, and loved ones are built on trust, honesty, and loyalty.

38. I make an effort to create and nourish positive relationships and get to know people better.

39. My close relationships contribute to increased happiness for both me and the other people involved.

40. I radiate and project positive energy, which attracts high quality people and relationships to me.

41. I relish the moments that I spend with my partner, friends, and family.

42. I put effort into creating opportunities to strengthen the bonds between me and the people I love.

43. I love laughing with my loved ones because it is good for my mental and physical health.

44. I am there for my social and personal connections when they need me.

45. I make an effort to do things for my partner, friends, and family that make them happy.

46. My passion and positivity inspire others around me to feel joy and happiness.

47. I happily celebrate and recognize the successes of my peers.

48. I make myself available to talk to and emotionally support my loved ones whenever they need me.

49. I build trust in my personal and work relationships by delivering on my promises.

50. I freely give compliments to others to improve their happiness, outlook and self-esteem.

51. I form and nurture relationships by creating and participating in social events regularly.

52. I interact more with people who matter most in my life, than I do with screens and electronic devices.

53. I voluntarily reach out to others and offer help even if they have not asked me for it.

54. When it comes to others' happiness, I make an effort to be aware of their needs.

55. I expand other people's networks by bringing people together.

56. I create opportunities for me and my loved ones to enjoy doing things together that we love.

57. I work well with others in professional environments.

58. I have strong connections with the people I work with.

59. I make an effort to regularly call the people I love and remind them that I care.

60. I always find thoughtful ways to show my significant other that I care.

61. I share things that make me happy with other people so it can also make them happy and brighten their day.

62. I make an attempt to meet new individuals who have interests in common with me.

63. My time is my most valuable asset, and I show others that I love them when I choose to spend it with them.

64. I use my talents and ideas to help others.

65. I strengthen my relationships when I share my gifts with others, rather than keep them to myself.

66. I sometimes make healthy sacrifices for the people close to me in order to make them happy.

67. I make an effort to dedicate time to talking and listening to my partner, friends, and family.

68. I make myself emotionally available to my loved ones.

69. I openly express gratitude to my loved ones to thank them for all they've done for me.

70. Whenever I am with a loved one, I am fully physically, mentally, and emotionally present.

71. I constantly look for and discover ways to connect with people over similar interests.

72. I look for ways to help others to decrease their stress and lessen their burdens.

73. I look for ways to help make other people happier.

74. I acknowledge the importance of communication in any successful relationship.

75. My communication abilities are continuously being refined, and I am continually striving for improvement.

76. I spontaneously plan fun, shared experiences with my loved ones to bring us closer.

77. I am there for my loved ones in times of sickness and in health.

78. I am a reliable source of positive energy to others in their darkest times of need.

79. I let my loved ones know I care through my actions as well as my words.

80. I take joy in creating opportunities to bring others joy.

81. No matter how busy I get, I always set aside time for the people I love.

82. When it comes to my spouse, friends, and family, I make an effort to be attentive to their needs.

83. My life is more fulfilling because of my wonderful relationships.

84. I am positive and encouraging to everyone, which makes people love being around me.

85. I offer positive and constructive feedback to people without being negative or overly critical.

86. I amplify my enjoyment of the things I love by sharing them with the people I love.

87. I do good things for others without being asked.

88. I am a strong, positive influence on others, and I help people cultivate a positive mindset.

89. I make an effort to provide emotional support for others when they are not at their best.

90. I am fun to be around because I am happy.

91. I make an effort not to isolate myself because being around others brings me joy.

92. I am a ray of sunshine, who brightens other's people's days when they are feeling down.

93. I find that I am happier in my romantic relationships because of my optimism.

94. I am able to provide emotional support for other people and still maintain my positivity and optimism at the same time.

95. I find and share positive solutions to other people's problems with ease.

96. I realize that everyone has the right to express their own point of view.

97. It is easy for me to constantly meet new people and cultivate new friendships.

98. I enjoy meeting people from different backgrounds because it makes me more empathetic and open minded.

99. I believe in my partner, friends, and family and I motivate them to do and achieve their best.

100. My effortlessly social nature and positive attitude make it easy to meet people for romantic relationships.

101. My effortlessly social nature and positive attitude make it easy to meet people for platonic relationships.

102. I realize that everyone has the right to express their own point of view.

103. I accept people who think and believe differently than I do.

104. I respect the privacy and personal time for both me and the people I am in relationships with.

105. I keep an open mind and avoid being judgmental of others.

106. I know that good relationships take work and I am willing and able to happily put the work in.

107. My positive attitude provides strength and longevity for my relationships.

108. I take good care of myself, which helps me more easily attract good romantic and platonic relationships.

109. I always find time and ways to send positive messages to the people I love and care about.

110. I accept my loved ones for who they are and respect opinions that differ from my own.

111. I accept my loved ones for who they are and respect their choices that differ from my own.

112. I choose to only spend time in my life with supportive, positive, and uplifting people.

113. I make an effort to fully show up in my life and relationships.

114. I accept myself, which allows me to accept others.

115. I have a strong professional network that supports and contributes to my career success.

116. I make an effort to make gestures, big and small, to show love for my loved ones.

117. I have a romantic partner who fully supports and loves me, and I do the same for them.

118. I sometimes put my own desires aside and do things I don't want to do because I know it is important to a person I love.

119. I am always honest because trust is the foundation of my personal relationships.

Chapter 19
Affirmations for Taking Accountability and Responsibility

Now that you are aware of your core values, it is time to reframe the way you see your mistakes. No matter how conscious you are of your primary principles, you will make mistakes from time to time. However, mistakes on their own have no power to upset your mental balance or water down the progress you've made so far in building a healthy self-esteem; it is your rationalization of these mistakes that has a devastating effects on it.

Trying to live your life by the high, incomprehensible or unrealistic standards of your parents or society is one reason why you feel the way you do about mistakes. If you've always heard that you should not spend money on different personal products as they are vanity. You will find yourself feeling bad and regretting the few times you went against that rule and trying your best to avoid making such a "mistake" again.

You believe your critic when it tells you that the mistakes you've made are proof of how worthless you are. But the truth is, mistakes are inevitable, and you can't be perfect at all times—which is okay. You need to consciously work on how you view mistakes.

The best way to handle mistakes is to start seeing them as:

1. **A learning process:** stop ruminating on previous errors and berating yourself for them, reminding yourself that you should just have done things differently in the future. You've learned your lesson and are less likely to make the same mistake again. If you had known what you know now, you probably wouldn't have behaved in such a reckless manner in the first place. Don't stop yourself from being spontaneous or trying new things

because you fear failing or making a mistake. Your mindset should be: "if I get it wrong, I'll at least learn the right way to do it next time."

2. **A natural part of your life:** No one in life is perfect, which is natural. Feel free to express your thoughts and do what you want. If your words or actions disappoint someone or make you feel awkward, remember that you cannot always be perfect – you can either learn from the mistakes or move on.

The Affirmations

1. I am here today as a result of the actions I took yesterday.
2. If I don't like something in my life, I will change it.
3. Things only change when my actions change.
4. Things only change when my attitude changes.
5. I am responsible for all results that happen as a result of my actions.
6. I am in control of my thoughts and I choose to think positively.
7. I take the steps necessary to ensure that I am mentally free and clear enough to achieve achievement.
8. I take a step each day to grow wealth tomorrow.
9. The problems in my life are my fault and not the fault of others.
10. There is no such thing as luck, I create my own fortune.
11. My financial success depends on my own actions, not on the economy.

12. My financial success depends on my own actions, not on the political climate.

13. My financial success depends on my own actions, not my upbringing.

14. My financial success depends on my own actions, not others around me.

15. I control my own financial future and I choose prosperity.

16. I create my own reality with my own thoughts.

17. I can change the circumstances around me with right thought and action.

18. I believe I can, I am certain that I can, and I will.

19. I have complete control over my destiny.

20. I will do whatever it takes within moral and ethical reason to succeed.

21. When I do something wrong, I take action to make it right.

22. Talk is cheap; I grow my success by action and results.

23. I accept each new challenge as an opportunity for growth.

24. I take responsibility for who I am today.

25. I accept that I have created the bad as well as the good in my life.

26. If I don't like the way my life is going, it is my responsibility to do something about it.

27. I am responsible for changing my own life; nobody else can do it for me.

28. Takers lose and givers win. I choose to be a giver.

29. It is my own actions that decide my level of success in every aspect of my life.

30. When I provide value to others, I receive money and financial success in return.

31. I am responsible for how I perceive adversity.

32. I am responsible for how I respond to adversity.

33. I am in control of my reactions to situations around me.

34. I am in control of my habits and impulses.

35. I have the ability to create good new habits and get rid of bad old ones.

36. I am in control of my mood and temper and always find a positive way to react to any situation.

37. I alone am responsible for my happiness.

38. I am responsible for my career situation and will change it if I don't like it.

39. I accept that everything I did before has lead me to the point where I am today.

40. For better or worse, I am the sum total of all of my choices.

41. If I want my life to be better, I have to make better decisions.

42. My own health is in my control.

43. I accept responsibility for any failures in my life.

44. I learn from each apparent failure in my life.

45. I choose to reframe what seems like failure as a lesson I will use to succeed next time.

46. I am responsible for the income I generate.

47. No matter the outcome of my life, I either created it or allowed it.

48. No matter my circumstances, I have the ability to turn my life around.

49. I am responsible for using my unique gifts and talents to the maximum extent possible.

50. I take responsibility to learn the skills and gain the education I need to achieve success.

51. I take responsibility for listening to others when they offer constructive criticism.

52. I am responsible for my current financial situation and will take specific actions to change it if I am not happy about it.

53. I am solely accountable for the words that come out of my lips, which have the potential to negatively affect my professional or commercial performance.

54. I am responsible for the quality of the thoughts in my head.

55. The problems I perceive in my life are all fixable.

56. I adopt a wealth mentality to ensure my financial success.

57. I am responsible for my past.

58. I am responsible for my present.

59. I am responsible for my future.

60. I want to do all in my ability to guarantee that my future is as bright as possible.

61. I have total power over how I react to whatever occurs in my life at any time.

62. I have the power to turn any negative into a positive.

63. I have the power to perceive any negative as a positive.

64. The life that I am leading is the life that I chose through my actions.

65. It is my responsibility to take action to correct any mistakes that I have made.

66. I take responsibility for seeing the good in other people.

67. I choose to speak kindly about others.

68. I take responsibility for the price I must pay for success.

69. If there is a better way to do something, I realize I must discover this for myself.

70. I own my mistakes and take action to correct them.

71. I accept responsibility for my physical health and recognize that I alone can change it.

72. I accept responsibility for the status of my relationships and recognize that I alone can change them.

73. I am responsible for my feelings.

74. I am in control of my emotions.

75. I take action to maintain mental strength and clarity.

76. I own my energy.

77. I am responsible for where I am in my life, not my friends.

78. I am responsible for where I am in my life, not my family.

79. I am responsible for where I am in my life, not my government.

80. I am responsible for where I am in my life, not my boss.

81. I point the finger at myself first, not others.

82. I always find a way to make it happen.

83. I make results, not excuses.

84. Nothing holds me back from achieving success.

85. No one holds me back from achieving success.

86. Every single day I take at least one step to become more responsible over my own life.

87. I choose my response in the face of a challenge.

88. I cannot control other people and how they perceive me, but I can put my best foot forward at all times.

89. I am responsible for always being prepared.

90. I am responsible for saving money for financial emergencies.

91. I am responsible for my own fate and do not depend on anyone else to keep my ship afloat.

92. I am responsible for the people I allow into my life.

93. No one is coming to save me, I have to better my own life if I want it to be better.

94. I take full responsibility for the person I become tomorrow as a result of the actions I am taking today.

95. I choose to better my surroundings with right thought and action.

96. I live a life of no excuses and no regrets.

97. I am not responsible for the circumstances I was born into, but I am responsible for every action I've taken since.

98. I always have a choice.

99. My past negative experiences have no bearing on my future success.

100. I am strong and in complete control of my own destiny.

101. I am a shot taker and a way maker.

102. I depend only on myself for my financial success.

103. Anything I want, I can create.

104. I confront challenges head on.

105. Past failures and struggles are a result of my attitude, which I take full responsibility for now.

106. Past failures and struggles are a result of my actions, which I take full responsibility for now.

107. I recognize that if my life isn't going right, I am the one who needs to change.

108. Whenever I don't like the way I feel, I change the behaviors that cause those feelings.

109. I choose to adopt a positive attitude each and every single day.

110. I embrace change as an opportunity for growth.

111. I always see the positive in everything that happens.

112. I always see the positive in every person I cross paths with.

113. The problems in my life are all temporary and easier to overcome than I think.

114. I am the only one who can change how I feel inside.

115. I do not compare myself to others.

116. I understand that I am running my own race.

117. I take responsibility for remaining humble and true to myself as my wealth increases.

118. I replace scattered thinking with specific goals to improve my life.

119. I refuse to engage in self-pity.

120. I do not manipulate others by trying to get them to feel pity for me.

121. When under pressure, I maintain my cool and composure.

122. I am flexible and resourceful when things don't go my way.

123. I am social and friendly and take initiative in social situations.

124. I have a healthy social life that helps keep my mind on positive things.

125. I fill each of my days with joy and laughter.

126. I replace thoughts of self-pity with concern for others.

127. I am responsible for providing the service to others that leads to my own wealth.

128. There is always money to be made, and I will not let external circumstances control my fate.

129. I replace impatience with persistence and hard work.

130. I am honest, and people are honest with me.

131. I take action to ensure that I am always full of energy and vitality.

132. I wake up each day feeling optimism, hope, and love.

133. I can and will change any situation that I don't like.

134. I am always open to change and embrace it.

135. I accept assistance from others when I am in need of it.

136. I seek answers when I don't already know them.

137. I am open to the idea that someone else may know more than me.

138. I am open to the idea that someone else may know better than me.

139. I am responsible for making every moment of every day fulfilling.

140. I move forward past fear when it arises.

141. I am confident and optimistic about my future.

142. I am passionate about my life, present and future.

143. I realize that every decision I've made up to this point has led me to where I am right now.

144. I keep my mind fixed on positive and uplifting things.

145. I guard my mind and only allow positive thoughts and images to enter it.

146. It can be done, and I can do it.

147. I don't let anything stop me from moving towards my goals.

148. What I see in my mind, I create in my life, so I take full responsibility for my life vision.

149. When I feel frustration, I calmly find a way forward.

150. When I need assistance or support, I seek it.

151. I offer help and support when I am able to.

152. I am reliable and dependable.

153. I keep my promises to others.

154. I take my commitments seriously.

155. I own my reputation and every part I played in creating it.

156. I am responsible for keeping my mind in a happy state.

157. What I perceive to be problems in my life can all be used to my advantage.

158. Anything that is wrong, I can make right.

159. There are no limitations to what I am capable of

160. I am a good steward of my finances.

161. I am responsible for responsible spending.

162. I always live within my financial means.

163. I am deliberate about filling my time with activities that push me forward.

164. I am deliberate about filling my time with activities that I enjoy.

165. I am intentional about spending my time with positive people that I love.

166. I alone control my attitude about money, success, and prosperity.

167. Instead of living on auto-pilot, I take direct control over my outcomes.

168. I choose to seek and find opportunities instead of obstacles.

169. I seek joy; therefore, I find joy.

170. I seek love; therefore, I find love.

171. I seek success; therefore, I find success.

172. For the sake of success, I am prepared to set my ego aside and do whatever it takes.

173. I am responsible for acting with maximum efficiency and efficacy.

174. It is up to me to improve my skills as needed.

175. My financial success is not controlled by big corporations or big government.

176. I am willing to pay the short-term price for long-term success.

177. I accept the consequences for all of my actions.

178. I am prepared to be the first to provide a helping hand if someone needs it.

179. I always pay it forward.

180. I make the first move, and don't wait for others to.

181. I am strong enough to overcome any and every obstacle I face with grace.

Chapter 20
Affirmations for Self-Confidence

The biggest contributor to success and happiness is the ability to be yourself - to boldly display your personality and make choices that are faithful to your own beliefs. It comes from making a positive difference in the world by using your particular talents. It's important to stand out and make your voice heard, even if what you're about to say will be controversial. Always remain true to yourself no matter what. These things are all indicative of the confidence that allows people to get ahead in their careers, enjoy amazing personal relationships, and acquire a high self-esteem and personal inner peace.

So many of us are afraid of making connections with others for fear of rejection, thinking that when people love us, we will love ourselves, and if people accept us, we will be confident—when it is the other way around. When we love ourselves, people will love us. And if we are confident, people will accept us. It all boils down to confidence.

We are all born with confidence, but over time, as we transition through adolescence and adulthood, rejections, difficulties, and cruel people of the world we encounter growing up whittle away at it, causing social anxiety, unhealthy self-criticism, and feelings of inadequacy. And while we go about our daily lives, we are frequently unaware of the negative ideas and sentiments that are ingrained in our subconscious, which further undermines our self-confidence, causing even further psychological damage to our psyches.

To regain your self-confidence and believe that you are sufficient, you must first believe in yourself by retraining and reprogramming your brain. The use of affirmations is a highly efficient method of doing this. Affirmations can quite literally rewire your mind, by physically affecting the neural pathways in your brain. Affirmations, when spoken coupled with the feeling one would feel if they honestly believed them to be true, can be extremely powerful tools in improving and changing your life.

If you would like to them as meditation, before you begin, find a quiet place where you will remain undisturbed for the entire length of the audio. Then, remove all distractions. Turn off your phone, eliminate as much noise as possible, close the door to where ever you are, and alert anyone around you not to disturb you for the next two hours. When you're ready to begin, find a comfortable position, either sitting up or laying down, and be sure to remove all physical tension from your body.

Choose a position comfortable enough for you to allow the muscles of your body to relax but that will also ensure you stay awake. Many people like to sit with their legs crossed and their hands resting palms up or down on their knees. Some people prefer to lay on their backs, with their palms up by their sides. Choose whichever is best for you.

Then, once you are settled into position, you can either choose a spot to look at and drop your eyelids and soften your gaze; or you can close your eyes altogether. Begin clearing your mind of all past, present, and future thoughts and worries and deepen your relaxed state by slowing your breathing to long breaths, fully inhaling then fully exhaling. When you feel you are adequately relaxed, let the words seep into your mind and your consciousness, or repeat them in your head at intervals.

It doesn't matter how you choose to meditate, as all of methods can be effective and make a noticeable difference in your state of mind and future success. With meditation through affirmations, you can not only consciously absorb these thoughts, but you can simultaneously subconsciously absorb them as well. The essential thing to remember is to maintain consistency. Whatever you do, make sure you do it every day—even multiple times a day if you have time.

You can begin your day with affirmations and end it with meditation and meditation. But just keep doing it. Change will not happen overnight. It will really take time to retrain your mind to think in a more productive manner, but I guarantee you that the work will be well worth it.

The Affirmations

1. I will never apologize for being my true self.
2. I am a strong and confident person.
3. I live my life unaffected by fear.
4. I live my life unaffected by doubt.
5. I can make it through anything.
6. Resilience and perseverance are part of who I am.
7. I have perfect health mentally, emotionally and physically.
8. No matter what happens, I can always make the best of it.
9. No matter what happens, I will always make the best of it.
10. I can have anything I want in this life.
11. I can do anything I want in this life.
12. I can become anything I want in this life.
13. My conscience is trustworthy, and I will lean on it for guidance and peace.
14. My views and opinions are all important and they have value to others and myself.
15. I speak up for what I believe in, regardless of what other people think.

16. I can become successful at anything I put my mind to.

17. I am unafraid to express my feelings.

18. I boldly express my thoughts.

19. All of my thoughts are rooted in self-confidence and love.

20. Where I am today is exactly where I am meant to be.

21. I only attract and allow amazing and loving people into my life.

22. I act as a magnet for wealth and success, attracting them to me.

23. I am worthy of all things that will lift me up and improve my life.

24. I attract love into my life by the power of the love I have for myself.

25. I own my weakness and mistakes with confidence and pride.

26. I know that everything will always work out for me in the end.

27. I possess wisdom, to the benefit of myself and others.

28. My inner self is not bound by the limitations of my physical body.

29. I deserve a bright and abundant future and it is coming my way.

30. I have the mental strength to handle all of life's challenges.

31. I live my life with certainty and confidence.

32. I have confidence in where I am and where I am going.

33. I am productive and efficient in all of my tasks that lead me towards my ultimate goals.

34. I have an abundance of talents that will serve to elevate my life in the best way possible.

35. I have an abundance of talents that will elevate the lives of others.

36. I am unapologetic about who I am.

37. I am unapologetic about what I can accomplish.

38. I have what it takes to achieve whatever I desire.

39. I will overcome any and all obstacles that try to stand in my way.

40. Success is just who I am.

41. Success is inevitable for me.

42. Nothing can ever keep me from achieving my dreams.

43. I am stronger than fear.

44. I am stronger than doubt.

45. Fear and doubt are not strong enough to discourage me from forging ahead.

46. I make the most of my talents and natural abilities.

47. I trust my internal wisdom to guide me towards prudent decisions.

48. I easily handle criticism and feedback with grace.

49. I love my talents no matter what others may think.

50. I am intelligent and attractive and this is how I am viewed by everyone.

51. I am fully comfortable in my own skin.

52. I believe in myself in a way that is palpable to others.

53. My skills and abilities will inevitably lead me to professional success.

54. I am respected and admired by others.

55. I do meaningful, important, and rewarding work.

56. I make significant contributions to the world in ways that only I can.

57. The work that I do with my natural talents positively impacts others around me.

58. I wholeheartedly believe in my ability to make a positive impact through my work.

59. I am capable of creating intelligent and effective plans for my future.

60. I attract wealth and prosperity in abundance.

61. The future is in my hands.

62. I pursue my deepest desires regardless of any resistance that may arise.

63. I love myself and every part of me, and others do too.

64. I am never a victim, and I always take control and responsibility over my life.

65. I can turn around any situation or circumstance for the better.

66. My circumstances are subject to the amount of faith and effort I put in to change them.

67. I easily find new ways of thinking and solving problems.

68. I am only in competition with myself.

69. I never give up on myself, no matter what.

70. I am more than good enough.

71. I am a decent person with a nice heart.

72. I commit to praising myself for who I am.

73. I am only critical of myself to the point where it is helpful.

74. Where ever I put focus and effort, I can see success.

75. I always hold on to my desires.

76. I consistently take action towards the realization of my dreams.

77. Everything that I try can work as long as I put work in.

78. My past does not hold any power over my present self-belief.

79. Everything that I need to accomplish my goals will come to me at the right moment.

80. Every opportunity can be an opportunity for advancement.

81. My high self-confidence will lead me down a very rewarding path of abundance.

82. I truly believe that all things will work themselves out for my benefit.

83. I am filled with courage and bravery.

84. My confidence results in an optimistic mindset in all situations.

85. I am at peace with my faith in myself and my abilities.

86. My confidence in myself strengthens and grows every single day.

87. I am an overcomer by nature.

88. I am a winner with a winner's mentality.

89. I possess infinite creative power and ability.

90. Right now, I am already a success.

91. I have no choice but to be successful.

92. Success is my only option.

93. My belief in myself inspires others to believe in themselves.

94. I inspire others around me to be the best version of who they are.

95. My potential is absolutely limitless.

96. I will never, ever quit.

97. I will never, ever give up.

98. I will never, ever stop short of my goals.

99. Persistence is an innate quality for me.

100. Perseverance is an innate quality for me.

101. Resilience is an innate quality for me.

102. I can adapt and overcome.

103. I am resourceful, and I always find the right tools, connections, and opportunities to better myself.

104. I have the intellect to come up with new strategies for solving any problem.

105. Every situation is an opportunity to bring forth my very best.

106. I easily let go of old thoughts patterns that are holding me back from being my absolute best.

107. I easily let go of unhealthy beliefs that are holding me back from being my absolute best.

108. Whatever it is, I can do it.

109. Whatever I do, I can do well.

110. I have the strength to make positive change.

111. I confidently make choices that will improve my life.

112. I have a positive mindset that benefits me in everything I do.

113. I am bold and confident.

114. I am optimistic and fearless.

115. I am in control of my life.

116. I am in control of myself.

117. I have the power to make things better.

118. I confidently embrace all of my imperfections.

119. I was born to be a success.

120. Everything that I do is aligned with my highest potential.

121. My confidence and belief in myself are always growing.

122. I am decisive and make good decisions with confidence.

123. My belief in who I am gives me motivation and energy.

124. I grow day by day through the fuel that is my self-confidence.

125. I move through my life with high self-confidence, and make and execute plans accordingly.

126. Doing my best comes easily to me.

127. I always act from an empowered place of confidence.

128. I always act from an empowered place of abundance.

129. I always act from an empowered place of strength.

130. Greatness is always my result.

131. I am willing and able to do whatever I need to do to see my dreams to fruition.

132. Feeling great about who I am is natural for me.

133. Doing my absolute best is all that I need to succeed.

134. I know that there are no limits on my success.

135. I know that there is no ceiling on my future.

136. I always act out of respect for myself no matter what.

137. I look forward to the amazing future that I have in store.

138. My best is yet to come.

139. I am loveable, and I am loved.

140. I will always make it to the other side.

141. I am a very self-disciplined person who knows how to accomplish what I want.

142. Making mistakes is normal, and I will not beat myself up over it.

143. I turn every mistake into a triumph.

144. I transform every negative into a positive.

145. I am a special being with talents that only I can express.

146. I believe in my ability to reach my desired outcome, no matter what things may look like.

147. My self-confidence is contagious and magnetic.

148. I will inevitably reach my highest potential.

149. I believe in the power of my dreams.

150. My confidence increases each and every single day.

151. I will always do what I set out to do, no excuses.

152. My confidence is unwavering.

153. I only seek to be my best self.

154. I have an immeasurable amount of potential for growth.

155. Today, I commit to building my self-confidence to even greater heights.

156. The more belief I have in who I am, the more other people believe in me.

157. I am entirely content with my skin and appearance.

158. I am totally at ease in my own skin.

159. Each day, I discover more about who I am and what is possible for me.

160. I take consistent productive action, and it is leading me to positive results.

161. Through my confidence, there is no limit on what I can accomplish.

162. Other people see my confidence as a part of who I am.

163. I can succeed in any environment.

164. I am very proud of my growth and excited about my prosperous future.

165. I am intelligent and skilled, but I know there is always more room for growth.

166. I am as confident in my personal morals and values and I am in my personal strengths and talents.

167. I always act in accordance with my ethics.

168. I am confident in my abilities, but I do not hold myself to impossible standards.

169. I love where I am and where I am going.

170. I am committed to moving ahead at my own unique pace.

171. I am unaffected by people who challenge my self-worth.

172. My self-discipline is an expression of my self-confidence in what I am striving to achieve.

173. All of my success flows from my confidence.

174. I have control over my life's outcomes and I take that control with confidence and boldness.

175. I possess the mental strength to get through anything.

176. I have the emotional resilience to come out the other side of any situation.

177. I am strong enough to turn any situation.

178. No matter what is happening, there is always something I can do to make it better.

179. I have the wisdom to choose what is best for me.

180. I have the mental clarity to make wise decisions in life and work.

181. Daily positive habits of thought continually lead me towards my best and most confident self.

182. I find confidence in my uniqueness.

183. Only I can express my gifts in my own special way.

184. My self-worth is determined by my identity inside, not my successes or failures.

185. I draw confidence from all the times that I persevered through hardships.

186. Momentary setbacks don't crush my self-esteem or confidence.

187. I will always remain committed to personal development.

188. I can achieve anything, even if it is beyond my grasp.

189. I have the persistence to overcome resistance.

190. Resistance in pursuit of my dreams is inevitable, and so is my ability to get past it.

191. Nobody can determine or limit who I am and what I am capable of accomplishing in this life.

192. I start each and every day by establishing my confidence and belief in myself.

193. When challenged, I stay committed to my values and my personal belief in myself.

194. My views and opinions matter and are held in high esteem by everyone around me.

195. I am confident enough to say no to situations or pressures that are not best for me.

196. I am not obligated to give in to other people's demands for my time and energy.

197. Though I am skilled and knowledgeable, I know when to seek help.

198. My confidence in myself makes it easy for me to share love with others.

199. I am a naturally positive person, fully aware of what I can accomplish.

200. I am always discovering new personal skills and talents.

201. All things are possible for me simply because I believe it to be so.

202. I have an ocean of creative ability within me.

203. I am confident enough to let go of anything or anyone that is not helpful for me.

204. Endless miracles are manifesting in my life.

205. I can express who I am easily and I have faith in my talent.

206. I always attract the very best of situations, people and opportunities.

207. I am brave, and my personal power is unlimited.

208. I am the creator of my own circumstances.

209. I have a steadfast faith in my innate abilities.

210. I will face and overcome all of my fears.

211. I handle pressure with focus, clarity, and calmness.

212. I always find the motivation needed to push through difficulties and pressure.

213. I am living out my highest calling for my life.

214. All of the prosperity and abundance that I crave is on the other side of my fears.

215. I have available to me limitless opportunities to advance my career.

216. My confidence in myself always shines through in an obvious way to others.

217. I am surrounded by new opportunities for advancement in my career.

218. My belief in myself makes me a great leader and motivator.

219. I am confident enough to accept what I cannot change.

220. I always feel a strong sense of calm and focus when taking on a new challenge.

221. I have no problem recognizing and working to improve my flaws.

222. Others are amazed by how easily I handle tough situations.

223. I immediately squash negative thoughts before they have the chance to grow bigger.

224. I will create a beautiful life for myself.

225. I can take on any leadership role with ease and comfort.

226. My self-confidence allows me to stand out from others.

227. My success and upward mobility are inevitable.

228. My mind is growing stronger each and every day.

229. I am a continual source of inspiration for others on how to believe strongly in who you are.

230. I always operate out of abundance, strength, security, and positivity.

231. I consciously let go of habits that are no longer serving me in my life.

232. I am ready for any challenge that comes my way.

233. I take consistent and deliberate actions that bring me closer to my goals.

234. Through my profound self-confidence, I continue to live my life with purpose and motivation.

235. My confidence always gives me a chance to make a comeback.

236. I understand that life is a journey, and I am always growing.

237. Every word I speak comes from a confident and capable version of myself.

238. My past failures are nothing but fuel for my future successes.

239. I can adapt to or change any circumstance.

240. As my beliefs about myself change, my world and experience also begin to change.

241. My potential has no limits.

242. I will accomplish whatever I desire.

243. Success is so easily drawn to me because I believe in myself.

244. I always bounce back from disappointments with even more confidence because it just makes me more determined.

245. I enjoy new challenges because it is an opportunity to sharpen my self-confidence.

246. I choose to live in confidence over fear.

247. Today, I am declaring victory over my circumstances and everything that I face.

248. I walk into each day with the expectation of success and high achievement.

249. Establishing good habits is easy for me.

250. Eradicating bad habits is easy for me.

251. My confidence is obvious to others in the way that I carry myself.

252. I always walk around with my head held high.

253. Every step I take gets me closer to my ultimate destiny.

254. Amazing things lie ahead for me.

255. I confidently take the reins in my life to take control of my future.

256. My self-esteem is a source of optimism in the face of setbacks.

257. I choose to see myself as the best version of myself and I know that in time I will get there.

258. I have strong and beneficial habits that steer me closer in the direction of my goals.

259. I never operate out of desperation because I know my value.

260. I have an inner compass that I trust to guide me to the right decisions.

261. I believe in myself and all that I am able to do.

262. I am prepared and destined to succeed.

263. I put forth excellence because I am worthy of excellence.

264. Extremely high levels of success await me.

265. I have an endless amount of positive qualities and talents.

266. I know I am a winner on the inside and the world can see it on the outside.

267. I ignore naysayers and simply continue moving along my own unique path.

268. My priorities are strongly in place, and I trust myself to follow through and commit to them.

269. I am solely responsible for the way I feel.

270. I have the self-assurance to give credit and praise to other people in my life where credit and praise are due.

271. The way that I talk to myself will always be positive and kind.

272. I remain confident in myself even when I see others succeed.

273. I have a "can do" and a "will do" attitude in pursuit of my dreams.

274. I have a champion's mindset and a winning belief system.

275. I perform well under pressure.

276. Everything I have to offer serves a unique and excellent purpose.

277. I move excitedly in the direction of nervousness because it means I am challenging myself to grow.

278. I have full confidence that everything difficult now will soon get easier in the future.

279. My lowest moments are not a reflection of who I truly am.

280. I am able to release my anxiety with confidence and focus on the moment.

281. I fully accept responsibility for all of my actions.

282. I have no problem apologizing for my mistakes and admitting my faults.

283. My confidence allows me to see the best in every single circumstance.

284. I am strong in the face of loss because I know ultimately things are working out for my benefit.

285. I am capable of leading myself and leading others to success.

286. The best things will come to me at the right time and at the right moment.

287. I have the skill to gracefully handle inner conflict.

288. I have the skill to gracefully handle external conflict.

289. What other people say about me does not shape who I am.

290. I am not the sum of other people's opinions.

291. Only I have the power to mold my self-image and self-worth.

292. I do what I say, and I say what I mean.

293. I am confident in what I bring to the table in all situations.

294. My self-assurance shows itself nonverbal and verbal ways.

295. There is a reason for everything and I know that there is a greater purpose for me.

296. I accept my circumstances as they are, as I work to change the parts I can control.

297. When people try to tear me down with their words, it only makes me better.

298. When people try to tear me down with their actions, it only makes me better.

299. I am able to consistently perform at my best regardless of how I feel.

300. I can change my thoughts and feelings at any time.

301. I can be confident in any and every situation I choose.

302. The confidence I have in myself makes other people confident in me.

303. My belief in myself is strong enough to withstand criticism from others.

304. I am in control of my thoughts, and, therefore, I am in control of my actions.

305. I am in control of my actions, and, therefore, I am in control of my outcomes.

306. I am in control of my outcomes, and, therefore, I am in control of my life.

307. I always make plans in expectation of a positive future.

308. I refuse to settle in any area of my life.

309. I visualize my future self as an unstoppable success.

310. The more confident I feel, the easier it is to be confident.

311. I have unstoppable momentum in the direction of my goals.

Chapter 21
Affirmations for Increasing Productivity and Improving Decision Making

Close your eyes. Imagine you're in a room where things are everywhere. It's supposed to be a bedroom, but with every single surface and furniture item covered, it's hard to tell. All around the room are heaps of filthy clothing in every corner, empty boxes on the floor, dirty dishes strewn about, a ball of wrinkled bedding on top of an unmade bed, unorganized paperwork covering the surface of what is intended to be a work desk, and everything is disorganized and out of control.

Everywhere you look, you see something that's supposed to be clean, folded, in a closet, or in a drawer. But it's not. And this is the room that you must sleep in and do work in. How does it make you feel? Stressed? Overwhelmed? Irritable? Confused? When our space is cluttered, it's hard to get things done and even harder to think straight. Our brains are no different.

Modern times have countless things constantly competing for our attention, demanding our focus, and ultimately taking up our mental space: calls, text messages, social media, phone notifications, pop-ups, media, news, and advertisements, just to name a few. And that's on top of the concerns and responsibilities that go along with everyday life. All of this together contributes to the cacophony of noise in our heads. With all these things constantly swirling through our brains, it's no wonder that focus and productivity are so difficult to achieve, and brain fog has seemingly become the norm.

Having a clear understanding of what to do but being unable to do it for whatever reason may be quite frustrating. You can't manage to keep your gaze fixed on the work at hand long enough to focus and accomplish it. You are unable to make choices since your mental clarity is insufficient. You are unable to be productive. Your low level of productivity has a negative impact on your self-esteem. You are unable to find mental tranquility. The next thing that's going to happen, not happen, or go wrong is clouding your ability to think clearly and rationally.

How can you mentally get back on track? By taking time away from all the noise and reprogramming your brain and resetting your mindset to make you feel calm, confident, optimistic, focused, and productive.

Your mindset makes all the difference. We often don't even realize the psychological and practical damage being done by disempowering negative thoughts rooted in our subconscious. In addition to causing feelings of helplessness and hopelessness that ding your self-confidence, negative thoughts also make you not want to take action towards your goals, a surefire way to eliminate all chance of success. That's why training your brain with intention can easily be the difference between attaining success and happiness, and not attaining success and happiness.

The use of affirmations is a highly efficient method of doing this. Affirmations can quite literally rewire your mind by physically affecting the neural pathways in your brain. Affirmations, when spoken coupled with the feeling one would feel if they honestly believed them to be true can be extremely powerful tools in improving and changing your life.

The Affirmations

1. Whatever I need to do, I do it now because the only time I have is the present moment.

2. My best future begins today with my current actions.

3. I am confident because I keep my promises to myself.

4. I like the satisfaction I get from accomplishing a job that I set out to achieve.

5. I do not give in to fear disguised as procrastination.

6. I am a well of wisdom, getting wiser every day.

7. I am clear on where I'm going, and clear on how to get there.

8. I make decisions based on my ultimate vision.

9. I prioritize what's necessary for the future over what's easy for right now.

10. I am okay feeling uncomfortable now so that I can feel comfortable later.

11. I unapologetically say no to things that are not in line with my goals and vision for myself.

12. I unapologetically say no to people that are not in line with my goals and vision for myself.

13. Although I am unstoppable, I take rest when needed.

14. I know the distinction between well-needed rest and laziness.

15. The sooner I complete a task, the sooner it is off my mind.

16. I am always learning from people about how to be more productive in my job.

17. I do what's best for me, without worrying about other people's opinions.

18. My environment is clean and organized, and supports my productivity.

19. I start today because some day never comes.

20. I focus on my personal priorities without guilt or shame.

21. I maintain simplicity in all areas of my life, which keeps my mind clear.

22. I am always growing and transforming for the better through the changes of life.

23. If I just start a project, the "how" always comes to me.

24. I do not need to know all the answers to get started.

25. My confidence, curiosity, and problem-solving skills show me that I have the ability to learn as I go along.

26. I work quickly and efficiently towards my goals.

27. I am able to stay focused on the task in front of me until it is complete.

28. I intuitively break down larger tasks into smaller, manageable pieces to avoid overwhelm.

29. I always have a clear list of things I need to get done.

30. I keep my mind clear by keeping my to do list on paper, not in my head.

31. I recruit the assistance of others to achieve my objectives.

32. I am a master delegator.

33. I'm proud of myself because I do what I say I'm going to do.

34. I can remain focused on the task at hand even in a room full of distractions.

35. My focus comes from within and I can tap into it where ever I go.

36. I maintain a distraction free work zone.

37. I know that when I really want to get something done, I can finish any task.

38. I'm not one to get mired down in the finer points.

39. I find it easy to zero in on something that needs doing.

40. I never spend too much time on a single task.

41. I know when it is time to move forward to the next step.

42. I know how to let good enough be good enough, and move on.

43. I pay attention to detail while maintaining my momentum.

44. I find it easy to focus on the target I have set for myself.

45. I can easily shift focus when necessary to accommodate changes while maintaining momentum.

46. My focus is unbreakable.

47. I put in the work now for the benefit of my future self.

48. I naturally know what to do to make my workflow more efficient.

49. Through the power of delegation, I am able to get many tasks completed at the same time.

50. I always maintain a high quality of work, no matter the caliber of task before me.

51. I can think my way out of any difficult problem.

52. I work with people who share my commitment to competence and excellence.

53. My work environment is full of great people who are dedicated to good work and success.

54. When I grow weary, I am grateful to have a team of people I can rely on.

55. I know there is more than one way to skin a cat so I do not get hung up on one particular strategy.

56. I quickly and seamlessly adapt to changes in strategy.

57. If something does not work, I quickly move on without missing a beat.

58. My diligence and focus serve as a great example to others.

59. I am productive, but I enjoy my work at the same time.

60. I do what's best for the long term, not just the short term.

61. Once I get the ball rolling, I become unstoppable.

62. My attention is only on what I am working on in this exact moment.

63. When a project gets started, it becomes easier for me to gain momentum in other projects.

64. My success in one area of my life helps me to have success in other areas of my life.

65. Getting items crossed off my to-do list is one of my favorite feelings.

66. I am a master of getting things done.

67. I feel calm when I am focused.

68. I pick and choose what projects and events are best for me to take on, rather than saying yes to everything.

69. When I set a goal, I move forward with confidence even though I may not know everything.

70. Perfectionism is just another form of procrastination.

71. I don't need all the answers to take the first step.

72. I know how and when to say no, which prevents me from spreading my time and energy too thin.

73. My body is my most important tool for a healthy, successful life so I take great care of it.

74. I think fast on my feet and solve unexpected problems quickly.

75. I am a quick critical thinker and can always find the right solution.

76. I am able to collaborate with different types of personalities to achieve the task at hand.

77. When I start something, I finish it.

78. The answers to my problems unfold as I take action.

79. I live a life driven by my commitments, not my emotions.

80. When it comes to time management, I am a dependable and prompt individual.

81. I make fast decisions, allowing me to work efficiently towards the goal at hand.

82. I finish what I start.

83. My future is decided by the work I put in now.

84. My future is decided by the decisions I make now.

85. I have the power to commit to a project and see it through until the very end.

86. I have my own system of organization that works wonders for me.

87. I prioritize proper sleep and healthy eating to give my mind and body sufficient fuel.

88. I always wake up with a plan for the day and execute accordingly.

89. I am known for my follow through.

90. I am known for my ceaseless dedication.

91. My excellent work ethic is well-known among my peers.

92. I cherish my time and make good use of it.

93. I value my energy and use it wisely.

94. I have a natural talent for managing my time wisely so that I complete everything I set out to do.

95. My time is valuable, and I spend it in a way that aligns with my life goals.

96. I know when it is time to start a project, when it is time to shift and when it is time to stop.

97. I am successful because I find it easy to balance my commitments.

98. I know how to make observations to see what is working, so I can do more of it.

99. I know how to make observations to see what is not working, so I can do less of it.

100. I always leave myself ample to time to complete the task at hand.

101. I eliminate unnecessary stress by starting projects early.

102. I am conscious of not taking on so much to where I compromise what is already on my plate.

103. I am aware of the areas I can improve on and do my best to get better.

104. When I feel like I hit a wall, I keep pushing until I get through it.

105. I am proactive about making changes in my schedule as needed to ensure both my productivity and my happiness.

106. I am aware enough to know when I need to do something and when someone else can be delegated to do something.

107. It feels good to sometimes trust others to make decisions.

108. My time is my most important commodity, and I do everything in my power to protect its value.

109. My discipline allows me to resist temptation when something important needs finishing.

110. As soon as I know all the information I need for the next step, I make a decision and act with haste.

111. I am 100% clear on what I want out of life.

112. I don't have to feel pressured to make every decision immediately.

113. If something comes up that I don't yet know how to approach, it is okay to take some time to find a solution.

114. I know how to be patient with myself when needed and act with urgency when needed.

115. Success may be achieved via a variety of means, and I want to discover my own without regard for the views of others.

116. Action and momentum will get me to my goal. Perfection and over-planning will not.

117. I deserve to rest without guilt after periods of productive work.

118. I put in the work to create the future I want and deserve.

119. What I put in, I will get out.

120. I know what I want and know how to achieve whatever I set my mind on.

121. I only focus on whichever task is in front of me at that moment.

122. I speak up for myself when I want or need something.

123. I listen to my intuition and trust it to guide me to the best decisions for me.

124. I know when it is time to consult another person in order to work through an obstacle quickly, efficiently, and confidently.

125. Though I sometimes seek the counsel of others, ultimately the final say is mine.

126. Just because other people don't agree with my decision, it doesn't make it wrong.

127. There is profound wisdom in me and all around me that helps me make solid decisions.

128. I am confident that I will make the right choice.

129. I am capable of making difficult decisions within a reasonable amount of time.

130. I know how long is too long to deliberate on a decision.

131. I approach new choices with confidence.

132. I know how to make decisions that are mutually beneficial to everyone involved.

133. I make decisions with logic and empathy.

134. I am capable of finding a good balance between rational thinking and creative thinking.

135. I am determined to complete what I have started.

136. I take my commitments seriously.

137. I am capable of finding my way through difficult tasks.

138. When I do my best, I can let go, knowing I did all I could do.

139. I am a leader and can guide myself and others toward success.

140. I revel in the sense of accomplishment I feel when I finish a project.

141. My self-confidence and self-esteem increase with each project I finish.

142. I believe in my choices and stand by my decisions.

143. I am comfortable with making important decisions.

144. I welcome criticism with grace and take action on the feedback I receive.

145. I am self-aware and conscious enough to know what I need to do next.

146. I am intentional about my actions and make each move with progress in mind.

147. I will pass through this day with intent.

148. I know what I want out of my life and know what it takes to get there.

149. I have reasonable expectations of myself and others.

150. I know what matters most to me, and choose to focus my time and energy on that alone.

151. I don't have to do everything, I only do what matters.

152. I work more efficiently when I am well-rested, so I make good sleep a priority.

153. My healthy routines are essential to my ability to focus.

154. If I have an "off day," I know I can get back on track tomorrow.

155. I place boundaries around my work time so I can get things done.

156. I place boundaries around my work space so I can get things done.

157. It's more important for me to keep moving forward than to be perfect.

158. There is a time to think, and there is a time to act.

159. There is no such thing as perfect.

160. I am greatly rewarded for my discipline.

161. I am capable of creating excellent projects and products in my work and business.

162. I have a habit of excellence.

163. I succeed in everything I do.

164. I reap the benefits from my dedication to my commitments.

165. I do what it takes to see things through to the end so I can get the results I desire.

166. It's better to be imperfect in motion than to be perfect and still.

167. I am respected, revered, and sought after by my professional peers.

168. I am known for delivering consistently great results in my work.

169. I work smart, not just hard.

170. I do not have to do everything; I get help when I need it.

171. There are people who are ready and willing to help me with my problems, and I attract them easily.

172. I have great intuition for knowing what step to do next.

173. I trust my instincts and believe they will guide me to success.

174. Everything is solvable.

175. I make changes in my life for the better every day.

176. I get closer and closer to greatness with every step I take.

177. My organizational skills help me maintain control over my life.

178. I feel strong because I do what I set out to do.

179. I only focus on today's work, today.

180. I leave tomorrow's work for tomorrow.

181. I become more and more clear on my direction as I grow and learn from my mistakes as well as my successes.

182. I achieve more when I move forward with an imperfect plan, than when I don't move with a perfect plan.

183. I appreciate my work ethic and my ability to problem solve.

184. I can solve problems quickly, efficiently, and effortlessly.

185. I can quickly troubleshoot my way around any obstacle that comes up.

186. I become more and more clear on what I want as each day passes.

187. I can and will do whatever it takes to fulfill my destiny.

188. I will get out what I put in.

189. When something comes up that I haven't experienced before, I am patient with myself as I come up with a solution.

190. When I am stuck, I enlist the help of others more skilled than me.

191. I am skilled at finding people whose strengths supplement my weaknesses.

192. I know what I need and I trust what I know.

193. I am great at coming up with strategy and deciding the best next step forward.

194. I have the power to create new and innovative things.

195. I trust in my ability to make decisions that lead to productivity and prosperity.

196. I work actively on what I can control and release all cares about what I cannot.

197. I wake up every day, renewing and honoring my commitments to myself.

198. Action is the best source of motivation, so now I am an action taker.

199. I always move forward confidently on my projects and goals.

200. Ideas show up when I do, so I show up to put my work in towards my goals.

201. I am an endless well of creative ideas.

202. I have a calm mind, so solutions easily come to me.

203. I trust my plan of action, and move forward with confidence.

Chapter 22
Affirmations for Success

Having objectives is one thing, but achieving goals is quite another thing entirely. You may have the strong desire to quit abusing drugs for instance, learn a new skill, or become compassionate, but you may discover that those desires never become a reality. You will feel dissatisfied, helpless and unhappy because it is our natural inclination to grow. Creating the kind of life you want based on your core values strengthens your self-esteem.

Accepting yourself becomes easier when you are able to create changes and achieve your goals. As someone who is still struggling with poor self-esteem, you may keep finding reasons not to put in the amount of effort required like a lack of time, adequate information, or believing that success is out of reach. You can overcome these stumbling blocks by doing the following:

1. Make adequate plan

You will get confused or overwhelmed by the steps you have to take to reach your goals if you dive straight into them without a sufficient plan. Achieving your goal become easier when you take time to analyze and break it down into bits - the steps that will help you arrive. What are the skills, experience, resources or equipment you will need and how can you get them? Answering questions like these will make for a better plan and prevent you from getting stuck, frustrated, or confused halfway through achieving your goal.

2. Gather essential information

Of course, there is no way you can successfully achieve a goal if you lack the basic knowledge needed. However, stop using this as an excuse when you can find the necessary information by simply searching for it.

Sign up for training, find a mentor, read books, or carry out research on the internet.

3. Manage your time properly

Even if you gather essential information and make adequate plans, you will still be unable to achieve your goals if you never have extra time on your hands. What activities do you engage in every day? Take stock of your daily activities; you may find yourself guilty of allowing tasks that are less important overshadow the important ones.

Learn to prioritize: take care of the most important tasks first and leave the least important ones for later. For instance, you could move painting the house to the bottom of your to-do list and ascribe number one position to helping your kids with their homework. Creating a list of your daily tasks will help you know which ones to do away with to make space for better goals.

Another important (really) skill to develop is the ability to say no. Sort the requests into categories depending upon their urgency or reasonableness.

4. Imagine the worst

When you find yourself giving in to the fear of failure by not making any substantial effort to achieve your goal, ask yourself: "what's the worst that could happen?" So, you acquire the job and get fired in a matter of weeks because they discover that you are a flop, or you summon the courage to go on stage and give a presentation but end up not making any sense. Okay, that's the worst that could happen! You don't know for sure how it will turn out until you try. Besides, what if you lose the job? You get another job.

5. Stop trying to be perfect

You really should stop trying to be perfect. Remember that mistakes are inevitable and do not add to or take away your self-worth unless you let them. Do what you can at the moment, one step at a time. Hold on to your core values and don't give in to the pressure of living by other people's standards.

You can also apply the following techniques in addition to the above tips:

- **Visualize that you've already achieved your goals:** Practice visualizing the way you will look and act when you've achieved your goals. Create scenes in your mind in which you are in a satisfying relationship, no longer an alcoholic, learning how to code, have lost 50 pounds, more confident and doing whatever it is you want to. The act of visualization reprograms the negative way you see yourself in your mind and causes you to act out what you already have in your subconscious. Believe it or not, visualization is a very effective tool you can use to bring yourself closer to achieving your dreams. Remember poor self-esteem stems from seeing yourself as lesser than other human beings. It never crosses your mind for once that you are equal, so you keep choosing negative routes and negative people. Visualizing yourself differently can change it all.
How do you practice visualization? By simply finding a quiet spot that you can let yourself relax and simply breathe. Focus on breathing and playing the scenes you planned to visualize. Imagine yourself doing whatever you usually do every day—waking up, brushing your teeth and so on and then see yourself taking small, positive steps to achieve your goals. Definitely, distracting thoughts will come. The trick is to observe those thoughts without pursuing them and refocusing on the positive picture.

  Practice visualization at least twice a day, once in the morning and at night before you sleep.

- **Have someone who will be checking up on you**: Another helpful technique is to share your short or long-term goals with a friend or family member and ask them to check up on you every week or so. Let the person know the steps you have to take to reach your goals as well as the timeframe that each step will demand. You will be driven to stay committed to your goals as you will want to have a progressive report to give that friend or family member every week.

The Affirmations

1. I am constantly working hard and building my skill set to advance my professional success.

2. I do not judge my level of success by the amount of money I make, but rather by the level of satisfaction I have with my life.

3. I do not measure my success by the amount of money I earn, but the quality of people with which I surround myself.

4. I have a healthy work-life balance that promotes my mental and emotional health.

5. I show initiative and dedication by arriving to work early every day.

6. I possess the resiliency and fortitude to recover from my mistakes and move forward.

7. I enhance my life with hobbies and leisure activities outside of work that make me happy.

8. I have the courage and capability to conquer all the challenges that come my way.

9. I easily remain focused on completing my daily tasks.

10. I always have opportunities to be successful because I do my best.

11. I challenge myself to improve a little each day, which increases my chances of success.

12. I do not allow the fear of failure to stop me from chasing my dreams.

13. I overcome excuses and do whatever it takes to achieve my goals.

14. All of my perceived handicaps are actually gifts that make me and my story unique.

15. I am not happy because I am successful, I am successful because I am happy.

16. I banish doubt and hesitation in favor of confidence and action.

17. I'm on a mission to become the greatest version of myself possible.

18. I know that things don't have to be perfect in order for me to be successful.

19. I keep my eyes on my prize no matter what is going on around me.

20. I dress for success because presenting a good appearance makes me feel good.

21. I make an effort to maintain a professional look so that I can always make a good first impression.

22. I practice the skills I want to hone a little each day, so I become more proficient.

23. I cast a wide net and broaden my horizons to explore the various available opportunities.

24. I set realistic and achievable goals for myself that I am accomplishing with ease and happiness.

25. I constantly expand my knowledge by learning more every day through reading and research.

26. I have the willpower and self-control to finish tasks even when they present challenges or stress.

27. I possess the wisdom and courage to make decisions that will improve my life.

28. I experience more success in my career when I possess a positive attitude.

29. I am consciously creating a happy, well-rounded, and productive life for myself.

30. My physical performance is at a peak when my mental performance is also.

31. I focus on being happy, which is a key factor in achieving success.

32. I do not quantify my success by the material possessions I own, but by the happiness that I feel.

33. I seek out interesting side projects that help keep my mind happy and productive outside of work.

34. I ensure my personal happiness first and foremost, and as a result, personal success easily follows.

35. I possess strong leadership qualities.

36. I have the capacity to make a positive impact in this world.

37. I am always learning, always growing, and always improving in every area of my life.

38. I have the drive to follow through on my ideas and finish what I start.

39. I devote my time and attention to concentrating on the measures that will enable me to reach my objectives.

40. I am an achiever in every area of life.

41. The more I have, the easier it is for me to get even more.

42. I trust, know, and believe that my hard work always pays off.

43. I know that if I work hard, wealth, prosperity, and abundance will be the result.

44. Each day, I discover new ways I can become more successful.

45. I can gain power and use it wisely to help others.

46. Regardless of the situation, I will always keep the door open for new chances.

47. I will never stop growing my wealth and prosperity.

48. It is important to me that I perceive the world through the eyes of an entrepreneur to guarantee that I never miss an opportunity to generate money.

49. My growing prosperity opens new doors to greater opportunity.

50. I work hard now knowing that there is unlimited success for me ahead.

51. I deserve wealth and abundance for the hard work I put in.

52. Everything that I try to do, I am able to excel in.

53. My relationships are just as full as my bank account.

54. I am in love with the life that I am leading.

55. I am blessed and successful beyond measure.

56. Seeing new opportunities is easy for me.

57. I generate what I want, when I want it, and in the manner that I want.

58. I have a life that is balanced, whole, and amazing.

59. I am currently living my own personal definition of success.

60. I place no limits on what I can achieve and am willing to pay the price to get there.

61. I recognize that growth has a price and I am willing to pay it.

62. Abundance flows to me in unlimited amounts when I work hard to achieve it.

63. I can earn any amount of money I want by putting in the work.

64. I recognize opportunities and convert them into money and riches.

65. I am always on a quest for personal growth, which serves me in all areas of my life.

66. I move forward towards wealth without overthinking things.

67. I have a mind that is clear, alert, and focused, which helps me achieve success.

68. I have a well-rounded, successful life.

69. My mental peace is just as much an indicator of my success as my bank account.

70. Everything I do leads to more success for me.

71. I am proud of what I have achieved.

72. I can increase my streams of income whenever I so decide.

73. I multiply my success by working smarter, not harder.

74. We can all be wealthy if we work smart.

75. I always find a way to be successful no matter what.

76. My lifestyle is a reflection of the success I have attained.

77. Success is better when shared and I always find ways to share it.

78. I rejoice in the things I enjoy as a result of my work.

79. I spread happiness, joy, and abundance.

80. Helping others is always an opportunity for success and creating a better life.

81. I have everything it takes to seize every opportunity.

82. Every business I create will flourish because I will do what it takes to ensure that.

83. I am swift to action, and my bank account reflects that.

84. I'm living the life of my dreams thanks to the help of others.

85. I can afford anything I want because I have put in the work to build wealth.

86. I feel satisfied each day knowing I am working to secure my future.

87. Wealth and abundance are available in unlimited amounts for people like me who are willing to work for it.

88. I can build and create my dream home.

89. I can build and create my dream lifestyle.

90. I can build and create my dream life.

91. I am proud of the life that I have created for myself.

92. When I put in work, there is no limit to what I can achieve.

93. I grab opportunities and turn them into wealth magnets.

94. I am the kind of person who succeeds in everything I do.

95. I am comfortable with money and wealth because I've earned it.

96. At the end of the day, hard effort is always rewarded.

97. I can't lose because I do what it takes to win.

98. I am successful, resourceful, and efficient because I focus on solutions instead of dwelling on problems.

99. I constantly expose myself to new ideas, unique viewpoints, and different ways of approaching situations.

100. I am complementary and supportive of those who I work with.

101. I choose to focus on solving problems and finding solutions.

102. I effortlessly feed my body only with things that make me feel good, productive, and mentally alert.

103. Everything I put in my body makes me feel healthier and happier in life and work.

104. I have a clear vision and always maintain sight of my goals.

105. I easily come up with action plans to accomplish my goals successfully and effortlessly.

106. Whenever I'm faced with a problem I cannot yet solve, a mentor appears to help me through.

107. I solicit the counsel of experienced people who can help guide me on the right path.

108. I take pride in maintaining a professional, put together appearance.

109. I have control over the urge to procrastinate.

110. I effortlessly meet deadlines in a timely manner without stress or anxiety.

111. A significant part of my personal success is giving back to others in a positive, impactful way.

112. I communicate well with the people I work with.

113. All my goals are within reach.

114. I always seek the opportunity to learn and grow more within my field.

115. I am grateful to work with people I respect for their integrity.

116. I am grateful to work with people I admire for their achievements.

117. I use my talents to teach and help others to find success.

118. I follow bliss, not money.

119. I take pride in preparing and educating myself thoroughly so I can do my best.

120. I take advantage of opportunities for professional development without hesitation as they arise.

121. I constantly seek opportunities to further my education and knowledge in my career.

122. I love to get out of my own comfort zone because I know that is where growth happens.

123. I dream big and act fast.

124. My positive habit of regular physical activity has a positive impact on my work.

125. I have the ability to become the top, most successful person in my field.

126. My positive attitude allows me to get more work done—faster, better, and more efficiently.

127. My enthusiastic attitude drives my success in work and boosts my motivation.

128. I effortlessly remain focused and stay on task in my work.

129. I am proud of how far I have come on my professional journey, and I look forward to going even further.

130. I approach each day with purpose and passion.

131. I take charge of my life, and I take responsibility for its outcome.

132. I have the energy to work tirelessly to accomplish the goals that I set for myself.

133. I set a positive example for others through my strong work ethic.

134. I have a clear vision of my own personal version of success.

135. I consistently take the necessary steps for me to reach my goals.

136. My strong and effective communication skills contribute to my career success.

137. I embrace challenges fearlessly and never back down from them.

138. I am constantly checking off goals that I've achieved.

139. My consistent accomplishments make me feel happy, proud, and fulfilled.

140.   I think ahead and plan wisely for long-term success in addition to short-term.

141.   I put my full effort and energy into everything I do.

142.   I keep up with innovation in my field so I can remain ahead of the curve.

143.   I always master new technologies in my field so I can remain competitive.

144.   I create a positive environment for those I work with.

145.   My energy motivates people to work harder, which contributes to our collective success.

146.   I usually surround myself with things that excite and inspire me to continue my journey.

147.   My positivity boosts my energy levels and aids me in being more productive.

148.   I am proud to have built a meaningful career that helps contribute to the happiness of others.

149.   The advantages of having a happy view on life are continually being reaped in unexpected ways.

150.   I devote my time to complete projects that I start, and my efforts are paying off.

151.   I look forward to working and enjoy what I do.

152.   I take advantage of my personal strengths to help me make progress every day.

153. I am unafraid to push myself and I respond well to professional challenges.

154. No matter what, I remain disciplined and keep my eyes on the prize.

155. I am capable of succeeding beyond my wildest imagination in any career path.

156. My hopeful and optimistic outlook makes it easy for opportunities to find me.

157. I am fueled by a sense of purpose, which ensures my success in my endeavors.

158. I feel like a success because I love every part of my life.

159. I commit myself fully to my projects until they are completed with excellence.

160. I am a go-getter, and I take action and go after the things I want in my life.

161. Whatever I see in my mind or visualize in my life, I can attract and attain.

162. I am constantly getting better every day because of my commitment to constant improvement.

163. I go for what I want and expect the best, regardless of the potential outcomes.

164. The success of others inspires and motivates me.

165. I have incredible self-discipline that causes success in every area of my life.

166. My good attitude and ambition move me closer to prosperity every day.

167. I happily put in time on a consistent basis to realize my goals.

168. My efforts are worth it, and I am constantly rewarded for my persistence.

169. I attain better results in my work by staying motivated.

170. I am surrounded by positive, encouraging people who want success as much as I do.

171. I have the ability to make wise decisions quickly and follow through with them quickly.

172. I stay on top of my work and start and finish things earlier than planned.

173. I have full faith and unshakeable confidence that I am able to achieve my goals.

174. I have wonderful friends, family, and relationships, which is its own success.

175. I trust my intuition and follow my gut instincts because they are always right.

176. I only see success in my future, and success is my only option.

177. My past achievements motivate me to keep pushing forward to achieve even greater things.

178. I keep my work space clear, which keeps my mental space clear for maximum productivity.

179. I make terrific first impressions on everyone I encounter because of my positive attitude.

180. I possess the necessary traits needed for upward mobility in society and life.

181. I am conscious of the way I mentally and emotionally approach every goal.

182. I know that my attitude has a direct correlation to my performance and outcome.

183. My positive attitude allows me to excel in endeavors both inside and outside of work.

184. I concentrate on big picture thinking and don't get held down by small details.

185. I always go above and beyond the call of duty, for which my efforts are always rewarded.

186. I lead by example and cultivate a positive culture in my workplace.

Chapter 23
Affirmations for Building, Keeping, and Growing Wealth

What makes the wealthy, wealthy? What makes the successful, successful? And why is it that the rich seem to get richer and the more successful people become even more successful? It all stems from the mind. Your actions will never go where your thoughts have not already been, and the fact is that wealthy people think differently. The millionaire mindset begins with a positive relationship with money and a positive view of money. It often requires eliminating the negative programming around money that has been put into our heads by our parents, friends, society, and the media....

"Money is the root of all evil."

"Rich people are dishonest and selfish."

"It's bad to want to be rich."

"There's not enough for everyone to be rich."

"Everyone who's rich either got lucky, cheated their way there, or was born that way."

"It's not possible for people like me to be rich."

Thoughts and embedded beliefs like these repel wealth and make it impossible to reach greater financial heights. Wealthy people know that the desire to be rich is simply the desire to maximize their potential, gain the resources to allow them and their loved ones to live their best lives. It can help those in need on a large scale in a way only money can do and provide products and services that are so valuable and helpful that consumers are happy to exchange money for them. The wealthy know that a healthy desire for money, a positive relationship with money, honest work, and proper stewardship over your finances is the best way to get there.

The road to wealth and success for most is often impeded by a poverty mentality shaped by unconscious programs in our minds. We are wired to carry out the ideas put in our heads a long time ago by outside influences. But a poverty mentality is not just about negative thoughts and beliefs about money. It is about being trapped with an "I can't" attitude. It's a thought process that often blames others for the present circumstances, whether your spouse, your boss, the president, or the economy.

Poverty is a state of mind, and people who remain in financial poverty are the type who always find reasons why they can't. They have an endless supply of excuses, stories about what they should have done, and rants about what they could have done if it weren't for some external force outside of themselves they blame for their shortcomings and unrealized dreams.

Successful people with the millionaire mindset take responsibility and control over themselves, their actions, and their outcomes, which in turn gives them control over their lives. While others talk about doing things, they take action and never blame others or external forces for their circumstances. They don't wait around for luck, the economy to turn around, that perfect business partner to walk into their lives, their bank account to magically double, etc. They change what they don't like and believe they can do so.

They are leaders, who take control and lead themselves, businesses, projects, and other people on the path towards success. They are decisive and like to be in control rather than sitting on the sidelines because they are actually very confident in their ability to make good decisions with positive outcomes.

Whether we like it or not, we are all leaders: it's just a matter of whether we are good or bad leaders. Leadership begins at home, so to be a leader, you need to be a leader of yourself first and foremost. This begins by becoming a master at your time management and owning your productivity. It also means taking pride in your work and bringing excellence to everything you do on every level, as you make your climb to the top, no matter who is looking.

People destined for success have good, foundational habits that they apply in their daily lives, whether that means showing up early to a meeting, being the first to volunteer for a task at work, or taking small daily action steps toward their entrepreneurial dreams. It is from these basic habitual actions and a foundational attitude that everything flows.

And while successful people make a lot of money, they know that material riches are not the only important type to have. They know that wealth reaches far beyond money alone. Success is about more than financial success. So they prioritize the people in their lives by balancing work with family, relationships, recreation, and their personal lives. They are cheerful givers with an attitude of service within their work, and an attitude of charity outside it.

Sometimes, it seems that we're doing all the right things and taking all the right actions to move toward our goals, but we still can't see progress. It is your frame of mind that makes all the difference. Disempowering ideas will make you feel powerless and hopeless, and they can be difficult to overcome. And since these negative beliefs are often anchored in our subconscious, we are often unaware of the psychological harm we are causing ourselves. But training your brain to be positive, optimistic, and expect good things to happen can be the difference between seeing success and not seeing it.

It's time to think big and stop being plagued and crippled by limiting beliefs. There is limitless potential and unlimited abundance for everyone who desires success and wealth. It is time to join those with the millionaire mindset. Hard work always pays off, and there are unlimited opportunities to create wealth. Anyone and everyone can become successful, including you.

It's time to adopt the thought processes of the rich and use affirmations to drive these thoughts into your subconscious. Affirmations will help you develop the right attitudes and habits for success. Because from new thoughts will spring new actions that will lead you on the right path to wealth in every area of your life.

The Affirmations

1. I have unlimited income potential.
2. I have multiple streams of income.
3. I make passive income as a result of the wise investment decisions I make.
4. I am creative and use my creativity to solve people's problems, generating wealth.
5. I act on my creative ideas and turn them into wealth.
6. I know that the only way to true wealth is not to trade my time for money.
7. I know that the only way to true wealth is providing value to the marketplace.
8. I know that the only way to true wealth is to sell valuable products and services.
9. I know that the only way to true wealth is to have my own business.
10. I love my business because it puts me in total control of my income.

11. I sell valuable products and services that improve people's lives.

12. Selling is good because it helps people to solve their problems.

13. Selling is good because it provides unlimited income potential for me.

14. My business allows me to choose what I do with my time.

15. I have financial security because I constantly have money coming in from multiple sources.

16. I leverage my time and the time of others to multiply my productivity.

17. I know there is only so much time in the day, so I have a team of people working towards my goals.

18. Wealth comes to me daily through various sources.

19. I can create wealth whenever I want or need to.

20. I have wealth that will take care of my family for generations.

21. I am a magnet for prosperity.

22. All of my efforts result in income.

23. I am completely deserving of all of the money I make.

24. My goals are in alignment with the creation of wealth and prosperity.

25. My mind is in alignment with the creation of wealth and prosperity.

26. My spirit is in alignment with the creation of wealth and prosperity.

27. My actions are in alignment with the creation of wealth and prosperity.

28. The more I get, the more I give.

29. The richer I get, the richer I make others.

30. I will improve the service I provide to humankind every single day.

31. I am determined to provide the best product or service that I possibly can.

32. I invest money back into my business to constantly grow it.

33. I invest money back into my business to constantly improve it.

34. My bank account is filled with money and always growing.

35. I can create wealth and money on command, by providing or improving the service I provide to others.

36. I fulfill the needs of others and generate wealth in the process.

37. I allow myself to receive as much wealth as I deserve, which is unlimited.

38. I create prosperity and share it with others.

39. Nothing will stop me from creating as much wealth as possible.

40. The more I give, the more I seem to get.

41. It is my joy to share my wealth.

42. Sharing my money makes it multiply.

43. I am grateful for the freedom that my business affords me.

44. Wealth is a state of mind, so even if restarting from nothing, I can always rebuild it.

45. I do not hoard money because through its use, I achieve prosperity and liberty.

46. I satisfy greater needs of the people and bring greater wealth into my life in return.

47. I generate wealth by helping people get what they want.

48. I expect to be paid in proportion to the service I provide others, and I will gladly provide that service.

49. My business allows me to live my ultimate lifestyle.

50. I live my life with a win-win philosophy and generate wealth in a way both my customers and I will benefit.

51. I only increase my prices when I increase the quality or value of the product or service I provide.

52. I always bring my absolute best to whatever I do.

53. Every single task or position deserves my best and that is what I bring.

54. I am open to receiving as much wealth as I am blessed with.

55. There is an infinite amount of wealth to go around.

56. I trust that my hard work will always pay off some way, some day.

57. I am grateful for every person who plays a role in making my dreams a reality.

58. I treat everyone with respect who helps contribute to the realization of my vision.

59. I am diligent and responsible with my income no matter what level it is right now.

60. I save and invest my money at all times, at all income levels.

61. I have no limits for my life and wealth.

62. I know that real wealth exists in the mind and those who have it can create it with ease even if all their money is taken from them.

63. I can create material wealth without limit.

64. Despite my financial success, I always have time and energy for my most cherished relationships and hobbies.

65. I have the knowledge to create real wealth at any time that I want.

66. I give back with abundance in amazing ways, and it returns to me ten-fold.

67. I have an entrepreneurial mindset and live independently on my own terms.

68. I am creative and create wealth and prosperity through the creative process.

69. I have the ability to profitably monetize all of my ideas.

70. I am wealthy because I turn the ideas in my head into action.

71. I am always wealthy because wealth is a state of mind.

72. I can create money at will because my abundance lies in my creativity.

73. My business allows me to live a life of my choosing.

74. I only compete with myself in improving my own products and services.

75. Every single day is an opportunity to serve others and create wealth in the process.

76. Wealth flows into my life continuously and effortlessly.

77. I have the wisdom to make profitable investments with my money.

78. Serving others through charity requires wealth, and I generate wealth to help the unfortunate.

79. We all have the right and ability to be wealthy; we just have to ask for it.

80. I speak up and make my needs and desires known, so I get them.

81. No matter the career, profession, or business I choose, I will rise to the top and be prosperous.

82. There are no limits to abundance, and everyone can be wealthy if they choose.

83. I choose to be wealthy and will provide service to others in return.

84. More money just makes you more of what you already are, and I am already kind and generous.

85. I deserve the money I receive because I serve others with love and without hesitation.

86. I deserve whatever I put in the work to earn.

87. The more money I make, the better because the more I can help myself and others.

88. As I grow myself on my personal development journey, my bank account grows.

89. Wealth is not a thing. It's a mindset, and I have the mindset of wealth, which can never be taken away from me.

90. I can grow wealth at any time and place, and the amount of my choosing.

91. I am proud of being rich.

92. I love being rich, and I use my riches to help others.

93. I am always attracting huge amounts of money into my life.

94. I always have an abundance of money because I have an abundance mindset.

95. I always have enough money to meet and exceed my personal financial obligations.

96. I will not be stopped in my quest to shamelessly create as much money as I want.

97. Gaining wealth is a good thing that benefits me and others.

98. Being wealthy allows me to help those in need on a massive scale.

99. I will move past any obstacle that prevents me from earning as much wealth as possible.

100. It's okay to value money and want more of it.

101. I expect to grow with each new project I embark upon.

102. I constantly expect bigger and better things in my life.

103. The system is rigged in my favor and the world wants me to be rich.

104. I seize opportunities that come my way with both hands.

105. I use the wealth I generate to generate even more wealth for me.

106. I give myself permission to become rich and successful in every area of life.

107. Constant growth requires constant change, and I am willing to pay that price.

108. How rich I am inside directly correlates to how rich I am outside.

109. My capacity to grow and expand in every way is unlimited.

110. Through wealth, I create abundance, and through abundance, I create freedom.

111. I freely share the knowledge of how to become wealthy with others.

112. I accept money into my life because I deserve it.

113. I already own all of the resources necessary to generate money in abundance.

114. I can create unlimited prosperity and the choice to do so is mine.

115. I am grateful for the talents and traits I have that allow me to build unlimited amounts of wealth.

116. No person, thing, circumstance, or obstacle will ever stop me from achieving my goal of wealth.

117. Money is available to anyone who seeks it.

118. I attract others who share my wealth mindset and we support each other in creating unlimited abundance.

119. I have the ability to recognize opportunities where others perceive challenges, which enables me to earn money when others are unable to do so.

120. I consciously remove any obstacles, physical or mental, to wealth and prosperity.

121. I consciously remove any obstacles, real or imagined, to wealth and prosperity.

122. I applaud the success of others and use it as inspiration for what is possible for me.

123. I think big and believe I can do anything I put my mind to.

124. I admire the successful and seek to emulate what they do to create my own success.

125. I respect those who are able to earn their own wealth and become rich.

126. I seek to be like those who are self-sufficient and create wealth on command.

127. Making money can be easy and doesn't have to be hard.

128. I am willing to put in the work to become rich, no matter how easy or hard it turns out to be.

129. I have a positive attitude about money and love it without shame.

130. Big life changes are opportunities to make big life changes.

131. When life brings change, it brings with it an opportunity for me to grow in every way.

132. I love unexpected change because it forces me to increase in every area of my life.

133. Money is an amplifier—if I am sincere and good, I will only become more so.

134. Everyone has the right to become wealthy, myself included.

135. Money is not the root of all evil, it is the generator of all wealth.

136. My ability to generate wealth is without limit.

137. No matter how much wealth I generate, I always help others to become rich with me.

138. It is a human right to become wealthy, but only I can exercise that right.

139. Being rich, wealthy, and abundant is in alignment with my spiritual beliefs.

140. I owe it to my creator to become and achieve all that I can, making use of the gifts I have been given.

141. They are unlimited resources out there to help me become wealthy.

142. I will never stop my service to mankind and therefore will always receive wealth in return.

143. I will never stop loving humankind, and being generous with my wealth.

144. I am not ashamed of making money.

145. I do not need to shamefully hide my success, because it can serve as a motivator to others.

146. When people see my success, it opens their eyes to what is possible for them.

147. My mind is always focused on the positive things money can bring.

148. I do not love money for its own sake, but for the positive things it can do for myself and others.

149. I am persistent and will overcome any obstacle that stands in the way of my financial future.

150. I am creative enough to always find quick, creative solutions to apparent problems in my business.

151. All of my actions are in congruence with my financial goal of attaining wealth.

152. I believe in myself and in my own capacity to generate wealth and prosperity.

153. Those who envy me only fuel me even more toward my goals of success.

154. Those who doubt me only fuel me even more toward my goals of success.

155. I follow the examples of others who are already living the life I want to live.

156. I accept the fact that those who are wealthier must be providing more value.

157. The confidence I need to create wealth is already within me.

158. I am proud of the product or service I provide to others in exchange for money.

159. I don't make excuses when obstacles show up in my path towards my goals.

160. Other people's negativity does not deter me from reaching my goals.

161. What others perceive as limits on them has nothing to do with me.

162. I set my own personal possibilities, not the opinions of others.

163. As I master my ability to generate wealth on command, I give back by teaching others what I know.

164. I love sharing knowledge and I love sharing wealth.

165. Money is the root of all prosperity.

166. I have a burning passion for growing my business.

167. The money I earn allows me to enjoy all the amazing things life has to offer.

168. Liberty is my most prized possession, and money is the most powerful way to preserve it.

169. I am dedicated to becoming all I can in life and in business.

170. I grow my money through wise investment decisions.

171. I gravitate towards those who are successful and admire the wealth and abundance they create.

172. Those who provide value to others deserve the money and success they receive in return.

173. Persistence pays off and I am a persistent person in pursuit of my goals.

174. I never give up when I am pursuing what is good and just.

175. Money obtained in the service of others is good and well-deserved.

176. I am willing to do the work required to change my family's financial future for the better.

177. Every day, I do something that gets me closer to achieving the success and abundance I desire.

178. I enjoy working when work it is in the service of others.

179. I enjoy earning money when I know it is in response to my service of others.

180. I deserve the rewards that come in return of giving service and value to others.

181. I have definite clear plans that will lead to my goal of generating wealth and abundance.

182. I fully commit to my plan to generate wealth and abundance.

183. I pursue my good ideas so they turn into money for me and value for others.

184. I am resourceful and always find answers to any questions I have.

185. I am resourceful enough to always be able to find a solution to any problem.

186. I am always able to seek and find the help I need when obstacles arise.

187. The attainment of wealth is possible at any age, no matter how young or old.

188. Everywhere I look, I see opportunities conspiring to help me achieve my goals of success.

189. I see ways of making money all around me, all the time.

190. I am building an empire of wealth that will give me all the money I need and help me enrich the lives of others.

191. I am capable of generating all the money I will ever need.

192. I am creative, happy, and living in a world of unlimited abundance.

193. I effortlessly find money-making opportunities.

194. I am limitless and unstoppable when it comes to getting rich.

195. I am rich not just in finances, but also in my relationships.

196. When I perceive an opportunity to earn money, I jump at the chance to seize it.

197. I have what it takes to become rich.

198. I am thankful for the financial freedom that being wealthy brings.

199. I can bring freedom to myself and to others by generating unlimited amounts of wealth.

200. My family and friends are happy to see me succeed.

201. I can have whatever I want whenever I want it.

202. I seem to be at the right place at the right moment all of the time.

203. There is more money available than any of us can even imagine.

204. I am not just lucky—I deserve all the money I work to generate.

205. I attract more and more money with each passing year.

206. I am so happy to have met and exceeded my financial goals.

207. I am grateful to have more money than I know what to do with. I will use it to provide greater service to humankind.

208. I can be whoever and whatever I want for the rest of my life.

209. I can do whatever I want for the rest of my life.

210. I can have whatever I want for the rest of my life.

211. I am a natural born success.

212. There is no such thing as luck—I earned everything I have.

213. I am destined to be rich.

214. I am destined to be wealthy.

215. I am destined to be successful.

216. Every day that goes by, I get richer and richer.

217. I am a powerful creative force, which is why it is easy for me to create wealth.

218. I share my talents and execute ideas with the world, and receive lots of money in return.

219. I have a clear idea of how much money I want to earn and what I am going to do to earn it.

220. I believe in my ability to make massive amounts of money.

221. I have the ability to create a million dollars over and over again.

222. Wealth is a mindset and I am wealthy inside and out.

223. Wealth outside comes from wealth within, and I have wealth within.

224. Money is a constantly renewing resource for me.

225. I am unified with wealth and prosperity.

226. My money is always multiplying.

227. I transform the lives of others with the money I attract into my life.

228. Money always flows into my life like a rushing river.

229. Wealth and prosperity are my birthright.

230. I was born rich on the inside, so I can easily get rich on the outside.

231. My external wealth is a reflection of my internal wealth.

232. I am willing to make whatever changes or improvements needed in myself to reach my financial goals.

233. It is fun to be rich and enjoy financial freedom.

234. My success breeds more success.

235. My wealth breeds more wealth.

236. My investments continually multiply, bringing me more money than I imagined.

237. I make money in my sleep with the power of my investments.

238. I make money in my sleep with the power of my passive income vehicles.

239. I can manifest millions.

240. I am excited about generating millions of dollars in my life.

241. I love money and money loves me.

242. I am good and money is too.

243. I easily achieve my financial goals.

244. I always knew I would become rich.

245. I love money because money allows me to do what I love.

246. My bank accounts grow constantly without limit.

247. I am living my perfect life.

248. I am rich and confident.

249. I am prosperous and love helping others.

250. All of my businesses are successful.

251. Everything I touch turns to gold.

252. I attract successful people who work in harmony with me.

253. I am growing richer and richer and am able to easily provide for my family.

254. I have enough wealth to take care of my family for the rest of their lives.

255. Because I am rich, I decide what I will do with my time.

256. I have unlimited amounts of wealth and can share it with others and generate even more wealth.

257. My choices are unlimited, and I can help others without limit.

258. I enjoy being a multi-millionaire.

259. I allow myself to feel success and enjoy the fruits of my labor.

260. I feel like a success, I act like a success, I am a success.

261. I have no problems going out and claiming what is mine, and wealth is mine.

262. I expect prosperity and riches to flow to me.

263. I joyously accept the money that flows into my life.

264. Money is only a tool that allows me to live the life of freedom that I want.

265. Success is my new normal.

266. Wealth is my new normal.

267. Abundance is my new normal.

268. I am amazed at how easily unlimited amounts of money come into my life.

269. I am attracted to money the way magnets are attracted to each other.

270. It was always my destiny to become rich.

271. Wealth generating ideas continually flow into my head.

272. Every success I enjoy generates a new success.

273. Every dollar I earn turns into another.

274. Prosperity is my natural state of being.

275. I am a magnet for millions of dollars.

276. I deserve to make millions.

277. Rich people are good people, and I am both.

278. Wealth is nothing more than energy, and I am continually drawing it towards me.

279. I can create a million dollars at will.

280. I am debt free and prosperous.

281. Everything that I need has been provided for me.

282. I can realize all my dreams.

283. Money is not just for others: it is for me.

284. I am confident in my abilities to grow my money resources.

285. I enjoy the rewards I earn from the service I provide to others.

286. Success is all around me.

287. I am both happy and rich.

288. I am at peace with my wealth and my ability to maintain it.

289. I am at peace with my wealth and my ability to grow it.

290. My hard work pays off with financial rewards.

291. Earning money has always been easy for me.

292. Getting rich is a skill of mine.

293. Making money is easy when you provide value to others.

294. I alone am responsible for my relationship with money.

295. I alone am responsible for my attitude toward money.

296. My talents and persistence guarantee my success.

297. Abundance is a natural part of my life.

298. I can always generate the money I need or want.

299. Money is my friend: it will help me to help others.

300. I am highly motivated in the pursuit of my financial goals.

301. I know that I will receive money in proportion to the value I provide others.

302. I do not always have to work for money because my money works for me.

303. I am always attracting prosperous investment opportunities.

304. I am happy that I benefit financially from lucrative investments.

305. I am motivated to do a great job and get my work done on time.

306. I will always earn more than enough money than I need to survive.

307. The value I provide others translates into money I deserve.

308. I have a lot to offer others and will be compensated in direct proportion to what I choose to provide.

309. I am deserving of the wealth I am constantly creating.

310. My talents are a gift to this world, and I deserve the money they generate for me and my family.

311. My unique talents benefit those around me and help us all excel to the best of our abilities.

312. I trust in my ability to generate money and prosperity and I will get it done.

313. I believe in my ability to keep going when things get tough.

314. I trust in my ability to amass wealth regardless of the political climate.

315. I trust in my ability to amass wealth no matter the state of the economy.

316. I bring in wealth from all corners of the world.

317. I am connected to the global economy and have customers all over the globe.

318. I trust myself to make wise and prosperous financial decisions.

319. Money always has and always will come naturally to me.

320. My mind is strong and helps me generate new ideas that attract money.

321. I don't earn money: I attract it in direct proportion to the amount of value that I provide.

322. I refuse to let others place limits on the amount of money that I can attain in my life.

323. There are no limits to the level to which I can monetize my talents.

324. There are no limits to the level to which I can monetize my ideas.

325. My exceptional intuition guides me when it comes to deciding what to do with my money.

326. I have everything required to become a success.

327. Success, wealth, and financial prosperity are natural and my birthright.

328. I am proud of the money I earn because I know I deserve it.

329. I am happy to be rich because I believe I am worth it.

330. I am just as deserving as others are of becoming wealthy and financially free.

331. I am always making money, whether I am actively working or not.

332. I am following the path toward more wealth and riches.

333. I can create any amount of money that anyone can name.

334. I easily learn new skills that help me earn more money.

335. I am intuitively pointed in the direction of wealth.

336. I am grateful to have the money to spend on things that will enrich and improve my life.

337. I am always planting seeds to help me earn more money in the future.

338. I love my work and the financial reward it brings.

339. I take action each and every day that will increase my income.

340. I am grateful to have plenty of money to invest in my own mental health.

341. I am grateful to have plenty of money to invest in my own spiritual health.

342. I am grateful to have plenty of money to invest in my own physical health.

343. I love treating myself and the people I love with the money I have.

344. My wealth is constantly compounding over time.

Chapter 24
Affirmations for Attitude and Relationship with Money

Your attitude toward money has a significant impact on whether or not you attract money into your life. If you grew up in an atmosphere that destroyed your self-esteem and left you lacking in desire and ambition, it will be more difficult for you to attract financial resources.

In addition, if you believe you do not deserve to be rich or that money is corrupt, you are likely to believe that you do not deserve to have sufficient financial resources, even if you consciously wish you had more.

If you have a bad attitude about money, you will not put up the effort necessary to get it. You will not pay attention to opportunities, and you may even make some mistakes in judgment that result in losing money.

With repeatedly repeating affirmations intended to change your attitude toward money, your subconscious mind will ultimately accept them as real, and a negative attitude toward money will gradually be replaced by a good attitude.

The Affirmations

1. It is never a problem for me to have more than enough money to suit my requirements.

2. I pay myself first, but I always share my money to help others who need help.

3. I deserve to be wealthy.

4. My wealth grows in proportion to the service I provide others.

5. My wealth grows in proportion to the value I provide others.

6. I can afford anything and everything my heart desires.

7. I am drawing money toward me all the time.

8. I have the power to create all the wealth my family needs.

9. I deserve financial abundance and material prosperity.

10. I own money, but money does not own me.

11. I find it easy to attract money into my life.

12. I choose to be rich and powerful but will use it to make a positive impact in the lives of others.

13. I know that my wealth is not just for me but for the betterment of others as well.

14. The world is full of riches, and I know that I will get my share.

15. I attract money wherever I go - no matter what I am doing.

16. I love money and feel the good that comes from it.

17. I am the one who has complete control over the amount of money I have in my life.

18. I choose to be wealthy and recognize that life is magnificent.

19. Money is good when it is used for good.

20. I am increasing my wealth, which gives me the power to increase my freedom.

21. I use money to open new doors to more success.

22. Money is a tool that I can use to create my best life.

23. Money is a tool that I can use to support others in living their best life.

24. Having or wanting money is nothing to feel guilt or shame over.

25. Money is a seed, which when planted properly, will grow.

26. I freely invest money into my business, knowing that I will always make a significant return.

27. I freely invest money into myself, knowing that I will always make a significant return.

28. I am responsible with my money, and I always find ways to make it grow.

29. I use and invest my money responsibly.

30. I enjoy the power that comes from financial independence.

31. I am always growing my wealth, no matter the state of the economy.

32. I am always growing my wealth, no matter the political climate.

33. I act on my ideas that create prosperity.

34. My wealth is growing every single day.

35. I am just as capable of creating, growing, and maintaining wealth as anyone else.

36. It is possible for money to come and flow to me easily.

37. I choose to share my wealth with others.

38. I find it easy to make money and make more and more with each passing day.

39. I attract wealth to me from all corners of the world.

40. I am strong enough to grow wealth despite my upbringing.

41. I have a positive mental attitude around money.

42. I have a healthy relationship with money.

43. I am in control of money, not the other way around.

44. I am unstoppable when it comes to generating massive wealth.

45. I enjoy making money.

46. My income is always effortlessly increasing.

47. I don't always have to work for money, I make my money work for me.

48. I put my money to work in profitable investments.

49. I make passive income from my money.

50. While I sleep and play, my money is still working and growing for me.

51. I can make lots of money without trading my time for it.

52. The actions I do today will result in more wealth, prosperity, and abundance.

53. I feel good, joyous, and positive when it comes to money.

54. Money is not the only thing that brings me happiness and fulfilment.

55. It is okay to feel happy and excited about making money.

56. It is okay to be wealthy.

57. It is my right to be rich.

58. My bank account continues to grow more than I ever thought possible.

59. I use the money I have to make more money.

60. I have all the wealth I could ever need or want.

61. I am surrounded by wealth and abundance.

62. My relationships are just as rich as my bank account.

63. I am always receiving wealth because I am willing to ask for it.

64. I am always receiving wealth because I am willing to work for it.

65. My inputs result in increase.

66. Having money gives me options, which is a good thing.

67. Wealth allows me to choose what I want for my life, while poverty would make my choices for me.

68. I have the ability to attract money and wealth to myself.

69. I have so much wealth I can share it with others effortlessly.

70. I can create and produce whatever amount of money I need at will.

71. I have the money I want and need because I ask for the money I want and need.

72. I am surrounded by opportunities to make more money.

73. I already have the ideas I need to make more money, I just need to act on them.

74. The world has all the money I could ever want.

75. I earn my money, fair and square.

76. I can make a lot of money and still be a good person.

77. I have my own positive opinions of money despite the opinions of others from my past.

78. I have my own positive relationship to money despite others from my past.

79. I can be both rich and humble.

80. I can be both rich and kind.

81. I can be both rich and loving.

82. I can be both rich and generous.

83. I can be both rich and honest.

84. I provide value and service to others in my work, which results in more money and wealth for me.

85. I have the capability to be responsible with my wealth.

86. I have the capability to grow my wealth.

87. As my professional service and contribution grow, as does my bank account.

88. I never take more in monetary value from others than value I provide them.

89. I deserve the wealth that I am receiving.

90. Whether it take a short or a long time to grow my wealth, I am as patient as I need to be.

91. Money is drawn to me and I accept it with gratitude.

92. I respect money and recognize it as a tool that provides liberty, prosperity, and freedom.

93. Money gives me opportunities in life to do, have, and become things that most can only dream of.

94. I enjoy money, wealth, and prosperity.

95. I am comfortable with having wealth and riches.

96. I deserve financial independence and financial abundance.

97. If I wish to raise my income, I must also raise my living standards, as well.

98. In order for my money to grow, I must grow.

99. I am always able to figure out ways to make money.

100. I am free of debt.

101. Anything I want, I can pay for in full.

102. I surround myself with people who are financially responsible.

103. I have an abundance of money that can help me handle any life situation that comes up.

104. I am master over my money, not the other way around.

105. I will always be wealthy.

106. Everyone deserves to have money to live their best life, and I will take my share without guilt.

107. I see a way to make money from new ideas every day.

108. I am comfortable with the money that hard work brings.

109. I have so much money that I always feel financially secure.

110. Money is good because it brings security to my family.

111. Money is good: it makes it easier for me to help others.

112. My mind is clear and calm because my financial needs are taken care of.

113. Money provides me with the opportunity to accomplish what I want, rather than merely what I am required to do.

114. Money is a ticket that allows me to do whatever I want in life.

115. Being wealthy allows me to make decisions based on growth and desire, not desperation and restriction.

116. What I earn has absolutely nothing to do with how well the economy is doing right now.

117. I thrive in economic times where others panic.

118. There are opportunities all around me to grow wealth.

119. Money is generously given to me and I generously give it to others.

120. I trust that I will always have more than enough money to meet my needs.

121. I love the feeling I get when I receive money well-earned.

122. I am thankful and appreciative when I receive money because I know that others don't always have it.

123. I find it easy to meet my financial goals.

124. My financial security makes it possible to help others.

125. My money allows me to better support my health.

126. Every single day, the amount of money I have grows.

127. I feel light and happy when I think about money.

128. The thing I love the most about money is how it enables me to change the world.

129. The stronger I am the more money I attract.

130. I deserve any amount of money I could wish for.

131. I have all the money I could possibly dream of.

132. I am proud and deserving of the wealth and money I have earned.

133. My wealthy mindset enables me to create money.

134. I admire the wealthy and successful and strive to be more like them.

135. I learn from rich and successful people who teach me about wealth generation.

136. My heart is open to receiving wealth, money, and prosperity.

137. I am getting closer and closer to my financial goals every day.

138. I allow and welcome wealth and money to enter into my life.

139. Financial increase is constant and inevitable for me.

140. I am comfortable looking at my bank account and seeing it grow.

141. I can earn as much money as I want and need.

142. Being wealthy and prosperous is my natural state of being.

143. I set financial goals and always achieve them faster than I thought I would.

144. Money can help buy happiness because it buys opportunity and freedom of choice.

145. I give myself permission to be rich.

146. It's okay for me to maximize my potential by making as much money as I possibly can.

147. I do the world a favor by making as much money as I possibly can.

148. I do my loved ones a favor by making as much money as I possibly can.

149. I do myself a favor by making as much money as I possibly can.

150. It goes without saying that the more money I earn, the more money I can contribute.

151. The more money I earn, the more money I am able to give away.

152. My ability to grow wealth is inspiring to others.

153. Pursuing wealth makes me a better person because I have to grow as a person for my money to grow.

154. Money is good and helps others.

155. I am responsible with my money, but I also enjoy it.

156. I gladly allow wealth to enter my life.

157. I can and will become rich, solely because I choose to.

158. I spend money without guilt or shame.

159. I love spending money on others to help them get what they need and desire.

160. I deserve all the money I have and even more.

161. I deserve all the money that is coming to me, and even more.

162. I give myself permission to openly receive all the money that is coming to me.

163. I feel good about money and enjoy it.

164. My heart is completely open to abundance and prosperity.

165. Money flows into my life without me asking for it because I am a magnet for money.

166. I am grateful for the money that keeps flowing into my life and I will use it for good.

167. I effortlessly attract money into my life through the service that I provide others.

168. I earn my money and my wealth because I make myself a valuable asset to the world.

169. I enjoy investing and love using my money to grow more money.

170. I take calculated financial risks because I am confident I can make them pay off.

171. In my professional life, I fulfill the needs of others in a moral way, and receive money in return.

172. The abundance I have makes me feel light and stress free.

173. I believe I have the ability to earn as much money as I desire.

174. I am mentally strong, so I can earn money in any way that I set out to.

175. I am resourceful, so I can earn money in any way that I set out to.

176. Every single day, I wake up with more money than I had the day before.

177. Every day, my income and my professional success are growing.

178. Attaining financial prosperity is my right and responsibility.

179. It is easy for me to manifest wealth.

180. I help others get the money they desire and deserve because there is plenty for everyone to succeed.

181. I admire honest, wealthy people and value the positive example they provide.

182. I learn from others how to increase my own wealth.

183. I am financially rewarded in proportion to the quality of work I do.

184. My mind and conscience are at ease when I spend money.

185. My mind and conscience are at ease when I grow money.

186. I can boldly say that I love making money.

187. I can boldly say that I love having money.

188. I can boldly say that I love spending money.

189. I can boldly say that I love saving money.

190. I can boldly say that I love growing money.

191. I am comfortable with spending and enjoying my money because I know more is always coming my way.

192. Money is a resource that is always renewing for me.

193. It is okay for me to spend money on the things I want.

194. It is okay for me to spend money on others.

195. I save and invest out of responsibility not fear because I know more is always coming to me.

196. I always exceed my financial goals and make more money than I want.

197. I grow wealth in every type of economic or political climate.

198. The world is full of money-making opportunities and I always seize them.

199. I can afford to spend lots of money on personal care because of my wealth.

200. I use my money to create the best life for myself and others.

201. Generating wealth is on auto pilot for me.

202. I love money and wealth.

203. I celebrate being able to buy a wonderful home for myself and my family.

204. I enjoy my financial blessings.

205. I use money to learn more and educate myself, to increase my value to others.

206. I have more than enough money and share my overflow with others.

207. I am a positive example for others to embrace money and the freedom it provides.

208. I love to give money away because I can easily create more.

209. I could regenerate my wealth from scratch if I had to.

210. I have a wealth mindset and have a positive attitude about money.

211. I find it easy to make money on demand.

212. The ability to help others motivates me to grow my wealth even more.

213. I am rich, wealth, and prosperous.

214. My investments always yield long term profits.

215. I am growing richer by the day.

216. I am skilled in creating and generating money.

217. I can create money-making opportunities for myself and for others.

218. I share money making opportunities with others because there is more than enough money to go around.

219. I am always discovering new money-making opportunities.

220. I have the power to generate my own money, regardless of what is going on in my environment.

221. It is okay for money to make me feel happy.

222. My subconscious acts in alignment with my conscious efforts to earn and grow wealth.

223. I have the power to create money through my mind and can do so whenever I need to.

224. I have the power to attract money into my life and increase prosperity.

225. I have the power to forever defeat debt and poverty.

226. I feel joy and satisfaction when I have the money to spend on things I want and need.

227. Wealth is the natural state of my life.

228. Having lots of money is the natural state of my life.

229. With every new day, I will claim the money-making opportunities it brings.

230. I choose to feel good about money, and the prosperity and security it can bring.

231. I choose to feel good about money, and the mental peace it can bring.

232. I love all the money I earn and every dollar in my bank account.

233. I cultivate positive feelings about money every day.

234. Money supports my life and dreams in every possible way.

235. I choose to let go of the negative feelings I have about money and wealth.

236. I choose to let go of the negative perceptions I have about money that I got from other people.

237. I use my leadership abilities and intelligence to attract money.

238. To receive money in the future, I will render services to others while expecting nothing in return.

239. I use seed money to plant new riches to be realized in the future.

240. I donate to worthy causes out of the goodness of my heart.

241. I feel myself becoming more and more wealthy each passing day.

242. Pursing financial goals is a worthy pursuit.

243. I make sound financial decisions.

244. I have gratitude for all the wealth and money I have received, created, and built.

245. I make lots of money and deserve every dollar of it.

246. I give away money every month to help realize other people's dreams and make the world a better place

Chapter 25
Affirmations for Handling Professional, Work, and Business Stress

Just as you can't stop mistakes from occurring, you can't also stop people from criticizing you. Like mistakes, criticism will influence your self-esteem only if you let them. Don't allow criticism to make you forget your self-esteem or core values.

To prevent criticism from having a damaging impact on your self-esteem, you have to learn how to cope with it. This segment will teach you how to respond to critics in an effective manner. But before that, there are a number of things you should understand about reality:

1. **People are different:** they see things differently, have different tastes, beliefs, behavior patterns and psychological makeup. You shouldn't regard their critical statements as the complete truth. For instance, someone who is naturally outgoing won't understand why you don't mingle with people. The person will immediately criticize you for being boring or too shy because he/she is unable to understand that your introversion is okay.

2. **Emotions color people's perceptions:** When people are feeling a certain way, their emotions color their words or actions. Your girlfriend may have called you wasteful for using up the remaining supplies because she just got fired and is feeling paranoid. If you start going over his criticism in your head and believing that you lack judgment, your self-esteem suffers for something that is not even the truth.

In conclusion, before you accept any critical remark as the ultimate truth about yourself, first reflect on the critic's overall makeup. And when responding to criticism, be neither passive nor aggressive; rather acknowledge the criticism by telling the person that they are right and provide an explanation if necessary. That is the only way to stop criticism instantly.

The Affirmations

1. I am doing my best at work and that is the best that I can do.
2. I am a valuable asset to any professional team.
3. I can get through any project if I just take things one step at a time.
4. The only thing I focus on is the task in front of me right now.
5. I am productive and focused and I easily check things off my to-do list.
6. I have more than enough time to accomplish the things I need to accomplish.
7. I will find my ideal career and make it mine.
8. I will create my ideal business if that is my desire.
9. My income is always increasing from the work that I do.
10. I radiate energy and confidence when I am at work.
11. My career does not take over my life.
12. Other areas of my life are just as important as the way I make money.
13. I am grateful to have found and realized my professional dreams.

14. The contacts that I need to help me advance professionally are on their way to me.

15. I attract positive mentors who guide me towards success in my chosen field.

16. I am grateful to have a lucrative source of income that supports my dream lifestyle.

17. I am always finding opportunities to grow and expand in my career.

18. I know I will always excel no matter what I do.

19. I am recognized for the quality work I contribute to my field.

20. Even better opportunities are always just around the corner.

21. I am in control of my professional path.

22. I will shape my career to be the way I want it to be.

23. I make great professional connections because I am confident in my abilities.

24. If I decide to change my career, it will lead me to something bigger and better.

25. I am fulfilled by my work.

26. I am challenged by my work in a positive and productive way.

27. I get excited to get to go to work each day.

28. I lead my team with humility and grace.

29. My career helps me grow into becoming a better person.

30. There is a successful business owner inside me who can manage a business to perfection.

31. I will find my way to the top of any field.

32. I am able to learn the skills I may need to learn to get the job done.

33. I bring excellence to every task, no matter how big or small.

34. I am calmly confident in my ability to manage my business and make it highly successful.

35. Today is the day that opportunity will knock, and I will open the door.

36. I perform my work with integrity no matter what.

37. I perform my work with pride no matter what.

38. I perform my work with excellence no matter what.

39. I am wealthy because of the dedicated efforts I have put in.

40. I get closer and closer to my business goals every day.

41. I am successful in my career because I take action.

42. I do what it takes to turn my ideas into reality.

43. I am constantly growing my business and professional income.

44. All of my career success just breeds more success.

45. I have a strong network of contacts and am well-regarded in my profession.

46. I always attract positive thinking people to work with me.

47. I always attract hard working people to work with me.

48. I am always learning new ways to do my work faster and better.

49. My professional efficiency increases every day.

50. I have the ability to be the best in whichever profession I choose.

51. I consciously release any and all negative thoughts that will impede my success.

52. I believe in myself and what I am capable of doing.

53. New opportunities are waiting for me and I am ready to grab them.

54. My communication abilities are continuously being refined, and I am continually striving for improvement.

55. Today is going to be a great day at work and every tomorrow will be too.

56. I am my own best motivator.

57. I capitalize on my opportunities by taking action.

58. I will explore all new avenues to success whenever they present themselves.

59. Each new idea is a gift and I will treat it as such.

60. Every day, I will look for new opportunities for further success.

61. Whenever I need assistance, I can attract the best resources possible to fit my needs.

62. Whenever I need assistance, I can attract the best people possible to fit my needs.

63. Whenever I need assistance, I can attract the best solutions possible to fit my needs.

64. I am proficient at time management, which allows me to attain my objectives.

65. I am effective at organization, which helps me achieve my goals.

66. I always find a way to enjoy my work.

67. I am grateful to have a means of making great money.

68. I make sure that my values and ambitions work with each other, not against each other.

69. My work surrounds me with inspiring people who push me to do better.

70. I am grateful to work with people who share in my enthusiasm for the work we do.

71. I welcome new work challenges with calm confidence.

72. I am naturally good at finding solutions to problems.

73. I surround myself with people who are highly successful and who encourage me to be the same.

74. I see a new chance for success in every new challenge I face.

75. Overcoming challenges is a way to improve my self-esteem and self-confidence.

76. When obstacles show up, it's a chance for me to show people what I'm made of.

77. I always take time to celebrate my successes and victories.

78. I trust my intuition to help me make wise professional decisions.

79. I am always in tune and intuitively know the best next step to take.

80. Today will bring an abundance of new ideas that I will use to my advantage.

81. I consistently expect winning solutions, and I always attract good outcomes.

82. I am happy with my growth in my career and expect more to come in the future.

83. I deserve and demand respect in my career.

84. My career path is the best one for me, no matter what other people are doing.

85. I am steadily climbing the ranks in my field.

86. By being myself, I bring something unique and wonderful to my work.

87. I am a successful person by nature.

88. I will remain consistent in my efforts, and will therefore achieve the results I want.

89. I achieve the goals I set out to achieve.

90. I am ambitious by nature.

91. I have a knack for succeeding at everything I do.

92. I am doing my best at work and that is good enough.

93. I keep my dreams alive with my positive attitude.

94. I always go the extra mile, and it always pays off.

95. I know that my dedication will lead to promotion and increase.

96. I have the energy of a winner because I am a winner.

97. I have the energy of a success because I am a success.

98. I bring joy and light into my workplace with my positive attitude and winning smile.

99. I only speak positively about those that I work with.

100. I have healthy, fulfilling, positive relationships with the people I work with.

101. I speak up boldly and ask intelligent questions when needed.

102. I create my own opportunities and don't just wait for them to come to me.

103. My repertoire of skills is constantly expanding.

104. I put consistent effort and energy into becoming better at what I do.

105. People take notice of my skill and work ethic.

106. I appreciate everyone, both above and below me, who helps contribute to my success.

107. I get what I want in my work by helping other people get what they want.

108. I keep my workspace clean so my mind will be clean.

109. I keep my workspace organized so my mind will be organized.

110. I always see the fruits of my labor.

111. Seeing other people ahead of me simply drives me to be better.

112. I always persist and never quit because things get too hard.

113. I have the wisdom to know when to try a different tactic.

114. I am especially gifted at what I do.

115. I will maintain a positive outlook at work today no matter what happens.

116. Communication with those that I work with is something I do very well.

117. I am only finished with a project when I know it is the best I could have done.

118. The work I do is always done to the best of my ability.

119. I only turn in quality projects, done with care.

120. I set a great example for other people in my field.

121. I'm always learning, so I can stay relevant in my field.

122. I have the power to make today a good day or a bad day and I choose to have a good day at work today.

123. All of the work that I do is important and significant.

124. I radiate confidence in my abilities, which gets me noticed.

125. I am open to doing whatever it takes to get the job done.

126. I deserve to be financially stable and I will do what I need to do to get there.

127. I always have the best team to work with.

128. I work with a team of people with unique and valuable skills.

129. I always bring the best out of the people I work with.

130. I am trusted in my field as an honest leader.

Chapter 26
Affirmations for Protecting and Improving Your Mental State and Confidence

Your influence, dear black man, has the power to transform the world. You've influenced generations. You've commanded armies. You've governed whole countries. Presidents, billionaires, physicians, attorneys, accountants, entrepreneurs, tradespeople, farmers, dads, brothers, and cousins are among the people you've become. Examine your local environment and seek to improve yourself and the people around you. Look for ways to improve your financial literacy and gain economic power. As powerful as an ocean current and as furious and relentless as the wind, be a positive, inspiring force. You, black guy, are a game-changer. Face the challenge.

To start believing your realistic self-description, write a new description of yourself that you will read out to yourself every day for a month till it drowns out the voice of that vicious inner critic you've been listening to for years. The new description should incorporate the tips outlined above: no use of pejoratives, generalization, exaggeration, or vagueness.

Make sure you defend yourself with positive affirmations of your strength whenever your critic starts bombarding you with negativity. Sure, the critic can be cunny and relentless, attacking you with memories or thoughts that are hard to ignore, making your attempts at accurate thinking useless. Let the rebuttal voice of your accepting friend, rational teacher, healthy coach, or compassionate mentor do the talking.

But you can still emerge a victor in this war against the critic. Distancing yourself from your mind or thoughts is another weapon you can add to the special arsenal you have for fighting the critic.

The Affirmations

1. Things don't have to be flawless in order to be successful.
2. I work calmly because I know things will ultimately work out.
3. I believe that everything will work out as it should.
4. I only use my own measurements for success, not someone else's.
5. Based on my personal definition of success, I know I am on the right path for myself.
6. When something difficult comes my way, I am entirely capable of navigating my way through it.
7. The answers I am seeking are already inside me.
8. Every issue has a solution, and I will be the one to uncover it.
9. My thoughts are centered, and my will is strong.
10. I always remain mentally calm despite what's going on around me.
11. I am impervious to drama and negativity because I have the emotional intelligence to not take anything personally.
12. I have the power to calm my mind and put myself at ease at any time.
13. I work towards my goals with relaxation and ease.

14. I have peace in knowing that I have an instinct that guides me towards success.

15. Contentment and calmness come naturally to me.

16. Mental peace and clarity come naturally to me.

17. Ideas and solutions come naturally to me.

18. I relinquish the concept that I must bear the full weight of things on my shoulders.

19. I reframe failure as a positive thing that is necessary for success.

20. Failure is really just a lesson on how to do better next time.

21. I do not over-inflate problems to be bigger than they are.

22. My calmness puts people around me at ease.

23. I attract other people who are also mentally calm.

24. I love moments of solitude as opportunities to mentally reset.

25. I love moments of solitude as opportunities to calm my mind.

26. I love moments of solitude as opportunities to replenish my spirit.

27. I am unapologetic with taking and protecting my alone time.

28. I am more than good enough for the rewards that come from my dedication.

29. I am fully deserving of reaping the benefits of the fruits of my labor.

30. I take the steps necessary to maintain a good energy field around myself.

31. In this moment, everything is okay.

32. I easily get into flow states of unstoppable creativity.

33. Getting in the zone mentally is easy for me.

34. I know how to channel myself into any attitude necessary for the task at hand.

35. I have the ability to clear my mind on command.

36. I have complete control over my thoughts.

37. I take full responsibility for my thoughts.

38. I have complete control over my emotions.

39. I take full responsibility for my emotions.

40. I have complete control over my reactions.

41. I take full responsibility for my reactions.

42. I only utilize my mental energy for what is in front of me right now.

43. I tackle things one thing at a time to avoid overwhelm.

44. Mental stillness and meditation are a frequent practice of mine.

45. I have the power to find peace within myself.

46. In times of turmoil, I go back to my breath to regain my calm.

47. I feel at peace with everything in my life.

48. I am completely and fully in the present moment.

49. Failure is beneficial because it teaches me what not to do in the future.

50. I live and operate only in the now.

51. When the time comes, the future will take care of itself and will also take care of me, if I let it.

52. I do not have to identify with every thought that comes through my head.

53. I do not have to believe every thought that comes through my head.

54. I do not have to succumb emotionally to every thought that comes through my head.

55. I choose to only believe things that are helpful and beneficial to me in some way.

56. I have the power to just let a thought pass by if it does not serve me.

57. My mind is kind to me and shows me that I am deserving of peace.

58. Tranquility is my natural state.

59. My mental peace is my priority.

60. I am emotionally strong and mentally fit.

61. I can find a complete state of serenity at will whenever needed.

62. Even when there is chaos around me, I am calm and tranquil within me.

63. Throughout the day, my subconscious mind is always working in my favor.

64. Though I strive for more, I am content with what I have.

65. I am patient and willing to wait for my greatest blessings to unfold in their due time.

66. If I put in the work, I know I will reap the reward.

67. I welcome failure and all the lessons it brings.

68. Whenever I think of all the things I'm grateful for, I immediately feel better.

69. I have a habitual practice of gratitude.

70. I am capable of making choices that will bring more goodness into my life.

71. I am working to become better, but I am happy about who I am.

72. When new issues arise, I remain calm and focused as the solution finds its way to me.

73. Each failure just gets me closer to a success.

74. I am capable of learning whatever I need to learn to do whatever I need to do.

75. There is no success without failure.

76. I am mentally strong enough to work through distractions that would normally derail others.

77. I am mentally strong enough to work through obstacles that would normally derail others.

78. I am mentally strong enough to overcome failures that would normally derail others.

79. I do what needs to be done immediately so I can keep my mental space clear.

80. My mind is my greatest tool, so I protect it fiercely.

81. My peace is my greatest asset, so I protect it fiercely.

82. I can activate my concentration on command.

83. My concentration skills are getting better each day.

84. I consciously engage only in healthy thought patterns.

85. I keep my body in top condition so I can keep my mind in top condition.

86. I take breaks without guilt, and always return to my task with renewed focus and energy.

87. I can quickly refocus myself when my mind wanders.

88. Momentary failure does not exempt me from ultimate success.

89. My mind stays clear because I do what I know I should do when I know I should do it.

90. I am able to separate myself from my constant inner monologue.

91. I am ruler over the background noise in my head.

92. I control my thoughts, my thoughts do not control me.

93. I conduct myself thoughtfully and consciously.

94. My healthy lifestyle empowers me by giving me the physical and mental energy I need.

95. In times of big decisions, I am patient with myself as I determine the best way to move forward.

96. I know I do my best, which is the only validation I need.

97. It is more important for something to be complete than be perfect.

98. I act with consideration but without hesitation because I trust my instincts.

99. I feel happier and more positive when I take initiative and take action.

100. I am able to put my head down and work on the process, and let the result work itself out.

101. I can call on my focus at will to gain momentum on whatever I need to do.

102. My mind is sharp and alert.

103. My mind is present and focused on the task at hand.

104. When my environment is decluttered, so is my head.

105. I love the feeling of making something complete over making something perfect.

106. When I focus on the present moment, I feel calm and ready to take on anything.

107. I am motivated and excited, yet relaxed in all that I do.

108. Whatever I put my focus on expands, so I choose where I put my focus wisely.

109. A better body means a better mind, so I am diligent in taking care of my body.

110. I feed healthy foods to my body and healthy thoughts to my brain.

111. The more I push myself mentally, the stronger I become.

112. The stronger mentally that I become, the easier it is for me to do what I need to do.

113. I am capable of pushing past my perceived limits.

114. I am so excited to meet the version of myself that lives on the other side of my current mental barriers.

115. My mind is better because of the respect that I show my body.

116. I am disciplined in my self-care because I know how great it makes me feel and perform.

117. I am empathetic with myself when I have a bad day.

118. I do not perform at the same level every day, but I do my best every day, and that is good enough for me.

119. Because I am active, my brain is active.

120. A healthy body equals a healthy mind.

121. I can put aside tomorrow's cares in order to focus on today's tasks.

122. My mental clarity allows me to make wise decisions for my work and personal life.

123. I have the mental wherewithal to do what I said I was going to do whether I feel like it or not.

124. Excuses don't stop me from doing what I know I need to do.

125. I take action based on my commitments, not my feelings.

126. I follow through on what I say. I'm going to do what I say I'm going to do when I say I'm going to do it.

127. I have confidence in my abilities because I know I can count on myself to do what I say I'll do.

128. I take care of my environment and workspace to promote a better state of mental well-being.

129. The state of my physical space is a reflection of the state of my mental space.

130. I only own things that make my life easier and happier.

131. I fully trust those that I delegate tasks to, relieving myself of mental load.

132. Everything does not have to go exactly according to my plan.

133. My only focus is meeting my expectations of myself, not the expectations others have of me.

134. I am in tune to when I need to make a shift or change in my life.

135. I trust my intuition and my gut feelings.

136. I settle my nerves by following my instincts.

137. My body carries my mind, and for that, I treat it well.

138. My emotional and mental well-being are supported by my physical health and nutrition.

139. I know when it is best to let go rather than try to control every person and situation around me.

140. I take care of my space as a means of taking care of my mind.

141. When I clean up the mess in my space, I clean up the mess in my head.

142. Every day will not be a great and perfect day, and that is okay.

143. It's never too late for me to get back on track.

144. I can easily make up for what feels like lost time in the pursuit of my goals.

145. If I keep moving forward, I will arrive at my goal destination right on time.

146. I do what I need to do to keep my spirits up and my mood high.

147. Despite the fact that I am not perfect, I am still amazing.

148. I accept myself fully for all my imperfections.

149. My clean and clear environment make for a clean and clear mind.

150. I dedicate time to relaxing as well as working.

151. My relationships and hobbies are just as important as my professional contributions to the world.

152. I always allow myself a mental reset before going back into another taxing project.

153. A healthy diet and exercise regimen keep me focused and clear-headed.

154. Everything will be okay if something does not go completely as planned.

155. My perception of my own actions is in my control.

156. All good things take time, and I am willing to wait, while taking action.

157. I am in a process and will respect that process.

158. I cannot control how everything will turn out, but I can control how it will control me.

Chapter 27
Affirmations for Gratitude

One of the most beneficial personal development exercises you may engage in is the practice of daily gratitude affirmations, which can be done at any time of day. You will experience pleasure, happiness, and tranquility in your life if you are grateful. It also actually assists you in achieving your objectives and fulfilling your aspirations.

Positive affirmations rewire your brain to think in a more productive way. When you combine positive affirmations with appreciation, you have superpowers for manifesting your dreams and desires in your life.

Gratitude is the most ever powerful human emotion, and it has the ability to improve your attitude, health, and whole life experience. A regular practice of gratitude affirmations may have a profound impact on your overall well-being on several levels, also including the physical, mental or emotional, and energy.

As a result, your energy vibration, mood, hormone levels, and overall health are all impacted negatively. Maintaining a good attitude not only makes life simpler and more enjoyable, but it also has a favorable impact on your physical health.

Your body actually secretes stress hormones such as cortisol and adrenaline when you are worried, furious, terrified, or apprehensive in order to assist you in dealing with the perceived threat by either fleeing or combating it.

The fight-or-flight reaction, which has been around for thousands of years, is still present in people today. The trouble is that if you are always worried or nervous, a little quantity of these hormones is being released into your bloodstream on a continuous basis, which is harmful.

These hormones cause inflammation, which in turn contributes to a slew of chronic health disorders.

Chronic stress also slows your metabolism, makes it difficult to lose weight, prevents you from getting enough sleep, and creates brain fog, exhaustion, and a lack of enthusiasm. Cultivating a regular practice of thankfulness affirmations may help to reduce the stress response in the body. As a consequence, you will feel more energized, healthier, lighter, well-rested, and encouraged to continue working toward your objectives.

The Affirmations

1. I keep an inventory of things I am grateful for every single day.

2. My happiness and mental state are improved because I express gratitude regularly.

3. I am grateful to have family and friends in my life who love and support me.

4. I am thankful that expressing gratitude allows me to tap into a well of positive emotions.

5. I appreciate that gratitude and love can boost my self-worth and self-confidence.

6. I am grateful for the level of education and wisdom that I have attained thus far.

7. I appreciate the ability gratitude has to strengthen my personal relationships.

8. I am fortunate to have gratitude, because it gives me a brighter, more optimistic outlook.

9. I am grateful for the chance to make a positive difference in the lives of others in both big and small ways.

10. I appreciate that I have the opportunity to work hard and improve the lives of others.

11. I am grateful for my health and a sound mind.

12. I am fortunate to have family and friends who are there for me when I need help and support.

13. I appreciate my insatiable curiosity and childlike wonder for life.

14. I am grateful to see life in a way that is always interesting and enjoyable.

15. I enjoy every bit of my life's journey, and appreciate even the small moments of joy it brings.

16. I am happy to have the freedom to make my own choices.

17. I am glad that I am always in control of the direction of my life.

18. I am grateful to be the unique combination of external and internal traits that make me, me.

19. I am grateful for the warmth and life giving powers of the sun.

20. I am grateful for the natural processes of nature that make the world run smoothly.

21. I am grateful that nature provides all the resources that I need to survive.

22. I am grateful for the planet that I live on and the natural gifts it provides.

23. I am grateful to have empathy and compassion for the predicaments of others.

24. I am grateful to be able to relate to the feelings of others, as it makes my human connections stronger.

25. I am grateful that no matter how much or how little I have, I always have something to give or help others with.

26. I am glad for the chance to spend time with folks that make me feel good about myself and my life.

27. I appreciate the generosity of my family, friends, and partner that enhance my life.

28. the immense gratitude I feel makes me humble, and makes me appreciate everything I have.

29. I am fortunate to have a good sense of humor that helps brighten my days.

30. I am fortunate to have a happy disposition that helps brighten the lives of those around me.

31. I am grateful for the connectedness of the world and the opportunity to travel to enjoy different cultures and experiences.

32. Internet access and the infinite, easy source of information it gives are two things for which I am thankful.

33. I am fortunate to be in an era in which knowledge is freely accessible at the touch of a button on a computer or mobile device.

34. I am grateful to have personal freedom to express myself the way I want.

35. I am grateful expressing my gratitude improves my health and emotional well-being.

36. I am thankful for all my personal teachers who have shown up along the way and made a positive difference in my life.

37. I appreciate that feeling gratitude reduces stress and anxiety.

38. I am grateful for the opportunity to nurture my existing relationships.

39. I am thankful for the diversity and beauty in nature.

40. I always consider myself lucky to have been the recipient of generosity from others.

41. I am grateful that you don't need a lot of money to be happy.

42. I am thankful that the best things in life are free.

43. Feelings of gratitude create feelings of happiness, and happiness leads to success.

44. I am grateful that this world is filled with beauty that costs me nothing to experience and enjoy.

45. I am grateful that sunshine always follows every storm.

46. I appreciate the opportunity to experience things I already love, and also discover new things.

47. I am thankful for the simple moments I can share with the special people in my life.

48. I am grateful for the time I have to spend with the loved ones who matter most.

49. I am fortunate to have honest and loyal, close friends and family.

50. I feel grateful for all the experiences that bring me lasting moments of joy.

51. I appreciate the selflessness of people who work in service jobs that enhance my quality of life.

52. I appreciate the people who don't even know me who work every day to keep me safe.

53. I appreciate the selflessness of everyday heroes who sacrifice their own personal freedom in order to protect mine.

54. I am thankful for all the positive memories I have accumulated over my lifetime of experiences.

55. I am grateful for positive memories that help me vividly and joyously remember loved ones even after they are gone.

56. I am grateful that there is always something amazing to look forward to in my life.

57. I feel grateful for my strength and ability to overcome adversity.

58. I am grateful for the power to forgive and for the forgiveness of others.

59. I appreciate the parents, guardians, and mentors that have instilled positive values in me.

60. I am grateful for the parental figures in my life who have looked out for my best interest and ensured that I was on the right path.

61. I am thankful for the free opportunity every day to experience beautiful sunrises and sunsets.

62. I am grateful that even if I do not have a lot of money that I can always give of my time to make someone else's life better.

63. I appreciate the guidance and wisdom dispensed to me by my family and my mentors.

64. I am blessed to have folks in my life who are willing to provide a hand when I need it.

65. I feel grateful for the feelings of benevolence that motivate me to do good things for others.

66. I appreciate artists who dedicate their lives to sharing their talents by creating images, music, and media that I can enjoy.

67. I am thankful for the relaxing sounds of nature that I can experience any time for free just by going outside.

68. I appreciate the healing power of music and how easily accessible it is.

69. I am grateful to have easy access to information and documentaries that open my mind.

70. I am grateful for being surrounded by new ways of looking at things.

71. I am fortunate to have the ability to communicate my feelings and concerns with others.

72. I am grateful for the ability to spend quality time with the people I love.

73. I am thankful to be able to support my health with both modern and natural medicine.

74. I appreciate all weather because I know that all seasons serve a purpose.

75. I am grateful for pets and animals, and their ability to instantly cultivate feelings of joy and love.

76. I am fortunate to feel hopeful for a brighter future.

77. I am thankful for the holidays that bring my family and friends together.

78. I appreciate all the gifts I have received throughout the years from thoughtful people.

79. I appreciate the sensation of a warm shower on a cold morning.

80. I am grateful for a warm jacket on a winter night.

81. I am grateful for a warm cup of tea on a cold evening.

82. I am grateful for a cool shower on a hot day.

83. I am grateful to have power and control over my mind.

84. I am thankful to have my mental health and emotional well-being.

85. I am grateful for the power and ability I have to set goals and achieve them.

86. I am thankful for the strength and resilience to carry on after temporary setbacks.

87. I am fortunate to have shelter and to have a roof over my head.

88. I am grateful to have access to transportation and the ability to get around to where I need to go.

89. I appreciate the true heroes out there who put their lives at risk to save others.

90. I feel grateful for the simple pleasures in life like fresh new flowers blooming in spring.

91. I like the shifting of the seasons, as well as the explosion of vibrant color that occurs in the autumn.

92. I am fortunate to be alive, and I make the most of every single day I am given.

93. I appreciate moments of solitude that bring me inner peace.

94. I appreciate moments of communion with others who bring me happiness.

95. In gratitude for the chance to learn from my mistakes, I express my gratitude to you.

96. I am thankful for those who use their beautiful words to inspire me and others.

97. I am grateful for the endless career possibilities that I have.

98. I feel fortunate to have loved ones who know just what to say or do to cheer me up.

99. I am grateful that there are those who are concerned enough to inquire about my well-being.

100. I am grateful for all the hobbies and interests that I am passionate about.

101. I am thankful for all of the successes I have had so far in my life.

102. I feel fortunate for all the happy moments I have to cherish.

103. I feel grateful that positive thinking is always a choice available to me.

104. I am grateful for the days when I am able to disconnect and decompress.

105. I am grateful that after the winter, spring always returns, bringing forth new life and beauty.

106. I feel fortunate to live a life filled with meaning and purpose.

107. I am thankful for the chance to become part of something bigger than myself.

108. I appreciate finding pleasant moments when they are least expected.

109. I am already grateful for the amazing moments that are coming in my future.

110. I am thankful to be able to use every experience in my life to make me a better person.

111. I am thankful to be able to use every experience in my life to teach others to be better people.

112. I am grateful for the nutrition and deliciousness that food provides to make me look and feel good.

113. I appreciate the freedom I have to choose my own path in life.

114. I appreciate every compliment I receive from others to brighten my day.

115. I am thankful for the ability to envision success and the conviction to follow through and make it happen.

116. I feel grateful that there are always opportunities available to me to better myself.

117. I appreciate having access to conveniences I often take for granted like clean drinking water, indoor plumbing, and electricity.

118. I am grateful to have enough food to maintain the health and nourishment of my body.

119. I make an effort to thank every single person who has made a positive impact on my life.

120. I am thankful for all the adventures I have embarked upon.

121. I feel grateful for kind gestures from the random strangers that I meet.

122. I feel fortunate for the overflowing happiness that I have to offer others.

123. I am grateful for every day I wake up to greet the sunrise.

124. I appreciate the satisfied feeling that comes with an honest day's hard work.

125. I am thankful for all the special things, big and small, that make life worth living.

126. I am grateful that something as simple as saying "thank you" can lead to happiness.

127. I feel grateful to live in a time when I can instantly and easily communicate with my friends, family, and loved ones.

128. I appreciate my daily routines that start and end my days right.

129. I am grateful for the quality content that other people have shared on the internet that opens my mind to new things.

130. I am grateful for a time of rest after a time of work.

131. I am thankful to have people in my life who love me unconditionally.

132. I appreciate my freedom to be myself and express my individuality.

133. I am grateful for the technological innovations that make my life more convenient.

134. I feel fortunate for all the role models who have served as a positive influence in my life.

135. For the insight I acquire from people who have gone through what I am currently going through, I am really grateful to them.

136. I am grateful for my ability to find the silver lining in everything.

137. I am thankful for life's teachable moments that provide me with valuable lessons.

138. I appreciate overcast days because they make me even more grateful for sunny weather.

Chapter 28
Financial Affirmations for Every Day

Financial affirmations are brief phrases you may repeat to yourself to feel better about money. Money mantras and abundance affirmations are two more names for financial affirmations that you may come across. The idea is to keep yourself motivated as you go through your financial path. A money mantra may help you remain on track to achieve your financial objectives, no matter where you are at in the process of achieving them.

It is important to remember that financial affirmations should always be delivered in a positive manner. You should refrain from being continuously judgmental of your decisions or your financial situation. Instead, adopting a positive attitude will assist you in being pleased with your financial decisions. A negative mantra might lead to bad financial choices in the future.

Maintaining a positive frame of mind should make a significant difference while trying to stay on track with your money. Although it is easy to get consumed by bad feelings when it comes to money, this negativity will not serve you well in the long run. In fact, having a negative frame of mind might keep you trapped in the same financial behaviors that aren't serving you well.

When you have a positive frame of mind, you may locate excellent things because you are actively seeking them. Instead of focusing only on your lack of progress or faults, you'll discover that it's far simpler to remark on the steps you've taken to get there.

The Affirmations

1. I am financially secure.

2. The joy I feel knows no bounds.
3. I'm capable of dealing with whatever that comes my way.
4. I always have a nice chunk of money in the bank.
5. My relationship with money is healthy and loving.
6. I am not afraid to ask for a raise when I deserve one.
7. Every day, in every aspect, I'm improving and becoming better and better.
8. I am prepared to go to any length to achieve self-sufficiency in my life.
9. I am a genius who can handle anything that comes my way.
10. I am easily able to save a portion of my income each month.
11. I have more talent inside of me than I know what to do with.
12. I deserve a good night's sleep after a long day of hard work.
13. I feel deserving of all the abundance that life has to offer.
14. I make a lot of money but never find myself lacking anything.
15. I set financial goals and work hard each day to achieve them.
16. It is easy for me to prioritize my needs and put myself first.
17. People compliment me on my hair, clothes, and spending habits.
18. All of my hard work finally paying off is an incredible feeling.

19. My best is always good enough; others recognize my worthiness.

20. being so concerned about my financial future has really paid off.

21. Every thought I think creates a new reality for me to experience.

22. In order to see my aspirations realized, I am prepared to go to any length to achieve them.

23. I measure my success by the love and happiness I have in my life.

24. I feel confident that my financial future is secure and promising.

25. I am financially independent and feel free in all aspects of money.

26. My family and friends; they are very proud of how well I handle money matters.

27. My tax obligations are up to date and I always pay my bills on time.

28. I am a genius, and everything I need to prosper is already within me.

29. I value whether or not I can afford something, not how much it costs.

30. I am able to see opportunities when they arise and capitalize on them.

31. I have the ability to negotiate my salary and never sell myself short.

32. I have achieved great success and satisfaction in every aspect of my life to date.

33. The more successful I become, the less time I have for boredom or worry.

34. I have the power and will never give up or let anyone tell me otherwise.

35. I'm grateful for this moment, but it doesn't define where I'll be tomorrow.

36. As I learn more about managing money, my money skills increase even further.

37. I can be as great as I want to be, if only I believe in my power to achieve.

38. I deserve to be successful in all aspects of my life, especially with money.

39. My income is higher than my expenses and I am not struggling to stay afloat.

40. I use money to express myself in whatever way I want and make the most of it.

41. I am aware of the impact that making good financial choices can have on my life.

42. I am becoming more financially stable every day, as long as I keep working hard.

43. My worth does not come from how much money I make but from who I am as a person.

44. I am able to actually provide for my family and make them proud with what I have achieved.

45. Every day, I am grateful for all of the opportunities that hard work has given me.

46. I am able to stay grounded when thinking about money and make decisions with ease.

47. Today I will do what others won't, so tomorrow I can accomplish what others can't.

48. It feels good to have my own savings put away and I enjoy how it builds up each day.

49. Money now flows to me freely and without effort. I am open to receiving it in whatever shape that it may take.

50. I am open-minded when thinking about money and willing to learn more about the topic.

51. Spending money on others brings me a lot of joy, but it's important to save some too.

52. I feel a sense of pride in all that I have accomplished and the time it took to do so.

53. Money doesn't make me happy or sad, but I feel really good when spending it on others.

54. There is really no obstacle that big enough to stop me from succeeding at whatever I choose to do.

55. I am determined to build wealth so one day I can help those less fortunate than myself.

56. I have a healthy relationship with money and make smart choices in how I spend my money.

57. My savings account is as full as it was the day it started and every penny of it is mine.

58. Each month, I have a budget that allows me to put at least 5% of my income toward savings.

59. I deserve financial abundance and I trust in the universe to give me opportunities for it.

60. Sometimes, I make peace with my past financial mistakes and work hard to never repeat them.

61. I always learn from my mistakes because each one teaches me how not to act next time around.

62. It feels great to invest in myself by taking a course or class on a topic that interests me.

63. Other people are able to look up to me as a great role model when it comes to money matters.

64. The best investment can make is in yourself by continuously learning and honing your skills.

65. There are plenty of opportunities for everyone willing to get off their ass and go get them.

66. When it comes to properly managing my finances, I have a great deal of satisfaction in my accomplishments.

67. If I have problems, they are tiny and insignificant compared to the size of my heart and soul.

68. As a result of my fantastic credit score, I have no concern about the possibility of ever requiring good credit for anything significant.

69. Finally, the only person who stands between you and your goals is you.

70. It feels wonderful to succeed at saving money instead of spending everything I make each month.

71. Today, I make a commitment to learn about how to better handle money while having fun doing it.

72. When faced with financial decisions, I consider all available options before making a decision.

73. I am a channel of divine energy. I use my energy to manifest the life that I desire and deserve.

74. Sometimes, if an opportunity comes up that would cause me to overspend, I choose not to take it.

75. As I learn more about managing my money, I look for new ways to improve upon what I already know.

76. If I am not sure how to handle a financial situation, I ask for help from those that know better.

77. I am pleased with how much I have learnt about investing my money in various ventures throughout the course of my career.

78. I put myself first in line when thinking about spending money and wasting it on unimportant things.

79. It feels good to spend time away from home with people that are close to me enjoying life together.

80. I never go into debt without having a solid plan in place that allows me to pay off my debt quickly.

81. Saving money every month is a huge achievement and it makes me feel great to accomplish such a goal.

82. When handling my finances, it is important to be realistic about how much I have versus what I need.

83. I feel great about all of my savings accounts because they represent how much hard work has paid off.

84. I value how much enjoyment I get out of spending money on meaningful things while still being frugal.

85. I work hard at keeping my financial house in order so one day I might be able to purchase my own home.

86. When going over my finances, I am able to keep a clear head and understand where all of my money goes.

87. I am able to ask for help when I need it and know there are resources available to me when I need them.

88. When it comes to acquiring money, where you start is less important than where you want to end up at the conclusion of the process.

89. Every little bit counts when trying to build wealth because every penny saved eventually becomes dollars.

90. My checking account is often overflowing and there is always a healthy sum of cash in my savings account.

91. All of my ideas are valid regardless of how others may perceive them, especially when it comes to finances.

92. I'm grateful for what this moment brings but even more excited about all the ones still waiting ahead of me.

93. Living below your means doesn't just benefit you financially; it also improves your overall quality of life.

94. I am surrounded by abundance on all levels of my life - financially, spiritually, emotionally, and physically.

95. I leave money on the table when I could be making more by taking advantage of opportunities that come my way.

96. I never regret trusting my instincts when it comes to money matters and know that it is always best to do so.

97. Sometimes what you have to do isn't fun, but it has to be done because the result is worth all of the effort.

98. When it comes to saving money, I always make sure to budget everything out and not go overboard with spending.

99. Having good credit represents how responsible I have been overall with my finances which also means a lot to me.

100. Although I am not perfect with money management, I know that I am always improving myself more and more each day.

101. I am proud of my new-found financial knowledge and how much more comfortable it has made me feel about my future.

102. I love the feeling of freedom that money provides me with. The less I worry about money, the more freedom I have.

103. Investing in myself by learning new skills or getting certifications look great on paper when applying for a job.

104. I realized that being broke isn't about how much you earn or spend, but rather what mindset is attached to it all.

105. The more relaxed I am about money, the wealthier I become. I am abundant and can receive more whenever I want it.

106. Every day brings new opportunities for me. The more I relax about money, the more money comes into my experience.

107. I never ever let money stand in the way of something that is important to me and feel lucky to be able to afford it all.

108. Just because I don't have a lot of money doesn't mean that I can't enjoy my life and appreciate everything around me.

109. Just because my bank account isn't overflowing with cash doesn't mean I can't still celebrate all I have in life.

110. When faced with financial problems, I consider every option available and find the best one suited for me.

111. Combining my finances with someone else's is very stressful and makes me uncomfortable, so I keep them separate for now.

112. I am making choices today that will positively impact my financial state tomorrow. Save now so you can spend more later.

113. Being financially secure allows me the freedom to work on achieving other life goals such as buying a house or traveling.

114. Debt relief is like to climbing a mountain; it's tedious and arduous, but the view from the summit is well worth it.

115. When thinking about financial problems, I take a step back and examine all of my options before making any rash decisions.

116. Being broke sucks, but there are many like me who can relate to how difficult life is when you have no money in your pocket.

117. I am grateful for all the money I have right now. As I focus on having more, it comes into my life easily and effortlessly.

118. I really don't need a lot of money to be happy, I just prefer having more than enough because life is easier when you have options.

119. Reaching out for help is a sign of strength not weakness, and knowing I have a solid support system makes everything easier.

120. Every month, I put aside a particular amount of money for savings first, before spending the remaining on bills and other frivolous expenditures like entertainment.

121. I am grateful for money because it gives me the freedom to do whatever I want without worrying about how much anything costs.

122. I am always very proud of how well I handle money matters because being financially responsible helps me succeed in all parts of my life.

123. Every day miracles happen in my life, including financial miracles. I am grateful for all the money coming to me right now.

124. My roommate/landlord/significant other understands my situation and helps me out until things get better financially on my end.

125. It has been shown that taking care of myself physically helps me feel better emotionally, so I indulge myself by purchasing something expensive every now and again to reward myself.

126. When you're fit and healthy, you're able to be productive. This is essential for business and will help me make more money.

127. Having a lot of free time allows me to relax and unwind without feeling guilty about wasting too much time doing nothing at all.

128. When faced with financial problems, I take a step back and analyze my options instead of panicking and doing something I will regret.

129. My relationship with money is joyful and completely free of fear. Money comes easily to me now, and there's plenty for everyone.

130. When faced with financial problems, I take a step back and contemplate what the best decision would be for my overall well-being.

131. Getting over financial problems is not as stressful as before now that I know what needs to be done in order to improve upon them.

132. My job is fun because it's a way of expressing myself and sharing what I have to offer with others.

133. I am making plans for increasing my income. I create new ideas every day that will help me gain more money, without hurting anyone.

134. It's okay if things don't go according to plan sometimes because the only way to learn from our mistakes is through trial and error.

135. My past mistakes taught me a lot about making better decisions moving forward without repeating the same, self-destructive behavior.

136. Even though my bank account doesn't reflect my financial success, I know that with enough time my efforts will show tangible results.

137. Money is always a good servant but a bad master. I choose to let go of any greed, jealousy or envy so that I can experience true prosperity.

138. When giving to others, I make sure it is something they really need instead of something I want to give them because I can afford it.

139. In order to make more sustainable financial progress, I need focus on all aspects of budgeting from spending to saving to giving back.

140. My personal relationships are very important, and I would never jeopardize them for money at all because I value them much more than that.

141. The money that I have now is bringing me comfort and security, and the extra advice of my accountant is helping me to plan for my future.

142. It is amazing how much money I am able to save and spend on things by simply planning ahead. It's just so easy when you know what you're doing.

143. I am open to receiving all the money I deserve and more, as life struggles make me stronger and help me grow wiser and cleverer each day.

144. Money is a neutral force in my life that neither brings me happiness nor sadness, but sometimes it makes me happy when spending it on others.

145. Every day I get better at managing what belongs to me... including money. As I grow wealthy, everyone benefits from being associated with me.

146. Happiness always comes from within and not from materialistic items that cost a bunch of money that will only bring me temporary satisfaction anyway.

147. I am consistently working towards my financial goals and targets because I enjoy the feeling of success that comes when I receive a paycheck.

148. Being financially free means that you don't ever have to answer to anyone or do something that you don't want to do in order to earn your keep.

149. I am realizing that my own deeds are the only ones that can affect how much money will come to me – no one gets rich by sitting on their hands.

150. People die with their wealth too often than not, so if I continue to save then someday, I'll be able to leave something behind for other people.

151. People love me unconditionally just as I love myself unconditionally. We all have our own different flaws, but we also have so many wonderful qualities too.

152. Even though I can't afford it right now, I don't let that stop me from wanting to buy the things that brighten up my day and add value to my life.

153. Figuring out how much I can save each month has been tough, but if it's challenging then it must mean that the rewards are proportionally greater?

154. I allow abundance into my life easily and effortlessly now. It is my divine right to have an overflow of wealth, happiness, health, and prosperity.

155. I am doing my best every day with money because it's the only way to ensure a comfortable life. Money isn't everything; but you can't buy happiness.

156. I am growing in knowledge about money every day, and this helps me plan for the future. My savings will work hard to provide for me later on in life.

157. It's easy to save money when you remember that everything is temporary. It all comes and goes, so why should the things that matter be any different?

158. I am talented in many areas that I fail to recognize. I take this opportunity now to uncover my talents and use them for the greater good of humanity.

159. I don't need a lot of money or expensive possessions to prove that I'm rich because being rich means having about the freedom to do whatever makes me happy.

160. My whole life I've been learning about money, and it's finally paying off in a big way. At this rate, my children will probably be wealthier than I am.

161. When I learn how to make money work for me, it's amazing. It's taken a lot of effort on my part, but I can see the payoff more and more as time goes on.

162. My new thoughts and feelings create the reality of my dreams. Every day miracles happen in my life, as long as I focus on all that is good and positive.

163. I am always doing my best every day with money because I know that it dictates how I'll live in the future. Money isn't one's everything, but it sure is a lot of fun.

164. I deserve to be happy with money in my life like everyone else. Sure, it isn't the most essential thing in the world, but why should it be handled any differently from the rest of life?

165. The one and the only thing stopping me from being rich is my ability to earn money, so I'm going to continue doing just that until one day I finally succeed big time.

166. I deserve the best now. I accept only good things into my life now. Abundance flows naturally to me. I am wealthy because I affirm myself as being wealthy.

167. I deserve to be happy with my money, and I'm going to go out of my way to treat myself more often. Life is just too brief not to take pleasure in things such as large purchases.

168. The most important decision you will ever make is who you allow in your life, no matter how much money you or they have or what their material possessions might be.

169.   When you invest your savings properly, you should see it work hard for you. This means that you can take a step back and let it do its thing while you relax.

170.   It feels amazing once you finally start earning an income because now you can do things without feeling guilty or scared about spending your hard-earned money.

171. When I spend time thinking about my savings, it makes me so happy. It really is a lot of money, and I feel so fortunate to have been able to save all of it up.

172.   I am really enjoying the fruits of my labor as I start dreaming about what's next. My hard work is working hard for me now, and even better things will be coming soon.

173.   I am working hard with money so that I can enjoy life's luxuries later on in life. If you cut back now, you'll have plenty of room to splurge when you're older.

174.   Before I go to sleep every day, I read an article about how to attract money while sleeping. The more I learn about the laws of the universe, the better my life will run.

175.   My money-making opportunities are increasing by the day, as well as my income. The right time to make a lucrative deal is approaching, and I am ready to seize it.

176.   The more responsibility I gain at work, the more money I can make. My boss is counting on me, which means he will give me all the opportunities I need to succeed.

177.   I am learning how to save money every day so that I can enjoy all the things I really want later on. You can't go anywhere if you don't have any money, so save up.

178. I happily complete all tasks that come up on my path. All those who surround me are happy because we have a healthy relationship with each other and our finances.

179. Some of the most important lessons you'll encounter in life are learned through mistakes, but it's our actions or reactions after making those mistakes that define who we truly are.

180. When it comes down to it, the harder I work for money, the more money I'll be able to make because effort eventually turns into results when enough time has passed.

181. I am taking care of my money now so that it can help me later on. It's easy to save if you just say no when tempted to buy something that isn't absolutely necessary.

182. I am learning about the importance of money in my life, and I am getting better at managing it every day. Money isn't going be your everything, but it is necessary to know when to utilize it effectively.

183. It feels amazing when I buy things for myself because it means I'm taking care of myself. When it comes to life, what's the purpose if you don't indulge yourself every now and then?

184. When I build my savings account slowly over time, there's something quite satisfying about watching it grow. It's very nice to have a nest egg in case anything awful happens.

185. Building wealth isn't easy, but neither is any worthwhile endeavor, and if success were as simple as working hard then everyone would actually attain their dreams easily.

186. My finances are steadily increasing as my business expands and becomes more profitable. The more people I reach with my products and services, the more I am able to earn.

187. The first step towards financial success is to simply stop spending money on things that don't matter and wasting money on living a lifestyle that doesn't suit your needs.

188. I am doing my very best every day with money because looking after your future is so very important. If you cut back now, you'll have plenty of room to splurge when you're older.

189. I am grateful for all the money coming to me right now, bringing me freedom from the bondage of old beliefs. Money flows into my life with ease, abundance and prosperity.

190. I am doing my best to be responsible with money so that I can enjoy all of life's luxuries later on in life. Sometimes you have to work for a little while before you can play.

191. I am always doing my very best every day with money because financial security is so very important. You will actually never know what life will throw at you, so having savings on hand just makes sense.

192. I deserve to be happy with money in my life, and I'm going to make sure that happens by following a budget and cutting all of the unnecessary costs. It's easier than it sounds.

193. I deserve to feel good about myself, and I'm going to make a point of getting what I want out of life. Money comes first: you can't enjoy yourself if you don't have any money.

194. Living below our means affords us room in our budget to save for future purchases or invest in ourselves. We are

selective with what we buy because we value our time and money.

195. Money is nothing but a tool that allows us to make our dreams come true. Each and every dollar has spiritual value. I am rich, and money comes to me easily and effortlessly now.

196. At this point in my life my bank account is empty, but I still have all of my internal resources available so it's just a matter of time before financial success is finally mine.

197. When I learn more about investing, I am filled with a sense of power. By learning what works and what doesn't, I am giving myself the chance to really improve my money situation.

198. When we start earning more, we think we can spend our way into happiness, but eventually we learn that the more money you make the more you end up spending it instead of saving it.

199. I deserve to be happy about my savings, and I'm going to make sure that happens by using coupons and only buying the things that I need. It's a great feeling when you get it right.

200. I'm learning so much about money every day, but I still have so much more to learn. There's always something new about numbers, even if you've been studying them for over 10 years.

201. Once my job is decentralized, I will be able to work anywhere in the world. I am becoming more financially stable by expanding my abilities and opening myself up to new experiences.

202. When I finally understand the financial markets and how they work, it's a huge relief. Knowing that there's someone

else who can help me with money and investments would be amazing.

203. I am doing everything I can to make sure I'm financially responsible because it's the only way to ensure a comfortable life. Money isn't everything since you can't buy happiness.

204. I deserve to be happy with my financial situation because everyone else is. There's no point falling behind on your savings and investments because it takes a long time to catch up.

205. I know how to create a budget that works because I take control of my finances now. My income exceeds my expenditures; I allow myself to indulge in small ways because of what I save.

206. I am always doing my very best every day with money because looking after your future is so very important. You will never ever know what life will throw at you, so having savings on hand just makes sense.

207. Getting out of debt is like climbing out from underneath a huge pile of dirt; at first it seems impossible but as soon as you make some progress, everything becomes easier and clearer.

208. My income is increasing by taking on more responsibility. I am finding that this makes my work days much more enjoyable. There is nothing better than knowing you're good at your job.

209. When I make tough decisions about my finances and they work out for the best, it feels amazing. I know that it's the result of long-term planning, and that really is making a difference.

210. I am working towards my dreams every day, and the financial gain is an ongoing perk of doing what I love. The sooner you start following your passion, the better off you'll be financially.

211. I deserve to be happy about my spending habits, and I'm going to make sure that happens by using coupons and only buying the things that I need. It's a great feeling when you get it right.

212. I am doing my best every day with money because looking after your future is more important than anything else. If you cut back now, you'll have plenty of room to splurge when you're older.

213. We value our financial assets wisely. I responsibly save my money now. Spending less than you earn is the road to wealth; saving more than you spend will always be rewarded in the future.

214. I deserve to be happy with what I have because everyone deserves a little luxury now and then. It feels so great to treat yourself to something nice every now and again, I'm so glad that I can.

215. Every day, I put out my best effort in terms of finances since financial stability is something that everyone deserves. Because you will never know what life may throw at you, it is always a good idea to have some money saved up.

216. I am taking care of my mental health every day by eating right and exercising regularly. When everything inside of me is in working order, not only is my body healthier, but my mind is also lot more at peace.

217. Money flows through me with ease and grace. Everything works out well for me. Each time I spend money, even on simple pleasures, I get something back in return... usually something better.

218. The literal definition of being successful is simply to have succeeded, so even though I haven't achieved everything I want to right now, I still believe that one day my efforts will pay off.

219. I trust that as the energy of money flows into my life, it will provide all I need. As I take responsibility for managing what already belongs to me, even better things come to me now.

220. My hobbies and passions are expensive, but that doesn't mean that I shouldn't keep doing them even if they aren't always affordable. The cost of fun isn't equivalent to the value of happiness.

221. The more money I have, the less important my physical needs become. As I become more prosperous, others benefit from being associated with me because they know that they will also be rich.

222. I deserve the best in life just like everyone else, and that includes having a proper savings account for emergencies. When life is difficult, you want to depend on friends and family.

223. I know how to set boundaries with people, places, and things. No one can make me feel loved or worthy unless I allow it. With great power comes great responsibility- so I responsibly choose love.

224. When I think about how much money I have waiting for me from my retirement fund, it makes me so happy. It really is a lot of money, and I feel so fortunate to have been able to save all of it up.

225. I'm taking full advantage of all life has to offer, without a care in the world about the future or any regrets about the past. Money is coming into my life in many different ways, and I will enjoy spending it when the time comes.

226. I am proud of my efforts towards self-improvement every day, but I will continue to work hard until I am the best version of myself. This old cliché is true: you can never be too rich or too thin.

227. When I think about how much money I have waiting for me from my retirement fund, it's so overwhelming. It really is a lot of money, and I feel so privileged to have been able to save all of it up.

228. Charity really does feel good. Knowing that by spending time or money on someone else, I'm making a difference, lifts my spirits. In our world, so many people need help, and it is a very rewarding experience to be able to help them.

229. There are no problems with my finances now...only solutions. The more responsible we are with our spending habits, the easier it is to save. I know that money comes easily and effortlessly to me now.

230. I am doing my best every day with money because looking after your future is more important than anything else. It's nice to know that if something awful happens, I can at least rely on my savings for support.

231. Every day, I put out my best effort in terms of finances since planning for your future is quite vital. You don't want to pass on debts and problems onto your children and grandchildren because you were irresponsible.

232. The more time I devote to my goals, the more likely it is that they will appear in my life. The universe is now giving me everything I want and desire. Life loves me, and money comes easily to those who love life.

233. My goal is always to make more money instead of spending money on items that are not important or necessary for happiness. My family wants for nothing because we know how to be happy without retail therapy.

234. I deserve to be happy with my financial situation because everyone else is. There's no point in being stuck in debt when there are so many other options available to you, especially if you work hard to improve it.

235. As I express gratitude for what money has already brought me, it exponentially increases in my life. Money flows from many sources. Every day more and more opportunities come my way, which brings me wealth.

236. Life has been hard for me in the past, but now it has been easy since I have learned from those circumstances. In the end, there is really no need for me to be anxious about things that are beyond of my control since everything will work out in my favor in due course.

237. We are smart about our finances; we use cash instead of credit cards. Wealth flows naturally to me now. Money comes easily and effortlessly to us now; we see money everywhere. Retirement accounts grow bigger and bigger.

238. I am grateful for this healthy relationship with money, which further strengthens our connection. Whatever my mind conceives and believes, my body experiences. Whatever I feel in my body affects every aspect of my being.

239. We are smart about our finances; we use cash instead of credit cards. Wealth flows naturally to me now. Money comes easily and effortlessly to us now; it's never scarce or lacking. We all deserve to be happy with what we have.

240. I am smart about how I invest my money so that it can last forever. I take responsibility for how much money is in my bank account. We all deserve to be financially secure and comfortable with no debt and a healthy savings account.

241. I do not want to become a billionaire solely for the purpose of being a millionaire; rather, I want to be able to live comfortably with enough savings and assets built so that I will never ever have to worry about anything else in my life.

242. We are intelligent about our investments. The more we invest, the more money we see in our bank accounts. I avoid buying luxury items because they aren't important to me. I choose to spend my money on experiences with loved ones instead.

243. I give myself permission to be open. I give myself permission to express my love, and joy. As I am open to new possibilities, the world opens up for me. The more I am open with my true self, the easier it is to connect with others.

244. The universe provides for me; money flows easily into my life now. Money comes to me freely and effortlessly right when I need it. If there is a delay in manifesting money, it is because the universe knows I have better things to do with my time.

245. Everyone on this planet is connected by an infinite source of supply. This supply never runs out; it can only multiply like a snowball rolling down a mountain. As I focus on

the abundance of this universe, it naturally transfers into my own life.

246. I am rich, and money comes to me easily and effortlessly now. Money is not here for us to judge; it's a tool that allows us to make our dreams come true. I always have enough money to cover all of life's expenses- so I don't worry about the future.

247. I trust that as the energy of money flows into my life, it will provide all that I need. As I take responsibility for managing what already belongs to me, even better things come to me now. My income keeps increasing, bringing more and more abundance with it.

248. In the evening, I always read an article on how to attract money while sleeping before going to bed. The more I learn about the laws of the universe, the better my life will run. My relationship with money is joyful and completely free of fear. Money comes easily to me now, and there's plenty for everyone.

249. My spending habits are healthy because they bring joy and nourishment to my body and mind. Money isn't earned to be saved: its purpose is to flow freely between human beings so we just can all benefit from each other's talents.

250. I will receive everything back from life tenfold. Money comes easily to me now, without my having to work for it all day long. In fact, one could say that money works for me. The more values I share with the world, the more valuable I feel. Everything I give away makes room for something better in my life.

251. Everything I give away makes room for something greater to flow in.

252.   People feel comfortable around me because they know I will never judge them or ask anything from them. Money flows toward those who do not cling to it like a child with a new toy, but those who project an attitude of gratitude toward the material things. The more we give away, the richer our lives become.

253.   It feels natural for me to help people in need because they are part of me. There is no "other" here, just existence coming through all beings continuously. you give what you want to receive, and I want to give love. As I express my gratitude, all that is mine by divine right flows back to me in generous measure.

254.   Anything I put my attention on seems to expand in front of me. The more money I make, the easier it is for me to make even more money. This cycle actually just repeats itself over and over again. My job is fun because it's a way of expressing myself and sharing what I have to offer with others. Today, as gladly as possible,

255.   I am smart about my finances; I use cash instead of credit card debts. Wealth flows naturally to me now. The universe rewards us for being responsible with our spending habits by always having enough to cover all of life's expenses - so I don't worry about the future. I am safe, secure, and taken care of 100% of the time.

256.   My creativity comes up with new ideas for earning money. The more I earn, the more I can give away. All good things come to me easily now. Everything in the universe is energy, including money. If I believe it and feel it, it will be so. The very fact that I have a good attitude about money has made my life full of happiness and fun.

257. I am at peace with money and what it represents: freedom and power. Money allows me to travel the world, spend time with friends and family, enjoy nature, pursue hobbies, and pay bills without worrying about not having enough. We all desire for a good life just as long as we use cash instead of credit cards so we can stay out of debt.

258. I deserve to be well paid for my work, and I am open to receiving more tasks that fulfill me and make the world a better place. As I focus on my abundance, I allow myself to accept more opportunities like this. They come to all those who believe in their own worth and take care of their finances. The universe is abundant; there is always enough for everyone.

259. I am a magnet for financial abundance. The more I give, the greater I get. Money is now flowing to me freely and readily. I have enough money to save for retirement or buy whatever I desire without worrying about not being able to pay my bills. My talent is living well below our means. We all deserve a luxurious life just as long as we don't go into debt doing so.

260. My income keeps increasing, bringing more and more abundance. My spending habits are healthy because they bring joy and nourishment to my body and mind.

261. The more responsible we are with our spending, the easier it is to save money. We breathe easy knowing that our families will always come first, so we save enough money for them without worry. There are delays in the manifestation of my finances only when they are perfectly aligned for my highest good and not because there is lack or scarcity. Each and every dollar has spiritual value.

262. We all breathe easy knowing our financial futures are never uncertain. We breathe easy knowing that our families will always come first, so we save enough money for them without

worry. The more responsible we are with our spending habits, the easier it is to save money. The universe rewards us for being responsible with our spending habits by always having enough money to cover all of life's expenses.

263. The more our gratitude for what we have, the more prosperous our lives become. There is abundance in everything - not just material things. We know that experiences with family and friends are what truly matter; therefor, our incomes allow us to travel whenever possible. We all deserve a luxurious life as long as we don't go into debt doing so. The universe has my back when it comes to my finances. I trust myself totally.

264. I am always financially secure, no matter what. I really deserve to live a life of abundance, and money comes to me easily and effortlessly now. Money is energy; it has no power over me because everything I need always comes to me, right at the perfect time. There are delays in the manifestation of my finances only when they are perfectly aligned for my highest good and not because there is lack or scarcity. I love how abundant my life truly is.

265. We find joy in saving money we earned because we know financial freedom will always come to us if we keep diligent with our spending habits. My family has learned the power of non-materialistic happiness, which allows us to give generously to others without worry. Money now pours into my life freely and readily; it is never sparse or missing in my life anymore. If there are delays, it is because the universe knows that life is short - so spend your time wisely doing what makes you happy.

266. Our lives are abundant in happiness, love, and gratitude; the more thankful we are for what we have, the wealthier life becomes. Money is nothing but a tool that allows us to make dreams come true. Recognizing that every dollar has spiritual significance, we accept responsibility for our own financial

well-being. Every dollar is an opportunity to practice mindfulness in action. If there are delays, it's because the universe knows that patience is always rewarded when you invest in your future self. We all deserve to be happy with what we have.

267.   There are delays in the manifestation of my finances only when they are perfectly aligned for my highest good- not because there is lack or scarcity. Money is nothing but a tool that allows us to make dreams come true. Recognizing that every dollar has spiritual significance, we accept responsibility for our own financial well-being. Every dollar is an opportunity to practice mindfulness in action. If there are delays, it's because the universe knows that patience is always rewarded when you invest in your future self. There is abundance in everything, not just material things. We deserve to live a life of luxury and opulence as long as we don't go into debt doing so. Money comes easily and effortlessly to us now; it's never scarce or lacking.

Chapter 29
Breaking Bad Habits

Habits are instilled behaviors. They have been repeated so many times, day after day, that they resemble mechanical functions. You don't have to think about your habits before engaging in them. You will learn the importance of knowing which of your behaviors must be eliminated. You can learn to mine the good aspects of complex behavior since it can have both good and bad effects.

In his book, Affirmations, Wilde suggests that the world around us actively works to undermine or destroy our power or sense of personal control. Then, affirmations of strength and control allow their bearer to overcome society's most imposing obstacles (Wilde, 2009). The affirmations will focus on the often lengthy and arduous process of reprogramming one's behavior. While difficult, this process is imminently worthwhile.

The Affirmations

   1. *Your behavior is completely within your control.*

It is important to realize that how we behave is entirely within our control despite what we may think. Except for yourself, there is no one else to blame for the things you do and say in your life. You need to take responsibility.

   2. *Everything you do should improve your life and the lives of others.*

Your actions should be purposeful. Why act without purpose? You are how you behave; and every action you take should in some way reflect your deepest values and desires. Give thought to your actions. Why are you behaving this way? Should you modify your behavior?

   3. *You will stop behaving in destructive ways.*

Identify the moments in your life in which you act in harmful ways to yourself or the people around you. Do you know that you are in complete control of the actions you take, so why behave in destructive ways? You have no excuse for behaving poorly. It's on you.

    4. If you repeat a bad behavior, simply notice and ask yourself to do differently next time. You understand and forgive yourself.

You must not treat yourself harshly. You will learn best from reinforcing good behaviors, not from punishing yourself for bad ones.

    5. With time and perseverance, you will transform yourself.

Confidence in your ability to attain your objectives is essential. Believing that you are capable is powerful and will help you to manifest your desired result more easily and in less time. You are capable of it.

    6. Make a list of your bad habits. You understand that to combat bad behaviors, you must first acknowledge them.

What habits do you wish to rid yourself of? What are the effects of these habits? In recognizing the specific nature of our most destructive habits, we can better confront them. You don't have to be scared of your behaviors. Put them to paper, and in so doing realize how small they are.

    7. You will slowly abandon all of the most harmful parts of yourself. You will feel freer.

There is nothing quite so freeing as proving to yourself that the behavioral loops you feel "stuck" within don't have so great a hold on you. You are capable of change. People do change. All it takes is a certain strength and willingness.

    8. You are capable of overcoming established habits. It only takes time.

the secret is time. You must strive to never lose patience with or hope for yourself. You must never give up. The only obstacle to your enduring and meaningful change is you.

9. *Today, you are grateful to yourself for trying to change for the better.*

It is important to recognize the effort you expend and the strides (however great or small) you make. Too often, we forget to reward ourselves or to appreciate ourselves for our work. Make sure you don't.

10. *You will learn more about yourself and your habits every day.*

You are observant and intelligent. That's not an opinion: it's a fact. You are capable of learning and growing; you are capable. Make a conscious effort to notice the way you act and think. Every bit of information can help you.

11. *You can unlearn your most destructive behaviors. You will.*

Believe in yourself. It will take time, but you have that time to give. Destructive behaviors can be rooted deep within ourselves. It takes hard work and sometimes a struggle to unlearn awful habits. You have to know that you are capable of it.

12. *Your willingness to evaluate yourself is admirable.*

A lot of people have trouble with honestly confronting their worst habits. We are hyper-critical, but at the same time, unwilling to tackle the parts of ourselves that are truly detrimental. Make sure you are not like that and you confront and eliminate your worst qualities.

13. *You have made a difference in yourself and the way you move through this world. You will continue to do so.*

Notice and appreciate, from time to time, the strides you have made. You are a different person than you were a couple of weeks ago. How do you feel about these small changes? What changes do you want to see a couple of weeks from now?

14. *You are embracing every small chance to improve yourself.*

Sometimes, we let the chance to change pass us by. Not today. Whenever there's an opportunity to behave in a way that aligns with your goals, seize it. You make sure that every one of your actions counts.

15. You are dynamic.

You are not doomed to remain the same forever. In fact, remaining the same is a near-impossible thing to do. Take control of the change in yourself and push yourself to change in the manner you want.

16. You will determine which of your negative habits and deconstruct those.

You can identify the habits that are harmful to you or rooted in a harmful attitude. You can then discourage yourself from behaving in that way again.

17. Your behavior changes as your thoughts change. You will think more positive and helpful ways. You will give yourself credit for having beneficial thought processes.

It's not always possible to be self-aware all the time, to know for certain why we are doing certain things. However, it is possible to encourage yourself to think more positively. This positive thinking will affect your actions in a similarly positive way.

18. You will let go of the thoughts that are holding you back from your full potential.

Once you have identified a thought process that only serves to harm you, banish it from your mind and heart. You do not want to create more obstacles for yourself. Make room for new, more helpful thoughts.

19. You are making room for new, constructive habits.

Breaking old habits means making new ones that promote your success. See the good that comes, or could potentially come, from cutting out bad habits and bad frames of mind.

20. Your day is filled with wonderful change.

Change is such a beautiful thing. You know that your life is surrounded by, and infused by, a wonderful dynamicity. Observe the change you see in your environment or in the people all around you. Be this change.

21. Habits are entrenched behaviors. You recognize that unraveling these will take a great deal of time.

Patience, patience, patience. You've got all the patience in the world, my friend. Trust in yourself and your ability to get to where you are going. Nothing you desire should come to you immediately. Where is the lesson in immediate gratification?

22. You are not controlled or defined by your most negative habits.

Your negative habits are a part of you, but they do not define you. You are so much more than a few paltry bad habits.

23. You are proud of yourself for your valiant and consistent efforts.

It takes a lot out of a person, being strong and courageous every day. Yet somehow, you can manage it. Take today to be proud of your strength of body and mind. You deserve to take pride in who you are.

24. You are stronger than your worst habits and your most consuming addictions. You will overcome them.

No matter the behavior, you can stop it. No matter what. Any belief toward the contrary is a straight-up fallacy. Close your eyes and say it once more: You are stronger. You will overcome.

25. You choose to improve yourself and feel better for having done so.

There's a lot of power in choice. These changes in you are all a product of your choices. You choose the change. Remember that and make good choices every single day.

26. You consciously recognize the most pervasive of your bad behaviors. Slowly, you make sure even these are completely eliminated.

To get rid of your bad behaviors, you must be conscious of them. You have to point them out to yourself whenever they recur and ask yourself to do better next time. This is the only way.

27. You overcome adversity. You welcome the challenge.
It's all about your state of mind. Any difficult task is far less imposing if you become excited by the prospect of victory. Let yourself get competitive. Let yourself be electrified at the idea of winning.

28. You are grateful for your ability to change and grow.
Imagine always being the same. You are grateful that the world doesn't work that way and that you have the power to be whatever you want to be.

29. You will release the habits that no longer or never have propped you up.
You do not need useless and ugly things. You let go. You're better for having let go.

Chapter 30
Building Constructive Habits

Now that you have deconstructed destructive behaviors, it's time to move on to replace them with new, more productive behaviors. At the start, sticking to your habits can be extremely challenging. When you are building a new habit, the most labor-intensive period is the phase of establishment. You must expend conscious thought and effort to repeat the desirable behavior. After this period has ended, however, you will be able to repeat the behavior without consciously thinking about it. When a desirable behavior becomes a habit, it is no longer difficult to keep it up.

In their study, "Pro-Environmental Actions, Climate Change, and Defensiveness: Do Self-Affirmations Make a Difference to People's Motives and Beliefs About Making a Difference?" authors Sparks, Jessop, Chapman, and Holmes found that self-affirmations had a real, demonstrable effect on the participants. Those who used self-affirmations to motivate their behavior and manipulate their intentions showed increased engagement with desirable behaviors.

Specifically, the authors observe that positive self-affirmations can push people to recycle more frequently. There is a scientific basis for the effectiveness of positive self-affirmation. When we tap into the potential of positive self-talk, we can improve our behaviors and build long-lasting habits that promote our health and productivity.

The Affirmations

1. *You are determined to build good habits that help you to live a better, more fulfilling life.*

Never underestimate the importance of determination. This is the quality that will carry you to the finish line. You refuse to quit! You refuse to let those obstacles overwhelm you as you strive to meet your goals! Nothing can stop you if you don't allow it to!

2. *You will do right by yourself today.*

To "do right by yourself" means acting in ways that honor your desires and your basic needs. You should strive to do right by yourself every day, and thus act in ways that align with your goals.

3. *You will give your body adequate food and rest.*

In pursuit of broader, less tangible goals, we might forget to honor our bodies. Your mind requires adequate nutrition and rest to function properly. Make sure that you are eating and sleeping enough. Make certain that what you consume will leave you feeling well in the long run.

4. *You are creative and inventive. You will determine what habits are most enriching for you.*

You cannot expect to implement the best possible habits overnight. It takes thought to figure out what habits you would most like to learn. It also takes trial and error. You will discover, over time, what works well for you in your life.

5. *Your habits will reflect on you positively.*

When you have developed the right and most positive habits, people will notice and admire you for it. Your mannerisms will set you apart from the rest of the group. They will make you a desirable partner, friend, and family member.

6. *You will only engage in behaviors that help you lead a better life.*

Today, focus your energy on your goals so that you can behave in the best possible ways. The more you practice this focus, the stronger it will become and the better your behavior will be. Have faith in your process.

7. *You will respect the work you put in to develop good habits.*

Don't let anyone, least of all yourself, make you doubt yourself. You are trying to become better. So, every day, become a little better than the day before. Internalize this fact. Allow no one to deceive you into believing anything that is not true.

> 8. *You establish healthy and productive habits on a daily basis. You are filled with determination.*

Consistency is key. There is consistency in many things it is all around you. For example, you can be sure the sun will rise tomorrow. You can be sure the seasons will change. If your heart continues to beat, you may be certain that you are still alive. So, be sure that your effort to change remains consistent.

> 9. *You are taking control of the way you behave.*

It is satisfying to take control. Once you've done it, you'll wonder why you hadn't started the process years ago. If you want to get things started, there is no better moment than right now. Take a deep breath, and concentrate on trying to change one, simple thing you've decided needs to change. You can do it.

> 10. *You feel good for working to change yourself in small ways.*

You have earned the right to feel good. You deserve to think about your efforts and to be glad. With all that you have done, the least you deserve is that. So, smile and pat yourself on the back. Things are looking up.

> 11. *You find better ways to communicate your ideas with others.*

Sometimes, we struggle to articulate our thoughts inarticulate, sincere, and respectful ways. Work to communicate your ideas in the best way possible, today. People will be more receptive to your ideas and suggestions if you learn to speak well.

> 12. *You practice healthy behaviors that improve your body and mood.*

Focus on your bodily health and the quality of your mood. How might you improve these? How motivated are you to improve these?

Recognize that both of these things are incredibly important to your continued success and productivity.

> 13. *You empower yourself by taking charge of your life. You are incredible.*

Feeling in control is powerful stuff. When you know you are in control and feel that power, it becomes much easier to act that way. You are no longer enslaved by the idea that you are powerless. You are no longer in your way.

> 14. *Your peers will recognize the changes you continue to make in yourself. You will feel pride in your accomplishments.*

Let others inspire you to work harder and be better. Your peers notice your continued improvement. Once in a while, they will pay you compliments for it, and you will feel great pride in the changes you have made in your life.

> 15. *You will remember to be patient with yourself. You know it takes time to develop the most useful habits to you.*

Don't rush yourself. The best things and things of the best quality take time to polish and perfect. Your progress is not too slow. If anything, know when it would be valuable to slow yourself down a bit more.

> 16. *You challenge yourself to remain constant in your focus, dedication, and patience.*

Consistency is important. You have to remember to reinforce good behaviors every day. The repetition of a desirable action will cement it as a habit, and habits drive you toward your goals. Remember that you are a dedicated person. You don't give up on your aspirations.

> 17. *Your efforts are inspiring. Give yourself the credit that you deserve.*

It takes courage and hope to work toward positive change. Be happy that you are courageous and hopeful. Drive forward in this world with the awareness that you can improve yourself with every breath you take.

18. *You know there is nothing wrong with having pride in your accomplishments.*

Be aware of your faults, be humbled by them, and proud of what you can do for yourself and others. There is nothing wrong with pride. In combination with self-awareness, Pride is a useful tool that awards us an understanding of our strenuous efforts.

19. *Today, the world is filled with opportunity. You will grasp opportunities with both hands. You will act with dignity and grace.*

Today, make sure that you focus intently. If we lose focus, great opportunities will pass us by, and we won't even notice. Make sure you do what you can for yourself.

20. *Your good habits speak to what you most value and work to make you a better person.*

You can depend on your good habits if they can depend on you. Even when you are tired, follow through on your promises to yourself. With time, it will get simpler and easier to do. Not a short time, by any means, but the ease of doing these good things is worth the work and the wait.

21. *You value yourself enough to make yourself better.*

It's a testament to your self-respect that you work hard to improve. Notice the kindness you show yourself and be grateful for it. You treat yourself well and you should be proud that you do. Understand that treating yourself with respect and consideration will help you improve.

22. *You recognize that you can improve yourself in some small way every day. You recognize that you are valuable throughout the process of self-improvement.*

Do not value the attainment of the goal more than the work you put in to get there. The work can be as pleasurable as the finished product. If you enjoy the process, the process will seem easier and will pass by more smoothly. Make every effort to discover the asset in your job.

23. *You love the way you are.*

You loved yourself then: you love yourself now. Do not reserve your love for who you will be. Love every version of yourself as you work to change. You aren't working to change because you hate your current self. You're working to change because you love self-improvement.

24. *The habits you have built make you stand out to the people around you. You are remarkable.*

People lose focus. While your peers struggle to remain mindful of their continual change, you will not. Not you. You are well aware of what is most essential. You know what you have to do to reach your goals.

25. *You will continually acknowledge your progress and reward yourself for it.*

Don't let your improvement go unnoticed. Your progress deserves recognition and adequate reward. This reward may come in many forms: a piece of chocolate cake, a new tattoo, a day without work. Be extra indulgent, today.

26. *You are determined to transform. Your concentrated willpower can achieve incredible results.*

Your determination is staggering. You know that you can do wonderful things for yourself and for others when you concentrate. Today, remind yourself that you are filled with determination. Remind yourself that your goals truly matter.

27. *You will let destructive urges pass over you. You will examine them with interest. You will not indulge them.*

Why do we have destructive urges? Try to unveil the root cause of your strange thoughts and desires to act poorly today. Discover why these things are a part of you. Then, ask yourself if you can do something to prevent these desires from recurring.

28. *You will indulge in ambitious ideas. You work toward achieving your behavioral goals.*

You may have ideas or goals that seem completely unachievable right now. That doesn't mean you will never achieve them: it means it will take your best, most amazing effort.

29. You are active and intelligent.
You are. You move, act, think. Recognize the strangeness of this miracle.

30. You are passionate and genuine.
You are. You should seek out what you are passionate about. You should say what you genuinely believe.

31. You have fantastic self-control.
Today, practice your self-control. Like anything, self-control requires a great deal of practice.

Chapter 31
On Sadness

We will all experience periods of deep sadness in our lifetimes. Some of us will experience these periods more frequently than others, but all of us will know what it means to feel deeply sad, lost, and confused. On the whole, our society does a very poor job of instructing us on how to cope with feelings of inadequacy and isolation. You will be able to experience sadness without guilt and address your sadness with the utmost effectiveness. I'm sorry to say it, but sometimes sadness needs to be felt. Through these various affirmations, you will give yourself full permission to feel sad. You will also give yourself the tools required to eventually overcome melancholy.

In their study, "Attributions and Affirmations for Overcoming Anxiety and Depression," Kinnier, Hofsess, Pongratz and Lambert (2009) discovered that positive affirmations induced in their bearers a sense of normalcy (as it relates to depression and anxiety) and were helpful to their participants' recoveries.

The Affirmations

1. *You will not blame yourself for feeling unhappy. You will not blame anyone.*

Blame is another thing that does little good, especially when it comes to addressing feelings of sadness. Do not waste your energy on finding someone to blame or making yourself feel all the worse by blaming yourself. Get rid of blame.

2. *You deserve to indulge in feelings of unhappiness from time to time.*

Sometimes being unhappy is unavoidable. Sometimes it is, but repressing that feeling will only lead to trouble down the road. Let yourself be unhappy once in a while. Letting yourself feel unhappy will help you to heal and let go of self-pity, resentment, and regret.

3. *Your unhappiness does not define you.*

You will be unhappy. That does not mean you are an unhappy person or your mood will dictate how you behave. You can overcome feelings of sadness, just as you can overcome every other feeling. It takes work and time, like everything else.

4. *You understand that feeling unhappy is normal. You understand that you are a strong person.*

You are not alone in your unhappiness. People become unhappy, sometimes. It's not actually something to be ashamed of; it's not something that will alienate you from your friends (unless you let it.) You are perfectly normal.

5. *You will appreciate negative feelings for their positive influence on you.*

Feelings of inadequacy are based on nothing at all. Still, that does not mean they are useless. Since they exist, you reframe them and use them to push yourself to improve. You may think, "I'm not fit enough." Because of that thought, you now know that you need to find a new physical activity that brings you joy. You are fit enough. However, if you want to become a better fit, there is a way to achieve it

6. *You are not alone in your unhappiness. You can comfort others; they can comfort you.*

The fact of the matter is actually that this is one of the most important things for you to remember in your most tough moments. Other people understand. Other people know what you are feeling and may talk to you about it, if only you reach out to them. For your own sake, you should do so.

7. *You understand that your sadness will end.*

Everything ends, and sadness is no different. You will not have to endure this unhappy feeling forever. Hold on for those precious moments of joy, contentedness, gratitude, and love. They are worth the wait.

> 8. *You accept what you cannot change. You move on.*

You have complete control over your behavior. In fact, that is all you have complete control over. There are going to be things around you that you don't like and that you can't change. Sometimes, you have to graciously accept the world for what it is. You can only do so much.

> 9. *Your sadness does not make you weak. You have emotional depth.*

There's nothing wrong with being sad. There's nothing abnormal about being sad. Do not compound your unhappiness by feeling ashamed of your sadness. There is absolutely nothing to be embarrassed of. Give yourself time and kindness, and you will recover.

> 10. *You discover the root of your unhappiness and examine it. You decide if you can make a positive change that will address these unhappy feelings.*

You can notice these feelings and ask, "Why is it I feel this way?" You can continue to ask this question until you uncover the real truth of the matter. Then, when you know the truth, you can determine if anything can be done to change the way you feel. There is no harm in trying this potentially beneficial exercise.

> 11. *You do not linger too long in sadness. You act to overcome these negative feelings.*

You should not dwell on the same, sad things. It's okay to be sad, but you can choose to step away from that sadness. You will really be able to dedicate more of your time and energy to other, more successful projects as a result. Sometimes, feelings of sadness will abate if you stop focusing on them.

> 12. *You understand the power of open spaces. You breathe in the fresh air with an appreciation for your ability to do so.*

Nothing is guaranteed, not even life itself. You are aware of the temporary nature of life and of everything in your life. You are ultimately grateful for what you have.

> 13. *You understand the power of the community. You lean on others when you need emotional support. This does not make you weak.*

From time to time, you are going to need a little help from your friends. Every one of us needs a little extra assistance. They can help push you to overcome feelings of melancholy.

> 14. *You endure sadness. You understand that even negative feelings can help you to improve yourself.*

It takes a lot of strength to outlast feelings of sadness. These feelings are so powerful, and devastating that they threaten to overwhelm us. However, you know you have the strength it takes to endure these feelings. No matter how long it takes, you will endure.

> 15. *You know that you will appreciate moments of joy all the more for having experienced moments of melancholy.*

To experience the highest highs of life, you have to experience the lowest lows. There is no ecstasy without suffering. There is no beauty without ugliness. There is no light without darkness. Make peace with this: You cannot appreciate the best things in life without going through the worst.

> 16. *You respect yourself in your sadness. You address your sadness in the ways you find to be the kindest and appropriate.*

Do not berate yourself for feeling inadequate. This will only compound the feeling. Do not berate yourself for feeling sad. This will only compound the sadness. Know that it is all right to feel sad. Treat yourself with the utmost respect.

> 17. *You know that life is the most valuable thing.*

Life is the only thing. There is nothing so precious as life. Please don't let anybody or anything to make you question this for a single second.

The world is a wonderful place despite its horrors, and you want to be here.

18. You are grateful for the moments of melancholy. They show you how strong you are.

It takes strength and incredible patience to get through periods of sadness. After that sadness subsides, you will know how strong you are. You will actually have a greater understanding of the power of your character.

19. You do not resent your sadness. You make the most of your emotions.

You can choose to use your sadness as fuel. Sadness has been known to make people funnier, more creative, or more inventive. See what benefits you can find in your sadness. You might as well practice productivity in the most unfavorable circumstances.

20. You let their caring lift your spirits.

The people in your life can lift you out from the pits of despair if you let them. You should know that these people care about you. You should understand that they want the best for you. So long as they are here, you will never be alone.

21. You avoid self-pity at all costs. It is not helpful to you.

Do not pity yourself for your sadness. You are not a pitiable thing. You are strong and in control, even in moments of weakness. Be sad if you must be, but never feel bad for yourself. This pain is only temporary. You can handle it.

22. You know that healing takes time. You don't rush the process.

Just as you practice patience for yourself in all other areas, you are patient while you are healing. It does take a good deal of time. You are ready to wait in silence. You are ready to wait a long, long time if you must.

23. When faced with adversity, you know you will get through it.

It is not blind confidence. You know yourself and your abilities intimately. Know that this period, however daunting, will not grind you down into the dust. You will bounce back stronger and more self-assured than ever before.

> 24. *You know that nothing worth having should come easily to you. You put the work in.*

You wouldn't enjoy attaining something you didn't work hard to attain. Because you know this, you don't begrudge having to work hard. You know the results will absolutely be worth this struggle and hardship!

> 25. *You forgive yourself for being sad. You recognize, now, that your sadness was reasonable all along.*

If you are suffering from depression, try not to be too hard on yourself. Everyone struggles with these emotions. You are not abnormal or weak for hosting negative feelings. No one should speak down to you for feeling this way.

> 26. *Write about what you are unhappy about, today. Work through these feelings.*

The written word is an amazing thing. Use it to your advantage, today. Write, write, write, and clarify the murky business of your soul. Why are you sad? How do you best fight your own sadness?

> 27. *You are not isolated. You know you can go to others and let their happiness be yours, too.*

You are empathetic. You know that you can instantly be cheered up when you witness happiness in other people's expressions. Your loved ones' happiness is particularly valuable. Seek out your loved ones in this trying time.

> 28. *You confront feelings of shame and discover their true source. You know that to overcome shame, you must recognize it.*

You should not feel ashamed. If you do, confront that feeling head on. Discover precisely why you feel the way you do, and find a solution. Demolish this feeling.

29. In the end, your sadness will better you.
You can learn from sadness. You can use your sadness to drive you to achieve something. In some way, your sadness will help you in your quest to improve.

30. You are a determined individual.
You are determined to endure the worst this world can throw at you.

Chapter 32
On Happiness

Happiness is elusive, bizarre, and even escapes description. It's one of the things that we as a society most value. We are taught to pursue what make us happy. However, we don't often know what makes us enduringly happy. Sometimes, we achieve a goal and are filled with disappointment because we expected it would make us happier than it did.

This indicates a misunderstanding of what makes us happy and what happiness really is. The truth is that happiness doesn't last. Nobody is ever completely pleased with their lives, no matter how successful they are. We will always want a new and better result than what we have achieved up until that point. That is okay. We have to teach ourselves to understand and be happy while progressing toward our goals. We will never stop progressing, and that is beautiful. If you let it, progress can be the key to your happiness.

Even Al Franken's Saturday Night Live character, Stuart Smalley, realizes the importance of overcoming your critical inner voice. In their book, I'm Good Enough, I'm Smart Enough, and Doggone It, People Like Me!: Daily Affirmations by Stuart Smalley, Franken (1992) describes the struggle with that critical inner voice and the eventual realization that you can accept and appreciate its existence without believing the things this critical inner voice espouses.

The Affirmations

1. *The world is wonderful. You are grateful for this day, no matter what it brings.*

Yes, no matter how hard our lives become, the world is still an incredible miracle. The world is a chance - a transient chance - to do something meaningful. Your life is the best thing, the only thing that you have. It would be best if you treasured every breath you take.

2. *There is beauty in everything around you, if only you give yourself the time to find it.*

From time to time, we all lose our sense of perspective. The world seems dark and cruel and filled with small-minded people. If it seems that way, know it won't seem that way forever. There are beautiful things and situations within your line of sight every day. You can choose to notice these things.

3. *Happy moments are always on their way. When one has gone, another one is coming to take its place. You simply have to actually wait a short period of time.*

Never lose faith in good times and positive feelings. Things will improve, despite the fact that it may not seem to be the case at the moment. You know they will because you are working to improve. Don't worry. The pendulum will swing back, and you will be happy again.

4. *You appreciate the little, valuable, wonderful things in your life. When you recognize one of these things, you smile. It would be best if you thanked them.*

Practice recognition and gratitude. We are imperfect and at times cynical. It can be difficult for us to see what makes our lives worth living. Put in the effort, every day, to see these things and to appreciate them.

5. *You understand that the secret to enduring happiness is gratitude and empathy.*

There is no permanent happiness. There are only moments that seem to pass too soon. That said, you can make your moments of happiness last a little longer, or a lot longer, by practicing genuine gratitude for the good things in your life. You can also be grateful for the bad. You learn and grow most in periods of adversity.

6. *You understand that the pursuit of happiness can make you very unhappy. Instead, you appreciate the things in your life right now that bring you joy.*

We don't know what makes us truly happy. If we hang all our hopes on the wrong thing, believing it will make us happy - and it doesn't - this can be absolutely devastating. Do not chase happiness. Do not believe that achieving your goals will make you permanently happy. Happiness is more complicated than that.

7. *Happiness is not only on the horizon. It surrounds you every day.*

You can find bits of happiness in your life, every day. You can notice how often you are happy, instead of letting these moments pass and convincing yourself you were never happy at all. Be self-aware enough to notice your happiness.

8. *You understand the positive power of a smile. You smile for yourself.*

Smiling more frequently can indeed improve your mood. Smiling is an easy, free, simple way to become a little happier. So, why aren't you smiling? Why aren't you trying to make your loved ones smile?

9. *You are a happy individual. You are a happy individual.*

Don't allow yourself or anybody else to convince you differently. You are happy. You see the things worth celebrating and worth being thankful for in your life. You know that sadness passes, and you work to improve yourself every day. You are, on the whole, a happy person.

10. *You promote happiness in others and feel happy for having done so.*

To try and make others smile or laugh is admirable. It is such a kind and considerate thing to do. You understand the importance of happiness and its fickle nature. You can make others happy. You want to because you are a kind and empathetic human being.

11. *You find happiness in the happiness of others. You share their joy.*

The joy of others is beautiful. You see it and your heart, too, will be filled with it. Let your appreciation for the happiness of others benefit you in this way.

12. *Make a list of the things and people you are grateful for in your life. You know that these things/people are wonderful aspects of your life.*

Gratitude will help you to find happiness and stay happy. While you are counting your blessings, keep in mind that you might be deprived of them at any time. It would be best if you appreciated what you have while you have it.

13. *You value hope and hard work. You recognize that you are hopeful and hard-working.*

You are able to work hard and for long periods of time because you have beautiful hope. You are inspired to keep working for yourself in the hopes that happiness is on the horizon. Indeed, happiness is on the horizon. You only have to wait for it.

14. *Your happiness is organic and precious.*

There is no use in attempting to force oneself to be joyful. It will not feel right. In fact, it may aggravate the problem. Instead, do things that have made you happy in the past and promote happiness in others. This will help to make you happier.

15. *You spend time with happy people. You appreciate their influence on your mood.*

Find joy for yourself in the joy of others. People who are happy are good influences. Especially in times of distress, surround yourself with these cheerful people to help remind you that there are things worth being happy about in the world.

> 16. *You know that happiness lasts longer when you recognize and give thanks for it.*

We can forget that we were ever happy if we do not properly recognize moments of happiness. When you are happy, stop for a moment and say it. Tell people you are happy. Remember, later on, that you were happy at that moment.

> 17. *Your happiness is important. It helps you to remain positive and productive.*

Your happiness is a tool. When you are happy, it is easy to do the things that honor your short and long-term goals. Furthermore, honoring your short and long-term goals makes you happy. It's a wonderful cycle.

> 18. *You are generous with your friends and loved ones. You are happy when you have made them happy.*

You know that the people in your life deserve to be happy. So, try to make them that way. You are kind and loving toward the important people in your life because they deserve it. Besides, they have and will continue to return the favor.

> 19. *You love your own happiness. You know that you deserve to feel happy and fulfilled in your life.*

Romanticize your happiness. Know that you are your best self when you are fully, purely happy. Happiness may be difficult to maintain now, but in practicing gratitude, you ensure that you will feel it more often and more powerfully.

> 20. *You are focused on having a positive mindset. Everything is colored by your thoughts.*

The same situation can have entirely different outcomes, depending upon the people involved. The pessimist tends to learn very little and to gain very little. On the other hand, the optimist learns and grows in spite of the circumstances.

21. You are working to become happier, to appreciate happiness more.

You deserve congratulations for your hard work. People work all their lives, they pursue happiness for as long as they can. You are participating in this age-old pursuit. However, you are changing it, too. You are managing your perception of what happiness is. In so doing, you make sure you will be happy.

22. Today is another chance to notice the things and people that make you happy.

Do not go around blind to the things that really matter. Notice and love. Let yourself notice and love in every moment of every day.

23. You are worthy of happiness.

You do not deserve to feel sad. You deserve to feel content. Let yourself be happy. Do not spend a single moment depriving yourself of that most valuable emotion. Completely reject the idea that you are unworthy.

24. Yours is a success story.

Have faith in the story that you're telling. You may not see it yet, but that's because you don't know the ending. One day, everything will make sense to you. When everything finally comes together, you'll feel complete and content with yourself. Be sure of it.

25. Your life is full of joy.

There is joy all around you, at all times of the year. You need only look for it. There are always things in your life to be happy about. Remember how precious and rare the phenomena around you are - your life, itself, should cause you to rejoice.

26. Happiness helps you to be more productive.

When you are satisfied with your work, you will do more. So, why shouldn't you be happy all the time? Accept happiness when it comes, and see how productive you can be.

>   27. *You believe in moments of true, undiluted happiness. You notice and appreciate them when they occur.*

There are such beautiful, happy moments in this world. You know they exist. You wait for them with bated breath.

>   28. *You are good. You are happy with who you are.*

You deserve to be satisfied with yourself. You are a wonderful thing.

>   29. *You will lead a happy life.*

Every moment of today, tomorrow, and the following day will be jam-packed with happy occurrences. You will manifest happiness.

Chapter 33
Setting Short-Term Goals

Short-term goals are vital to our happiness and productivity day to day. They push us to develop better habits and continue forth toward larger, more challenging goals. You will learn through the repetition of these many affirmations that short-term goals are critically important to your mental and physical well-being. You will discover over several days how good it feels to consistently achieve something. You will then reinforce this positive behavior through congratulatory affirmations.

I know that it is difficult to keep your eyes on the prize. It's even more difficult to remain focused when you are not practiced in doing so. You cannot expect yourself to meet a demanding and effort-intensive goal when you haven't taken your first "baby-steps." You aren't a sprinter right now because you haven't even crawled yet. It will take time to build the abilities that will allow you to consistently attain your broad objectives.

With these affirmations, you will set short-term goals that train your body and mind to work steadily. You will learn that you are capable of setting and meeting goals. You will build up toward the goals that are most challenging and most important to you.

The Affirmations

1. *You will set a goal this morning. You will have reached this goal by nighttime. You will be proud of yourself for this small victory.*

It doesn't have to be a large, impressive goal. Just do something you would not otherwise have done, something that benefits you in a small way. You deserve to accomplish something, however small, today. Small accomplishments add up over time.

2. *You can set and meet a short-term fitness goal today. You might take a walk, go for a bike ride, or do another refreshing activity. That is within your power.*

Honor your body. You need fresh air and to get your heart pumping a little faster. You'll benefit from the adrenaline rush. If you want to sharpen your mind, keep yourself in good physical shape. You'll be happier for putting in that effort.

3. *Today is yours to make of it what you will.*

Take charge! What do you want to do today? What do you want to achieve? You will decide to make this day an empowering one. You can prove to yourself what you are made of. You can make today an incredible day!

4. *Make a list of your short-term goals somewhere. You recognize the importance of putting something on paper. Your goals are real. You remind yourself of them whenever you look at that page.*

Putting your thoughts to paper can be a powerful tool. When you do it, you in some way make the words and the ideas more real than they may have been before. It can be easier to realize your goals after you have written them down.

5. *You value your progress toward achieving short-term goals.*

The process is as important and influential to your development as the achievement itself, if not more so. You should appreciate the moments leading up to the achievement for all they are worth, not only the end result.

6. *You celebrate appropriately once you have met one of your goals. You understand the power of positive reinforcement.*

It's all about positive reinforcement! When you have accomplished something, reward yourself appropriately. You deserve to recognize your achievements fully. Moreover, rewarding yourself for exhibiting good behavior will encourage you to behave that way in the future.

7. *You are proud of the goals that you have set for yourself. You carry them with you with pride.*

Remember what you have achieved. Too quickly and too often, we might forget the things which make us proud of ourselves. If you have to, make a list of the things you accomplish. Add to that list every day, as you work hard to meet your goals.

8. *Your goals are achievable. You work to achieve them every day.*

You can reach your goals. It's vitally important that you trust yourself to meet them, even when they seem so far out of reach. You can do it. That slogan should be repeated over and over in your head. You can. You have no room for doubt in your mind.

9. *Your goals are meaningful to you. They make you feel good.*

Working toward your goals is an honorable thing. Make sure you continue to understand how important your goals are and why. Your goals are rooted in your deepest desires. You honor them and yourself with your work.

10. *Your goals reflect well on you. You inspire others when you share your goals and progress with them.*

It feels good to share your passions and accomplishments with others. Further, it can help you to reach your goals faster and more easily when you have expressed your pride in them to others. The process can seem shorter and less arduous when you remind yourself of how much the goal means to you.

11. *Short-term goals help to ensure that you will reach your long-term goals. You are disciplined and self-assured.*

You know that meeting small goals first will help you to reach larger ones later. Further, these smaller goals can be a part of the larger goals you have set for yourself. Meet your smaller goals with the knowledge that they prepare you for larger ones.

12. *You find your progress toward your goals fulfilling. You know that working toward goals is what makes you better.*

Your progress is exciting and new. You know you can learn things about yourself throughout your progress, which can help you to refine your strategies. You can pursue success a little more swiftly every day.

13. *You will establish healthy and sustainable goals.*

You must make sure that the goals you are dedicating yourself to are worthy of your time and effort. If they do not make you a better person, you should abandon them as quickly as possible. Each of your goals should be worthwhile.

14. *Once you have met one goal, you will discover another, new goal to pursue. You recognize that continual self-improvement is possible. You know that you can always be a little better than you were before.*

You'll strive to be better until you die. That's the best sort of life. At no point should you be idle because there are always going to be parts of ourselves that could use a tad more work? Don't be scared of this reality. There's nothing nobler than changing for the better.

15. *You are powerful. You prove it with every day of hard work.*

It takes power to achieve all you have done. It takes power to continue to push forward and achieve more. You are an immensely powerful person. Be proud of you who are and who you will eventually become.

16. *You are motivated to meaningful goals. Write down a few more!*

You can never have enough goals, so long as you can honor them all simultaneously. Make sure your goals do not conflict in any way.

17. *You know that the goals you make help to determine the kind of person you are. You make meaningful and attainable short-term goals.*

You are in the process of changing this very minute. Similarly, you are in pursuit of your goals in this very minute. The goals you choose to pursue will determine the direction of your personal growth.

18. You evaluate the importance of your short-term goals. You understand why you are fighting to achieve each one.

Never lose perspective. Remind yourself constantly of the importance of your goals and why your goals are meaningful. If you remind yourself, you will not lose sight of your goals.

19. Working toward your goals brings you joy.

Hard effort and devotion will bring about a sense of fulfillment. Find it. Know that your work has a value that merits celebration. Joy should not be reserved for when all the work is over but should be present throughout every stage of the process.

20. Your short-term goals bring immeasurable value to your life.

Short-term goals can help you in numerous ways, and you recognize that. You want to make the most of your short-term goals, so you ask what benefits you can gain in the pursuit of each. Incorporating this question into your work helps you to improve more quickly.

21. You will embrace difficult tasks today.

No matter how grueling, strenuous, or stressful, the task will seem simple today. You are ready for it. You are excited to tackle this wondrous challenge. Take on more than your share today and know that you will be all the stronger for having done so.

22. You will learn to concentrate your efforts toward achieving something important.

To focus is a hugely valuable and transferable skill. Each day, you lengthen your attention span. You work to make your focus sharper as you fight to meet your goals. As a result of a clearer focus, you are more productive and successful.

23. *You are on the right track. You trust that you are on the right track.*

Never doubt it: this is where you are meant to be at this place in time. You will choose where to go from here and where to go from there and so on. You are making the best choices you can. You are learning, changing, and growing happier.

24. *You are committed to making real change in your life. You are committed to achieving great things.*

This commitment will shine through you in all that you do and all that you achieve. People will know when they see you that you are formidable in your focus and nerve. They will know that you are a person prepped to do powerful things.

25. *You know how to chase what you want.*

Through trial and error, you have developed an effective way to pursue your goals. You continue to perfect your method as you work.

26. *You visualize your success. You know how it will feel and what it will mean. You know it is worth it to you.*

Success will mean a lot to you. You eagerly pursue it, excited by the prospect of the additional happiness it will bring. You know it will make you happy and mean that you are dynamic and strong. You know it is worth the world.

27. *Your short-term goals help to improve your discipline.*

Discipline will serve you well in all areas of life. You are grateful that the way you move through the world and learn affords you greater discipline.

28. *Your short-term goals give you additional self-confidence.*

Because you set and meet your short-term goals consistently, you are filled with confidence. You know that you can be trusted. You know that you can get the job done.

29. *You are grateful that you are able to work to achieve your goals.*

Some don't pursue their goals. Some can't pursue their goals. You, however, belong to neither of these groups. You are able to honor your goals through the active pursuit of them. You are able to make yourself the very best you can be.

30. *Your goals show you what you are made of.*

You test your mettle every day as you pursue your short-term goals. Through this process, you learn what type of man you are. You learn what type of man you are to become.

31. *You are choosing to meet your goals.*

You do have the choice. Whether you meet your goals or fail is entirely up to you. Choose wisely.

Chapter 34
Setting Long-Term Goals

Words and genuine beliefs are powerful, powerful things. You can manifest your success and happiness by using the right words. Studies consistently prove that self-affirmations are valuable to the body and mind. Yogananda, in his book Scientific Healing Affirmations, even goes so far as to suggest that positive affirmations can affect the physical body's ability to heal itself. He contests that repeated affirmations can activate inactive "life energy". Admittedly, that's a little out there. However, the positive effects of affirmations have been documented extensively. They may not be able to heal your physical wounds, but they can certainly, without a doubt, heal your mental and emotional ones.

The focus here is on helping you overcome obstacles to reach your long-term goals. The affirmations will help you shed your past behaviors and hang-ups to do what is right for you now. Over many days, you will learn that your goals, however impressive, are indeed within reach. You can unlock the version of yourself that will meet your goals. Every affirmation deals with the nerve and resilience required to faithfully pursue your long-term goals.

The Affirmations

1. *Every day is an opportunity to take a small step toward achieving remarkable change.*

You are working for drastic results. You understand that drastic results take time, and you don't want or need to rush it. You will figure things out in time. Make small changes that eventually accumulate into larger ones.

2. *You will be patient with yourself as you work toward your goals.*

Very few goals worth reaching come easily. It takes so much time. It takes everyone time to become the best versions of you. Understand this and embrace the slow and, at times, unsteady nature of the progress.

    3. *The process toward achieving your goals is as useful to you as actually achieving them.*

It's true what they say: it's not about getting anywhere; it's about getting there. Start loving the work because that's what life is composed of. A life lived well is a constant process of self-improvement.

    4. *You understand that your ambition is what makes you a better individual.*

Ambition can make you selfish, but like most qualities, it is two-sided. It can hurt you, and it can help you. Ambition sometimes gets a bad rep, but people neglect to notice that ambition drives people to improve and succeed. Your ambition is powerful.

    5. *Your long-term goals are meaningful to you.*

Keep your sights set on your goals. People sometimes forget their aspirations if they fail to remind themselves of what is important. Allow yourself to not become one of those individuals. Remind yourself of your goals and why you want to pursue them. Then, do something productive that will help you meet your goal.

    6. *Make a list of your long-term goals. You are aware of how effective it may be to write down your objectives and then read them back to yourself.*

Realize that the written word has a sort of magic to it. When filled with purpose and intention, it can remind you of what is most important. It can push you to work and to succeed. Let this exercise give you strength today.

    7. *Your long-term goals are important to you. You trust yourself to meet these goals.*

You trust and know that one day you will meet your goal. You have dispensed with doubt because, frankly, it was never useful to you. You pursue your goals with a headstrong vitality. You know that you deserve to meet these goals.

8. *Your goals are empowering. You know that it is endlessly useful to set long-term goals and keep them in your mind.*

Your goals are tools. They keep you busy, productive, and happy. To have goals is to have reasons to live, act, and love. Recognize that your goals are an important part of your identity. Recognize that you determine your goals and how you go about achieving them.

9. *You are the driving force responsible for making progress, little by little, toward your most lofty goals.*

It is important to realize and reaffirm your total agency. You call the shots, chief. Every one of your actions, good or bad, aligned with your goals or misaligned, is yours. You decided to do that. Try to make good decisions.

10. *You are happy that you have these goals to guide you in your life.*

Goals are so vital to leading a good life. You count your goals as blessings because they are just that. Make sure you continue to set and meet small goals. Make sure you continue to set and meet larger ones, too. These are what push you to improve.

11. *Long-term goals help you to keep your life in perspective. You are a strong and dependable person.*

You know you are strong and dependable because you have to be to set and meet these long-term goals. These goals require slow, forceful, consistent work. You put the work in, and in so doing, prove yourself. You know you will meet your goals.

12. *You appreciate slow progress. You know that self-improvement, and life in general, is an endurance sport.*

Life is not a sprint: it's a marathon. You must maintain a speedy but consistent pace. You have to pace yourself to be as successful as possible. If you push too hard at the start, you risk having to stop and give up entirely.

> 13. *Your long-term goals are always on your mind. You are dedicated and intelligent. You will meet these goals in time.*

You remember the most important things. You know what is driving you forward in this life. Your long-term goals are always in the back of your mind, informing everything you do or say. They help you to behave in the best way.

> 14. *You feel happiest when you behave in a way aligned with your goals.*

You derive happiness from the pursuit of your long-term goals. These are the aspirations that define the very core of who you are. You are pleased to have the opportunity to work toward them. You are happy that they have entered into your mind and changed it.

> 15. *You love the potential you are filled with.*

There's something so beautiful about potential. The thought that you can do anything, be anyone, is so wonderfully freeing. Internalize that you are free to do whatever will make you happiest. You are free to become a greater self.

> 16. *You find happiness in the pursuit of your long-term goals.*

Attempting to improve yourself will ensure that you are happier because you have trained yourself to find the beauty in good things. Being productive makes you enduringly happy. You will fight to stay productive.

> 17. *You understand that the happiest people are constantly pursuing a new goal. The happiest of people improve themselves constantly.*

Your long-term goals are infused with a promise of happiness. However, so is their pursuit. You look to your friends and loved ones, and you see that the happiest and most successful are never completely still. They have goals that align with their deepest values.

18. Your goals make a difference in the quality of your day.
Having goals will make your day feel more meaningful. It will make your day happier. It will make you feel more fulfilled as you travel through the world. All that is required is that you remind yourself of your objectives.

19. You share your goals with others. Your friends can help you improve upon these goals and/or build new goals altogether.
Collaboration with trusted friends is a great way to encourage your continued improvement. The individuals in your life who are concerned about you will aid you in determining the best course of action for you. Even better than you do, they may know what sorts of goals will make you happiest.

20. Your long-term goals are achievable. You make progress toward them little by little, day by day.
Trust that your goals are possible to achieve. If you work hard enough, and if your goals are truly reflective of your innermost values, you can reach your goals. You are not scared of the time or strength it will take. You have enough time and strength in abundance.

21. You are a disciplined and remarkable person.
Do not forget that you are strong and important. You are incredible. You can do all the things you wish to do to become the person you want to become.

22. Your long-term goals make you excited about your future and whatever it will bring.
While the present is the most important time, your future is also important. Your long-term goals ensure that you are headed toward a desirable future filled with astonishing success.

23. You work consistently and intelligently to reach your goals.

Work smart. You have to be self-aware enough throughout the process to realize the quality of your work and whether something needs to change. If you need to rest, then rest. If you need to work more quickly, you do. Little adjustments should constantly be made.

24. You deserve success.

You are worthy of it. No matter what you may believe at present, you are a wonderful person deserving of every single one of your laurels. Allow yourself to celebrate. Allow yourself to be happy and to feel fulfilled. Your success is well-earned.

25. Even a lack of progress, or lateral movement, will help you discover your priorities.

Every adjustment is an opportunity to see what you are aiming for more clearly. Your values are obscured, hidden deep within you. When you modify a goal, you are doing so to honor that deep value. Keep your eyes peeled and see what it is you are truly hoping to achieve. See what you are aiming for.

26. You can do fantastic things.

You have done and you will do great things. Great things for yourself, and, better yet, great things for others. Work hard and be generous.

27. Your future is bright.

You are so lucky to have the prospects you have. You are working to improve every part of yourself and every aspect of your life! Naturally, your future is brilliantly bright, filled with the happiness you have yet to feel.

28. Your goals are worth the extra energy you expend. You are a fighter.

Do not become tired and do not become overwhelmed by stress or the amount of work you have. You can do this. You can do it, no matter how long it takes. Instead of feeling doubt or fear, feel the excitement. This work is so meaningful to you.

29. You are passionate. You put everything into your work. You give it your all because you know it's important. You know that valiant efforts define your life.

Conclusion

Was there a change in yourself this year that you were surprised by? It's incredible that you can make monumental strides when you dedicate your mind to it. It might take everything you have to remain focused and remind yourself of your deepest desires every hour of the day, but when you do, the results are absolutely incredible. This book is about positive change. It's about how difficult it is to change and how beautiful it is when you do. It is a book that seeks to motivate black men to make changes. I hope it did that for you.

Take this time to reflect upon the person you were before you read this book. You should have improved your self-esteem, taken on better habits and goals, and gained a more mature understanding of your emotional state and physical needs. Is that right? As you look back on this year of progress, of slow and sure change, do you feel happy? Have you learned that the process is as beautiful as the finished result? Indeed, what is the most important lesson you have learned this year?

These questions are not for my sake. I cannot hear or ponder your responses at all. The final exercise of this book is to take an honest look at what you can achieve. Take the time to evaluate yourself and the rate of change you eventually settle into. Approach it like a scientist might, determining the energy expenditure needed for the tangible, positive results. I hope you found it an interesting read. Only you know that. If it was, please read on. If it not, perhaps affirmations are not for you right now. That's all right, too. You'll find something that works better this season.

Affirmations are only as powerful as your belief in them. You are still reading because you maintained a great faith in affirmations and in yourself. That is a remarkable feat of psychological strength. You should be incredibly proud of yourself for sticking through to the end. Many others gave up part way through. You persisted, and that speaks volumes about your character. It speaks volumes about your value and ability to achieve drastic, positive change. The affirmations were successful because you are a self-aware and brilliant person. I take no credit for your results: it was all you.

If these affirmations were helpful, here is what you do next: think back on the commitments that had the most significant effect on you. Make a list of them. Once you have accumulated a large list, try to determine why these affirmations were potent. Determine what in these words drove you to change in positive ways.

Once you have isolated the common denominators, develop your affirmations based on this idea. You will then have created a shortlist of affirmations tailored specifically to you. You can continue to build affirmations for yourself in this way and thus have even more purposeful and productive days. Make sure that the affirmations you create are rooted deeply in kindness. While they are concerned first and foremost with your continued productivity, they must be prevailingly kind.

In the short-term, cruel words might motivate you to push yourself harder; but in the long-term, they will destroy you and leave you empty. I don't mean to scare you; I mean to wake you up. Don't speak to yourself if what you have to say isn't coated in love and acceptance.

This book should have helped to recalibrate your mind. It should have pushed you to work on something new every month and to better yourself every day. Do not let time away from these affirmations ruin all the progress you have made. Stick true to your values and the behaviors that work for you.

This book focused a great deal on the importance of determination and consistency. Frankly, the importance of these two characteristics cannot be overstated or repeated too many times. Your decision led you through this book, through the various affirmations, improving yourself all the while. More importantly, you were consistent. You came back day after day, even though you were exhausted, and it became more difficult. You demonstrated throughout the reading process an incredible amount of strength. You astound people when you put your all into achieving your goals. I am astounded that you are still reading.

This book helped you to understand and value the most important things in your life. It encouraged you to love yourself, your goals, and the those dearest to you. Ultimately, these three aspects are most important to consider. They are the three things that you should never forget. I hope as we advance, you will honor these things with positive behaviors and the continued incorporation of affirmations into your daily life. Now, you must understand the incredible power of words to remind us of our values and inspire us to act well. It would be best if you respected these words. You must choose your words carefully and mean what you say.

Black Man, **YOU ARE** valuable to your family. The world may see you as "just another black man", but we see you as a necessity to the family structure. Why are you a necessity, you may ask? The answer is simple. It brings back balance to the family. Our young men need to see a healthy relationship between a man and a woman, just as our young girls need to see one.

We need you to teach our young men how to lead their family, our young girls how to respect themselves and the men in their lives. **TODAY IS THE DAY YOU** take control and decide how you are going to form a healthy relationship and rebuild the family unit.

www.ingramcontent.com/pod-product-compliance
Lightning Source LLC
Chambersburg PA
CBHW070450120526
44590CB00013B/637